India and Civilizational Futures

Backwaters Collective on Metaphysics
and Politics II

Edited by

VINAY LAL

OXFORD
UNIVERSITY PRESS

OXFORD
UNIVERSITY PRESS

Oxford University Press is a department of the University of Oxford.
It furthers the University's objective of excellence in research, scholarship,
and education by publishing worldwide. Oxford is a registered trademark of
Oxford University Press in the UK and in certain other countries.

Published in India by
Oxford University Press
22 Workspace, 2nd Floor, 1/22 Asaf Ali Road, New Delhi 110002

ISBN-13 (print edition): 978-0-19-949906-9
ISBN-10 (print edition): 0-19-949906-3

ISBN-13(eBook):978-0-19-099041-1
ISBN-10 (eBook): 0-19-099041-4

Typeset in ScalaPro 10/13
by Tranistics Data Technologies, Kolkata 700 091
Printed in India by Manipal Technologies Limited, Manipal

India and Civilizational Futures

To the memory of
S.M. Mohamed Idris
'Uncle' Idris to his many friends
and
The Grand Old Man of Penang
to the world
An intrepid fighter for justice
A dreamer with a cause
A relentless seeker of truth
An initiator nonpareil of social movements
A rigorous critic of imperialism in all its guises
and still
a kind, gentle, and devout man
The last of his kind

You inspire us all

CONTENTS

FIGURES

ACKNOWLEDGEMENTS

A civil war raged in Sri Lanka for something like three decades, and a little over one year after it was brought to an end in May 2009 a few individuals gathered together in Colombo to reflect on what had transpired in that little island and whether the intellectual and cultural resources of Indian civilization could be husbanded in some fashion to help us think about the sources of conflict, the peculiar anxieties generated by modernity in that part of the world, and the contours of the immense task of decolonization. In the olden days, before the advent of European colonialism, Sri Lanka was known by the name of Serendib; but it is, unluckily, not serendipity which brings to mind the events in that tear-drop shaped island at the tip of India. As I write these very words, the country is again in a state of acute turmoil, precipitated in this instance by orchestrated suicide bombings across several churches, hotels, and other sites. Some people were at once speculating that the bombings, which have claimed 250 lives and left at least twice as many people injured, were undertaken in retaliation for the attacks on two mosques by a white supremacist in New Zealand just weeks ago. There are other common narratives: though ISIS may have been eliminated, or largely decimated, in Syria, Iraq, and the area around these countries, its tentacles have spread to Asia. There has been the usual rehearsal of the tiresome thesis of 'the clash of civilizations', while a similar apocalyptic scenario has invoked the present religious strife as a modern-day instantiation of the Crusades.

The members of the Backwaters Collective on Metaphysics and Politics are not inspired by the tenor of such observations or most contemporary conversations about politics, history, or religion. We recognize that nationalism is a potent force, and is everywhere rearing its ugly head, but it holds out no attractions to any of us. The homilies of modern social science, which apparently will resolve the world's problems if the economists are given a free hand and if people will only behave rationally, move us not an iota. Those who conduct what is called 'research', which is nearly everything one can imagine and in some fields and departments has been reduced to surveys, questionnaires, and supposed debates over what is mistakenly called 'methodology', have generally persuaded themselves that more research will lead to a better world. Indeed, though most of the members of the Collective—whether their association with it has been confined to a meeting or two or is more enduring—are university professors or independent scholars, I doubt that anyone with the Collective is at all inclined to think that most scholarship has anything to offer that might even remotely ameliorate the profound social ills and political problems that seem to afflict nearly every country.

Only a handful of us gathered at Colombo and little did we imagine that the Collective would have this kind of longevity. The origins of the Collective, and our decision to convene more as a scholarly group, are part of the narrative that is recounted in the preceding volume of this series, *India and the Unthinkable* (2016). The interested reader will similarly find in the earlier volume a set of reflections on why the Collective came to style itself the 'Backwaters Collective on Metaphysics and Politics', and some clues to the various ideas—which are disparate and, oddly enough, converge as well—that animate the members of the Collective.

* * *

The Sree Narayana Mandira Samiti, Mumbai, has been the mainstay of our organization. It has been generous both in its funding and the institutional support it has so unstintingly offered over the course of nearly a decade. The Samiti has made absolutely no demands on the Collective, and it might be said that some of the themes that are echoed in this volume—an ecological conception of plurality, inter-communality, hospitality, to name a few—are exemplified in the manner in which the Samiti has played the role of a gracious host. Though the Backwaters Collective gratefully acknowledges the Samiti as a whole, it is particularly appreciative of the help extended by some of its office-bearers, including its chairman, Shri M.I. Damodaran; Shri N. Mohandas, vice chairman; Shri N. Sashidharan, president; and Shri N.S. Salim Kumar, general secretary.

I would be severely remiss if, speaking on behalf of the Backwaters Collective, I did not acknowledge the magnanimous assistance of Shri R.K. Krishna Kumar, trustee both of the Sir Dorabji Tata Trust and of the Sir Ratan Tata Trust. He has been supportive of our enterprise since its inception and has asked nothing of us in return. The gener-osity of Shri Kumar and the Tata Trusts has permitted the Collective to engage in the play of thought shorn of the financial anxieties that ordinarily bedevil groups such as ours, and the Collective's members are hopeful that the deliberations of the group, as well as this volume and the preceding one, furnish more than ample evidence of the Collective's judicious use of the funds placed at its disposal.

Many other organizations and individuals have extended a help-ing hand, and often much more, to the Backwaters Collective. The Collective has been pleased to partner with the Kochi Biennale Foundation (KBF) over the last few years and even hold events in common. I would like to thank, in particular, Bose Krishnamachari, an internationally acclaimed artist and co-founder and president of the KBF, and likewise Riyas Komu, who is not only an artist of great distinction but also a trustee of the KBF, curator, artistic entrepreneur, and intellectual voyager. Gautam Das, the assistant director of pro-gramming at the Kochi-Muziris Biennale, has always been helpful. Since around 2012, the Le Meridien Hotel in Kochi has served as the venue for the annual summer meeting of the Collective. The general manager of the hotel, Tejus Jose, has gone out of his way to accom-modate our group and, along with his staff, extended more than the common courtesies to make the stay of the conference participants comfortable, even memorable. No one thinks of a hotel as akin to a home: but if perchance one were moved to embrace such a possibility, the staff of the Le Meridien Hotel has done more than what one might have thought possible to generate such an outcome.

Anish Damodaran, Ashis Nandy, Dinakaran, and Roby Rajan have been with the Collective from the outset, and to this core group I would like to add D. Venkat Rao, who has been present at every gathering once the Collective reconvened as a scholarly group in 2011. They have made the Collective into what it is, namely, if I may put it somewhat immodestly, an arresting chapter in the annals of contemporary Indian intellectual history. My thanks to each of them. Anish arrives with an entourage and brings his friends to every gathering, and they have unfailingly enlivened the scene and offered a helping hand. I would like to thank them for their friendship and conviviality: Unnikrishna Madhavan, Bubesh Chand, and Dr Vinod Nair.

Finally, this volume is inscribed to the memory of S.M. Mohamed Idris, who was something of a legend in Penang, where he lived for the most of his 93 years. He passed away on 17 May, just before this book was to go to press. He was associated with many of the principal NGOs in Malaysia and especially Penang over the last five decades, including the Consumer Association of Penang, Third World Network, and Citizens International. It is wholly characteristic of Mohamed Idris that he should have obscured his own critical role in founding and nurturing some of the principal civic associations that have made Penang so singularly attractive to activists and dissenting thinkers. 'Uncle Idris', as he was known affectionately to his friends, was not present at any of the deliberations of our Collective though he was the moving force behind 'Multiversity', an initiative out of Penang for the decolonization of universities and a systematic inquiry into the imperialism of modern knowledge systems. As he put it to me in his own inimitable fashion on more than one occasion, 'We in the South would like to get the West off our backs.' Though Uncle Idris's disciplined and stern ways of being in the world were not entirely mine, he had the enviable gift of bringing out the best in everyone. I dedicate this volume to one who was so selfless with great admiration and not a little trepidation.

Vinay Lal
Los Angeles, 21 May 2019

I

INDIA AND THE CHALLENGE OF THE GLOBAL SOUTH
Some Thoughts on Pluralism, the Categories of Knowledge, and Hospitality

VINAY LAL

The Singularity of Bandung

The Afro-Asian Conference held at Bandung, Indonesia, in 1955 is now commonly held to be the origin of much of the thinking around what is called the Global South. That was not always the case: as late as 2004, the term, 'the Global South', appeared in fewer than fifty indexed publications in the humanities and social sciences,[1] and it is only in the last several years that the term has secured an assured place in critical thinking about not just international relations and area studies but also about the most pressing questions revolving around the growing disparities between the most affluent and the most impoverished countries, shifts in the global economy, and the increasingly bleak possibilities of social justice for the poor and the disenfranchised around the world. The idea of the Global South is usually thought to bear a family resemblance to other terms such as the 'Third World' or 'the developing world', but it is clear that 'the Global South' brings entirely new possibilities to the discussion, among them the idea of decolonization and the solidarities forged of anti-colonial struggles. Whatever the limitations—and those are much less evident to many than the accomplishments—of postcolonial scholarship over the course of the last four decades, one of its more signal contributions might well be that it helped facilitate a fundamental transition in thinking about the post–World War II period as one shaped predominantly by the geopolitical realities of the Cold War and super-power rivalry to an appreciation of decolonization as the motive force in the two to three decades following the end of World War II.

As the president of Indonesia—who played host to his counterparts from twenty-eight other nations[2] whose billion and a half people then accounted for 54 per cent of the world's population—Sukarno was in no doubt about what Bandung signified to the world, especially to countries whose people had only just been liberated from, and in some cases continued to live under, the yoke of colonialism. 'This is', Sukarno in his opening speech declaimed, 'the first international conference of coloured peoples in the history of mankind.'[3] A modern-day scholar with some appreciation of what Bandung stood for might nonetheless characterize Sukarno's observation as inaccurate. Two Asian Relations conferences had been held in New Delhi, the first in 1947, on the cusp of Independence, and again in 1949; long before, in 1927, the League against Imperialism and Colonial Oppression convened in Brussels.[4] One might also call to mind the lesser-known 'Congress of the Peoples of Europe, Asia and Africa', convened in Puteaux, France, in June 1948.[5] More tellingly, Asian delegations had gathered in 1926 under the umbrella of the International Conference for Peace at Bierville in northern France with the full awareness that even allegedly progressive peace movements were hobbled by a uniquely European parochialism: as their members wrote,

> There is one thing which cannot fail to strike anyone who studies the peace movements of Europe. It is the fact ... that when European people think of peace they think of it only in terms of Europe. In the imagination of European thinkers the world seems to be confined to the areas inhabited by European races. The vast continent of Asia ... and Africa, with its particular problems, do not come into the picture at all.[6]

These delegates would, I suspect, not have been surprised at the hierarchical arrangement of the continents in the Congress that met in June 1948, even if they had not given any explicit thought to the matter. Asia was, even in the liberal imagination of the West, a thoroughly effeminized zone: in India, at least, there were no real men according to Robert Orme, Thomas Macaulay, and a legion of other European writers, even if the colonial state later discovered what came to be known as 'the martial races'. The heathens and savages of Africa were but children, altogether bereft of the faculty of reasoning and incapable of even rudimentary forms of self-regulation. If I may put it this way, Europe, Asia, and Africa are listed in much the same way, and with precisely the same homologous effects, as we list 'men, women and children'. There has always been the supposition that as we move from men to women and then to children, we are in each case descending to an inferior species of being, from those who are fully formed to women who, as a general rule, are incomplete and finally to children who must painstakingly be socialized into becoming 'men' or 'women'.[7]

Yet, as a further perusal of Sukarno's speech suggests, he was perspicacious in his understanding of how Bandung had created a wholly new precedent, the ramifications of which, I would like to suggest, have largely escaped those who have turned their critical gaze on the idea of the Global South. 'It is a new departure in the history of the world', Sukarno explains, 'that leaders of Asian and African countries can meet together in their own countries to discuss and deliberate upon matters of common concern.' Until a few years ago, Sukarno goes on to say, all such meetings were held in European countries, or, as in New Delhi in March–April 1947, when the host country was still under the aegis of colonial rule; all such gatherings took place 'thousands of miles away, amidst foreign people, in a foreign country, in a foreign continent. [Such a meeting] was assembled there by choice, not by necessity.' This is not a complaint from a petulant nationalist, or a mere sentiment of unease about having to convene in the land of one's oppressor and partake of his food, but rather an expression of a fact that, six decades after Bandung, remains unimpeachably true. The vast majority of what are called South–South dialogues have, in some fashion or the other, been mediated by the West: when students from Nigeria, Malaysia, Bangladesh, Brazil, Egypt, India, and China meet at all, they do so at the doorsteps of American or English universities. Pakistani intellectuals and writers do not, in general, read the

works of Chinese, African, Iranian, or Brazilian writers; indeed, they
seldom even read the works of Indian writers. If I may be so bold as to
say so, and I shall return to this point later, the Pakistani feels particularly compelled to repudiate the Indian and Bangladeshi as part of his
moral and intellectual universe as the despised part of his own self.
Indians are not any less culpable: barring the names of Saadat Hasan
Manto and Faiz Ahmad Faiz, the Pakistani literary and intellectual
world remains entirely opaque to them,[8] and to middle-class educated
Indians the cultural scene in Pakistan can be reduced to whatever
is evoked by 'ghazals' and the Pakistani soap operas that have been
hugely successful in north India and are tolerated by the state as an
open channel of communication between estranged neighbours. The
same argument about the paucity of South–South intellectual conversations holds true, as a general rule, of the scholars and intellectuals
of the Muslim world: they may perhaps read each other, but they are
little if at all conversant in the works of their counterparts in China,
Africa, Latin America, or the vast world of non-Islamic South Asia.
One might be able to continue in this vein ad infinitum, to which
we may add the fact that the intellectual journeys into the heartland
of a country from the metropole have, in most nations of the Global
South, not been a whit easier. The Bengali intellectual of the late
nineteenth century, to take one example, found the Urdu-speaking
world of Muslim Lucknow and the courts of Rajputana of little interest but fancied that London and Oxbridge could nurture his soul; and
the world of the *adivasi*, to summon a modern-day example, is but a
foreign country to the educated elites of Delhi, Mumbai, Bengaluru,
or Chennai. In the cryptic formulation of Ngugi wa Thiong'o, 'The
links between Asia and Africa and South America have always been
present, but in our times made invisible by the fact that Europe is still
the central mediator of Afro-Asian-Latino discourse'.[9]

One may, quite reasonably, dispute whether Bandung was anything like that unmediated conversation between the peoples of the
South that Sukarno put forward as an illustration of the possibilities
of thinking anew about a world that, at least in the formal sense, was
about to be shorn of the curse of colonialism for the first time in
half a millennium. There is a poignancy in the characterization of
Bandung by the African American writer Richard Wright, himself the
member of a subject race eking out a living amidst its conquerors, as

a 'meeting of the rejected', a conclave of all those whose 'past relationship to the Western world' offered something akin to a 'kind of judgment upon that Western world!' The leaders of most of the nations
that were being represented 'had been political prisoners, men who
had lived lonely lives in exile', but Wright also detected something
else that he believed they had in common: 'The populations of almost
all the nations listed were deeply religious.'[10] Yet, beyond all this,
Wright found occasion to marvel at something else, something which
brought him closer to an appreciation of Sukarno's observation that
after Bandung not every conversation among the peoples of Asia and
Africa would have to be routed through the West. As the days wore on,
and the leaders came to know each other better,

> their fear and distrust evaporated. Living for centuries under colonial
> rule, they had become filled with a deep sense of how greatly they dif-
> fered from one another. But now, face to face, their ideological defenses
> dropped. Negative unity, bred by a feeling that they had to stand
> together against a rapacious West, turned into something that hinted
> of the positive. ... They could now feel that their white enemy was far,
> far away. ... Day after day dun-colored Trotskyites consorted with dark
> Moslems, yellow Indo-Chinese hobnobbed with brown Indonesians,
> black Africans mingled with swarthy Arabs, tan Burmese associated
> with dark brown Hindus, dusty nationalists palled around with yellow
> Communists, and Socialists talked to Buddhists.[11]

There may be more than a whiff of exoticism here, and I am
similarly inclined to question Wright's judgment, perhaps inspired
by his own upbringing in the Methodist and Seventh Day Adventist
churches, that the populations represented were all 'deeply religious'.
Enough of this timeless spirituality of the East! More recently, a number of scholars have drawn attention to the myth-making present in
The Color Curtain and suggested that Wright's unofficial narrative of
Bandung and his travels in Indonesia compel a different reading of
his canonical work.[12] Nevertheless, the thrust of Wright's remarks is
unmistakably clear, as is his invocation of a new dawn for what W. E.
B. DuBois had described as 'the darker races'.[13]

Let us, however, pursue further the very organization of the
Bandung conference, more so from the standpoint of unraveling
how the idea of area studies as it developed in post–World War II
USA in response to a tacit demand from policymakers that the

academy should instantiate, consolidate, and extend American hegemony might have constituted a repudiation of the ambitions of the
Bandung conference. The meeting was billed as a gathering of Asian
and African nations, yet nine of those countries belong to what, in
American parlance, is called the Middle East and, occasionally, though
far more so in scholarly circles rather than in popular discourse, the
Near East. We know that Asian American studies as it is constituted
in the USA has never encompassed the Middle East, and indeed even
South Asia has only very grudgingly been allowed into the portals of
Asian America. In Britain, by way of contrast, the category 'Asian' was
tacitly reserved for those from South Asia, and only more recently
have scholars of multicultural Britain broadened the scope of Asian
Britain to encompass the Chinese, Japanese, Vietnamese, and others
who are evidently of different racial stock than those from the Indian
subcontinent. In either case, the category 'Asian' has not incorporated
the Middle East, though evidently at Bandung a more expansive conception of 'Asia' was adopted.

I will not, for long, be detained here by the question of what is
signified by 'middle' in 'the Middle East', but it is necessary to at least
peripherally bring it to the fore of my deliberations. The most obvious answer, namely, that the Middle East constitutes the geographic
middle in some demonstrable sense between Europe and Asia, is of
course the least interesting of all the possible readings that come to
mind. As one moves eastward from the world of Christendom, one
encounters the world of Islam before entering the far remoter terrains of Hinduism, Jainism, Confucianism, Taoism, and Buddhism.
There is a long strand of Euro-American scholarship that has wavered
between the recognition of Islam as part of the inheritance of the
Western world and, on the other hand, the insistence that the cultural
mores of Muslim societies have much more in common with those
said to characterize 'Asian' societies.[14] Those who advocate for the
former position have dwelled on the commonalities of Abrahamic
faiths,[15] and in recent years Garry Wills is only one among many
highly respected public commentators in the USA who has sought
to diffuse tensions between Islam and Christendom by underscoring the inclusiveness of the prophetic vision of Muhammad.[16] The
latter view, which I would say has by far greater salience in the
popular imagination, adverts to those familiar features of Orientalist

discourse to highlight the essential convergence of Muslim societies with other Asian societies, from the Oriental's alleged incapacity to live outside the framework of political despotism and the sheer lack of the individual as an atom of being to the consignment of women to permanent second-class status. What indubitably emerges from these histories is another fact, namely, that the category which we describe as 'the Middle East' is a zone of immense anxiety and transgressive possibilities. This, as much as oil or geopolitics, points to why 'the Middle East', far from having the potentiality of representing some Archimedean point, remains a 'problem' for modern Western civilization.

Among the nations that were present at Bandung was the Kingdom of Afghanistan. In very recent years, a small number of American universities have seen fit to create a program in Central Asian studies.[17] Some might be inclined to argue that the inspiration for this was derived from the fracturing of the Soviet Union and the transformation of the former Soviet republics into new states that had to be accommodated within the area studies framework. But what seems to me to be the more pertinent consideration is that Afghanistan was for various reasons outside the pale and, if I may use a colloquialism, fell through the cracks, a point that was visibly brought home in the wake of the bombings of 11 September 2001, when the Americans found that virtually no one in their gargantuan political and military establishment had any knowledge of Afghanistan. I recall reading, and find it entirely plausible, that only one person in the State Department, military intelligence, and the CIA knew Pashto. To the best of my knowledge, not a single program in either South Asian Studies or Middle East Studies at that time embraced Afghanistan: what cannot be categorized cannot be studied. With their overweening pride as the guardians of Islamic history and teachings, the scholars of the Muslims societies of the Middle East showed that they had little use for the wild Pathans. In India, and among scholars of South Asian Studies, the memories of the long and extraordinarily complex links between India and the Afghan world—traces of which can be seen in the Mahabharata and linger on in the Sultanate- and early Mughal-period monuments that dot Delhi—had been eviscerated by two centuries of colonialism and the supposition that India had nothing to learn from its past, certainly not from its Muslim past.

Thus was Afghanistan condemned to obscurity in the American academy before the hegemon's obsession with what it stupidly calls the war on terror necessitated the withdrawal of a death warrant.[18]

South Asia in the Global South

Thankfully, Bandung was not hobbled by these constraints, and I have found Bandung a similarly invigorating occasion to think about the linkages between South and Southeast Asia. By and large, South and Southeast Asia are, at least in the American academy, distinct domains of study, even if scholars engaged in diaspora studies or Indian Ocean studies have sought to present them as a unified field. A handful of American institutions have conjoined South and Southeast Asia into a single 'field', but my own experience suggests to me that unfortunately the reasons for doing so have little to do with lofty intellectual reasoning and more to do with commanding numbers and gaining increased leverage with respect to allocation of funding and such matters. It is important, as well, to recognize that some Southeast Asian scholars may be deeply suspicious of efforts to link South and Southeast Asia together as a disguised attempt to impose some kind of nascent Indian imperialism. Though the entire thesis of the substantive Indic roots of Southeast Asian cultures remains attractive in various respects, the various hypotheses about the degree of Indianization of Southeast Asia, the various registers in which it took place, and the role of Kshatriyas (warriors), merchants, and Brahmin priests in acting as conduits for the dissemination of Sanskritic culture have all been ably called into question. 'The Indian influence is no longer regarded as the prime cause of cultural development' in Southeast Asia, two influential German scholars of Indian history have written, and yet they commence their discussion with the unequivocal assertion that 'the transmission of Indian culture to distant parts of Central Asia, China, Japan, and especially Southeast Asia is one of the greatest achievements of Indian history or even of the history of mankind'.[19] It is, to my mind, more than an accident that just as Indonesia played the host, so India was important in giving shape to the program at Bandung and, in the years ahead, becoming the public voice of the Non-Aligned Movement.

How, then, might we characterize the challenge posed by the Bandung conference, particularly in an effort to introduce some differentiations and subtleties into what has become a rather amorphous idea of the Global South? Bandung clearly cannot be read only as an endeavour to forge solidarity between formerly colonized subjects or to create a third path that would steer clear of both the West and what was then the Soviet bloc. One may, with only minimal effort, produce an inventory of the arguments that have been summoned to show that the experience of subjection to colonialism no more unites people today than patriarchy, even allowing for the various inflections it takes, has done anything to produce universal sisterhood. Nationalisms have produced sub-nationalisms and every attempt at secessionism is at first sought to be squashed with a brute display of force. It is an article of faith for postmodernists that there is no fundamental category—not race, not class, not gender—that resists further fragmentation. Another school of thought has sought to emasculate decisively the conception of the Global South with the argument that the entire world is captive to the ideology of neo-liberalism. We are, after all, living in the era of *homo economicus*. The proponents of the idea of the Global South were emboldened by the notion that the arrangement which is signified by the acronym 'BRICS' (Brazil, Russia, India, China [and South Africa]) would mount a significant structural challenge to the global economy; but less than a decade later it seems difficult to view BRICS as having any kind of emancipatory potential for the nations of the South. Even as the most strident critics from the South railed against the structural readjustment policies that the International Monetary Fund (IMF) deploys to punish recalcitrant states, every BRICS country contributed to the organization's $430 billion bailout, China to the tune of $43 billion and India, Russia, and Brazil each contributing an amount of $10 billion.[20] Or, if we may pick up a different narrative which points to the same difficulties, efforts to produce a third permanent seat on the UN Security Council for a BRICS country have come to naught. Russia, notwithstanding its frequent expressions of eternal friendship for India, or its stated ambition to minimize American influence, has been nearly categorical in its refusal to advocate on behalf of a BRICS nation as a Permanent Member of the Security Council. The supposition among India's foreign policymakers, who have long had a reputation in the

West for being romantic, ineffective, and, therefore, effete, that China might support India's bid for such a seat has absolutely no takers.[21]

It would be a truism to say that the BRICS nations are very much in competition with each other, but the failures of BRICS are not those which have been pointed out by policymakers, economists, or others who belong to what I term the realist junta of global politics. While this is not the occasion to excavate the entire history of the term and the various ways in which it insinuated itself into the vocabulary of the Global South, the notion of 'development' is perforce the hook on which the Global South, and then BRICS, was pegged. Most critiques of development have stressed only the fact that it has rarely been the case that the whole nation developed, and that most often development aided those who were in some position to participate in the global economy, could avail themselves of urban networks, or were placed to take advantage of government programs of redress and assistance. In other words, this critique zeroes in on the fact that even if development has aided the poor, it has seldom if ever aided those whose lives are characterized by the most grinding poverty. All of this is what scholars and commentators refer to as 'uneven development'; however, such a critique falls short of any systemic understanding of development as a modern ideology that (in the view of its harshest critics) is fundamentally genocidal, though not merely in its conception of the supposed beneficiaries of development as people who should meekly lay down their lives in the name of the well-being of the nation.[22] Development has no purpose other than to assure its targets that they only have to live out the history of someone else: their present is Europe's past, and their future—well, their future is to live out Europe's present.[23] If adherence to the idea of development—even a development that has been parsed in all its anodyne variants, including 'alternative development', 'development with a human face', 'indigenous development', even the much celebrated 'sustainable development'—was the bedrock of BRICS, and one of the fundamental impulses behind the Global South, it behooves us to ask whether the Global South holds out any hope for liberation from domination of the North and the possibility of at least proportional parity between nations?

To return to the question I have posed, namely, how might we construe the real challenge of Bandung, it can now be rephrased in this fashion: can the Global South mount an intellectual and socio-cultural defense that would facilitate the conditions for an ecologically genuine survival of plurality? In dwelling on this, I propose to join it at the hip to another query that, to the scholar of South Asian Studies, must remain paramount: What can South Asian Studies bring to the idea of the 'Global South'? Or, stated in yet another fashion, what might India and South Asia as a whole bring to the conversations now taking place about the Global South? What specifically does that part of the world bring to our understanding of the Global South, and how does it facilitate a political reading of the Global South that would be generative of a politics of knowledge that is fully cognizant of, and less compromised by, the imperialism of categories that has effectively reduced the social sciences in the Global South to sheer mimicry? I have long argued that no emancipatory work in any of the social sciences disciplines, or in area studies programs, is at all possible without an awareness of the fact that, even more so than Apple, Google, and McDonald's, or pop icons such as Madonna, Beyonce, and Jay Z, it is the entire edifice of Western social science that has been globalized.[24] The very categories through which we think about the world—our very conceptions of development, growth, literacy, poverty, planning, production, state, technology, well-being, to name just a few—have installed an imperialism that appears to be nearly insurmountable.[25] It is surely no accident that, to take the illustration of India, though every Indian language has proved to be a fecund ground for creative literature, equaling if not besting whatever fiction and poetry has appeared at the hands of Indian writers in English, no Indian language has been able to produce a modern social science literature of any substantive merit. Nor has any Indian language been able to draw upon Indian intellectual traditions to generate a vocabulary that would be sensitive to Indian conditions and responsive to the country's own multifarious histories. I would venture to say, at least from my conversations with social scientists whose work focuses on Africa, that precisely the same argument could be advanced apropos of every African language. Remarkably, even Ethiopia, one African country that was not colonized, appropriated the entire intellectual apparatus of the West in giving shape to its own educational institutions, legal systems, and administrative structures; indeed, the colonization of Ethiopia in these respects was not a jot less than what transpired in the rest of Africa that fell to one European power or another.[26] Though it has now become commonplace to trumpet the emergence of China as a superpower, can we point to any theoretical constructs that have emerged from the academic practice of Chinese social science that we could say have been globalized? Some others will point to 'Subaltern Studies' as at least one intellectual contribution of the Global South of note, but the most striking aspect of Subaltern Studies is its overwhelming reliance on various strands of French-inspired poststructuralism, British Marxism, semiotics, and nineteenth- and twentieth-century German philosophy.[27] This is apart from the consideration that Subaltern Studies, much like postcolonial theory, was seeded and flourished in the academy in the West—in Britain, Australia, and the USA.

Any consideration of what 'South Asia' may bring to the Global South must begin with an admission of the difficulties, which I shall enumerate briefly rather than explicate at length, that lie in the way. Proponents of the term, particularly in the American academy, are nevertheless deeply suspicious of the fact that South Asian studies in the USA is often little more than a politically correct moniker for Indian studies. I cannot recall that over the eight years, between 1984 and 1992, that I was a graduate student in the Department of South Asian Languages and Civilizations at the University of Chicago, which has arguably been the most influential site of South Asian studies in the USA, I ever heard any substantive discussion of Pakistan or Bangladesh. The history and politics of Pakistan were not, so to speak, on any syllabus. There was even less mention of Bangladesh, except when Barisal, the birthplace of the great poet Jibanananda Das, was invoked; and I do not at all recall hearing the name of Kazi Nazrul Islam, now often referred to as 'the Poet of Bangladesh'. One could not study Urdu literature, of course, without running into the names of Manto and Faiz, but it is unquestionably the case that South Asian Studies was by default Indian Studies. The effort in recent years, not without some success, to rectify this shortcoming and bring the countries of the subcontinent into the orbit of South Asian scholarship, and thus put some teeth into the term 'South Asia', is certainly admirable. Here, as elsewhere, practice has often preceded theory. There have been many activist networks in which Pakistanis, Indians, and Bangladeshis have worked alongside each other, but these collaborative exercises are barely to be witnessed in the academy. Moreover, among the progressive left activists who have long worked with diasporic South Asian communities in the USA, who are also mindful of the fact that most Americans remain oblivious to distinctions between Pakistanis, Indians, and Bangladeshis, not to mention sub-regional identities, the preferred term for South Asians was always 'desi'. This is one of many ways in which the received hierarchy was questioned.

However, if the endeavour to work with a more expansive conception of 'South Asia' is salutary, opening up that term to the histories that cannot be contained by the nation-state that we call India, I would also point to the desirability of a more critical awareness of the various ways in which 'South Asia' constricts the imagination. I will not now remonstrate, though there is plenty of reason to do so, against the origins of 'South Asia' and indeed the 'Middle East' as part of the administrative machinery of American governance and knowledge formation in the aftermath of the end of World War II. Many others have ably described the idea of area studies as a species of Orientalism.[28] My concern is quite different: where many have advocated for 'South Asia' as a way to circumscribe the reach of India-centric and Hindu-centric narratives, I would like to call attention to the fact that the notion of South Asia no less suggests a bounded space that obscures the extraordinarily rich histories of India's linkages with large parts of Asia. I have already suggested that there is little justification, notwithstanding some concerns about various theses that have hypothesized an outsized historical influence of India over the region, for viewing the histories of South Asia and Southeast Asia as distinct. But much the same argument can be made apropos of India's long-standing links with Afghanistan and Central Asia, and, not any less, with Iran. One of the most pathetic demonstrations of how the realist discourses which revolve around the apotheosis of the nation-state as the 'end of history' have trumped over a civilizational history where Iran and India are inextricably intertwined was on offer when, not so long ago, India joined hands with the so-called 'international community', which is nothing but a form of barbarism to inflict pain on countries that are recalcitrant to American hegemony, to rebuke Iran and have it declared a 'rogue state'. My objection to 'South Asia' is, thus, not only that we should be much less accommodating to the woefully limited American experience of the world. The category 'South Asia' contracts as much as it expands the world. Nor will it suffice to counter this with the argument that in construing the American academy, as well as the other institutions of the hegemon, as furnishing the template for social science scholarship, I am reinforcing the very imperialism of categories that I am seeking to put into question. In India, Pakistan, and indeed in much of the Global South, social science scholarship has for decades been integrated into the norms of American, or at best Anglo-American, scholarly work. More so than in other arenas of political and social life, it is in scholarly work that the idea of 'Empire'—an Empire that is all but American—reigns supreme and can be witnessed in all of its various manifestations, from the older orthodoxies of modernization theory to the more recent strands of work associated with postcolonial theory and other incarnations of poststructuralism.

There are yet other difficulties that inhere in the idea of South Asian area studies. The intellectual apparatus that developed in the American academy for the study and interpretation of South Asian societies was for the first several decades largely restrictive in its scope. The older departments of Sanskrit and Indic studies were, in a manner of speaking, revamped to make some room for the 'vernaculars', though the emphasis on the textual did not by any means disappear; at the other end, the anthropologists descended upon 'the village', that quintessential, timeless, and ubiquitous unit of Indian social life. Something called 'religion' had always been a preoccupation for colonial officials, not least because they were convinced that nowhere in the world did religion occupy so fundamental a place in the lives of ordinary people as in India. Whatever else an Indian might be, she or he was first and foremost the carrier of an intense if almost always unthinking and even instinctual religiosity. Moreover, the colonial state and its functionaries would become spectacularly successful in peddling the view, which to my mind has scarcely been dislodged in the common understanding in the West, howsoever hard some scholars have been labouring to establish otherwise, that the history of India was characterized by relentless and unremitting religious hostility which pitted Hindus against Muslims, Sikhs against Muslims, Hindus against Buddhists, Sunnis against Shias, and so on. The advocates of religion in India held, on the colonial view, an implacable hostility against adherents of other religions; religious animosity was always smoldering on the surface. The slightest provocation was enough to send Indians, who were easily excitable, into a rage against their religious adversaries.

It may be argued that scholars who work on the religious history of South Asia, who are located mainly in area studies departments rather than in religious studies departments or divinity schools, which everywhere in the academies of the West are to the present day dominated by scholars of Christianity and Judaism, have largely dispensed with these and other crude formulations that characterized the colonial readings of Indian religions and especially Hinduism. But I wonder if scholars of the life of religion in South Asia have not fallen—if inadvertently at times—into embracing a different fallacy, helping to shape a little-noticed feature of the academic landscape of Indian religions. Though of course there is a distinguished body of work by American and British scholars on Islam in India, and I refer to the work of Richard Eaton, Barbara Metcalfe, Francis Robinson, and Gail Minault among others, it is not accidental that it takes undivided and pre-independent India as its subject. The area studies specialists have tacitly adopted the view that, subsequent to India's attainment of independence and the vivisection of the country, Pakistan bears some kind of special responsibility for Islam, or, to put it differently, that Pakistan is Islam's special provenance in South Asia. Similarly, Sri Lanka bears the sword for Buddhism, much as India carries the burden of Hinduism.[29] There is, as well, a considerable acceptance of the view that the recrudescence of religious nationalism is a worldwide phenomenon, but whatever the merit of that observation, in South Asia its origins have everything to do with the particular manner in which religion has been tethered to the project of the nation-state. If there is a part of the world where religious inclusiveness was historically the norm, where, to take an instance, colonial officials routinely encountered communities such as 'the Husaini Brahmins' or the Meos that they were at a loss to classify,[30] it is unquestionably South Asia. The cussed and ignorant people of this part of the world refused to draw religious boundaries among themselves: as subjects of a nation-state, they would most assuredly have to learn to do so, even if they had to be brow-beaten into submission. It is largely for this reason that the religious nationalism that has been visibly on display in

recent years in all three countries has become such a potent force, taking on a virulent form and necessitating, in each case, public rituals
of exorcism. If the project in Pakistan is to produce a proper Pakistani
Muslim, one who looks westward to authenticate his Islam and now
disowns the Indic civilization that was his cradle as a contaminant, so
the project in India is to produce a proper Hindu, one who has shed
his effeminacy and will stand up to the Muslim bully, indeed a Hindu
that can and will claim all of the land as *matra bhoomi* (motherland),
rashtra bhoomi (national territory), and *punya bhoomi* (holy land).

India, the Global South, and Ecological Pluralism

To return, yet again, to the question of what South Asia brings to the
conception of the Global South, we may now pose the question thus:
Can Bandung help us to think in the idioms of a civilization, and, if
so, does it create a productive tension between India as a nation-state
and India as a civilization? It is perforce necessary to introduce two
caveats before entertaining any further thoughts on this subject. First,
I am more than aware of the many perils in deploying the discourse
of 'civilization'. We know that far too many people were subjugated
on the grounds that they were allegedly wanting in civilization, and
that European powers took it upon themselves to 'civilize' the primi-
tives, the heathens, and the barbarous. By the late eighteenth century,
and certainly no later than the first half of the nineteenth century, a
civilizational grid had been established as an evaluative scale to judge
the proximity of a given people to civilization. M. K. Gandhi was perhaps only the most unusual and prescient thinker of the twentieth
century to initiate a scathing critique of the pretensions of civilization,
having no regard at all for what are trumpeted as its achievements.
Hind Swaraj, his little tract of 1909, which then and for many years
thereafter seemed the bizarre manifesto of a Luddite, but now seems
eerily incandescent in its surreal predictions about what civilization
would be reduced to, has dozens of passages such as this one:

> Formerly, men travelled in wagons. Now, they fly through the air in
> trains at the rate of four hundred and more miles per day. This is con-
> sidered the height of civilization. It has been stated, as men progress,
> they shall be able to travel in airship and reach any part of the world in

a few hours. Men will not need the use of their hands and feet. They will press a button, and they will have clothing by their side. They will press another button, and they will have their newspaper. A third, and a motor-car will be in waiting for them. ... This is civilization.[31]

Had Gandhi not been writing over a century ago, and that too as a radical insurgent-in-the-making, we might be forgiven for thinking that he was positioning himself as something of a poster boy for a handful of the most iconic global corporations in the world. One has only to click on the Amazon app, log in as a 'Prime' member, and one will have clothing or whatever else one needs almost instantly by one's side; press another app, and one can have the *New York Times* or the newspaper of one's choice with one's morning tea or coffee. And we can scarcely overlook Uber, which can have a 'motor-car' in 'waiting' for us: this, Gandhi surmised, is what is 'civilization', which he judged and satirized as having purchase over humans by rendering unnecessary the use of our hands and feet. However, the fact that the discourse of civilization has been compromised is no reason why we should jettison it, and Gandhi also readily embraced the view that the civilizational ideal stood for something higher even if the notion of 'universal civilization' was derived from a Western narrative about progress. His critique of the nation-state and of industrial modernity stemmed from a reading of civilization as an intrinsically ecumenical entity that is permissive of dissent, ambiguity, and a genuine plurality.

Second, it must be allowed that, even as Bandung facilitated the idea of conversations among the nations of the South and signifies a form of internationalism that seems far more pluralist than anything that is available today, it paradoxically only wound up affirming the centrality of the nation-state. Consider, for example, that the communique issued by the heads of state at Bandung at the end of the conference gave unequivocal encouragement to each nation to seek its own path to—what else—development. However one interprets the idea of development, more particularly when it is set up as a 'national goal', it becomes inextricably tied to the ideology of the nation-state; indeed, it is in the name of development that the nation-state can commit its gravest excesses, usually with no consequences. Consider, too, that even as the nations at Bandung pledged their adherence to an international regime of human rights, the communique affirmed

in the strongest terms the absolute sovereignty of each postcolonial
state and laid down the principle of 'non-interference' in the affairs
of other states as part of the doctrine of *panchsheel* (five principles).
This in turn set the stage both for rivalries among postcolonial states
and, not less alarmingly, the suppression of minorities within each
nation-state. Whatever may have been intended by the signatories
of the Bandung communique, the developmentalist state that would
brook no resistance was enshrined as the logical outcome of the anti-
colonial struggle and the nationalist aspiration.

And, yet, despite all this, it seems to me that what emerged from
Bandung was not only a testament to anti-colonial struggles that in
Asia and increasingly Africa had driven the European colonizer from
power, but the possibility of a civilizational dialogue. South Asia is,
I would venture to say, uniquely positioned to initiate such a dialogue
and offer a new vocabulary, and the chapters in the present volume
are a testament to this hopeful outcome. This civilizational dialogue
can take many forms, some of them wholly unpredictable. To this
end, let me put forward, albeit briefly, a few possibilities—drawn
from India and elsewhere in the Global South—before a more considered discussion of at least one idea that it appears to me can be
recuperated in the service of such a civilizational dialogue. First, it is
widely recognized, even by those who are loathe to make too much of
the Indic substratum that informs the cultural mores and rhythms
of life in much of Southeast Asia, that the Indian epics have left a
lasting influence on art and cultural practices. Throughout this part
of the world, the Mahabharata, the Ramayana, and more widely the
puranic literatures have always been seen as civilizational texts, rather
than as religious works offering sets of prescriptions and injunctions.
Whatever difficulties the countries of Southeast Asia might have in
parleying with India, the epic literature furnishes common grounds
for conversation. In many respects, the Indian origins of these works
have even been obscured: much like cricket, which many in India
doubtless think of as an Indian game in its origins and essence,
played with much less passion in some distant lands such as England
and Australia, so the epic literature has now become intrinsic to the
cultural inheritance of Indonesia, Thailand, and most of the rest of
Southeast Asia.[32] In Indonesia, as in India, the characters drawn from
the Ramayana and the Mahabharata inhabit everyday life, and the

stories routinely inform discussions of politics, economics, ethics, and social mores. Indonesian writers, to take one instance, drew upon the 'mythical imagery and comic-book violence' found in the Indian epics to develop a notion of 'monkey masses' as a metaphor for 'the disenfranchised masses of Indonesia and Rahwana as a metaphor for [President] Suharto', thereby forging a literature of resistance to Suharto and his New Order regime.[33] It is understandable why the Sri Lankan writer, Anil de Silva, should have thought that 'the Ramayana and the Mahabharata, though born in India, belong to the "collective dream" of all of South East Asia'.[34]

Second, we cannot overestimate the reach of what is now termed Bollywood in nearly all of the Global South and beyond. I have read on countless occasions that Bollywood is increasingly to the Global South what Hollywood is to the Global North. It is immaterial that Bollywood's reach now extends to the Global North; the American market, in particular, is not only growing in importance as a market for new Bollywood films, but the USA has been emerging in many films over the course of the last two decades as the very landscape in which the narrative unfolds. The Non-Resident Indian American provides more than just revenues and rather has even become a key part of the plot. It may be too soon to say that 'diasporic India' has displaced 'village India', but the trend is unmistakable. The success of Bollywood in countries in the Middle East and Africa is often attributed to the fact that such films, for all their titillation and lasciviousness, are much less tolerant of nudity and open sexuality, and that viewers across the Global South are much more receptive to films that appear to embody the very values that they themselves embrace—values which are alleged to receive greater recognition outside the West, such as veneration for parents, respects for teachers and elders, the cultivation of proper demeanor, feminine modesty, and so on. These considerations appear to me to carry less weight than is supposed by such arguments; they are also somewhat comical in their rendering of the West as a spiritually barren landscape. I am similarly wary of the argument that the phenomenal success in China of *Dangal*,[35] the Aamir Khan film that revolves around a retired wrestler and the two daughters he grooms for the wrestling ring, suggests that though India has not prevailed against China in the geopolitical sphere, it may be able to leverage its 'soft power' more successfully.[36]

What is, however, remarkably true of Bollywood is that it is unabashed in its embrace of the marvelously fecund world of Indian myths. Viewers outside India where commercial Indian films have found large markets may be accessing this rich mythic world in a different language and through various forms of displacement.[37] Sudha Rajagopalan, in an intriguing study of the extraordinary reception given to Hindi-language films in the aftermath of the death of Stalin until the end of the Soviet period, has suggested that there was a constellation of reasons which led to the immense popularity of Indian cinema in the former Soviet Union. Many among those from whom she collected oral testimonies stated that they found the state-mandated socialist realism tradition of cinema tiresome; some stated that in Indian films they were 'confronted with the personal', as opposed to the ideological, 'for the first time'; and yet others discovered in Indian cinema 'a means to play with a world beyond the prescribed boundaries of their reality'. Rajagopalan characterizes the 'dull, unchanging and homogeneous reality' of Soviet cinema as perceived by the subjects of her study as 'Soviet monochrome'—a world of 'practicality and rationalism',[38] a world circumscribed by the rigorous dictates of history and rigidly beholden to the teleology of historical time. Though she does not quite put it this way, Indian cinema has been inventive and successful in generating a geography of affect, but its empire of myth is even more impressive. The irony of it is that middle-class educated Indians are convinced that, in the fashion of the West, they need to be more attentive to history-writing and that the battle in India against the forces of communalism and fascism will be won the day that scientific history triumphs over myths. Quite to the contrary, the battle has been already lost precisely because everything was surrendered to the terrain of the historians.[39] India needs to make much better use of its storehouse of mythic material: it is potent, it is fecund and generative, and regales in ambiguity and is thus civilizational in its impulse, intention, and import.

We could, in a similar fashion, advert at length to what may be called 'the varieties of Islam', more pronounced perhaps in India and Indonesia than anywhere else in the world, and what they bring to the global conversations about Muslim societies. Though Indonesia is predominantly Muslim, and larger than any other country that is a Muslim-majority state, it has had little trouble, as I have already hinted, accommodating Indian mythic material into the national cultural ethos. In one of Jakarta's largest public squares is to be found a massive sculptural representation of perhaps the most iconic scene from the Mahabharata, that is the delivery of the sermon known as the *Bhagavad Gita* from Krishna, who appears in the guise of a charioteer, to the Pandava prince Arjuna, urging him to be faithful in the performance of his duties.[40] How might one try to reconcile the Indonesian Muslim's world with the Islam of the Arabian Peninsula? While the 'leaders of the free world', such as they are, have lavished attention on ISIS and promised to eradicate it from the face of the earth, the far more insidious threat posed by the Wahhabi state of Saudi Arabia is overlooked, of course all in the name of 'national interest' and geopolitical compulsions. Is it not precisely because the Qawwali music that has come down from the Chisthi Sufi order is undeniably part of the inheritance of Islam in South Asia that the purists in Pakistan, who claim adherence only to Wahhabism, had to assassinate one of its greatest exponents, Amjad Sabri, with the specious argument that Islam forbids music?[41]

We might, as a final instance, turn to the contemporary problem of refugees in an effort to comprehend what the Global South, which today is merely seen in the capitals of the Global North as a vast cesspool from which refugees sputter out, has contributed, both by way of historical experience and the categories it has deployed to speak of the stranger at one's doorstep, to this discourse. In the received narrative, the Global South generates refugees and the Global North, in varying degrees of graciousness, receives them. Thus, as a singular instance, the story of Syria that has dominated the headlines for the last several years calls to mind a country that has forced out millions of people. There are countless number of reports in the media of the difficulties that the countries of Western Europe and the white Anglophone world have encountered in integrating these refugees into their societies, and many such reports celebrate the heroic and altruistic disposition of the hosts who are often described as being guided by their Christian faith. This narrative, in its most widely accepted form, occludes the fact that the Global North hosts a miniscule number of these refugees in comparison to those who are hosted by the neighbouring countries of Turkey, Lebanon, and Jordan. Over 3.5 million refugees from Syria were registered in Turkey alone by December 2017,

and another million in Lebanon; in Western Europe, Germany, which
has hosted about half a million refugees, is singularly alone in dis-
playing compassion toward refugees to a similar extent. Germany,
of course, knows a thing or two about inflicting holocausts, and
I am certain that theologians and cultural historians will pronounce
upon Lutheran guilt as the driving force behind the country's efforts
to seek redemption. In contrast, the USA, for all of its characteristically pompous and pathetically pious proclamations about the country's exceptional record in welcoming to its shores the wretched of
the earth, had settled 16,218 refugees by November 2016—and this
during the allegedly progressive presidency of Barack Obama. The
dominant narrative occludes, even more significantly, any awareness
of the historic role of Syria over the course of the last 200 years as a
haven for millions of refugees, from Circassians in the eighteenth
and nineteenth centuries and Armenians in the early twentieth century to Iraqis in the early twenty-first century.[42] By 1925, the Armenian
population of Aleppo had increased to over 200,000 from just 20,000
less than four years earlier, accounting for over a quarter of the city's
population.[43] At the end of 2010, before the onset of the civil war in
the following year, Syria played host to over a million refugees and
asylum-seekers from Iraq—dwarfing anything that has ever been
done by the USA for refugees.[44]

The Question of Hospitality: An Ethical
Framework for the Future

The problem is not merely or even that the countries of the Global
South are all too often ignorant of their own histories, or that
they have been much too permissive of dominant narratives. The
everyday experiences, life forms, and cultural norms were, in the
civilizational worlds of West Asia, central Asia, and South Asia,
conducive to an ethos of hospitality. This may appear to be an odd
if not cruel time for suggesting that the civilizational nexus of India
is fundamentally grounded in the principle of hospitality and that
such a principle can assist us in delivering an ethical framework for
the future. A Hindu nationalist government is in power, commands
a substantial majority in Parliament, and clearly has the support
of a substantial portion of the populace; the same government has

been permissive in allowing the naked abrogation of the rights of Dalits, Muslims, and various other constituencies, among them students, intellectuals, and human rights activists who are viewed as insufficiently supportive of the agenda of Hindu nationalism if not outright opposed to it. Dalits and Muslims have been lynched, and a system of targeted assassinations has sought to silence those who have dared to speak openly of the alarming descent of India into an authoritarian state. Hindu nationalism's most rabid supporters, whether organized as paramilitary groups, vigilantes who see themselves as the custodians of Hinduism, or merely hoodlums for hire, have created a culture of fear and terrorized many people into submission. Inclusiveness, as I argued in an opinion piece for the *Indian Express* on the anniversary of the assassination of Gandhi, is the touchstone of a Republic; but the Republic of India is increasingly exhibiting signs, which may be argued are intrinsic to the nation-state, of insularity and xenophobia.[45]

There is, nevertheless, yet a case to be made for 'hospitality', though others may wish to rest their case on the famous tendency of Indian voters to boot out incumbents and restore some order of civility. In arguing thus, I am also mindful of the fact that one must first contend with the indisputable fact that, like many of the richest words in (at least) the English language, 'hospitality' has been degraded by its present usage. The 'hospitality industry' has become one of the largest and profitable sectors of the corporate world, indeed the world-wide tourism boom: there are surely more students studying 'hospitality' than physics, astronomy, deconstruction, or postcolonial theory, most likely all of the four (and many more subjects) taken together. The present breed of middle-class Indians moving into the service sectors of the economy who have pounced upon hotel management and business administration with unbounded enthusiasm can perforce think of hospitality only when it is conjoined with 'industry', not showing—any more than others around the world who are all partaking of the gigantic 'hospitality industry'—the slightest awareness that the two terms in apposition have an agonistic relationship to each other. It is perhaps imperative to add that the allied and older discourse of 'tolerance' has also become an increasingly difficult even impossible terrain to negotiate. As the discussion of tolerance in Western literature since the time of

Erasmus and John Locke amply demonstrates, even the most ardent advocates of tolerance have often had to concede that tolerance implies 'tolerating' the other. Two radical critics of the monoculture of a global civil society have summed up the difficulties in an arresting formulation: 'Tolerance is but the "civilized" form of intolerance.'[46] In tolerating the other, perhaps one situates oneself in a hierarchical relationship to the other—though, in these times, it appears to me no mean task to even be able to tolerate the other, since there is no tolerating the other without some self-restraint.

What is, indeed, striking, at least in the public discourse of contemporary India, is the degree to which both the left and the right have demonstrated an acute intolerance for 'tolerance'. From the standpoint of Indian secularists and liberals, all talk of tolerance reeks of intolerable conceit on the part of the Hindu. In this scenario, the Hindu reels off an imaginary history of 'Hindu tolerance': Hinduism is conceived as a uniquely tolerant religion, hospitable not only to enormous even unfathomable variety within the fold of Hinduism but even to the faiths that are fundamentally alien to the Hindu spirit and 'way of life'. The barbarous treatment dished out to the lower castes over millennia, on the left view, is altogether forgotten, rationalized, or even defended on the most specious grounds. Hinduism, so argues these critics, is crowned in the discourse on 'Hindu tolerance' as the religion that stands at the apex of civilization—not because it delivers a straightforward message from a singular messiah, but precisely because it is permissive of many teachings, a multitude of gods, and an open-endedness that stands in stark contrast to the stern austerity that characterizes the unforgiving Semitic faiths. Surprisingly, however, the advocates of Hindu nationalism are even less accepting of the idea of Hindu tolerance. To them it was 'Hindu tolerance' that became the graveyard for tens of millions of Hindus over centuries of rule by rapacious foreigners and in particular the despotisms of successive Muslim dynasties. 'Hindu tolerance' and the laissez-faire dispositions of Hindu kings rendered their subjects vulnerable to foreign rulers, unaware as they were of the fact that the foreigners trooping into India were carriers of the most rigid forms of religious dogmatism. Hindu tolerance, so say the advocates of Hindu nationalism, is only for the weak and the effete: India has had enough of that to last many afterlives. Thus has intolerance for 'Hindu tolerance' united those who position them-selves as bitter foes.[47]

What, then, is to be said of hospitality? We have supposed that what are alleged to be the 'cosmopolitan' cultures of the West furnish the templates of hospitality to the rest of the world, but the South Asian ethos was permissive of hospitality in altogether different idioms than those that have become the currency of the day in liberal democracies. Two stories told by Rabindranath Tagore, during the course of a visit to China in 1924, are uniquely illustrative in this respect.[48] He was once traveling in his native Bengal and, at a place some 100 miles from Calcutta, his car overheated; every few miles he had to stop and ask for water so that he could cool down the engine. The entire area was suffering from a severe drought; time after time, through fifteen villages, Tagore had quite the same experience. Though the villagers had little water to spare, and almost none to drink, their sense of hos-pitality made it impossible for them to refuse him water. Elaborating upon this story in his Hibbert Lectures at Oxford in 1930 on the 'Religion of Man', Tagore notes that they had but to follow 'the inexo-rable law of demand supply', making a business deal out of it; 'the millionaire tourist', rushing through a village at sixty miles an hour, would have considered these poor, ignorant villagers as poorly versed in the laws of success, seriously in want of some manual on how one can move from being wretchedly poor to gloriously rich. It was their dharma, Tagore contends, that moved them to such generosity: it is the same dharma that made them reject the idea that they could, as a consequence, claim any merit or reward. What others were likely to mistake as the acts of simpletons arose from a 'simplicity [that] is the product of centuries of culture' and is 'difficult of imitation'; as Tagore further argues, 'to be absolutely simple in one's hospitality to one's enemy, or to a stranger, requires generations of training'.[49]

On the same trip to China in 1924, Tagore describes a Mahsud village in Afghanistan that was being 'pacified' from the air by the British. One of the fighter aircraft had to make an emergency landing in the middle of the village, and two airmen were pulled out of the burning wreckage; though they were surrounded by villagers who had lost some of their family members to the bombing and whose homes they had destroyed, the airmen were taken to a nearby cave where they were fed and nursed back to health before being allowed to depart.

'According to a Mahsud', Tagore explained to his audience,

hospitality is a quality by which he is known as a man and therefore he
cannot afford to miss his opportunity, even when dealing with someone who can be systematically relentless in enmity. From the practical
point of view, the Mahsud pays for this very dearly, as we must always
pay for that which we hold most valuable. It is the mission of civilization to set for us the right standard of valuation. The Mahsud may have
many faults for which he should be held accountable; but that, which
has imparted for him more value to hospitality than to revenge, may
not be called progress, but is certainly civilization.[50]

But hospitality beckons forth not only some histories: it is, I
would wager the thought, an epistemological category—suggestive
of how we know the other, and how we may become stranger to
ourselves such that the stranger to us becomes familiar—that is all but
unavailable to those who are conversant only in the language of the
nation-state. Hospitality, sad to say, is now nothing but that mangled
monster which is contained in the term 'hospitality industry'. It is as
a civilizational category that we shall have to recuperate 'hospitality'.
Thus, to extrapolate from this instance, might we be able to think of
generating categories of knowledge and being in the world which are
at least to some degree opaque to dominant knowledge systems? If
we do not do so, the 'Global South' will rapidly become what I fear
it is already in some measure, that is a hip term, which points to
the genius and remarkable tenacity of the American academy in its
capacity to defang, delimit, debilitate, and ultimately decimate any
idea that resonates with the slightest possibility of unmanageable
epistemological dissent.

Notes and References

1. Thomas Hylland Eriksen, 'What's Wrong with the Global North and the
   Global South?', in *Concepts of the Global South: Voices from around the
   World* (Global South Studies Center, University of Cologne, Germany),
   available at https://frontiers-of-solitude.org/blog/257 (accessed on 12
   April 2019).
2. Cyprus, which was not independent, was also present at the conference;
   South Africa, an apartheid state that was beginning to face the force of
   international ostracism, was represented by the African National Congress.

3. Opening Address of President Sukarno, 18 April 1955, in *Asia-Africa Speak from Bandung* (Djakarta: The Ministry of Foreign Affairs, Republic of Indonesia, 1955), 19–29.

4. Amitav Acharya, 'Studying the Bandung Conference from a Global IR Perspective', *Australian Journal of International Affairs* 70, no. 4 (2016), 342–57 at 343.

5. Anne-Isabel Richard, 'The Limits of Solidarity: Europeanism, anti-colonialism and socialism at the Congress of the Peoples of Europe, Asia and Africa in Puteaux, 1948', *European Review of History-Revue europeenne d'historie* 21, no. 4 (2014), 519–37.

6. Cited by A. Appadorai, 'The Bandung Conference: The Genesis of the Conference', in A. Appadorai, *The Bandung Conference* (New Delhi: The Indian Council of World Affairs, 1955), 1.

7. An elementary Google search, for all its faults, is illustrative of how deeply ingrained are the hierarchies I have suggested in the English language. The phrase 'Europe, Asia and Africa', with quotation marks, yielded 1,340,000 hits; by contrast, 'Africa, Asia, and Europe' shows up 524,000 times. The phrase 'men, women, and children' turns up 27,500,000 results; but the phrase 'children, women, and men' yielded only 279,000 hits, and 'women, men, and children' still turned up only 5,280,000 results, or less than 20 per cent of the results when the traditional phrase was used in the search. This data is from a search conducted on 14 June 2018.

8. I am aware that Pakistani writers such as Mohammed Hanif and Mohsin Hamid or, from an earlier generation, Hanif Kureishi and Bapsi Sidhwa, have acquired something of a following among Indians. These writers, however, are largely based abroad, even if they maintain residences in Pakistan: the more germane consideration is that Pakistani writers of the diaspora, as is true of the much larger number of Indian writers in diverse diasporic settings, work within the parameters of a highly anglicized conception of 'world literature'. It is not only that they write in English, but the subject matter of their fiction, and the sensibility that they bring to their writing, has already been shaped in the vortex of certain familiar conceptions of humanism, cosmopolitanism, and the 'liberal imagination'.

9. Ngugi wa Thion'o, 'Asia in My Life', *Frontline* 29, no. 10 (19 May–1 June 2012), available at http://www.frontline.in/static/html/fl2910/stories/20120601291012200.htm (accessed on 18 March 2019).

10. Richard Wright, *The Color Curtain: A Report on the Bandung Conference* [1956], reprinted in Richard Wright, *Black Power: Three Books from Exile*, with an introduction by Cornel West (New York: Harper Perennial, 2008), 437–8.

11. Wright, *The Color Curtain*, 572.

12. See *Indonesian Notebook: A Sourcebook on Richard Wright and the Bandung Conference*, eds. Brian Russell Roberts and Keith Foulcher (Durham, North Carolina: Duke University Press, 2016).

13. In 1910, W. E. B. DuBois assumed the editorship of *The Crisis: A Record of the Darker Races*, the journal of the National Association for the Advancement of Colored Peoples (NAACP).

14. Others, besides European and American scholars, have also gravitated toward the view that Islam occupies something of a middling place between the Judeo-Christian world and the 'Orient'. The most famous Japanese scholar of Islam, Okawa Shumei, later to gain notoriety as an apologist of Japanese imperialism in China, took this view. See Akira Usuki, 'A Japanese Asianist's View of Islam', *Annals of Japan Association for Middle East Studies* 28, no. 2 (January 2013), 59–84.

15. In my invocation of Abrahamic religions, I do not mean to suggest that the 'family of Abraham' is unproblematically singular or that we should uncritically adopt the term. However, whatever divides Judaism, Christianity, and Islam from each other, they also have much in common. For an intelligent discussion of these faiths and their varying interpretation of stories shared among them, see Carol Bakhos, *The Family of Abraham* (Cambridge, Mass.: Harvard University Press, 2014).

16. See, for example, Garry Wills, 'My Koran Problem', *New York Review of Books* (24 March 2016); and *What the Qur'an Meant, and Why It Matters* (New York: Viking, 2017).

17. My home institution, the University of California, Los Angeles (UCLA), is one of a handful of universities with a Program on Central Asia, though it is of recent vintage. The University of Nebraska at Omaha established the Center for Afghanistan Studies in 1972, which is described as the 'world's only permanent research center devoted entirely to the study of Afghanistan's geography, culture, and people'. (See https://www.unomaha.edu/international-studies-and-programs/center-for-afghanistan-studies/about-us/mission-and-history.php [accessed 10 June 2018].) The center, however, is less a research institution than a public service and advocacy organization, publishing and distributing textbooks in Afghanistan, facilitating cultural exchanges between Afghanistan and the USA, and conducting workshops on Afghan studies for American high school teachers. *The Journal of Afghanistan Studies*, the first of its kind, commenced publication in 2018 but is an initiative of another new organization, the American Institute of Afghanistan Studies (https://afghan-institute.org/).

18. For those who are puzzling over what this means, it may be worthwhile to recall the economist Joan Robinson's alleged pronouncement that 'the only thing that was worse than being colonized was not being colonized' (cited by Ashis Nandy, *The Illegitimacy of Nationalism: Rabindranath Tagore and the Politics of Self* [New Delhi: Oxford University Press, 1994], 3). I have not been able to identify this quotation in any of the writings of Robinson, though she did write something that appears to have the same weight: 'As we see nowadays in South-East Asia or the Caribbean', Robinson remarked in her 1962 book *Economic Philosophy*, 'the misery of being exploited by capitalists is nothing compared to the misery of not being exploited at all' (New York: Doubleday, 46). Whatever the exact meaning that one might impute to Robinson's remark, Nandy's formulation of it does not appear any less compelling merely because it is somewhat inaccurate. There are an ample number of writers who continue to take the view that colonialism was doubtless the most desirable outcome for Africa, though not unexpectedly the Africans squandered the benefits of colonialism upon freedom. As Paul Johnson once put it, 'Colonialism's Back—and Not a Moment Too Soon', *New York Times Magazine* (18 April 1993).

19. Hermann Kulke and Dietmar Rothermund, *A History of India*, 3rd ed. (London: Routledge, 1998), 43–5.

20. Annie Lowrey, 'I.M.F. Adds $430 Billion for Lending', *New York Times* (21 April 2012), B1; 'BRICS Pledges $75 Billion Contribution to IMF's Bailout Fund', *Times of India* (19 June 2012), available at https://timesofindia.indiatimes.com/business/india-business/BRICS-pledges-75-billion-contribution-to-IMFs-bailout-fund/articleshow/14266972.cms (accessed on 25 March 2018). South Africa, the fifth member of BRICS as of 2010, contributed the remaining $2 billion.

21. See Ian Bremmer, 'Brazil Wants Some Security Council Love. But It Won't Get It (Yet)', *Foreign Policy* (3 April 2012), available at http://foreignpolicy.com/2012/04/03/brazil-wants-some-security-council-love-but-it-wont-get-it-yet/(accessed on 28 March 2018); 'The BRICS without Mortar', *Stratfor Report* (23 October 2016), available at https://worldview.stratfor.com/article/brics-without-mortar (accessed on 28 March 2018); Ana Palacio, 'What Do the BRICS Mean for US Leadership', *World Economic Forum* (1 October 2015), available at https://www.weforum.org/agenda/2015/10/what-do-the-brics-mean-for-us-leadership/ (accessed on 28 March 2018).

22. There is a large and very radical body of critical work on development. See, in particular, Wolfgang Sachs, ed., *The Development Dictionary: A Guide to Knowledge as Power*, 2nd ed. (London: Zed Books, 2009), and

Majid Rahnema and Victoria Bawtree, eds., *The Post-Development Reader* (London: Zed Books, 1997).

23. For a further elaboration of this argument, see Vinay Lal, 'The Concentration Camp and Development: The Pasts and Future of Genocide', *Patterns of Prejudice* 39, no. 2 (2005), 220–43.

24. Vinay Lal, *Empire of Knowledge: Culture and Plurality in the Global Economy*, 2nd enlarged ed. (London: Pluto Press, 2002; New Delhi: Vistaar/Sage Publications, 2005).

25. See Vinay Lal and Ashis Nandy, eds., *The Future of Knowledge and Culture: A Dictionary for the 21st Century* (New Delhi: Viking Penguin, 2004).

26. Yirga Gelaw Woldeyes, *Education and the Economy of Violence against Traditions in Ethiopia* (Trenton, New Jersey: The Red Sea Press, 2017).

27. I have discussed this at length in Chapter 4 of my *The History of History: Politics and Scholarship in Modern India* (Delhi: Oxford University Press, 2003; 2nd rev. ed., 2005).

28. Rey Chow, 'The Politics and Pedagogy of Asian Literatures in American Universities', in *Writing Diaspora: Tactics of Intervention in Contemporary Cultural Studies* (Bloomington: Indiana University Press, 1993), 120–4.

29. I wish this insight had been mine; it is not. The idea is taken from Ashis Nandy, 'The Idea of South Asia: A Personal Note on Post-Bandung Blues', *Inter-Asia Cultural Studies* 6, no. 4 (2005), 541–5.

30. See M. Mujeeb, *The Indian Muslims* (London: George Allen & Unwin, 1971), 15–16; on the Meos, see Abhay Chawla, 'How Meos Shape Their Identity', *Economic and Political Weekly* 51, no. 10 (5 March 2016), who states quite bluntly, 'Outsiders were unable to understand their syncretistic practices. Diverse explanations are available regarding the Meos converting from Hinduism to Islam.' The online version can be found at https://www.epw.in/journal/2016/10/web-exclusives/how-meos-shape-their-identity.html (accessed on 26 January 2019). For a more expansive and detailed study of the Meos, see Shail Mayaram, *Resisting Regimes: Myth, Memory and the Shaping of a Muslim Identity* (New Delhi: Oxford University Press, 2000).

31. M.K. Gandhi, *Hind Swaraj or Indian Home Rule*, rev. new ed. (Ahmedabad: Navajivan Publishing House, 1939 [1909]), 32–3.

32. Among many works on this subject, see Vittorio Roveda, *In the Shadow of Rama: Murals of the Ramayana in Mainland Southeast Asia* (Bangkok: River Books Press, 2016); Singaravelu Sachithanantham, *The Ramayana Tradition in Southeast Asia* (Kuala Lumpur: University of Malaya Press, 2004); and Gauri Parimoo Krishnan, ed., *Ramayana in Focus: Visual and Performing Arts of Asia* (Singapore: Asian Civilisations Museum, 2010).

33. Marshall Clark, 'Shadow Boxing: Indonesian Writers and the Ramayana in the New Order', *Indonesia*, no. 72 (October 2001), 164.

34. Anil de Silva, 'The Collective Dream of a Continent', *UNESCO Courier*, Year 20 (December 1967), 13.

35. Rob Cain, '5 Key Reasons for Dangal's Massive Success in China', *Forbes* (31 May 2017), available at https://www.forbes.com/sites/robcain/2017/05/31/5-key-reasons-for-dangals-massive-success-in-china/#13b6474b35be (accessed on 28 May 2018).

36. Amy Qin, 'A Bollywood Smash with a Twist, in China's Cultural Battle with India', *New York Times* (30 September 2017), A10.

37. It is worth noting that among diasporic Indian communities, films in other Indian languages, such as Tamil and Malayalam, also have a considerable following. A case in point is the market for Tamil-language films in Malaysia, besides the other obvious example of Tamil speakers in Sri Lanka who have furnished a market for Tamil cinema. Interestingly, though Chennai is the hub of the Tamil film industry—dubbed Kollywood, a portmanteau of Kodambakkam, the neighbourhood where the studios are concentrated, and Hollywood—films in Tamil are also produced in increasingly growing numbers in Malaysia itself. However, one cannot speak of the globalization of Tamil cinema in quite the same vein as one speaks of the near worldwide audience for what is termed 'Bollywood'. Nor am I concerned for the present with whether Bollywood is at all the apt term for commercial Hindi-language cinema before the mid-1990s, when what is now termed 'Bollywood' might be said to have come into being with films such as *Dilwale Dulhaniya Le Jayenge* (1995).

38. Sudha Rajagopalan, *Indian Films in Soviet Cinemas: The Culture of Movie-Going after Stalin* (Bloomington, Indiana: Indiana University Press, 2008), 38–52.

39. The argument is extended in Vinay Lal, *The History of History: Politics and Scholarship in Modern India*, 2nd ed. (New Delhi: Oxford University Press, 2005).

40. The sculpture, *Wijaya Arjuna*, or 'The Victory of Arjuna', stands in central Jakarta against the backdrop of the twin towers of Bank Indonesia. Eleven horses are yoked to the chariot; the scene could reasonably be described as being drawn more generally from the Mahabharata rather than the Bhagavad Gita specifically; however, on a visit to Jakarta in 1999, I was told that at the sculpture's inauguration in 1987 President Suharto invoked the Gita and enjoined the audience present to follow its teachings on *nishkamkarma* (self-less action). See also I Gusti Made Dwi Guna, *Nyoman Nuarta: pematung internasional yang pantang menyerah* (Jakarta: Badan Pengembangan dan Pembinaan Bahasa, 2017), 16–18.

41. Vinay Lal, 'The Murder of a Sufi Qawwal and a Nation in Its Death-Throes' (25 June 2016), available at https://vinaylal.wordpress.com/2016/06/25/the-murder-of-a-sufi-qawwal-and-a-nation-sate-in-its-death-throes/ (accessed on 28 May 2018); and Khaled Abou El Fadl, 'Lamenting the Murder of One of the Sabri Brothers', UCLA Newsroom (30 June 2016), available at http://newsroom.ucla.edu/stories/ucla-faculty-voice-lamenting-the-murder-of-one-of-the-sabri-brothers (accessed on 28 May 2018).

42. Dawn Chatty, *Syria: The Making and Unmaking of a Refuge State* (London: C. Hurst & Co., 2018).

43. Richard G. Hovannisian, *The Armenian People from Ancient to Modern Times*, vol. 2, *Foreign Domination to Statehood: The Fifteenth Century to the Twentieth Century* (New York: Palgrave Macmillan, 2004), 425.

44. United Nations High Commission for Refugees, *UNHCR Global Report 2010*, 'Syrian Arab Republic', 189–93, available at http://www.unhcr.org/4dfdbf50b.html (accessed on 2 April 2018).

45. Vinay Lal, 'A Republic of Inhospitality', *Indian Express* (30 January 2018), available at https://indianexpress.com/article/opinion/republic-day-muslims-intolerance-beef-ban-bjp-dalits-hamid-ansari-5040847/ (accessed on 19 March 2019).

46. Gustavo Esteva and Madhu Suri Prakash, *Grassroots Post-Modernism: Remaking the Soil of Cultures* (London: Zed Books, 1998), 87.

47. For a much lengthier treatment of this subject, see Vinay Lal, 'Intolerance for "Hindu Tolerance": Hinduism, Religious Violence in Pre-modern India, and the Fate of a "Modern" Discourse', in *Religion und Gewalt: Konflikte, Rituale, Deutungen (1500–1800)*, edited by Kaspar von Greyerz and Kim Siebenhuner (Gottingen: Vandenhoeck & Ruprecht, 2006), 51–84.

48. Rabindranath Tagore, 'Talks in China' [1924], in *The English Writings of Rabindranath Tagore*, vol. 4, *Essays*, ed. Mohit K. Ray (New Delhi: Atlantic Publishers & Distributors, 2007), 741–805.

49. Rabindranath Tagore, *The Religion of Man* (London: George Allen & Unwin, 1931; reprint ed., Boston: Beacon Press, 1961), 149–50.

50. Tagore, 'Talks in China', 741–805.

2

LEARNING AND HAPPINESS
Sketches for an Alternative Theorization
of Indian Sociality*

VIVEK DHARESHWAR

The question how we can draw from Indian thought or intellectual
traditions to learn to live in our contemporary world is yet to find a
satisfactory articulation. Our problem is not simply that we no longer
employ terms such as *atman, avidya,* and dharma to reflect on our
experience; the terms that we do indeed use—sovereignty, secularism,
rights, civil society, political society, and corruption—seem to insulate
our experience from our reflection! The predicament we find ourselves
in will not even appear as a predicament until and unless we think
through the choice we have to make between (*a*) religion and tradition, (*b*) history and the past, (*c*) philosophy and *adhyatma,* and (*d*) the
caste-system and the practitional matrix. The task of reconceptualizing
Indian intellectual traditions and making them available for our reflection must begin by inquiring why the first term in each of the pairs
above stands for a domain of inquiries and disciplines that blocks and
distorts the element in which Indian thought moves. This chapter will
take an indirect route to explore the implications of that choice.[1]

---

* An earlier version of this article appeared in the inaugural issue of the
e-journal *Unbound.*

My research into Indian thought and social structure (which has
been necessarily comparative because one has to understand the
relationship between Western descriptions of India and the Western
culture, in all domains) has led me to formulate the hypothesis that
the intellectual traditions of India were (are?), without exception, concerned with discovering the meta-learning paths to understanding
the relationship between learning and happiness. In some form or
the other, the central question common to all the Indian intellectual
traditions is the relationship between learning and happiness. If my
claim is correct, exploring that question will allow us to understand
the extraordinary insights generated by the Indian traditions; by
learning to ask that question again we would at the same time be
continuing their pursuit.

Because of their insight into the ways and stages of learning
as well as into the nature of the learner, Indian traditions saw the
need to set up multiple sites of learning to encompass and articulate Indian sociality. The ambition was to make learning penetrate
all aspects of sociality (through what we now think of as ritual, art,
and other practical disciplines). In short, ethical learning was inseparable from sociality. When this extraordinarily complex and dynamic
configuration of learning came into confrontation with a religious
and moralizing culture, namely, the West, the latter had no resources
to understand it cognitively except to see its practices—the fine inter-
articulation of sociality and ethical learning—as immoral. Why the
Western frame is normative in this way is itself a research question:
when we look at 'the caste-system' or 'Hinduism' as normed prod-
ucts of the Western frame, rather than as theoretical entities whose
background theory we can reconstruct and understand, we will come
to the realization that 'the caste-system' or other such entities are
black boxes that obstruct our understanding of the meta-learning
paths that Indian sociality represents. While we need to understand
the pragmatic reasons for the perpetuation of these black-boxing
categories, it is vital for the reconceptualization task to realize that
they are not cognitively justified. When objections are raised to the
very possibility of an alternative knowledge system, all the objections
are unsurprisingly parasitic upon colonial descriptions, and these
parasitic discourses are threatened by what undermines their existence, namely, alternative knowledge.

The challenge that the framework I am excavating or articulating has to confront is: in what way can the learning or cognitive attitude deal effectively with parasitism? This chapter will argue that that is indeed the challenge Indian traditions give us the resources to tackle: the indirect route taken by this chapter will make clear how *swaraj*, parasitism, phantasy (*upadhi, maya*), desire, ignorance, learning and knowledge (avidya and *jnana*) are to be thought in terms that makes sense to us today. If we pursue this insight about how the Indian traditions sought to create a learning society,[2] we will be able to develop alternatives in all the domains where we are now saddled with normative theories, some disguised as 'social scientific' theories and others as political and legal doctrines, and some even as interpretations of 'Indian philosophy'.

My strategy in this chapter will be as follows. I will set out the framework within which to understand the link between practical knowledge and sociality. The framework will, I hope, enable us to understand the audacity and profundity of the attempts by Indian traditions to organize the social and natural spaces, relations, and events/acts as learning experiences. At the limit, everything—event, space, happening, acts, and structures—is sought to be encompassed by the learning attitude. The different traditions are distinguished by the different ways in which they go about achieving or elaborating such an attitude. Only when we achieve a conceptualization of this extraordinary process and the cognitive or learning attitude it nurtured will we begin to have a sense of the nature of practical knowledge. While the formulation of this hypothesis in this particular form is possibly novel, as my discussion of Gandhi and Tagore (and of their debate, in particular) will make clear, they were articulating it in other ways, both practitionally and theoretically. I will then turn to explaining why normativity is a problem and what kind of problem it is especially for Indians. The contrast between the learning attitude and normativization that I am setting up will enable us to formulate novel questions for future research as well.

Adhyatma as Reflection on Experience

There is a sense in which adhyatma is almost entirely an activity; whatever speculative or descriptive sense we might be tempted to

see in it through the metaphysical lens of onto-theology is entirely
subordinate to facilitating the particular kind of activity it engages
itself in. What kind of activity is it? In one formulation, we could say
that it is an activity that aims to fully realize experience. When talking about reflection on experience, it is important to realize that we
invariably use experience to refer to what occurs or happens (*bhava*)
as well as to the result of the activity of assimilating or understanding what happens, what we undergo (*anu-bhava*). How to turn the
happenings—sad or happy, ordinary or extraordinary, natural or
social—into experience constitutes the adhyatmic inquiry. Clearly
there are any number of ways of saliencing what is important and
how to transform that into experience. Elsewhere, I have coined the
term practitional matrix to conceptualize experiential inquiry that
characterizes the Indian intellectual traditions.[3] The thought behind
it is something like this: action is always action in a matrix, like a
gesture in a dance, sound in a raga, or offering in a ritual. You learn to
appease the ancestors and that involves engaging the past in a practitional matrix; you express your gratitude to the implements that have
helped in your interaction with the world, so *ayudha puja* is a practitional matrix that engages the implements. Since there are no events
or occurrences that are by themselves trivial or significant and there
may be multiple ways of engaging each event or aspect or dimension
of what occurs, diversity of practitions is a given. That is why too the
diversity of Indian traditions. The central inquiry though is about
awareness or self-consciousness—realizing the atman is the way one
tradition speaks of it (Vedantins), another might speak of 'standing
in awareness' (*arivinalli niluvu*, a phrase used by *vacanakaras* writing
in Kannada), but none speak of it as a 'religious' or 'mystical' event
only manifest to some, and actually attained by none, as is the case
with monasticization in Christianity. The theological or normative
frame has, unfortunately, turned the talk of atman into some sort of
revelation, and the Bhakti traditions (so-called popular Hinduism)
have been accorded the mystic status.

Every element that is potentially a way of completing experience
is also a way in which experience could get distorted or occluded
altogether. An architect concerned with understanding how space
can enhance living, or relationships of those who inhabit it, begins to
be parasitic on the real estate sector's exploitation of land for selling

phantasmatic ideas of living. A singer begins to make her musical pursuit secondary to the fame concerts bring in. A politician begins to love his own exploits for the rewards and fame it brings. A scientist becomes enamored of the junketing that international collaborations bring in. These are not unusual examples by any means since any of us could be, or are, in that position. What it highlights is the peculiar structure of parasitism. Doing things for fame or making it motivate your pursuit has ways of occluding and perhaps terminating the really important thing, namely, the pursuit itself, because the phantasy supporting the desire conceals the parasitic structure. This is the case even if you are a human being not pursuing anything such as science or music. The texture of the relationships could come under strain as one gets caught in a phantasmatic conception of oneself, say, as attractive or tough and so on. What the parasitism ultimately occludes is experience that enables you to have self-knowledge.[4] When Gandhi began to see that colonialism had begun to create parasitism through, for example, medicine, law, and the state, and that these institutions were distorting or occluding experience, he was not distinguishing, as Marxists and Liberals were to do later, colonialism as some material process with no effect on experience (taken in a narrow sense as subjective). The violence of colonialism, he realized, consisted in very deeply fragmenting the saliences that had organized the practitional matrix, thereby in the long run undermining the very integrity of experience. His attempt to reorganize the saliences drew from the same resources that had indeed enabled him to see how the violence of colonialism had a disintegrating effect on experience itself.[5] Stripped of the practitional structure, actions tended to be automatism, occurrences and incidents traumatic. The result was perhaps the last great concept to come out of Indian traditions, namely, *satyagraha*, yet another concept that resists translation.[6] Could the structure and activities that have become parasitic be transformed through satyagraha into sites of learning? How can new sites of learning be brought into being so that the automatism of actions and trauma of occurrences be transformed into experience, and the phantasy that conceals the parasitic nature and perpetuates desire be therapeutically engaged, if not removed? The crucial concept here is that of sites of learning. There is no limit to the kind of practical learnings there can be which enables one to transform structures, occurrences

and emotions into experiences. The body, time, relationships, place ...
all these can turn into *upadhis* or they could be transformed into sites
of learning. And what is a site of leaning for one tradition may not be
for another, or not in the same way. Erotics is a way of learning for
one tradition (think of Tantric traditions), for another it is austerity of
a certain kind.[7]

The concept 'practitional matrix' enables us to understand the
way experiential knowledge works and why it is necessarily an ever-
expanding field. It helps us model how a rich tradition of *kavyas* and
shastras emerge in the process of tackling multiple aspects of living,
whether it is engaging the past, arranging the living space, appre-
ciating beauty, incorporating considerations of taste and health,
elaborating erotics, and so on. The cultural learning that this process
creates does not consist in any doctrine it yields (the shastras are not
doctrines) but structures ways of doing things—practical knowledge,
in short. What the process also produces is what we might term
action-theoretic concepts, that is, concepts that one understands
only by understanding their function in the matrix.[8] Concepts such
as *manana*, *shravana*, *nidhidyasana*, or upadhi, avidya, maya too are
action-theoretic concepts; they are not (metaphysical or ontological)
descriptions of the world. Looking for translations of them as
though they are descriptions (even if metaphysical) of the world, has
the effect of turning them into obscure, mystic, religious entities.
Entities in the world do not come with upadhi written over them, for
instance. Whether my body or my past becomes an upadhi depends
on my relationship with it. Nor is any entity, action, or discipline
parasitic in itself. When, for example, I become parasitic on fame,
how am I supposed to understand 'fame'? What kind of upadhi is it?
What makes it one? If, however, we want to understand how upadhi
functioned in *advaita*, we do better by trying to understand parasitism in our contemporary experience. Are we thereby translating
upadhi? Or are we drawing on Indian thought to understand ourselves critically? Does recognizing the self-concealment of parasitic
structures and activities help us understand why maya was such a
powerful insight?

There is thus a disjuncture between the practice of the discipline of philosophy and the cultural learning that underlies Indian
thought and its diverse paths of organizing learning and reflection on

experience. This raises a large and difficult question about whether this claim implies that Western philosophy is inimical to experience or, less strongly, at least to certain ways of reflecting on it. Although the context of Indian thought regimented by philosophy has forced this way of formulating the question, it does nevertheless throw light on why there has been a significant strand of thinking within Western philosophy—from Marx and Nietzsche to Heidegger and Wittgenstein—which has sought the end of philosophy. It may well be that the destruction of the past goes hand in hand with the destruction of experience, if indeed it is not the same process. The unease generated by this process must have registered at some level and in some form in Western thinking. Indeed, both philosophy and history come to be regarded with profound distrust by many thinkers after Marx, the most prominent of them being Nietzsche, Heidegger, and Foucault (Wittgenstein[9] too, in a very different way, but his target was philosophy). It may be that our attempt—following Gandhi—to bring to bear the cultural learning on the practice of philosophy provides a different, experiential route to the task of clarifying where such a distrust springs from. The practitional matrix is not some fragment of history that is irretrievably lost. It designates the diverse ways in which adhyatmic activity completes experience: relationship to the past is achieved by transmitting the cultural learnings through *itihasa*, which is itself a variety of practitional matrix.

Indeed, by making the past external to us, history denies such learning. It is historicized away as nostalgia. We glibly say that the past cannot be retrieved, without realizing that we are disowning learning in our confused attempt to be historical. We regard figures such as Ramaksrishna Paramahamsa or Ramana Maharshi as mystics and even if we feel certain awe toward them we conceal that with an expression of condescension. Gandhi gets treated as a benign father of the nation, his thought and action finding no resonance in our thinking. Both history and philosophy, the new tools we proudly use, render them alien to us. We discuss concepts such as atman in the same way as we write commentaries on Hegel's essence and appearance. Without knowing how to understand the two traditions, we treat both traditions as charlatans. If history renders the past external and phantasmatic, philosophy insulates experience from reflection.

We are at home in thinking when our cultural learning is made available for articulation either as practitions or as theories. When, however, the disciplines of the human sciences actually make us disavow our cultural learning, and do so, moreover, without offering any new learning, we have no choice but to begin the slow work of re-understanding education as setting up of sites of learning, to recover, create, nurture, and articulate our cultural learnings. The issue of what that task involves formed the substance of the dialogue between Gandhi and Tagore.[10] It is instructive to rehearse that debate in the light of the framework I have sketched above. In many ways, they had sought to answer the question about how an action becomes part of a practition, how a genuine learning attitude emerges.

What Was the Gandhi–Tagore Debate About?

When reading Gandhi or Tagore, we rarely pause to consider the kind of intellectual struggle they engaged in while reconnecting to the life with concepts embodied in Indian traditions. This is in part because we tend to assume that when they employ concepts from Indian thought, their access to the semantic and epistemic horizon of those concepts is without any uncertainty or hesitation and that somehow those concepts are received by them fully formed. The assumption may be bolstered by our sense that when it comes to concepts of Indian thought we are more distant from them than they were. At any rate, there is evidence enough to show that Indian intellectuals, mistakenly perhaps, think of their relationship to Western concepts—rights, equality, freedom, civil and political society, nationalism, and so on—as unproblematic and their understanding of them impeccable, whereas they would be less confident about their relationship with and understanding of concepts from Indian thought. Whether or not this is indeed the case, when we read Gandhi or Tagore we rarely interrogate their thought with a view to understanding their struggle with concepts. We have to understand their divergences (as indeed their convergences) through their struggle with concepts. Tagore's argument that if we want to gain India in truth we have to make her more fully distinct in our minds informed all his intellectual activities (including the founding of the university, Visva-Bharati).

Gandhi's satyagraha was explicitly aimed at ethically strengthening the intellectual traditions that he thought had become hollowed as a result of colonialism.[11] *Hind Swaraj* is concerned with the particular kind of enslavement that colonialism had brought about and which was wrecking the intricate structures of the practical life evolved over a very long period of time.[12] The enslavement of Indians had a peculiar epistemic character: it taught them to ignore the kind of knowledge that organized the domains of practical life. Law, medicine, history, nationalism, and the state bring in a way of looking and certain conceptualizations that begin to cleave reflections from the form of practical life in which they are embedded. Thus health, to take an example dear to Gandhi, no longer functions as a matrix of practical action, related integrally and reflectively to ends that inform not only that matrix but other adjacent matrices (or possible new ones that can be fashioned). In any case, health is not the state of my bare body. Law is not a resource that helps me resolve my conflictual relationships in my familial matrix or in the domain of business in a reflective way, but an instrument that creates new disputes which I can only deal with in its terms which extrudes reflection. History brings in a perspective that begins to distort my relationship to the kavya and *purana* by transforming their function in the practical form of life. Similar considerations apply not only to nationalism, and to politics centered on the state, but to many more entities and conceptualizations that colonialism brought in. So let me speak of a cognitive/evaluative frame which, as it were, houses these entities and enslavement to which distorts, devalues, and veils the domain of practical life, which I will term the actional frame.[13]

When Tagore argues that the domain of modern education has rendered India indistinct and derivative, he was echoing Gandhi's diagnosis of the Indian predicament in not only education but in politics and economy too. Indeed, as we shall see, both of them locate the distinctiveness of Indian thought in the centrality that it accords to *learning*. The experiential conception of truth begins to acquire clarity and depth as both Gandhi and Tagore elaborate the idea that learning is what spiritualizes all domains of life, be it erotics or economics or education.

Tagore's diagnosis of the predicament of Indian thought was that colonialism and, in particular, colonial education had made the

Indian mind diffuse, helpless and obscure to itself. Consequently, India itself had become indistinct. How to make India 'distinct' was how Tagore formulates the task for himself and his contemporaries. Tagore reworks a thought from *Ishopanishad* to both characterize the predicament and find a creative way out. In what follows, I will make an attempt to reconstruct Tagore's argument and explore its philosophical depth, plausibility, and fruitfulness. That will make it easier for us to grasp the deep affinity between Gandhi's and Tagore's thought. Once the frame that shows the deep convergence of their views emerges with its distinctive horizon, we will be able to use that frame to grasp how the different domains of the colonial present they were confronting is normed and distorted by another frame that actively repulses the horizon of understanding these two thinkers were trying to elaborate through their struggle with Indian thought. I will call the former 'actional frame' and the latter 'quasi-cognitive/evaluative frame'. That is to say, a deeper under-standing of the convergent frame itself will provide us with the resources to reframe the debate between them in such a way that we can both see why their divergences pose a puzzle and explain how the divergences come about. The reframing, then, is at the same time an attempt to resume their remarkable struggle with the concepts and conceptual capacities of Indian thought, their own debate with one another illustrating the difficulties involved in making it available to understand the present.

The Education of Desire

The central insight of Tagore's thought enables us to conceptualize the link between social structures and the training of desires that characterizes Indian culture. What had begun to appear as exces-sive restrictions was anything but that: the elaborate set of actions that constitute sociality train desire in such a way that no residue is left behind. The learning that enables such actions to be invented, executed, and multiplied cannot be restricted to any domain; it is at the centre of all domains of activities. Hence, Tagore's poetic invocation of the figure of Saraswati sitting on the lotus to signal the centrality of learning to all spheres of life in Indian culture. What is special about this education? What sets it apart from the way education is conceived in the West? Learning directs action to assimilate truth, or what is the same thing, achieve person-end unity in such a way that it is impossible to imagine the person without the end. Tagore gives the example of the villagers who think nothing of offering water to his overheated car despite the fact that water is scarce. As Tagore puts it, these villagers cannot think of themselves without this end, generosity, which for them is not a special or supererogatory act. This kind of learning or education which involves 'assimilation of truth' takes centuries to achieve and when that learning disintegrates, what seemed inseparable, the person-end unity, begins to come apart. Understanding what causes this disintegration was an important intellectual task for Tagore. The person-end unity explains what it is for a person to become vague or indistinct to oneself. In another example Tagore gives we see this clearly: a child who has just got himself a new toy from an English shop refuses to join the children immersed in playing with whatever crude things they have devised. The play is what reveals the creativity, the dharma of childhood, not the toy, which now begins to 'obscure' the revelation of that dharma. In yet another example, we see the people of Mahsud protecting the pilot who was bombing their village but whose plane has crash landed in the village. Their 'ideal' of hospitality does not allow them to separate that truth from the rhythm of relationship they have assimilated it into. So dharma is this rhythm of relationship, the simplicity achieved by the complete assimilation of truth. This simplicity is, as Tagore puts it, 'the product of centuries of culture', and it is 'difficult of imitation'. When Tagore talks about learning being at the centre of life in all domains in India, he is pointing to the process that has created this rhythm of relationship, what I have been calling the person-end unity. He realizes that some process set in motion by colonialism is causing the disintegration of 'this rare fruit of a higher life'. He insists, therefore, that 'we must get to know this force of disintegration and how it works'.[14]

Responsiveness and the Assimilation of Truth

To say India has become indistinct is to say that the actional frame has become dormant, that it has, as I put it, become dispositional.

We are no longer able to learn/teach what Tagore calls the 'assimilation of truth'. To become distinct again or make India more one's
own is to understand how to *assimilate truth as one goes about in
different domains*. The fact is that the actional frame which has made
possible the kind of example Tagore gives illustrating the rhythm of
life, dharma, has so completely fractured that it does not organize the
saliences of our sociality anymore, nor does it have the resources to
create new practitional matrices. But, of course, it is present in some
form since, if it were not, the task would be nearly as impossible as
making the quasi-cognitive evaluative frame our own. Tagore's (and
Gandhi's) conviction was that the practices are still intact enough
for them to take the route of re-articulation or re-elaboration rather
than learning a new system such as the one colonialism brought
in: the quasi cognitive-evaluative frame. The central insight of their
reflection may well be that the latter and the concepts and baggage
that come with it are not learnable in the sense of 'assimilation of
truth'. Far from allowing for our responsiveness, they insulate our
experience from our reflection. So Tagore's (and Gandhi's) demand
that the intellectual centre and economic centre should not be separated. What about politics? Gandhi is clear there can be no separation there either. But Tagore? Tagore, as I have shown, should agree,
but he insists on the autonomy of economics (and by implication
politics too?). He seems not to understand what satyagraha is all
about—that it is a way to resist that very separation. Tagore's concern
that India had become indistinct is, therefore, related to the frame
argument; and he too sees it that way and yet succumbs to the framing effect himself in his argument with Gandhi. He is the one who
forcefully shows how Indian sociality must be regarded from the
actional frame, how the Indian past should not be regarded through
the conception of history, how the liberty that anchors the Western
institutions is not the freedom emerging through what appears to
be minutely structured practices—that which the actional frame
makes possible.

I have developed the matrix idea as a framework that presents
what is deeply convergent in the thinking of Gandhi and Tagore.
The convergent frame enables us to situate the very frame that has
generated the problem. It does so by showing how the conceptuality
that comes with the quasi-cognitive-evaluative frame—whether it

is political concepts or 'the caste system' and other such 'entities'—blocks our responsiveness to the conceptual world that was/is ours.[15] We can begin to understand what goes wrong when that responsiveness is missing or when we suffer from a loss of concepts and conceptual capacities.

It is not only that we had 'hit upon the device' of getting things cheap 'by proudly conducting our beggary in threatening tone', not only that we were 'ecstatic' because 'everything worth having in the political market was ticketed at half-price',[16] the indifference to the quality of what we were getting, to the nature of the pursuit—scientific, artistic, or political—that we were only imitating was concealed by the assumption of the quasi-cognitive-evaluative frame. Parasitism, therefore, did not involve only rent-seeking, or creaming off, or brokerage of Western agencies (as Gandhi put it), it had to block off the reflection on ends that was part of the actional frame. It's only when the language of modern economics or politics comes in that it becomes justifiable to say let 'the language of economic science' decide what we produce, or the language of politics—of political liberty—decide what institutional arrangement we should have. The reinforcement of the one by the other, the dependence of the one on the other could only be interrupted and functioning of the parasitic structure fully revealed only if the actional frame could be activated. As Tagore remarks, where we do not understand we cannot be just and where truth is imperfect love can never have its full sway. But if we are not able to resist and break the link between the structure of parasitism and the quasi-cognitive-evaluative frame, we will only be imitating the Western pursuits, whether in the sciences, the arts, or in other domains, becoming more obscure to ourselves. His worry was that we will perhaps gradually lose the cognitive ability to perceive this state of affairs too. Gandhi's satyagraha, the attempt to set up sites of ethical learning, was a concerted attempt to break that link and reveal the structure of parasitism. Tagore had seen that too:

> But before Asia is in a position to co-operate with the culture of Europe, she must base her own structure on a synthesis of all the different cultures which she has. When taking her stand on such a culture, she turns toward the West, she will take with a confident sense of mental freedom, her own view of truth, from own vantage-ground,

and open a new vista of thought to the world. Otherwise, she will allow her priceless inheritance to crumble into dust, and, trying to replace it clumsily with feeble imitations of the West, make herself superfluous, cheap and ludicrous. If she loses her individuality and her specific power to exist, will it in the least help the rest of the world? Will not her terrible bankruptcy involve also the Western mind? If the whole world grows at last into an exaggerated West, then such an illimitable parody of modern age will die, crushed beneath its own absurdity.[17]

Unfortunately, the feeble imitation of the West has come to stay, whichever domain we take, no longer feeble in the drive to be Western-like, becoming more ludicrous by the day. Or so it appears. Gandhi was the more consistent thinker who had no doubt that unless the actional frame and the experiential truth it makes possible provides the matrix to assimilate the pursuits we want to learn from the West by grasping and rethinking its deepest insights and discoveries, we will only be parasites and this parasitism, linked as it is to cognitive enslavement (indeed made possible by it), will in the end leave the actional frame without any nourishment.[18] So Gandhi's *charkha*, whose underlying truth, he said, the educated India still has not assimilated, is not a fact, not just avidya; nor for that matter are non-cooperation and swadeshi just facts. They were attempts to render India distinct so as to gain her in truth. It is difficult then to see how Tagore could have disagreed with Gandhi, but disagree he does, even at the cost of inconsistency, which he does not see because of the framing effect of colonialism. Once the insulation of the frames kicks in, there can no more be any responsiveness to the conceptual world of practical life. And the conceptuality that comes through the quasi-cognitive-evaluative frame is only capable of being deployed or used for manipulation. Tagore does not pause to examine his desire to see reason reinstated; reason is evidently in the service of holding in place the quasi-cognitive-evaluative frame, and from that frame the kind of reasoning/reflection involved in the actional frame, in the reflective shaping of the practitional matrix that unites persons and ends, the assimilation of truth into the rhythm of life and relationship, is not even recognizable as reason/reflection. That's the point Gandhi is making when he says that the educated Indian mind has not assimilated the truth of the charkha (so it cannot be said to be truly educated, as Tagore had pointed out in his discussion of the villagers' dharma).

Reflection and Practical Form of Life

How to rediscover or how to reinvent the deepest rhythms of the practical life is the common question facing both these thinkers. Whether it is to learn to act again, relearn the conceptual surrounds of the actional frame, or whether it is to relearn how to train desire and re-elaborate sociality—festivals of seasons, of places, ancestors, gods, and Tagore's attempt to sing their significance into being again, the issue cannot be reinstating reason. The kind of reflection needed to sustain the goings about that makes possible experiential knowledge, and truth has no bearing on whether something is scientific or not (in some scientistic sense of the term). It's strange, then, why Tagore takes objection to Gandhi's remark about the earthquake as unscientific. If there was anyone who could appreciate that Gandhi was not making a causal statement about the world, but engaging in reflection about a particular kind of world and the problem it was facing, it would be Tagore. Rather than trying to validate or endorse Gandhi's remark, I simply want to undermine the impulse to call it 'unscientific'. When Tagore contrasts the obscene pursuit of wealth in New York City with the wealth that Lakshmi transmutes into well-being, it would be sheer scientistic crudity to criticize him for being unscientific. Whether we feel we are able to endorse his judgment or not, we certainly cannot be thinking that there is some science that will help us decide. The contrast has to do with the world that the actional frame brings into being. We know this graceful goddess, we know the stories about her, and we have the practice of offering puja to her. It may be that she helps to regard wealth in certain way, as Tagore so insightfully brings out when, elsewhere, he contrasts Lakshmi with Kubera, inducing the kind of reflection on ends that practical life requires. In any case, it is to miss the point to call that remark unscientific or superstitious.

While it is important to reject the strange scientism that underlies the general incomprehension of Gandhi's remark, there is a deeper, perhaps more elusive, aspect to Gandhi's attitude that we need to foreground.[19] This has to with the relationship between anu-bhava and practition. As I had claimed earlier, building or elaborating practitions is the way Indian traditions try to encompass events, happenings, and spaces as learnable. An event or happening like the earthquake does not make experience if we insist on seeing it as an event describable or explainable by say geography. It has to be rendered experiential. Gandhi's remark, however misleading it may seem, is an attempt to initiate, at that historical moment, a process of reflection by which this 'happening' becomes experiential. At another moment, when perhaps practitions were flourishing instead of being broken under colonialism, the reflection on such event might have taken a different form. For Gandhi, whose satyagraha was a concerted attempt to revitalize the practitions, the way to assimilate the earthquake into truth was to inquire into the ways the practitions have become unjust or violent, and are no longer in that sense practitions. When colonialism attacks Indian ways of life for being steeped in 'superstition', what it is targeting is the idiom of experience, the practitional modes of making events and happenings experiential.[20] The assimilation of truth that Tagore saw underlying the three concepts his examples (discussed earlier) illustrated—hospitality, generosity, play—is also what is at work in Gandhi's response to the earthquake. The question then is: why Tagore does not see it that way and why we too fall back on some indefensible scientism to distance ourselves from what we regard as Gandhi succumbing to superstition (or, even worse, Gandhi pretending to be superstitious in order to make the masses fall in line).

On all the issues that divide them, Tagore, as we have seen, is consistently inconsistent. It is because of this 'consistency' that the two frames idea had to be invoked. That idea has a greater generality going some way toward locating, if not explaining, the predicament that Indian thought finds itself in. Sometimes, however, Tagore seems to shift the problem onto the followers of Gandhi, as though they will not see what Gandhi sees. He admits that Gandhi is truth itself rather than a walking quotation (such as other intellectuals and his own compatriots), someone who has been able to speak the language of the people. Nonetheless, the people, he fears, might be misled by Gandhi's own idiom, whether that involves charkha, superstitious talk, or ascetic negativity. What he doesn't see is that, only because of such a common language could Gandhi achieve responsiveness to the conceptual world he was certain they still accessed. For Gandhi thinking with concepts evolved from Indian thought was continuous with the effort to break with cognitive enslavement; these concepts once developed would not be simply Indian, they could be employed by anyone. The rejection of the division between economics and ethics, or politics and ethics, would be based on developing concepts that would show why economics and politics as they are today lead to the violence of separating persons and ends. Therefore, when I say Tagore succumbs to the framing effect of colonialism, it is to imply that somewhere Tagore is unable to sustain his effort to think with Indian concepts and through the practitonal mode. The default language he reaches for is the language that saturates the colonial present (and our present too), the language that conceals the parasitic social structure of which he is so critical. Tagore's switching between frames is instructive for us because that is our predicament too, except that Tagore, when he was in the actional frame, did create resources to both imagine and access the practical form of life whereas our recourse to it now is almost dispositional, and our view of it is from the distorting lens of the other frame.[21] Domains like economics and politics repulse reflection of the kind Gandhi and Tagore were trying to bring into being. We would rather ask if the charkha makes economic sense;[22] we do not wish to undertake an inquiry into experiential truth, like Gandhi did, and ask if economics makes sense. Utilitarian consequentialism, which has given the philosophical basis to economics, has made it perfectly natural for moral philosophy to ask if it is rational to be moral, whereas both Gandhi and Tagore would have sought to reflect if it is ethical to be rational if that means the violent separation of person and end. Such reflection will not be an alternative Gandhian economics or politics in some doctrinal sense, but it will honour non-violence as a way of discovering experiential truth.

Practical form of life makes it possible for those living in it to discover experiential truth. The practical form of life was able to structure multiple ways for people to learn to live with desire or learn to be happy or learn to train desire without residue. Those multiple ways involved sites of learning and teachers who implicitly or explicitly instructed one how to use them. The learner was conceptually (which does not necessarily mean propositionally) equipped to assess where one is, what is the appropriate way to pursue wealth such that Lakshmi 'transmutes it into well-being', or power such that one discovers dharma. Do I pursue a path of erotic learning or do I practice absti-nence as way of learning about desire? That form, as I say, enables one or equips one to assess one's life. The reflective pursuit is helped along by many things: stories, elders, the elaborate kinship system, the temples, the festivals. In a way these are props or devices that help lead that life, take a learning attitude to living, but in principle it could be done in another surrounding, with some other props that get set up. The question that Gandhi and Tagore asked and debated, then, needs to be asked again with some urgency because the parasitical and experience-occluding structures are smothering the pursuit of a happy, learning, or inquiring life that makes everything new because it connects with the real (*sat*).

There is one question that may seem inescapable at this stage: if Tagore had not succumbed to the framing effect and had fully shared in the Gandhian attempt not only to seek a cultural explanation of our present from the actional perspective, but also to engage with that pres-ent to discover experiential truth, could he still have disagreed with Gandhi on the very same issues? What form would or could that differ-ence have taken? I am not sure if this counterfactual question can really be answered. However, it might make some kind of speculative sense to argue that such a disagreement would have made the debate fully a part of the Indian conceptual world, in the way, for example, the debate between Budhhists and Vedantins, or Advaitins and Dvaitins was part of that world. This is simply another way of putting the more obvious consequence of my attempt to reframe the debate between Gandhi and Tagore: we need to re-engage with the conceptual resources of Indian intellectual traditions to develop knowledge that helps overcome the violence of separation (maya) everywhere in the world, but beginning at home makes sense because the resources are in some form still avail-able and because Gandhi and Tagore have illustrated both the possibili-ties and pitfalls of that attempt. But the task is to make such a resource intellectually available to everyone, such that experiential knowledge begins to reshape the human sciences.

For Gandhi, the practical form of life and experiential truth go together; their separation generates violence. The 'genius of Indian civilization', he thought, consisted in integrating the two. Through the discovery of experiential truth he wanted to write new things on what he called the Indian slate. Tagore showed how for Indian thought there can be no justice or love without understanding permeating all areas of life; his attempt was to revitalize that thought. We need to expand that area of understanding, because the practical form of life makes us realize that there is happiness in understanding. There are areas in contemporary life bereft of reflection; perhaps all of us need to rethink the old in a new language even as we look for new culturality (new socializing resources or devices) to deepen our reflections and extend it to new areas. That way we will better understand how the old practical form of life arranged its culturality to aid inquiry and reflection. Gandhi and Tagore were part of a movement that was largely political; though they did see the intellectual dimension of the movement, pragmatically politics took priority since they were battling the colonial power. By reframing their debate I am hoping their reflections will become part of a movement that will now be primarily intellectual (rather than social or political) because to extend reflection and understanding to new areas involves freeing ourselves from the language that insulates those areas from reflection.

We cannot do so unless we are able to break the quasi-evaluative/cognitive frame that seems to have entrenched itself.

Normativization

There is little doubt that the hardest problem we encounter in the comparative task of reconceptualizing the domain of the human sciences is theorizing normativity. It stands to reason why that is so: the moral domain is unintelligible to Indians. Even today the questions that moral philosophy struggles with does not make intuitive sense to us. The paradox at the heart of morality—one can only be immoral if one is already moral—is driven by the dynamic of secularization. In some way analogous to the Christological dilemma—Christianity must lose its properties to make its truth acceptable to all, but the more it loses its properties, the less Christian it becomes—the paradox of morality seeks to absorb other domains within itself. The moral person enacts in the secular realm the endless process of *conversio* that the priest undergoes in the monastery. Morality is the secularization

of the monasticization process, but without the benefit of the theological resources which rendered the monasticization process meaningful to the priest. If Protestantism abolishes priesthood by making
everyone a priest (as Marx expresses it), the modern citizen is the
secular priest, giving norms to himself. As Christianity begins to be
ascendant, the pagan world of Greece and Rome become subjected
to the dynamic of secularization. It is my argument that this process
of secularization takes the form of normativizing all domains that it
encounters. Indeed, at the limit, all human action is subject to mor-
alization. These domains, their problematizations and actions, begin
to be broken down, rebundled or transformed in a peculiar way with
the emergence and spread of Christianity. Normativization begins to
supplant problematization. What does normativization involve? What
happens when experience is brought under a norm? In his *The Uses of
Pleasure*, which should be considered the first significant work on the
norming of experience, Foucault begins by noting that 'sexuality'—the
term or its equivalent, the thing and the discourse—did not exist in
pre-Christian Europe (or in non-European cultures).²³ Foucault then
proceeds to show how 'sexuality' is what emerges when diverse and
distinct domains of practice and reflection about them—*dietetics* (diet
and regimen), economy (the household and the relationship between
husband and wife), erotics (reflections on the relationship with boys),
and finally wisdom in relation to erotic love—when these areas or
domains are clubbed together or unified by norming or moralizing
them. The transformation—as much historical as it is discursive—
results in the ontologically peculiar entity called 'sexuality'. This thing
does not exist in India or China; it, however, seems to exist for the
West. They 'experience' it, talk about it incessantly; its scope is ever
expanding, though in a repetitious, monotonous way. It is the introduction of (a distinctive notion of) truth and norm by Christianity in
the pagan milieu that drives this historical and cultural transformation that is still incomplete.

In the last decade of his life Foucault's research focussed on
highlighting the radical difference between Christianity and the
Hellenic–Romanic thought. Truth, of course, is at the heart of what
he uncovers. With Christianity, there emerges a conception of truth
totally at odds with the conception that had organized the 'care of the
self' culture.²⁴ If self-knowledge in the latter was access to a reality that

was not the object of knowing, in Christianity, knowing (*connaissance*) is entirely and exclusively intellectual or theoretical. The examination of conscience, for example, is a knowing of the kind that Christianity brings into being, as is the endless decipherment of the self as an object, a domain. When Christianity begins to attack domains such as economics and erotics that were integrated into the conditions of spirituality as part of the access to truth, those domains get opened up for knowing through the rational reflection of theology. A peculiar combination of rationality and morality begin looking for 'truths' in these domains, truths that allegedly provide the subject with the knowledge about how he ought to act or what he ought to avoid. This combination of rationality and morality is what I would like to term 'normativization', the unique contribution of Christianity. If problematization was the route that the many spiritual movements used to seek access to truth, Christianity fashions normativization as the route for the salvation of souls.[25] The extraordinarily detailed genealogical picture of the ancient world that Foucault draws is meant to highlight the later emergence of domains such as sexuality, economy, and politics that are ontologically peculiar in that they distort experience by insulating it from reflection.

I can now complete the argument: under colonialism, the secularization process sought to transform the domains it encountered in India. The practitional matrices (whose idealized structure I have sought to delineate) were experienced normatively as the caste system. Once the matrix idea is in place it is possible to argue how 'the caste system' is the product of a frame that comes with colonialism. To say this is to say that the entities in that frame are not amenable to theorization—we know as much or as little about the caste system as we did in let's say the eighteenth century. The more interesting question is why that frame brings up entities that are of this nature, that is, they are incapable of being understood or theorized. Because they are incapable of being understood, their deployment effectively stifles any creative responsiveness the practical form of life needs to nourish itself.

* * *

Let me state as emphatically as I can what I have argued for and what I have not, so there is no confusion: I am not offering another,

Foucauldian view of the caste system; I am arguing that like 'sexuality', 'the caste-system' is a product of the normativization process which is specific to the West.[26] Does it exist in some sense of exist? I have suggested that it existed for the West, as an entity in their experiential world. This argument opens up a deeper inquiry about the relationship between experience and normativity. I have often in the past referred to such entities as ontologically peculiar. However, given the framework outlined here, that inquiry into the relationship between normativity and experience will have to be an adhyatmic one. I am aware that the argument I have developed and the methodology I have implicitly employed will have left many conceptual and empirical questions unanswered. It might be thought that in the oppositions I propose—past/history, adhyatma/philosophy, tradition/religion, practitions/the caste system—there is no place for art, law, and, indeed, politics. What are they displacing or obscuring or occluding? It is a legitimate question and the answer too is already contained in the concept I have proposed to articulate Indian sociality, namely, practition. As we enrich that concept, which would involve becoming adept at creating and elaborating new practitions, we will be able to realize the sense in which domains such as politics, law, and art are experience-transcendent in the West, as they have their roots and justification in religion. The hope is that those questions can eventually be answered if the argumentative strategy has enabled me to formulate the domain problems any research project that seeks to reconceptualize Indian traditions has to confront. To what extent do the domains we take for granted in our thinking perpetuate the discourse of normativity? How does the latter persist long after colonialism? Does our persistence with the use of domain talk (inherited from the existing human sciences, legal and political discourse) in some way perpetuate normativity? Or is it the case that the learning attitude that underlies practical mode of knowledge has something to do with this persistence? In the absence of the cultural conditions that drives normativization, how do discursive structures of norms reproduce themselves in India (if indeed they do)? Furthermore, if normativity actively repulses or occludes experience, it would be reasonable to assume that a culture nourished on experiential knowledge would find ways of resisting it. Would it be possible to formulate a hypothesis regarding the forms that such a resistance would take?[27]

Finally, if spirituality is knowledge—what I have been calling experiential knowledge—then the issue cannot be only one of resistance to normativity and preservation of practitional matrices. Are there new ways of inter-articulating cultural knowledge and sociality? I have been using the term 'cultural learning'—Tagore's assimilation of truth and Gandhi's Swaraj are examples—whenever I have spoken of spiritual or experiential knowledge. The reason for that should have been obvious. That learning is intrinsically linked to happiness; however, the conditions of spirituality and access to truth have no one path. There are innumerable ways and heuristics to discover or invent to seek access to truth which brings about transformation in the subject, brings about happiness. Consequently, the sociality articulated by that cultural learning too tends to be richly layered and pluralized. When, therefore, the religious–secular world of colonialism/capitalism has begun to strip sociality of all cultural learning, the urgent question for both practical–spiritual knowledge and intellectual knowledge is: how can we articulate new cultural learnings that find expression in the articulation of sociality itself? Will the learning attitude be able to radically reconceive politics as the creation of sites of ethical learning?

Glossary

advaita	non-dualism (of Vedanta)
adhyatma	the term for Vedantic thinking (experiential search for enduring happiness)
anu-bhava	translated as experience, it literally means in accord with what is/happens
atman	traditionally (and misleadingly) translated as self or soul. The concept designates the real (contrasted with what exists)
ayudha puja	offerings to weapons/implements
avidya	ignorance
charkha	spinning wheel
itihasa	used as an Indian term for history, it means 'thus indeed it was'. Both *Puranas* and *Kavyas* are forms of *Itihasa*
dvaita	dualism (of Vedanta)

jnana	knowledge
kavya	although currently used to translate the word 'poetry', it is the traditional name for a genre of writing that concerns the transmission of the past. For example, Ramayana and Mahabharata are regarded as *mahakavyas*
maya	refers to a structure that conceals the nature of the real
purana	misleadingly translated as mythology, it means ancient stories
swaraj	self-government
shravana, manana, nidhidyasana	stages in mediation: listening/mindful recall/ immersion
shastras	traditional treatises on various disciplines (dance, architecture, and others)
upadhi	translated variously as 'limitation', 'adjunct', or 'imposition'
Vedantins	those belonging to one of the six schools of classical Indian thought

Notes and References

1. Although I will touch on all the pairs, my focus will be on the last. Among contemporary thinkers, it is Ashis Nandy who first forced us to think about tradition and the past—a) and b) above—in a radically novel way. See his 'An Anti-Secularist Manifesto', *Seminar* 314 (1985): 14–24; 'History's Forgotten Doubles', *History and Theory* 34, no. 2 (1995): 44–66. The puzzle is why Nandy has not brought to bear the same radically revisionary perspective on the last two pairs too. It is a puzzle because, as I hope to show, making the choice in one case—say tradition over religion—will lead us to the choices presented in the other cases too.

   For the contrast between tradition and religion and the contrast between the past and history, I am indebted to S.N. Balagangadhara, 'How to Speak for the Indian Traditions: An Agenda for the Future'. *Journal of the American Academy of Religion* 73, no. 4 (2005): 987–1013; S.N. Balagangadhara, 'What Do Indians Need, a History or the Past? A Challenge or Two to Indian Historians', Maulana Azad Lecture 2014, available at http://ichr.ac.in/seminars_lecturers.html (accessed on 6 June 2015). More generally, I have drawn both from his unpublished writings on normativity and from the many stimulating conversations over the years on the need for reconceptualizing the human sciences. I doubt though that my formulation of the issues, my approach, and what I have made of his insights would be congenial to him.

2. The phrase is from Joseph Stiglitz and Bruce Greenwald, *Creating a Learning Society* (New York: Columbia University Press, 2015). The sense of learning implied in that work is rather different from what is sought to be articulated here. Stiglitz is concerned about how economic policy should be designed to preserve economic skills—use of complex financial instruments, for example—that have tendency to migrate with capital flight. Although his undefined notion of learning economy/society is proposed as an alternative to the neo-classical approach, he seems unable or unwilling to explore a notion of learning society outside of the economic conception of productivity. As my discussion of Gandhi's objection to the separation of ethics and economics will make clear, a genuinely learning society is one which brings to bear ethical learning on what we think of as economic or political activity.

3. Vivek Dhareshwar, 'Framing the Predicament of Indian Thought: Gandhi, the *Gita*, and Ethical Action', *Asian Philosophy*, 22, no. 3 (2012): 257–74.

4. Tagore speaks of the dangers of 'mental parasitism' that a poet becomes vulnerable to when, consciously or unconsciously, he develops a craving for reward and fame and feels injured when it is denied or withdrawn. See 'Letters to a Friend', in *The English Writings of Rabindranath Tagore*, vol. 6 (New Delhi: Atlantic Publishers, 2007), 408.

In a wonderfully lucid reflection on this phenomenon of 'mental parasitism' that obstructs one's own pursuit, the renowned Hindustani singer Ganapathi Bhat Hasanagi talks about how the concert circuit really distracted him from pursuing music; so he decided to go back to his village to be a farmer because that life allowed him to pursue music. I was struck by his realization that farming supported his search whereas the institution of concerts did not (*'Sangeeth Sant* Ganapathi Bhat *Avarondigina Odanatada Ondu Jhalak* [A Glimpse of the Interaction with Ganapathi Bhat], *Nirupane* [Narration], Vasanth Bhat Hasanagi, *Taranga* [*Ugadi Visheshanka* 2015], 142–6). One immediately thinks of contemporary academic life, whether here too the 'mental parasitism' of various kinds obstructs the intellectual pursuit. Of course, the issue is not simply fame or fame is not a simple thing (as perhaps money at some level is). There is a deeper question about the relationship between what one pursues and the form of life that supports or enables or which obstructs it, without making any assumption about any form of life being intrinsically free from phantasmatic veiling. It seems to me that what we call *adhyatma* with its concepts such as *maya* and *upadhi* is indeed about achieving insight into the phantasmatic veiling of experience. The examples from Tagore and Ganapathi Bhat Hasanagi show how that reflection is alive in shaping everyday living as a form of inquiry.

5. As we shall see, both Gandhi and Tagore insist on seeking explanations of the Indian predicament, its indistinction, its having disintegrated into facts, from within the actional frame, so that the very activity goes towards making the frame distinct, even as the explanation offered illuminates what has rendered India indistinct and helps in seeking ways to strengthen the dharmic activity. The actional frame is what Tagore calls the rhythm of dharmic activity that helps 'assimilate truth'.

6. Often mistranslated as passive resistance, it refers to a mode of struggle against injustices that involved expressing one's anger by standing in truth and thereby compelling those committing the unjust act to accept the truth. Though Gandhi popularized *satyagraha* as a method of protest against colonial rule, he held that it can be practised wherever truth is violated (even against one's parents, for example).

7. I have developed the concept of sites of learning to explain both Gandhi's response to colonialism and his understanding of ethical action in my 'Politics, Experience, and Cognitive Enslavement: Gandhi's *Hind Swaraj*', in *Democratic Culture: Historical and Philosophical essays*, edited by Akeel Bilgrami (New Delhi: Routledge, 2011).

8. There is nothing mysterious in this: think of 'cover drive' or 'square-cut' which cannot be understood except by having some understanding of the practitional matrix, namely cricket, within which that concept/action has sense. Bernard Williams once contrasted thin concepts such as 'right' with thick concepts that are action-guiding and world-guided. His claim was that under the sway of morality, thick concepts are disappearing. See Bernard Williams, *Ethics and the Limits of Philosophy* (Cambridge, MA: Harvard University Press, 1985), chapter 8.

   The action-theoretic concepts of the practitional world fit the bill better because they are truly action-guiding and world-guided. For a discussion of the practitional matrix in a comparative perspective, see my 'Critique, Genealogy and Ethical Action', *Marx, Gandhi and Modernity: Essays Presented to Javeed Alam*, edited by Akeel Bilgrami (New Delhi: Tulika, 2014).

9. See note 18 below.

10. Sabyasachi Bhattacharya, ed. *The Mahatma and the Poet: Letters and Debates between Gandhi and Tagore: 1915–1941* (New Delhi: NBT, 1997).

11. Although I present here textual reference for my interpretation of Tagore's arguments, my interpretation of Gandhi draws largely on my 'Politics, Experience, and Cognitive Enslavement'.

12. Mohandas. K. Gandhi, *Hind Swaraj*, edited by Anthony J. Parel (Cambridge: Cambridge University Press, 1997).

13. I have discussed the need for postulating these two frames in 'Framing the Predicament of Indian Thought'. It is significant that something like that idea is implicit in both Gandhi and Tagore, and that, furthermore, the explication of that idea helps in reframing the debate between them, thereby making that debate directly relevant to our own contemporary effort to overcome the framing effects of colonialism. For a discussion of how the two-frames idea may be of relevance to a comparative cultural understanding, see my 'Critique, Genealogy and Ethical Action'.

14. Rabindranath Tagore, 'Talks in China', in *The English Writings of Rabindranath Tagore*, vol. 5 (New Delhi: Atlantic Publishers, 2007), 722–4.

15. There is a question here for Tagore and Gandhi too. When they talk disapprovingly of some Western idea being 'mechanical', do they have in mind something like what I am saying here about the quasi-cognitive-evaluative frame? It seems perhaps that they do mean some force that turns ideas into entities that can be manipulated. Thus, their problem with nationalism, class, the state, and such others (which has a component of ideology or discursivity of some kind). They have no view which they counterpose to nationalism; their objection would indeed be that there could be 'views' of this kind (ideologies). It is instructive in this regard to compare Gandhi's *Hind Swaraj* with Tagore's 'Our *Swadeshi Samaj*', in *The Sky of Indian History: Themes and Thought of Rabindranath Tagore*, edited by S. Jeyseela Stephen (New Delhi: UBSPD, 2010).

16. Bhattacharya, *The Mahatma and the Poet*, 73.

17. Rabindranath Tagore, 'Creative Unity', in *The English Writings of Rabindranath Tagore*, vol. 5, 642.

18. Without a language or reflective dimension, but still a force as a disposition—we have here the phenomena of contemporary politics and business! Even resistance to that is without a language, as we witnessed in the anti-corruption movement of Anna Hazare.

19. Vinay Lal's wide-ranging comments on the draft prompted me to think more about Gandhi's remarks; Dilip da Cuhna's response to an earlier version of the chapter helped me see what was already there in the argument I had set out.

20. Among Western thinkers, perhaps Wittgenstein would have understood Gandhi's concern for the integrity of experience and his mode of dealing with what disrupts it. Especially in his *On Certainty* (edited by G.E.M

Anscombe and G.H. von Wright, translated by Denis Paul and G.E.M.
Anscombe [New York: Harper Torchbooks, 1972]), Wittgenstein attempts
to understand the philosophical incomprehension of the idioms of experience, while seeking a form of reflection as an activity that preserves
the integrity of experience. Here is Wittgenstein's ironic expression of
Gandhi's point: 'Men have judged that a king can make rain; we say this
contradicts all experience. Today they judge that aeroplanes and the
radio etc. are means for the closer contact of peoples and the spread of
culture' (On Certainty, no. 133). Both Gandhi and Wittgenstein pay close
attention to what people regard as contradicting experience and how they
arrive at that judgement.

Wittgenstein's experiential critique of the bewitchment of philosophy shows that the choice between philosophy and adhyatma does not
mean a choice between Indian and Western thought. I develop this at
greater length in my 'The Saddle of Experience: Wittgenstein and the
Bewitchment of Philosophy' (forthcoming).

21. Imagine a singer who engages with the world through sound losing his/
her conceptual capacities. Not only is he/she not able to sing—engage
the world—he/she cannot even respond to sound anymore or do so
only intermittently. The practitional matrix that made possible that
conceptual response simply withers, as there is no creative engagement
anymore. The singer no longer has the conceptual ability to enter that
matrix. Suppose we now extend this example to the world of Carnatic
or Hindustani classical music—the singers and the involved (that is,
educated) followers suffer a conceptual loss over a period of time: the
singers or listeners are barely able to engage with the complex practitional matrices that house the conceptual capacities, without which there
are no innovations, no new action. Suppose we now imagine the larger
practical domain of which the musical world is a subset (but also a
microcosm) undergoing a conceptual loss. The example of the musical
world is important for two very different reasons: one, music illustrates
very well the fact that the conceptual capacity involved is not propo-
sitional. Two, it is indeed remarkable that in the real world in which
the conceptual loss has happened, the musical world—whether that of
Carnatic or Hindustani—has survived as a genuine practical field with
vigorous innovations and creative explorations. It is not an exaggeration
to say that it is the only field in which we have witnessed genuine excellence in a sustained way for over a century now, precisely the period of
parasitism in other fields. Well, that is where we are; the example will,
I hope, bring to mind the enormous complexity of the practical form
of life, the senses in which its conceptual capacities organized the very

diverse learning and responsiveness that an experiential conception of truth demands.

22. As Amartya Sen asks in his essay on Tagore in Amartya Sen, 'Tagore and His India', in *The Argumentative Indian: Writings on Indian History, Culture and Identity* (New Delhi: Penguin Books, 2005), 101. Sen's anodyne portrait of Tagore as a defender of 'reason' and (of all things) anticipator of Hilary Putnam's 'internal' realism makes him into a nineteenth-century English liberal consequentialist with some mildly eccentric (hence embarrassing) views about religion. Sen wilfully ignores the Tagore of philosophical essays such as 'Our *Swadeshi Samaj*', 'The Centre of Indian Culture', 'Personality', 'The Fourfold Way of India', 'Creative Unity', or any number of letters and lectures where he explicitly develops what I have been calling an experiential conception of truth, which has no echo in Western philosophy. See volumes 4–6 of *The English Writings of Rabindranath Tagore*. The core of that conception makes clear how Tagore regards reason: 'For the reality of the world belongs to the personality of man and not to reasoning, which, useful and great though it be, is not the man himself' (Tagore, 'Personality', in *The English Writings of Rabindranath Tagore*, vol. 4, 368).

   What is depressing about Sen's essay is its dogged attempt to find Tagore 'reasonable' from a Western lens, filtering out, in the process, Tagore's attempt to think with Indian concepts. Ironically, the only place where Tagore insistently speaks about reason is in his critique of the charkha, which has generated for us the puzzle of why Tagore is occupying the frame—the quasi-cognitive-evaluative frame—which finds incomprehensible the actional frame that he (Tagore) himself is trying to revitalize. That Sen is firmly anchored in the same frame but without even suspecting the existence of another frame speaks to the predicament of Indian thought—illustrating no doubt the indistinctness that Tagore had spoken about.

23. Michel Foucault, *The Use of Pleasure*, translated by Robert Hurley (New York: Vintage Books, 1985). However, it should be noted that Foucault himself seems to be at best only obliquely aware of normativity as a cultural phenomenon that is specific to the West. See note 23.

24. For a discussion of the significance of the 'care of self' culture, see Michel Foucault, *The Hermeneutics of the Subject: Lectures at the College de France, 1981–1982*, translated by Graham Burchell (New York: Palgrave Macmillan, 2005).

24. The most difficult problem here is the relationship between truth and norm. Can that be investigated philosophically? It is clear that part of the reason for Foucault's rejection of philosophy in favour of genealogy has to

be that the philosophical route to that question will lead back to theology. Instead, he thought he could show how the ethical reflections of Greek and Roman schools and their exploration of the condition of spirituality as access to truth had nothing in common with the universally binding property of Christian morality (or its secularized versions) or with the Christian concept of Truth. Whereas the secularized version of Christian morality is relatively easy to track (think of Nietzsche's work), the secularized version of truth has posed a far more difficult challenge. Although Foucault did not always formulate his earlier inquiry as tracking secularization, it was evident when, for example, he discussed the vertical or in-depth Christianization (as distinct from its horizontal spread through proselytization) or welfare state as pastoral form of power; however, once he began his inquiry that produced the volumes on the history of sexuality, it was clear that he was indeed explicitly investigating the relationship between truth and norm as what structures the secularization process. Perhaps the only place where Foucault does explicitly use the term 'secularization' to designate the phenomenon of governmentalization is in his lecture, 'What Is Critique', in *The Politics of Truth*, Translated by L. Hochroth and Catherine Porter (Los Angeles: Semiotext(e), 2007), 44. For further discussion of this notion of secularization, see my 'Marx, Foucault and the Secularization of Western Culture', *Rethinking Marxism* 28, nos. 3–4 (December 2016).

26. It has often been suggested to me by readers who refuse to follow the methodological steps required to understand the argument about normativity that the term 'caste system' is the problem, whereas 'caste' is transparent, on the obvious understanding that it translates 'jaati'. Although this is not the place for a detailed elaboration, I want to suggest that it is 'jaati' that has been made to translate as 'caste', which cannot be understood outside of the normed entity, 'the caste-system'. There can be no theory of normed entities. Foucault does not, unlike Freud or Lacan, offer a theory of 'sexuality'.

27. I engage with these issues in my forthcoming book *Normativity and Experience*.

3

ANOTHER COSMOPOLIS
Living with Radical Diversities and Being One's Own Self[1]

ASHIS NANDY

As an unavoidable part of contemporary public life, the social sciences are getting professionalized and, thus, more self-contained and
self-referential. At times, one is tempted to get anthropomorphic and
predict that some of these disciplines are destined to live in the near
future within a solipsistic world. Economics, academic psychology,
and international relations rarely look beyond their own perimeters.
When they do, the efforts look naive and strained. Some of the other
disciplines rarely turn their critical gaze upon themselves. Historians
historicize historians not histories; and the anthropologists, even
when they plead for thick descriptions, often manage to look politically shallow or subservient to sponsored ideas floating around in
the culture of the global middle class. John Maynard Keynes knew
the exact human motives involved in economic decision-making
and never looked at other disciplines, organized around the study
of human motives, which might have something to say about these
motives. And the ethnography of Clifford Geertz in Indonesia dis-
misses the 'invisible' genocide, which took place under the patronage
of Geertz's own country, as a minor strife.

Willingly or unwillingly, these sciences buy into the categories that
deal with the play of national interest, security, economic development, international trade, and other such lofty, tangible forces with
which the first pages of serious newspapers and university departments seem perpetually occupied. Yet, most practitioners of these
disciplines are probably aware that underlying these tangible, well-
known, real-life forces there are less tangible subjectivities in the
form of cross-cutting perceptions, sentiments, images, and fantasies
that constitute the underside of the strategic visions in which the relationships among countries, communities, and cultures are grounded.
This is an exercise which deals with that underside.

One crucial part of these subjectivities is the tacit, ill-defined,
culturally inculcated belief in the right to be oneself. That right
includes the right to disapprove and dislike practices and conventions of communities and cultures that look, through the optics of
one's own culture, unjust, cruel, or even simply distasteful. However,
this right to disapprove does not bestow the right to hate or nurture
fantasies of annihilation or extermination. It is the argument of this
paper that the spread of the idea of cosmopolitanism shaped by the
Enlightenment values has gradually made it obligatory to disown all
hostility or even dislike of any artefact, tradition, or practice that is
culturally marked—from cuisine to sports, from marriage rituals to
religious rites, and from dress to ideas of personal hygiene. Unless,
of course, the target of rejection or dislike happens to be associated
with rich and powerful countries located in West Europe or North
America. You can fulminate against cola drinks but not convey your
dislike for Sri Lankan, Thai, or Chettinad cuisines, which routinely
bring steam out of one's ears. You may still perhaps make wry comments about English food in polite society, more so if you are English,
but it is becoming increasingly difficult to say anything nasty about
run-of-the-mill Bombay films if you are not an Indian. Yet, there are
at least as many Indians who passionately dislike such films as there
are English who disparage English food. That is the normal price of
multiculturalism today.

I believe it is possible to live with diversities without such a tough
version of cross-cultural amity or tolerance, as shown by many societies in the world, particularly the ones that are community-based and
have traditionally lived with radical diversities. This is a preliminary

attempt to recover and illustrate a few elements of this other form of cosmopolitanism in South Asia.

To do so, I use some scattered data from a study of the mass violence that broke out when British India was partitioned in 1947. One of the better-known features of the memories associated with that violence is the widespread use by the survivors of, what many call, memories of an idyllic, pre-Partition 'tranquillity'. Not so much as self-indulgent, romantic nostalgia but as a utopic vision of a desirable society and as a critique of the present fraught relationships among the major communities in South Asia now. Scholars have seen those memories as a near-mythic construction of the past with virtually no basis in empirical realities, though a few have gone and assiduously looked up the data on communal relations before and after Partition to test the proposition of the survivors. Both groups forget that locating utopias in the past has been a living tradition in the Indic civilization and so has been the use of such utopias as criticisms of the contemporary. Gandhi's Ramarajya is a reasonably good example. I, too, use them here as parts of an older approach to inter-community relations that may or may not stand our empirical and ethical scrutiny, but did probably once underwrite the capacity to live with apparently irreconcilable diversities.[2]

* * *

I turn now to snippets from a few interviews, ranging from casual, throw-away comments to relatively well-formulated principles behind which the respondents are willing to stand. First, there is Urvashi Butalia's moving account of Bir Bahadur Singh's visit to his ancestral village in Pakistan fifty years after Partition.[3] A more detailed psychological profile of him is now available from Shobna Sonpar and Asha Singh, both practising psychotherapists in New Delhi.[4] From it we come to know something of his family background and world view including ideological moorings that configure his memories of Partition.

Bir Bahadur as a child had witnessed a number of women in his family, including his sister, being beheaded by his father, a leader of the Sikh community at the foothills of the Himalayas in what is now Pakistan. The Sikhs, hopelessly outnumbered, feared an attack by the

Muslims and the Sikh women and few elderly men feared dishonour. They chose to die at the hands of their own. (Now called 'honour killings' and condemned as a cultural pathology of some communities, such practices had a different cultural status at the time. And a mix of fear and admiration for them endures.)

Bir Bahadur, around eighty when interviewed, survived the trauma, escaped to India, and made peace with his memories by recasting them in the form of a heroic saga. He routinely recites that saga at community gatherings in a Sikh temple. Assumption of that heroic posture has made Bir Bahadur fiercely anti-Muslim and a depot of stereotypes and prejudices. He is an office-bearer of the Bharatiya Janata Party and subscribes to its version of Hindu nationalism, not a politically correct choice for a Sikh these days. During the demolition of the Babri mosque, he led a squad that participated in the demolition of the mosque.

However, Bir Bahadur has always believed that the Hindu and Sikh commensal taboos that forbade them to eat with the Muslims—and to consider food or water even touched by a Muslim to be polluted—was a practice exceedingly humiliating to the Muslims. He considers such taboos evil. Though a victim of Partition, he has nurtured a deep sense of guilt about the social customs centring on purity and impurity. Butalia, who took him along with her Japanese friend Fujiwara Chiharu to Pakistan, describes in moving detail Bir Bahadur's meeting with his former Muslim neighbours and how he fulfilled his lifelong wish to drink water from his village well and share a meal with his childhood friends and neighbours.[5]

Bir Bahadur's beliefs are shared by a number of witnesses, most of them refugees from the former East Pakistan, and by scholars who have in recent times turned to studies of Partition violence with a vengeance. Social anthropologist Satish Saberwal has argued that the Hindu caste system was ultimately responsible for Partition itself.[6] Perhaps it was, but there are perplexing testimonies of those who directly experienced the Partition violence which seem to suggest a more complex attitude towards the Hindu caste system among at least some Muslims. Saberwal is embarrassed by the caste system and now that there is a growing consensus on its evils in modern South Asia, it is a safe villain to identify. Saberwal, like most well-educated South Asians, seems oblivious that the caste system may be evil, but

many communities in the region, taking advantage of it, have survived for centuries as what social anthropologist Imtiaz Ahmed calls
'bridge communities' between Hindus and Muslims and have also
sometimes cultivated world views and pursued vocations that their
formal religious affiliations should force them to reject.

For instance, in Rajasthan the Meos, who trace their ancestry to
the Mahabharatic clans, and the Langas and the Manganias, communities of musicians and minstrels, and in Bengal the Patuas or
Pat Chitrakars, who make their living by painting mostly Hindu
gods and goddesses, are examples of such communities among
Indian Muslims. Among Hindus, the Pranamis or Parnamis, and
the Hussaini Brahmins of Punjab and Gujarat, have developed
theologies in which Islam and Hinduism intersect. There are also
the well-known cults of Gazi Mian and Satya Pir in eastern India.[7]
Similar communities are found among the Buddhists and the Tamils
of Sri Lanka, and Buddhists and Hindus of Nepal. Very few know that
Gandhi's mother belonged to the Pranami sect, which Dominique
Khan has recently identified as a lost Shia sect, to the utter consterna-
tion of the Pranamis, who, after a massive slaughter of the community at Bhawalpur during Partition, have been trying hard to establish
themselves as an unalloyed Hindu sect. They have also stopped
showing their sacred text to outsiders.

Ian Talbot has a comparatively less one-dimensional approach but
while admitting that pre-Partition Hindu–Muslim relations in Punjab
were less troubled than they were to later become has to quickly add
that he does not share the 'romanticized' idea of pre-Partition Hindu–
Muslim amity in the testimonies of the victims of Partition. He tries
to skim history from memories of witnesses the way Saberwal seeks
to find 'truth' from history.[8]

We have also run into witnesses who seem to hold academically
incorrect views on such issues. For instance, Saba Khatak, a well-
known Pakistani political scientist, once shared the experience of
interviewing an elderly woman whose family had been the victim
of Partition violence and was twice displaced—from the United
Provinces in India to East Pakistan in 1947 and from Bangladesh to
Pakistan in 1971. Khatak asked her if the Hindu caste system, with
its ornate ideas of purity and pollution, did not distance the South
Asian Muslims from the Hindus. The respondent said 'no' and went

on with what she was saying. Khatak wanted to be doubly sure and, after a while, asked her the same question again. The answer was the same. But this time she added more firmly, 'Why should the caste rules on purity and pollution offend us? A Hindu does not even eat with most other Hindus.'

This does not mean that this was the refrain of most respondents or that such discrimination did not hurt at all. It means that people perhaps tried to look at such differences as strange peculiarities of a community rather than as deliberate attempts to humiliate. But perhaps even that explanation is not fully satisfactory. One is forced to return to a 'Personal Statement' of Raimundo Panikkar, a few sentences of which served as the epigraph in my psychological profile of Cochin. Panikkar invites us to believe that: 'Pluralism is not synonymous with tolerance of a variety of opinions. Pluralism amounts to the recognition of the unthinkable, the absurd, and up to a limit, intolerable.' He goes on to add: 'Reality does not need to be in itself transparent, intelligible.'[9]

Historian Anindita Mukhopadhyay's story of a Hindu refugee from East Pakistan, S.K. Talukdar, also revolves around the issue of commensality. But, in this instance, the respondent's experience cannot be dismissed as a casual comment of an ageing exile; it involves a more serious engagement with a social practice of another community that, by our standards, should be deeply humiliating to others. Talukdar remembers how, heeding the pleas of his close friend Sirajuddin Ahmed, Talukdar decided to go to the village home of Siraj before fleeing to India from East Pakistan. Sirajuddin wanted his friend to visit his village because he had sensed that Talukdar's departure could be final; he probably would not see Talukdar again. Also, Talukdar's father, who was by then dead, was very close to Sirajuddin's father; the friendship between the two young men was an extension of the close ties between the two families.

When Talukdar arrived at the village, Siraj's father was himself waiting to welcome his young guest to his vast village home. After the exchange of pleasantries, Siraj's father, being a prosperous landlord and knowing Hindu customs, offered to get the services of a Hindu cook for Talukdar or, alternatively, supply Talukdar rice, vegetables, pulses, and fish so that he could cook for himself. Talukdar chose the second option. However, he never actually had to cook, for the two friends secretly managed to convince Sirajuddin's mother to cook for them.

One day, Sirajuddin's father stumbled upon the two friends while they were eating together. He was furious with the two friends and was about to beat them up. After a while, tired of scolding them, he broke into tears and said to his son: 'What have you done? You have ruined the caste of your friend! How shall I tell his father [after I die and meet him], when he asks me about his son, that I have taken away his son's caste?'

Later, still deeply perturbed, he went to a local *pir*, a Muslim divine, to pray and atone for his unintended transgression and make an offering.

It is worth noting that both families were educated. Talukdar's was an urban, middle-class family of mainly professionals well-exposed to the modern world and Sirajuddin's was part of an upper-middle-class landed gentry and was also educated and stayed in a metropolis. The behaviour of neither could be easily attributed to lack of education or urban exposure. We may also note that in both Talukdar and Sirajuddin—and even perhaps in Sirajuddin's mother—the attitude towards the caste system was relaxed and, to some extent, subservient to human relations. But for Siraj's father it was a matter of serious ethical commitment; he considered it his religious duty to protect his friend's son's caste. The relaxed, casual attitude towards the caste system that angered Siraj's father is also important. He considered it his *religious* duty to protect his friend's son from apostasy. So probably did his pir. For, despite the bloodbath that was the backdrop of the story, the events speak of a time when religion had not yet probably become in South Asia a matter of tense negotiations and self-affirmation. The border lines were clear but they were differently defined.

I now illustrate that relaxed, easy-going relationship with faiths using an episode from psychologist Chavi Bhargava's interview with Shakuntala Devi, a refugee from Bhawalpur in Pakistan, devastated and embittered by the turn of events in 1947. Yet, despite her bitterness, Shakuntala was capable of begging her son-in-law, a pilot in the Indian Air Force, not to bomb Lahore during the India–Pakistan war of 1971, because it was her natal place. She still missed the presence of Muslims in her Jaipur neighbourhood; she was, she said, accustomed to living with them.

Eating with Muslims was a problem for Shakuntala, too, in her childhood. Her mother allowed her to play with her Muslim friends but beat her if she ate at any of their homes. Alas, Shakuntala liked their food more than what she ate at her home. One day she took her problem to a Muslim friend's mother, who solved it quickly. She asked Shakuntala if she knew any Hindu prayer or mantra; Shakuntala did. Her friend's mother then taught Shakuntala a *kalma* (the Muslim confession of faith), so that when she went to her friend she could recite it on the way and become a Muslim. She could then eat at any of her Muslim friends' place with impunity. On the way back, she could recite the Hindu prayer to become a Hindu again. That worked.

* * *

The works of both Sabarwal and Talbot might have gained if they had taken their witnesses, untutored in contemporary social sciences and history, more seriously. Memories have no obligation to follow the rules of social sciences; memory work, if I may call it so, is a technology of the self that, like Freud's dream work, is designed to grapple with life, not the theoretical concerns of the academe.[10] The job of utopia, even when you project it into the past and not into the future, is not to supply a guidebook the way economic forecasting does, but to critically assess the present and open up the future. In the study we did of the Partition violence, we found most of our witnesses—even when bent by life and unexposed to our intellectual universe—not merely socially sensitive but also ethical and life-affirming. The massive bloodbath, which contextualized this story, had changed the political topography of their lives radically but not their moral universe.

Let me tease out a few possible implications of the snippets I have supplied. My first proposition is that even when we reject Bir Bahadur's politics or his glorification of the killings in his family, we *are* more comfortable with his understanding of social hierarchy because we feel we have the correct categories for it. Our cognitive frame is populated by concepts such as feudalism, honour killing, primordial prejudices and stereotypes, and the gender inequalities supposedly inherent in traditional social orders. We are likely to dismiss the significance of the first two stories where inequalities do not look like inequalities to the protagonists, but as asymmetries arising out of peculiarities of community practices and cultural belief systems. As if these peculiarities were parts of the landscape and there was a silent expectation that the peculiarities of one's own community will be treated with similar respect by other communities.

What to Bir Bahadur, a modestly educated son of a village shop-keeper and moneylender, looked like humiliating hierarchies and obscene discrimination was for some others perplexing oddities of other communities. They have learnt to live with such practices over generations and accept them as cultural differences they must work around. Whether such acceptance goes with some degree of 'toler-ance' of the inequities and exploitation coupled with the caste system could be an important issue, but not when one is discussing the psy-chological and cultural skills to live with such differences in those outside the caste system. Such tolerance cannot be a self-conscious process. Brought into awareness, it will be probably become a source of inner tensions and raise new predictable questions on humiliation and dominance. You cannot breathe normally and at the same time count your breath.

This is not an indirect plea to suspend judgement on the ethics of commensal taboos or on Hindu ideas of purity and pollution. It is a plea to take seriously something many have observed in India but few have considered important. I first noticed this anomaly when working on a brief psychological biography of Cochin city.[11] Each of the communities with whom I interacted in the city believed that it was superior to the others and said so to me in no uncertain terms. Their quasi-mythical, ever-changing, *jati puranas* or caste epics, too, endorsed this belief. At the same time, each of the communities knew that other communities made similar claims of supremacy and had their own jati puranas to back their claims. Fortunately for Cochin, no ambitious historian has been tempted to write an authoritative history of the city or its inhabitants, to reconcile the conflicting claims of the different communities and to carefully apportion glory to the deserving and dismiss the false claims of the others. I suspect that the city's enviable record of communal amity has much to do with its flawed historiography and its fragmented, quasi-mythic, shared memories.

It is natural in this context that there is no demand for reciprocity. The resigned tolerance shown is non-ideological and does not even call itself tolerance. It is based on the acceptance and, in some cases, celebration of the otherness of others, not of the sameness of others, as the Zapatistas would put it. Hence, there is no laboured attempt to show that behind the otherness of the neighbours is hidden concordance. The acceptance comes from the rhythm of everyday life and can be seen as part of a silent, un-heroic cosmopolitanism. The dominant strand of cosmopolitanism—with its ideas of mainstream, national integration and multiculturalism—does not recognize its strange cousin and might like to legislate it out of existence. But that also is not easy. For it is all around us in different guises in different communities and in different spheres of life.

Years ago, historian Dipesh Chakrabarty noticed the consistent invocation, by many uprooted by the Partition, of the memories of an idyllic village where nature's bounty matched social and inter-religious harmony.[12] In our study of Partition violence, too, these happy memories of infinite amity is a running theme in most of the interviews. Chakrabarty's analysis covers memories of sophisticated intellectuals, some of them from the Left, ever eager to talk of class relations and the oppressive political economy of pre-Partition South Asia. This was Gandhi's reaction too. Anthropologist Nirmal K. Bose gave Gandhi the statistics on the highly skewed land distribution in Noakhali, where 80 per cent of the land was in the hands of 20 per cent Hindus. But can that explain away all the bittersweet memories of one's pre-Partition days? Or does it also gesture towards a semi-articulate critique of post-Partition Hindu–Muslim relations from the vantage ground of another model of neighbourliness?

A vital part of such homage to the past is the invisible, ill-defined struggle to be oneself and includes the right to disapprove and dislike not only individuals and groups but also cultures. However, for some reason, that disapproval does not turn into hatred or lead to fantasies of extermination. This is changing in South Asia. Competitive democracy in many places has sharpened community boundaries and some communities have begun to act more like nationalities than as religious, ethno-linguistic groups or castes. As a result, when communities clash these days, especially communities that have lived in peace and harmony for centuries and where even inter-community marriages were not uncommon, a different kind of extreme violence with exterminatory projects ranging from ethnic 'cleansing' to 'final' solutions come into play. And the psychological ambience of inter-community relations changes for ever. Murderous hatred, lovingly reared as a political technology, enters both the upper echelons of power and the everyday life of the ordinary citizens. When the unlamented, home-brewed, premodern cosmopolitanisms die, they unleash strange ghosts.[13]

I started with the observation that the growing pace of modernization—and now globalization—is making it almost obligatory to disown all hostility towards or even dislike of any artefact, tradition, or practice that is culturally marked—from cuisine to sports, from marriage rituals to religious rites, and from dress to ideas of personal hygiene. This assumption has also become part of the official version of multiculturalism.

I believe that it is possible to live with diversities without such a tough, sanitized version of multicultural living and many societies that are community-based have institutionalized that belief over the centuries. Diversity can mean not merely the acceptance of difference but also the refusal to bend one's deeper beliefs to accommodate a facile, skin-deep idea of national integration.

* * *

Our pathways to the future, Bruno Latour believes, wind their ways through the past. Breaking the shackles of history not merely intro-duces new disjunctions in the contemporary consciousness but also opens up the past outside the suzerainty of history. It sharpens the ability to work with multiple pasts and renegotiate politically with many imperfect pasts embedded in people's memory and, thus, frees the future in societies where the future has been either stolen, hijacked, or marginalized by the dominant imaginary.[14]

These humble, home-brewed cosmopolitanisms, pushed to periph-eries of our mindscape in recent centuries, do not share the popular belief in an irreversible, linear, diachronic movement from the pasto-ral to the civic. Nor do they presume that their versions of neighbourli-ness must conform to the ideals of a social-evolutionary version of progress and a strict division between the secular and the sacred. It insists that the present in dialogue with the past and the future may be more complete in itself and is perhaps healthier for that reason.

Categories of hospitality and co-living tolerance probably come to ordinary citizens less frequently from constitutional guarantees and ideals of citizenship; they come from personal faiths and from traditions of hospitality in their communities and cultures.

* * *

Nelson Mandela, in whose name this lecture series has been initiated, was associated with an exceedingly imaginative and ambitious project on reconciliation. That initiative, the Truth and Reconciliation Commission in South Africa, was based on the presumption that testimony was more important than the forensics of culpability. A testimony opens up or at least tries to open up the future by establishing a dialogue between the oppressor and the oppressed within a shared ethical frame that recognizes the humanity of both. A trial, even when necessary, can only establish guilt and, while bringing the oppressed within a frame that recognizes their humanity, tends to push the oppressor out of it. It can sometimes absolutize the differences between the two sides, probably more so, when the victim and the persecutor belong to different ethnic, religious, or racial groups and seek justice within a single, unbending legal frame.

I am aware of the many criticisms of the Truth and Reconciliation Commission, but I do believe that Nelson Mandel and Bishop Desmond Tutu—both fully exposed to Zulu cosmology, living with Zulu ideas of neighbourliness, justice, and cosmopolitanism—challenged our clear-cut divisions between victims and perpetrators, the killers and the killed, and between what Fyodor Dostoevsky called the anthropologists and their subjects. That challenge is itself a major contribution to the culture of public ethics in our times.

Notes and References

1. This is a much-revised, expanded version of the Nelson Mandela Lecture delivered under the auspices of the Bob Hawke Prime Ministerial Centre, the School of Law, at the University of South Australia and Oz Asia Festival, at Adelaide on 21 September 2010 and used as part of a presentation made at a conference organized by Asian Development Research Institute at Patna on 25 March 2017. I am grateful to Vinay Lal for his critical comments on an earlier draft of the chapter.

2. The practice of locating utopias both in the past and in the future is also alive in Sinic and Islamic civilizations and was also once known to European Christendom.

3. Urvashi Butalia, 'Community, State and Gender: On Women's Agency during Partition', *Economic and Political Weekly* 28, no. 17 (24 April 1993), pp. WS-12-22; and 'Persistence of Memory', *Civil Lines*, no. 5 (2001): 169–98.

4. Shobna Sonpar and Shalini Singh, *Life History Constructions and Mass Violence: A Psychological Perspective* (Delhi: Project on Reconstructing Lives, Centre for the Study of Developing Societies, 2002), unpublished report, 77–85.

5. Butalia, 'Persistence of Memory': 169–98.

6. Satish Saberwal, *Spirals of Contention: Why India Was Partitioned in 1947* (New Delhi: Routledge, 2008).

7. Two examples of recognized recent works on such bridge communities are Shail Mayaram, *Resisting Regimes: Myth, Memory and the Shaping of a Muslim Identity* (Delhi: Oxford University Press, 1997) and *Against History, against State: Counter-perspectives from the Margins* (New Delhi: Oxford University Press, 2004); and Shahid Amin, *Conquest and Community: The Afterlife of the Warrior Saint Gazi Mian* (New Delhi: Oxford University Press, 2015).

8. Ian Talbot, 'Pakistan and Sikh Nationalism: State Policy and Private Perceptions', *Sikh Formations* 6, no. 1 (2010): 63–76.

9. Ashis Nandy, 'Time Travel to a Possible Self: Searching for the Alternative Cosmopolitanism of Cochin', in *Time Warps: The Insistent Politics of Silent and Evasive Pasts* (Delhi: Permanent Black, 2002), 157. I cannot help regurgitating what I said in my paper on Cochin years ago in support of Panikkar's position: The growing demand that you must be perfectly impartial in matters of culture is a relatively modern development. So is the belief that cultural dislike and ethnic stereotyping must sometime or other lead to violence. This is not what experience tells us. For instance, 'the founder of Zegota, the one organization in Poland and in Europe as a whole that had as its sole purpose the saving of Jewish lives, was herself a zealous anti-Semite. She reportedly expressed her wish that the Jews she was protecting would disappear from Poland after the war.' István Deák, 'Heroes and Victims', 'The Politics of Retribution', *New York Review of Books*, 31 May 2001, pp. 52–6; p. 55. Stereotyping is not only the politics of the demagogues and the bloodthirsty; it is also often the sociology of the lesser mortals and part of normal life.

10. For a brief, introductory note on the idea of memory work as a crucial, under-socialized, psychological manoeuvre in the collective life

of communities, see Ashis Nandy, 'Memory Work', *Inter-Asia Cultural Studies* 16, no. 4 (2014): 598–606.

11. Nandy, 'Time Travel to a Possible Self', 157–209.

12. Dipesh Chakrabarty, 'Remembered Villages: Representation of Hindu-Bengali Memories in the Aftermath of the Partition', *Economic and Political Weekly* 31, no. 32 (10 August 1996): 2143–51.

13. Four random examples of extreme brutalization brought about by ruptured neighbourliness are E. Valentine Daniel, *Charred Lullabies: Chapters in an Anthropography of Violence* (Princeton, NJ: Princeton University Press, 1996); Gita Mehta's documentary film on Bangladesh killings, *Dateline Bangladesh* (1971), Rakesh Sharma's feature-length documentary film on the Gujarat riots, *Final Solution* (Bombay, 2003); and Joshua Oppenheimer's documentary *The Act of Killing* (2012) on the Indonesian genocide.

14. See, for instance, Ziauddin Sardar, 'The Problem of Future Studies', in *Rescuing All Our Futures: The Future of Future of Future Studies*, edited by Ziauddin Sardar (London: Adamantine, 1998), 9–18.

4

BACKWATER ECSTASIS
Truth, Destiny, and the Co-Existential Analytic

ROBY RAJAN

Liberal Benefactions

In an outburst of geopolitical punditry shortly after the outbreak
of the Syrian war, the leading liberal commentator and onetime
aspirant for Canada's prime ministership Michael Ignatieff was
moved to observe:

> When state order collapses, as it did in Yugoslavia in the 1990s, as it
> is doing now in Syria, chaos unleashes existential fear among all the
> groups who had once sheltered under the protection of the state. Such
> fear makes it difficult to sustain multi-confessional, pluralist, tolerant
> orders when dictatorship falls apart. When state order collapses, every
> confessional or ethnic group asks one question: Who will protect us
> now? As Sunni, Alawite, Christian, Druze, and Shia ask this question,
> they know the only possible answer is: themselves. In a Hobbesian
> situation—a war of all against all—each individual gravitates back to
> the security offered by their clan, sect or ethnic group ... they conclude,
> rationally enough, that they can only face these dilemmas alone, in the
> safety of their own group. Such was the case in the former Yugoslavia.
> Such is the case now in Syria. ... Common identities and loyalties
> rarely survive the rush to the protection of armed groups and the
> bitterness that results when these groups begin killing each other.[1]

Ignatieff's essay traces the contours of a drama, the opening scene of which features the collapse of a dictatorial state and the emergence of 'a security vacuum on top of a political one'. A multitude of ethnic and religious groups find themselves stricken with 'existential fear', scrambling hither and thither for protection before a common realization dawns: it's now each group for itself. The 'existential' action unfolding on the stage is interspersed with a running political commentary: 'In a state that had never permitted mobilization of political parties across sectarian, clan, or ethnic divides, none of these groups has learned to trust each other in a political order. ... What they lack is time, the experience of democracy, and the opportunity—it can take generations—to forge political alliances across confessional, sectarian, and clan lines.' Any 'common identity' they may have once shared under the aegis of the state dissolves 'in the face of the fear that overcomes all ethnic groups upon the collapse of state order'. As Scene I draws to a close, the question looming over everyone is: what next?

Enter the Grand Intervener wearing a pained expression and bearing 'humanitarian' gifts, but with a glint in the eye that bespeaks a steely determination to sort out the mess. There will be conditions of course: 'Intervention will not occur until interveners can identify with a cause that democratic electorates in Western states can make their own.' Flashback to the former Yugoslavia, where, the commentary reminds us, 'it was the Bosniak Sarajevans who understood this clearly and helped mobilize the outrage in western countries that eventually made intervention possible'. There the Intervener could arrive in full strength 'because international opinion identified the Bosniaks as worthy victims who could be assisted in the name of a general defense of "European values"'.

The scene then shifts improbably to the mid-western American town of Dayton, Ohio, where then US Assistant Secretary of State Richard Holbrooke is performing a set of complex diplomatic pirouettes to negotiate 'a peace that preserved Bosnia-Hercegovina as a state and forced institution-sharing upon unwilling enemies'. So did American diplomatic sagacity finally put Humpty Dumpty back together? Well, not quite, says Ignatieff: 'Western intervention did not succeed in recreating inter-ethnic tolerance and accommodation. It may have only locked ethnic hostility in place.' Wherein lies its 'success' then? Ignatieff's answer is modest: 'It did force ethnic groups to deal with each other politically and, to accept, over time, that limited cooperation was a better option than war. The fact remains that no one is dying today.' Ignatieff had begun his essay by lamenting the collapse of 'multi-confessional, pluralist, tolerant orders' in places such as Bosnia, but by this point in the drama the yardstick for measuring success has shrivelled to the bare fact that 'no one is dying in Bosnia', never mind the hostility that may well have been permanently 'locked in place'.

So what is it that the Bosniaks had 'clearly understood' which accounts for their 'success'? For Ignatieff, this consisted in collectively transforming themselves into 'worthy victims'—victims whose suffering was pathetic enough to tug at the conscience of Western publics, who then would be moved to intervene to uphold 'European values'. Cut now to the present, to the sad predicament of the 'free Syrian opposition' and their failure 'in making their cause a universal claim'. Why this 'failure', considering that the suffering there is much greater—at least going by the number dead which is many multiples the number that perished in Bosnia? Here Ignatieff brings truly bad tidings: it turns out that the Syrians labour under a double misfortune. The worthiness of victims measured by the quantum of suffering alone is no longer sufficient to trigger intervention because 'life has also changed for the intervening states' since the good old days of Bosnia and Kosovo. You see, 'the interventions in Bosnia—and later in Kosovo—were easily paid for by expansive European and North American societies whose economies were growing robustly'. The misfortune of Syria's victims, it turns out, is not that they were insufficiently worthy; it was that their predicament happened to coincide with the 'age of sequester, austerity, and deficit' in the West. Victimhood alone, no matter how worthy, was no longer sufficient to elicit intervention from the West's 'recession-weary publics'.

The scene now shifts abruptly to the economic and financial bureaucracies of the metropole where the questions being posed are of a wholly different tenor from Ignatieff's earlier moralizing: 'What interest does the United States actually have in intervening in Syria at all? Who cares which bunch of thugs runs the country?' A utilitarian calculus weighing the victim's suffering against the Intervenor's interest in propping up a 'bunch of thugs' is now displayed in raw form: 'Humanitarian suffering alone constitutes no clear principle

of triage, and it is a president's job to do triage, to apportion scarce
national resources and scarcer political capital to a few vital tasks.
Bloodshed and carnage alone will not—and should not—trigger the
dispatch of the Marines.' Thus runs Syria's woebegone path from
being a self-sustaining 'multi-confessional, pluralist, tolerant order'
to haemorrhaging blood on the Intervenor's operating table and at the
mercy of his cold calculus of triage.[2]

At the time Ignatieff offered us these glimpses of how the world
looks from the Intervenor's vantage point, he held the oddly named
'Edward R. Murrow Professorship of Practice' at Harvard. The 'practice'
in question was presumably of the political variety, a topic on which
Ignatieff had disquisitioned at some length a few years earlier while
belatedly introspecting on his misguided support for the American
invasion of Iraq:

> Politicians live by ideas just as much as professional thinkers do, but
> they can't afford the luxury of entertaining ideas that are merely inter-
> esting. They have to work with the small number of ideas that happen
> to be true and the even smaller number of ideas that happen to be
> applicable to real life. In academic life, false ideas are merely false,
> and useless ones can be fun to play with. In political life, false ideas
> can ruin the lives of millions and useless ones can waste precious
> resources. An intellectual's responsibility for his ideas is to follow their
> consequences wherever they may lead. A politician's responsibility is
> to master those consequences and prevent them from doing harm.
> I've learned that good judgment in politics looks different from good
> judgment in intellectual life. Among intellectuals, judgment is about
> generalizing and interpreting particular facts as instances of some
> big idea. In politics, everything is what it is and not another thing.
> Specifics matter more than generalities. Theory gets in the way.

This exercise begins with a mea culpa for chiming in with the general chorus to invade Iraq, but peters out in the end in a series of self-
justifications: after all it was not just him, 'everyone' was misled by
'faulty intelligence' about Saddam Hussain's possession of chemical
weapons. A jumbled taxonomy of ideas, judgment, and responsibility
is then mobilized in the service of self-exoneration: intellectuals can
afford the luxury of indulging themselves in 'interesting' ideas even
when they are 'false' or 'useless', whereas politicians have to work
with a small number of true ideas because 'false ideas can ruin the

lives of millions' and 'useless ideas can waste precious resources'; good judgement in intellectual life has to do with theorizing about particulars as instances of a larger general idea, whereas in political life, it is specifics all the way down because 'everything is what it is and not another thing' and theory only gets in the way; an intellectual's responsibility is to follow the consequences of ideas wherever they may lead, but a politician must 'master those consequences and prevent them from doing harm'. What is evaded throughout this convoluted exercise is that Ignatieff's own idea that Iraq could be liberated by the Intervenor's display of shock and awe had the dubious distinction of possessing all three characteristics: it was false, useless and uninteresting—*in addition to* 'ruining the lives of millions'.

'Everyone labored with the same faulty intelligence and lack of knowledge of Iraq's fissured sectarian history,' writes Ignatieff, with nary an acknowledgement that this 'fissured sectarian history' was produced by the very invasion he had served as lead cheerleader for. 'Faulty intelligence' and 'Iraq's fissured sectarian history' are put forward as two titbits of 'knowledge' that could have been improved upon by additional information gathering and historical research, which could, therefore, have averted the blunder of the invasion.[3] What we have here is a textbook case of disavowal: the 'sectarianism' the Intervenor perceives as the other's tortured 'history' is what the Intervenor has himself unleashed through his act of emancipatory intervention.

True to his calling as a professor of practice, Ignatieff declares that when it comes to matters of political judgement, 'theory gets in the way'; in retrospect, however, it is hard not to wonder whether a good dose of theory may not have been exactly what the doctor ordered to temper the professor's excessive zeal for practice.

The Existential Analytic and Its Discontents

Surprisingly, community is not a topic that many theorists have considered worthy of philosophical reflection. Jean-Luc Nancy is one of the few to venture beyond the limits of history, sociology, and anthropology to probe into the philosophical foundations of community. Nancy's starting point is the fundamental rethinking of subjectivity launched by Martin Heidegger's existential analytic in *Being and*

Time.[4] The task Heidegger sets himself is to free thought from the categorical apparatus of 'metaphysics' in which it has been trapped for a couple of millennia. This involves providing a phenomenological account of our engagement in a meaningful world-structure, in relation to which traditional metaphysics would be a derivative mode.[5]

'Dasein'—literally 'there-being'—is the word Heidegger uses to distance his conception of human being from the object-cognizing subject of epistemology so as to redirect our attention towards the question of being which had fallen into forgetfulness. Such a distancing is crucial for Heidegger because the centrepiece of his notion of Dasein is the claim that prior to the explicit act of cognizing, there exists a pre-understanding of Dasein's there-being in the world as a forestructure of meanings and existentially rooted dispositions that are constituent features of being-in-the-world. Among the most significant of these are our everyday pre-theoretical practical involvements and our social relations of being-with-others (*Mitsein*). Importantly for Heidegger, this 'being-with' is in no way an external prosthesis that is tacked on to some more fundamental 'being self': it is co-originary with the self.

Heidegger's point is that the notion that the subject first encounters objects and other selves, which he then grasps with his cognizing faculty falsifies the proper order of things. It is our engaged immersion in our practical involvements and with others that is primordial; every other mode of presence is secondary. The true problem then is not how to pass from mental representations of objects to the objects themselves, but that this was seen as a problem at all. Our being-in-the-world—our dealing with objects as ready-to-hand, our irreducible embeddedness in a network of meanings—is consubstantial with our always-already being-with-others, so that Dasein's being is inextricably interwoven with others. George Steiner puts the matter succinctly: 'Being-in-the-world, says Heidegger, is a being-with.'[6]

For Nancy too, metaphysics has for too long been trapped within a notion of 'individual' as self-present. The individual in this conception is atom-like, embodying what Nancy calls 'immanence'—by which is meant a self-enclosed essence, an 'absolute origin'.[7] As a foundation for being, Nancy holds such a conception of essence to be utterly fallacious: 'One cannot make a world of simple atoms. There has to be an inclination from one toward the other or from one to the other.'[8] But, as we have seen, this idea of 'being-with' as prior to the individualized subject is not originally Nancy's; it is already present in Heidegger's notion of Mitsein.[9]

However, Nancy maintains that this key insight is given short shrift by Heidegger as demonstrated by the fact that Dasein's co-originality with Mitsein is introduced only after the existential analytic of Dasein has been independently sketched out—as if, despite himself, Heidegger ends up treating the 'with' as an addendum to Dasein. Furthermore, Nancy points out that when we reach the famous Section 74 of *Being and Time*, this 'with' is determined in terms of the *Geschick* (destiny) of a *Volk* (a people)—two words that take on a deeply ominous ring when viewed in light of Heidegger's subsequent (albeit short-lived) enthusiasm for National Socialism.[10]

Nancy's rejoinder to Heidegger—whose entire corpus is pre-mised on the idea of humankind's 'forgetting of being'—is that it is Heidegger who forgets the truth that he himself had first unearthed: that there is no being that is not already co-original with being-with. For Nancy, this fateful oversight demands that *Being and Time* be rewritten from scratch: to 'take up again the ensemble of known indications from *Being and Time*, with the aim of suggesting a recom-position in which *Mitsein* would be *actually* coessential and originary. It is necessary to rewrite *Being and Time*. ... One can guess without much trouble that this necessity also belongs to the stakes of a politi-cal rewriting'.[11] In short, a rewriting of *Being and Time* with being-with as its foundation is essential for a rethinking of the political as well. It was Heidegger who first opened up this pathway, says Nancy, but 'the same Heidegger also went astray with his vision of a people and a destiny conceived at least in part as a subject, which proves no doubt that Dasein's "being-toward-death" was never radically implicated in being-with—in *Mitsein*—and it is this implication that remains to be thought'.[12]

Nancy's central move here is to extend his critique of what he calls 'immanentism' from the subject conceived as self-enclosed individual to the community conceived as substantial and sharing a common substance: 'Being-in-common is not a common being'[13] as Nancy cryptically puts it. Community is not a communion that fuses subjects into a substantial collectivity. Whenever community is thought of in terms of communion, that is when 'politics becomes the conduct of the history of this subject, its destiny, and its mission'.[14] For the question of the 'with' to be posed, says Nancy, any politics which rests on the claim to embody communal substantiality would first have to be withdrawn, and the presumed immanence of community 'unworked' so that the 'with' of being-with can shine forth and a renewed politics brought into being. This is held to occur through an 'interruption' of the myth that represents the community to itself in a common origin. When a community's myths are interrupted, this common origin undergoes a displacement, and the myth can no longer function as the ground of communal belonging, preventing the community from completing itself as a 'work'.

'Fundamental ontology' for Nancy is, therefore, not the question of being *a la* Heidegger; it is the question of being-in-the-world as co-original with being-with. Prior to every substantiality of individuality or communality is our 'thrownness' into a pure relationality of being-with. To distance himself from 'metaphysical' notions of individual and community, Nancy's preferred term for his non-immanent understanding of being is 'singularity', which occurs first and foremost by way of a leaning-toward rather than the side-by-sideness characteristic of atom-like individuals. Singularity is the being to which the ecstasy of being-outside-itself has always already occurred. This is why Nancy can assert: 'One could not properly say that the singular being is the subject of ecstasy, for ecstasy has no "subject" —but one must say that ecstasy (community) happens *to* the singular being.'[15]

Community then is not a 'collection' of beings; it is the 'spacing' of being as outside-of-itself and the relationality to other singularities that has occurred prior to any being's being-ness. The finitude of a singularity which is simultaneously an 'abandonment' to an excess-of-itself appears as an 'exposition' to other singularities to which Nancy gives the name 'communication'. Appearance in the world is, therefore, always a 'compearance' (co-appearance)—a phenomenon that is 'more originary than any other'.[16] For this to occur, there must already be a multiplicity of singularities that are mutually exposed in their compearance. Being comes to be only in a being's ecstasis of outside-of-itself that is in no way appropriable by it. This is why Nancy can say emphatically: '*Community does not sublate the finitude it exposes. Community itself, in sum, is nothing other than this exposition.*'[17] When Nancy characterizes the very nature of community as 'inoperative' (in his book of that title), what he means is that community cannot be turned into a 'work' that sublates the finitude of singularity, because it *is* nothing other than the exposition of finitude.

Exposition, then, is not a 'decision' on the part of singular being to extend itself: 'It is what it is, singular being, only through its extension ... and that makes it exist only by exposing it to an outside. This outside is in turn nothing other than the exposition of another singularity. ... Finitude compears, that is to say, it is exposed: such is the essence of community.'[18] The being that is outside-of-itself is therefore necessarily extended toward other singularities which are similarly extended and outside-of-themselves in the mutual 'exposing-sharing'[19] that is 'community'. But it is not only that there is a plurality of singularities; every singularity is itself traversed by plurality, and this reciprocity of plurality and singularity is what Nancy intends by his term 'singular plural'.[20]

Nancy is at pains to emphasize that 'singular plural' has nothing to do with 'intersubjectivity', which is entirely an instance of side-by-side *juxtaposition* of pre-given subjects rather than the mutual *exposition* of a 'with'.[21] Juxtaposition presupposes an existent, whereas exposition is prior to existence. A being is singular not because of any special properties that distinguish it from other beings, but because it is exposed in a singular way to other singularities. Singularity dwells on this shared edge as an 'offering', and not in any interiority or exteriority amenable to appropriation. What is shared between singularities is not a common substance but the sheer facticity of their mutual exposure. The 'with' or the 'in between' of singularities is neither a bridge between them nor an encompassing space; it *is* nothing but their mutual exposition. 'With' is not one mode among others the subject may choose for being in the world; it is anterior to any subjective intentionality because the 'with' is co-original with Dasein's 'there'. In Heidegger's terms, we are already 'thrown' into being-with before any work of gathering ourselves into a substantiality can commence. In this sense, being-with is the transcendental condition of possibility that opens up the space in which a politics can germinate. If 'politics' is a field of contestations between quasi-substantialized entities, then not only is Nancy's ontology pre-political, it also comes with the imperative that every substantialized notion of community be 'unworked' if political life is to be renewed.

Like other European philosophers of the post-war era, Nancy's theoretical labours are undertaken under the long shadow cast by the twentieth century's pseudo-events of fascism and Stalinism. His ontology of non-immanence is clearly meant to forestall any future descent into totalitarianism, whether in the name of the 'destiny' of a 'Volk' or as the imagined supersession of all social antagonisms in a 'workers' state', both of which he diagnoses as stemming from their aspirations to immanence. Nancy maintains that immanence is an impossibility, and that the inherent impediment to a realized immanence is our own primordial being-with that refuses to be corralled into a self-enclosed substantiality: 'Community is, in a sense, resistance itself: namely, resistance to immanence.'[22] Nancy fully recognizes that while immanence itself is an impossibility, the drive to immanence is very real—as are its destructive, even catastrophic, consequences. To keep these hazards at bay, the first gesture of politics for Nancy must be a paradoxical 'retreat from politics' so that all established formations of immanence may be unworked, and the 'with' that is their condition of possibility may disclose itself.

This is Nancy's version of Heidegger's 'ontological difference': a retreat from juxtaposed ontic entities towards an ontologically anterior being-with so that the political may be renewed in non-immanent form. Although he forswears any explicit conception of what such a politics might look like, the question itself is posed in all its clarity: 'how can the community without essence (the community that is neither "people" nor "nation", neither "destiny" nor "generic community") be presented as such? That is, what might a politics be that does not stem from the will to realize an essence?'[23] The underlying imperative is also clearly spelled out: 'Community is given to us—or we are given and abandoned to the community: a gift to be renewed and communicated, it is not a work to be done or produced. But it is a task, which is different—an infinite task at the heart of finitude.'[24] While being-with is inherently resistant to the drive to immanence, we are also enjoined to bring about the exposition of an ecstatic being-with if the self-destructive consequences of such a drive are to be averted. Nancy then proposes his *co*-existential analytic as the fundamental ontology that ought to supersede Heidegger's since the latter's analytic was merely existential and could not, therefore, accord the 'co-' the centrality that was due to it—a fateful oversight that was paid for with an incalculable political price.

But here precisely, at his point of deepest insight, it appears that Nancy may well have a thing or two to learn from the ruthless professor of practice we encountered at the outset. What appears to be missing in the philosopher's otherwise admirable co-existential analytic is some link between his ontology of being-in-common and the predominant feature of today's world: millions of refugees, asylum seekers, religious and ethnic minorities, internally displaced people, illegalized migrants, nomadic peoples, and all others who find themselves trapped between a universal 'human rights' proclaimed by 'the international community' and their stark reality as stateless inhabitants of refugee camps and internment centres. The redoubtable professor of practice is surely correct in his observation that as social order begins to unravel, the state is no longer in a position to offer any protection, and 'one's own group' is often the only recourse for a modicum of safety and security. The problem, however, is with the practice professor's supposition that it is the state which is the universal norm, and the turn to community an aberration that is occasioned by the state's 'failure'.

Failures Failures Everywhere

The precise extent of this 'failure' today may be gauged by a recent report of the United Nations Refugee Agency titled 'Global Trends'.[25] Wars and persecution have driven more people from their homes than at any time since the agency started keeping records. It noted that on average twenty-four people were forced to flee each minute in 2015, four times more than a decade earlier, when six people fled every sixty seconds. Every day 34,000 people are forcibly displaced as a result of conflict or persecution.[26]

The study which tracks forced displacement worldwide based on data from governments, partner agencies and the own reporting of United Nations High Commissioner for Refugees (UNHCR), found that a total of 65.3 million people were displaced at the end of 2015 (compared to 59.5 million just 12 months earlier), of whom 21.3 million were refugees, over half of whom were under the age of 18. It is the first time in the organization's history that the threshold of

60 million has been crossed. In addition, there are 10 million state-less people who are denied any nationality, and lack access to basic rights such as education, healthcare, employment, and freedom of movement.

'More people are being displaced by war and persecution and that's worrying in itself, but the factors that endanger refugees are multiplying too', said UN High Commissioner for Refugees Filippo Grandi. 'At sea, a frightening number of refugees and migrants are dying each year; on land, people fleeing war are finding their way blocked by closed borders. Closing borders does not solve the prob-lem.' The report found that, measured against the world's population of 7.4 billion people, one in every 113 people globally is now either an asylum-seeker, internally displaced, or a refugee—putting them at a level of risk for which UNHCR knows no precedent. To put it in per-spective, the tally is greater than the population of Canada, Australia, and New Zealand combined. A record 40.8 million people were forced to flee their homes but remained within the confines of their own countries—another record for the UN Refugee Agency.

Forced displacement has been on the rise since at least the mid-1990s in most regions, but over the past five years the rate has acceler-ated. While today's largest conflict is Syria, in the past five years at least fifteen conflicts have erupted or reignited: eight in Africa (Côte d'Ivoire, Central African Republic, Libya, Mali, northeastern Nigeria, Democratic Republic of Congo, South Sudan, and Burundi); three in the Middle East (Syria, Iraq, and Yemen); one in Europe (Ukraine); and four in Asia (Kyrgyzstan, and in several areas of Myanmar, India, and Pakistan). Thousands have also fled raging gang warfare and drug-related violence in Central America.

Almost nine out of every ten refugees (86 per cent) are in regions and countries considered economically less developed. Their pre-dicament is well encapsulated in the following remark by Hikmat, a Syrian farmer driven from his land by war, now living in tent outside a shopping centre in Lebanon with his wife and young children: 'We can't go on and we can't go back.' Children made up 51 per cent of the world's refugees in 2015, according to the data UNHCR was able to gather. Many were separated from their parents or travelling alone.

Globally, if all the refugees, internally displaced people, and those seeking asylum were to form the population of a country, it would be the world's twenty-fourth biggest. As if to acknowledge this grim milestone, ten refugees made history as members of the first-ever Refugee Olympic Team by traveling to Brazil to compete in the Rio Olympics in 2016. The team included two Syrian swimmers, two judokas from the Democratic Republic of the Congo, a marathoner from Ethiopia, and five middle-distance runners from South Sudan.

Last year, on average, each day saw another 42,500 people driven from their homes. If all of the world's displaced people formed a country, it would have the fastest-growing population and one of the youngest, with half the population under eighteen. But it would be among the worst nations for access to education, child mortality caused by preventable illnesses including pneumonia and malaria, and rates of child marriage and sexual abuse. Many refugees will live in exile for years to come, the report said: 'In effect, if you become a refugee today, your chances of going home are lower than at any time in more than 30 years.'

To say in light of all this that large parts of the world are 'failed states' must surely qualify as the mother of all euphemisms. It would be far more accurate to reverse predicate and subject, and arrive at the following proposition: *There are no failed states; state itself is failure.*[27] Nancy's generalized denunciation of states and communities as equally instances of 'immanentism' does not seem to be able to account for this overwhelming ontic feature of our time. Driven from home by poverty, rape, ostracization, and violence, becoming either 'internally displaced' or 'refugee' in an alien land where simple tasks such as crossing a border or reuniting with one's family can turn into an experience of extreme danger and despair—to say to someone trapped in such a fate and turning to his/her community for a modicum of protection that s/he should 'eschew the immanentism of his self-enclosed community' borders on the ethically obscene. Such glibness usually issues forth from those who themselves shelter behind states armed to the teeth, and often goes hand-in-hand with a theoretical approach to community that construes it as a 'site' of knowledge, memory, narrative, ritual, myth, even of insurrection, revolt, rebellion, resistance, defiance, dissent—but never of Truth.[28]

Truth and Universal History

Alain Badiou is only the most explicit of contemporary theorists to declare that any invocation of community 'works directly against Truths' because Truth can only be arrived at by 'subtracting the grip of the communal'.[29] Badiou does, however, make a useful distinction between Truth and Knowledge: Knowledge pertains to the positive order of reality, whereas Truth is correlative to an Event irreducible to the order of reality. Knowledge as knowledge of phenomenal reality is determined by causal mechanisms, but from time to time, an Event takes place that is out of reach for Knowledge. That is to say, it cannot be accounted for by Knowledge, except at the cost of occluding its 'evental' dimension by reducing it to just another occurrence in the normal flow of things.

For Knowledge, there are always problems to be solved, gaps to be filled in, perspectives to be accommodated, criticisms to be made, assumptions to be questioned—but the overall frame within which these inquiries are carried out is complete and closed. When faced with disturbances, Knowledge mobilizes the entire set of economic, political, cultural, psychological, and scientific causes in their 'complex interaction' to account for them. What Truth does, on the other hand, is to reveal these disturbances not as local malfunctions but as symptoms that crystallize the flaw in the totality as such. Truth is 'metaphysical' in the sense that it is *meta* with respect to what Knowledge takes to be 'reality'. The principal feature of a Truth-Event is non-determination by its context: there is an excess in the emergence of an Event which interrupts the regular chain of causality, and because of which it cannot be accounted for at the level of contextual causes and effects. Categories and methodologies derived from the social and narratological sciences that in any way presuppose a notion of extant 'reality' therefore lack the conceptual resources to account for the central feature of a Truth-Event: its autonomy from contextual determination.

How are we to know whether we are in Knowledge or in Truth? The short answer is that there is nothing intrinsic to the Truth-Event that makes it irreducible to Knowledge as the object of scientific, sociological, political, or psychological analysis. There is no neutral standpoint from which a Truth-Event can be unambiguously identified; it can be recognized as such only by the engaged subjective perspective on it. An Event exists only for those who discern in it traces of Truth; for the external observer, these traces are mere perturbances in the field of Knowledge. One of the great merits of Badiou's theory of the Event is that it pins us down to a precise site of Truth which, according to him, can only be four in number: politics, art, science, and love. Where does philosophy fit in this schema? For Badiou, philosophy is always conditioned by Events in these four domains; by itself, philosophy cannot generate any Truth. Philosophy's job is therefore limited to arriving at one of these four sites after an Event has occurred, and to try and make sense of this occurrence. Tying Truth down to a specific site of occurrence in this way has the infinite merit of holding our feet to the fire of an Event, and removing the temptation to academicism and pedantry.

To address the question of whether community could be a potential site of Truth, we could do no better than begin by turning to Nancy's axiom that it is relationality that must first be presupposed for community to be at all; a community is singular not because of specific properties that distinguish it from other communities, but because it is exposed in a singular way to them. A community's singularity is not an interiority or exteriority it can 'appropriate'; rather, it dwells on the edge it shares with other communities. What is 'shared' is not a common substance or a connecting bridge but the sheer facticity of their mutual exposure.

The central problem here is: how can a dynamic system emerge from this mutual exposure? It cannot be explained from the outside because it is not determined by any set of relations with an external other. The discord that introduces a dynamic into it must, therefore, be absolutely immanent; the system then starts to cause itself in a closed loop, and the singularities 'become what they are' by overcoming their immediacy.[30] For Hegel, the fundamental discord is that between the individual's 'infinite subjectivity' and the norms and practices of a society's collective life which constitute its *Sittlichkeit.* These norms and practices are not simply 'created' by individuals;

they must be 'found' as already present, even though they are sustained by the very activity of those who find it.

In the course of Hegelian historical progression, this substance gradually dissolves, but it will eventually be recovered mediatedly as the rationality embodied in three institutions of the modern world: the *family* in the domestic sphere, the public domain of *civil society* (which for Hegel is primarily determined by market relations), and the *constitutionalist state* which guarantees the citizen's freedom. For Hegel, freedom must be realized in actual institutions which must in turn be 'rational' to promote freedom. These institutions comprise the intermediate domain of 'Objective Spirit', lodged between 'Subjective Spirit' unaware of any relationality and 'Absolute Spirit', which is the supreme domain of art, religion, and philosophy. Progressing through each of these levels, Spirit becomes increasingly self-determining as it advances towards a fuller definition and actualization of freedom.

As Dieter Heinrich points out, the problem Hegel struggles with in *Philosophy of Right* is that a fully realized autonomy and freedom do not consist only in 'accepting and following the will's own law, but also involve requiring that there be a reality that corresponds structurally to the will's own structure. ... Hegel's answer is the rational state whose good constitution respects the freedom of its citizens. This is the *structure* in reality that corresponds to the internal structure of the will'.[31] Its subjects do not accept the state '*because* it provides for the fulfilment of all the needs of the natural individual. Instead, the will accepts the state because *only* with reference to it can the self-reference of the will's own structure be completed'.[32] The state is, therefore, not just an instrument of civil society designed to satisfy the needs of its citizens: 'The state is the actuality of the ethical Idea—the ethical spirit as substantial will, *manifest* and clear to itself, which thinks and knows itself and implements what it knows in so far as it knows it.'[33] In the state, 'freedom enters into its highest right in relation to individuals, whose *highest duty* is to be members of the state'.[34] But as Heinrich points out, it is not the state as such that is the absolute Idea for Hegel. Rather, 'what corresponds to his definition of the absolute Idea is the *structure* of correspondence *between the will and the state, rather than the institution of the state alone*'.[35] Hegel's notion of citizenship 'encompasses' family and civil society by 'preserving' the immediate affective ties of family and the independent individuality of civil society in the institution of the state.[36]

The underlying logic of dialectical development here is that of *Aufhebung* in which each stage is simultaneously annulled and preserved in the next stage which remedies the lack on account of which the previous stage could not stabilize itself. The institution of contract which governed civil society recognizes the individual's abstract personhood and capacity for labour; morality recognizes the collective good through abstract principles such as the categorical imperative; the family is a haven of affect-laden self-sacrificing relationships. Although civil society also promotes the common good through the workings of the market's invisible hand, it cannot by itself supply the larger sense of community that is necessary for freedom to flourish. It is, therefore, the universality of the state in which the immediacy of the family and the self-interested independence of civil society are surpassed and preserved ('sublated'): 'The principle of modern states has enormous strength and depth because it allows the principle of subjectivity to attain fulfilment in the *self-sufficient extreme* of personal particularity, while at the same time *bringing it back to substantial unity* and so preserving this unity in the principle of subjectivity itself.'[37]

But political identity within the rational state is not all; one's identity as member of a *Volk* sharing a common culture and tradition is just as important for Hegel:[38] '*Das Volk als Staat* is the spirit in its substantial rationality and immediate actuality and is therefore the absolute power on earth.'[39] Nation and state come together here in the nation-as-state in which a Volk constitute themselves as a state, and the state is in turn grounded in a shared culture. It is only as a state that a Volk can move from unreflective tradition to self-reflexivity and freedom. So also the state's constitution cannot be built entirely on formal principles but must reflect a Volk's particular tradition and history. A state built only on law would not be animated by the *Geist* of a Volk and cannot hope to command its full assent because it would turn into a purely utilitarian arrangement; on the other hand, law that flows directly from tradition can never be reflective enough to serve as its own justification.

The developmental trajectory of the Volk is roughly parallel to the
individual's:

> In its initial stage, a Volk is not a state, and the transition of a family,
> tribe, kinship group, mass (of people) etc. to the condition of a state
> constitutes the *formal* realization of the Idea in general within it. If the
> nation, as ethical substance—and this is what it is *in itself*—does not
> have this form, it lacks the objectivity of possessing a universal and
> universally valid existence for itself.[40]

Recognizing the value of persons as individuals rather than as
members of a cultural community is therefore fundamental to the
transition from nation to state. A Volk is just a tangled mass of customs and traditions unless it is able to articulate the distinct spheres
of family, civil society, and political representation into the reflective
structure of a rational state.

The state is the only way for a Volk to reflect on its collective inheritance and decide which of its traditions to endorse in light of the universal ideals of justice and freedom. The particular content of a Volk's
culture is thus combined with the universal form of the state in which
particularity, affect, reflexivity, and rationality can all be integrated.
Full 'recognition' then involves recognition of the other as contractual
partner, as moral agent, as family member, as member of a particular
Volk, all of which find their consummation in the citizenship of a constitutional state. This in turn opens up the domains of art, religion,
and philosophy through which Spirit comes to consciousness of itself
as Absolute. It is thanks to the logic of sublation that a particular can
come to see itself as part of the universal without wholly losing its
particularity while simultaneously going beyond itself, partaking of
world history, and contributing to the progress of freedom.

Thus, we get the Hegelian account of universal history beginning
with the immediacy of the Greek *polis*, broken up by the Roman
epoch in which the Greek substantial unity is lost, followed by the
medieval universe of total alienation in which reality gets transposed
into a Beyond of which this world is only a pale reflection, followed
in turn by nations built entirely around culture but lacking rational
institutions, which, therefore, had to come to grief in the abstract
negativity of the French Revolution, and eventually superseded by
the rational state that could reintegrate the ethical substance with

free subjectivity as its fundamental feature. The rational state thus restores the Sittlichkeit of public norms, but this time reflexively and therefore on a higher level at which reality is adequate to its concept: 'The principle of modern states has prodigious strength and depth because it allows the principle of subjectivity to progress to its culmination in the extreme of self-subsistent personal particularity, and yet at the same time brings it back to the substantive unity and so maintains the unity in the principle of subjectivity itself.'[41] 'The state is the self-conscious ethical substance' as Hegel puts it.[42] Even though the ethical substance can no longer be experienced immediately the way it was in traditional community, it is still crucial that this substance be recovered in a different form if the modern state was not to be experienced by the citizen as just another external arena ruled by competition and calculation.

In summary, for Hegel the subject must first be pried loose from the particular life-world he is immersed in and compelled to shift his fundamental allegiance away from his primary community toward a secondary community where his sense of belonging is no longer spontaneously given. However, Hegelian 'sublation' means that this does not involve a direct loss of the primary identification; rather, it is reintegrated into the secondary identification so that it starts to function as the form of appearance of the latter. By being a loving member of one's family, a productive member of one's profession, an active believer in one's faith, a helpful contributor to one's local community, one is partaking in the proper functioning of the state, whether one is aware of this or not. The rupture from the immediate substantiality of traditional community gives rise to the universal *Moralitat* of the individual's infinite subjectivity, but this morality must find concrete political expression in the modern rational state, or else it remains merely abstract.[43]

Writing in the high noon of modern optimism, Hegel could scarcely have imagined either the emergence of mega-corporations that would undermine the autonomy of civil society by forging a nexus with the state, or that the 'universality' of the modern state would soon come to host a particularism more virulent than anything the traditional communities had ever known. Instead of the citizen recognizing the essence of his freedom in the institutions of the state, the 'nation' moment which Hegel had envisaged as being subsumed under the state's rational totality resurfaces with a vengeance, seeking compensation for loss of primary identifications and demanding to subordinate the state to its secondary passion.

T.R.V. Murti's Field Guide to Changing the Past

The dialectical motor throughout the Hegelian schema is the cancelling-cum-preserving operation of sublation (*Aufhebung*) in which a 'lower stage' is both annulled and elevated in the 'reconciliation' that takes place at the 'higher stage'. But is Hegel's the only dialectical story that can be told? Does negativity have any destiny other than that of serving as handmaiden to sublation? And if so, how does that change our perspective on community?

For some illumination on this question, we can turn to the last master dialectician of India, T.R.V. Murti, and his half-forgotten *The Central Philosophy of Buddhism*[44], an immensely attractive feature of which is the fact that the words 'colonial', 'pre-colonial', and 'post-colonial' do not appear even once in its pages. What Murti offers us is a retelling of the story of Indian philosophy—but a retelling which is also a dialectical meta-philosophy. In our context, Murti's meta-philosophy is of particular interest because it sheds light on the question of whether it is possible to conceive of an alternative to the dialectic of sublation. This in turn raises further questions: how do two irreconcilably opposed perspectives on the 'same' totality emerge in the first place? Is it possible to have a 'synthesis' of these opposed perspectives? If not, what does it mean to say that these perspectives are incommensurable? In the course of addressing these questions, Murti also sheds light on how those of us who follow in the wake of an Event can come to grips with its Truth.[45]

Murti takes particular exception to Radhakrishnan's assertion that Buddhism is 'only a restatement of the thought of the Upanishads with a new emphasis'.[46] If that is so, Murti remarks dryly, then 'it is desirable to emphasize this "emphasis", especially because it is of a fundamentally metaphysical nature', and poses the following query: 'Is not a *fundamental metaphysical difference* the source of all other differences?'[47] After training his guns directly at Radhakrishnan's soft-pedalling of 'fundamental metaphysical difference' as a mere 'difference in emphasis', Murti proceeds to offer us a reconstruction that makes the past of Indian philosophy readable in an entirely different way from that of his teacher, who is none other than the greatest contemporary systematizer of Indian philosophy.[48] As is well known, for Radhakrishnan Buddhism is but a tributary of that gigantic river called Hinduism that has its headwaters in the *Vedas* and the Upanishads, flows through multiple *darsanas* (philosophical schools), and empties out into the great ocean of Advaita Vedanta.

In a classic dialectical move, Murti picks out Madhyamika from the whole tangled mass of metaphysical doctrines and elevates it as *the* defining moment of Indian philosophy. Not only did Madhyamika 'precede the revolution in the Upanishadic tradition by several centuries', says Murti, 'there is no doubt that it was the Madhyamika dialectic that paved the way for the other Absolutisms'.[49] In Murti's account, the highest development of Indian metaphysical systems in the form of their respective Absolutisms necessarily had to follow upon speculations of the earlier doctrines of Samkhya, Nyaya-Vaisesika, the Vedanta of ekatvavada, and the Abhidharma whose inconsistencies the Absolutisms subsequently denounced. Unlike the earlier doctrines, however, Madhyamika is not an independent account of 'ultimate reality' but rather a demonstration of how all previous systems necessarily engender contradictions when thought through to their conclusion; for Murti, Madhyamika is only the self-awareness of the traditional metaphysics as a system of immanent errors. Whereas the earlier doctrines had proposed various explanations of 'the true reality', Madhyamika is not a doctrine at all in this sense. Negating as it does all preceding doctrines, it cannot be accommodated within the field of their mutual disagreements.[50]

After Murti, all doctrines prior to the emergence of Madhyamika are disclosed as moving inexorably towards an impasse, and all that followed in its wake as a series of attempts to break out of this impasse. Although the *drstis* (dogmatic viewpoints) have between themselves engendered their own collective deadlock – and the Absolutisms of Advaita and Vijnanavada are derived by Murti as alternative ways of resolving this deadlock—there is no 'teleology' of any sort operating here. If by 'teleology' is meant an evolutionary logic in which the 'lower stage' already contains the seeds of the 'higher stage', then Murti's procedure is almost the exact opposite. For him, the previous 'stages' become readable as dogmatic (*drstivada*)—and the subsequent absolutisms as efforts to cope with their impasse—only through their retroactive placement on either side of the doctrinal voiding effectuated by Madhyamika.

Murti's project may therefore be characterized as one of retelling the development of Indian philosophy from the perspective of its 'becoming' by centring it on Madhyamika's irruption into the doctrinal field as a paradoxical doctrine of no-doctrine. The rise of Madhyamika, for Murti, marks a caesura in Indian philosophy: there can be no direct passage from the drstis that precede it to the Absolutisms that follow it. From this opening, Murti is able to generate all prior doctrines as being caught in their 'internal incongruity',[51] and all posterior doctrines as born of attempts to cope with Madhyamika's scandalous impact. By placing Madhyamika at its dead-centre, Murti resuscitates Indian philosophy in its becoming by reintroducing possibility into a process which, in accounts such as Radhakrishnan's, appears as a monotonous succession of doctrines that renders invisible the shattering encounter which engendered the development of the great Absolutisms.[52]

By opening up the past in this way, Murti restores to actuality its dimension of potentiality: he inserts possibility into reality by reintroducing contingency into the past and grasping it in its becoming.[53] Radhakrishnan, on the other hand, gives us a watertight account with the Upanishads serving as the all-englobing context for its unilinear unfolding—but at the cost of disavowing the principal impetus behind the development of the very Absolutisms he so prizes.[54] For Murti on the other hand, there is no primordial origin which determines once and for all the trajectory of Indian philosophy; rather, *context is always retroactively constituted by the reconstruction it is a 'context' for.* In Murti's retelling, a recontextualization of the context occurs through a drastic reduction of the doctrinal multiplicity to its minimal difference: the entire plurality of metaphysical doctrines and the discursive terrain they share is violently reduced to the bare Two of *atman* (substance) and *anatman* (no substance). The entirety of the past with all its proliferating multiplicity is reduced in one fell swoop to the presence or absence of a singular feature—atman—and how the various doctrines stand in relation to this.

It is crucial to note, however, that this reduction is in no sense an approximation of the 'true reality' of the doctrinal multiplicity. Murti puts the matter this way:

> It is customary to speak of the six orthodox and six heretical systems. The Samkhya, the Yoga, the Nyaya, the Vaisesika, the Purva Mimamsa, and the Vedanta (also called the Uttara Mimamsa) constitute the former; the four classical schools of Buddhism (the Vaibhaiska, the Sautrantika, the Vijnanavada, and the Madhyamika), Jainism, and the Carvaka make up the latter. This traditional enumeration errs by being at once too narrow *and* too wide; *too narrow*, as it does not include many other schools—the non-Advaitic schools of the Vedanta, the various Saiva systems, the philosophy of language, etc. which are not mentioned at all. If the intention is to include the basic systems only, then it is *too wide*. For there are only three basic systems (the Samkhya, the Nyaya-Vaisesika, and the Advaita Vedanta), and three (the Abhidharmika, the Madhyamika, and the Yogacara) belonging to Buddhism. The Jaina system may be taken as different from both groups.[55]

In short, any exercise aspiring to be a 'comprehensive representation' of Indian philosophical doctrines inevitably stumbles upon either a lack or an excess: no enumeration can ever quite be 'it' because some form of 'distortion' is always already at work. The reduction into the Two of atman and anatman is only a further contraction of an already constitutive distortion. Knowledge's response in the face of such a scission—typified by Radhakrishnan—is always to try and contain the damage by translating the Two back into the familiar terrain of a multiplicity circumscribed within a shared One.[56]

The Two is also not the embodiment of a 'conflict' between two 'really existent' social groups identifiable by their positive characteristics—there are no 'actual entities' which identify as *atmavadin* (adherent of the substance doctrine) and *anatmavadin* (adherent of the no-substance doctrine). Nonetheless, all determinate groups with their positively identifiable features are but an effect of the Two. The One as common ground for the proliferation of multiplicity gets cut from within by this virtuality of the Two, and the totality as such begins to appear differently structured when viewed from one or the other of the Two. There is no third neutral way that stands elevated above the Two from where the totality may be surveyed without distortion. Each of the Two now deploys its own notion of what the totality is as such—including its own role and that of the other in the totality.

It is not only that the Two perspectives 'disagree'; they disagree about their very disagreement. They can neither be brought to a common denominator nor harnessed to complement each other in a 'synthesis'. In Indian philosophy, what is ultimate enlightenment for one is sheer *avidya* (ignorance) for the other.[57] Each considers itself to be orthodoxy and the other heterodoxy. The disagreement here is not only about their difference; it is about how this 'difference' is itself differently inflected through the two incommensurable perspectives. The two differ in the very way in which they perceive the 'difference' that separates them. For anatmavada, the gap that separates it from *atmavada* is not the same as—is unacceptably different from—this same gap perceived from the atmavada standpoint. We move from a straight 'difference' between the multiple drstis—not to some under-lying 'identity' encompassing these differences but—to the difference of difference itself.

In the wake of Murti's reconstruction, we are also able to clearly discern the self-decontextualization of the *Prajnaparamitasutra* from its entanglement with other sundry sutras by voiding itself of all the Abhidharmic content, enacting a self-rupture with the *skandhas* (elements), and subordinating the entire field of the drstis to its own self-expansionary logic. What was once a part of the whole emerges not only as relating to the other but also as self-relating, subsuming the whole out of which it emerged as a subordinate moment in the movement of its contraction-expansion, throwing the totality into damaging imbalance and overdetermining the entire network of rela-tions. The determinative power of the extant causal chain is violently interrupted by a self-emptying of the doctrinal content and a self-decontextualizing from the entire field of the drstis.

The temporality of this kenosis is that of retroactivity—an effect that is not only in excess of its causal context, but retroactively causes its own cause. It is not that the drstis first existed and were subsequently negated; rather, *drsti only becomes drsti retroactively with Madhyamika's cutting into the heterogeneous doctrinal field and splitting it into Two.* There are no drstis that form a pre-given 'context' prior to the cut; *drsti qua drsti* only 'comes to be through being left behind'.[58]

Henceforth, the totality called 'Indian philosophy' possesses a minimal consistency only insofar as it is split; any appearance of a prelapsarian 'unity' it possessed prior to the splitting turns into an illusion pure and simple.

The Middle Way

Murti's own explicit stance towards the Hegelian operation of sublation—which, in his words, 'unifies and yet retains differences in its grip, subsumes particulars without annulling them'[59]—is that it is an instance of the *catuskoti*'s (tetralemma's) Third of 'conjoint affirmation' (*ubhayam*), and that such a combination is 'subject to the (same) difficulties urged with regard to each alternative'[60] and some additional ones besides. The Madhyamika's negation, on the other hand, is a 'universal negation' that breaks out of the entire fourfold delineated by the catuskoti. For Murti, the Madhyamika's negation is 'the negation *of* judgment (as such), and not one more judgment'[61] within the fourfold (*parapaksanirakaranam*)[62]: Madhyamika's *sunyata-sarva-dristinam*[63] implies a breaking out of the entire four-cornered field marked out by the mutually opposed dogmatisms (*sarva-dharmanam-bhuta-pratyaveksa*).[64]

This matter is cleared up further by the Japanese Buddhist philosopher Gadjin Nagao by returning us to the *mahavakya* (great saying) from the *Prajnaparamitasutra: rupam eva sunyata, sunyataiva rupam* (form is emptiness, emptiness is form).[65] For Nagao, 'form is emptiness, emptiness is form' is not a mere axiom of symmetry which says if A = B, then B = A. In the context of the drstis, the first part of the mahavakya ('Form is emptiness') does read like a standard claim about reality, here asserted to be 'empty'. However, Nagao's interest here is not in the mahavakya's claim about the nature of reality, but in the formal dialectical logic it traverses in the course of its unfolding.

As an intervention in the field of drstis, it is necessarily first (mis)recognized as yet another drsti about form, so the first task is to negate form and declare it to be empty. However, if we were to stop with this negation, emptiness would still stand in opposition to form. It would remain attached in a negative way to the very positivity of form which it negates. Ridding emptiness of this attachment therefore calls for a subsequent negation of the entire relation in which form remains opposed to emptiness as its other. With the first negation, we lose substantive form; with the second negation of the mutual implication of form and emptiness, we lose this very loss—to obtain what? 'Form' once again, but this time not 'form' as opposed to emptiness, but as the coincidence of the 'opposites' of form and emptiness: *emptiness itself is the new form.*

With this second negation, the very meaning of 'form' undergoes a radical transformation: from emptiness being opposed to form, it *becomes* the new form. We begin with a certain idea of form, but this idea itself undergoes a transformation and redefinition in the course of its actualization. The negation of the drstis traverses only the first negation performed in the mahavakya; it takes a second negation of that negation for the dialectic to reach fruition. In the trajectory of Indian philosophy, it is the early Yogacara that performs this second negation for Nagao.

Nagao's insight also holds for our dialectic of the Two. The first negation has to rebound back upon the Two as internal negation within each of the Two in a reflexive looping back of external difference into internal difference. In Murti's reconstruction, this coincidence of external and internal difference in the Two of atman and anatman is what explodes into Advaita on the one hand and Vijnanavada on the other, transforming the entire doctrinal terrain into a field of Absolutisms. Here, 'reconciliation' between the Two is brought about not by any sublation a la Hegel but in a redoubling of external into internal difference.

'The Middle is not a point between two extremes and cannot be found at a certain point', says Nagao, 'because the path is a total process, dynamic, and dialectical.'[66] It is the totality of the dialectical path—of negation, and negation of negation—that constitutes the Middle Way for Nagao. If, as Murti says, 'Hinduism and Buddhism belong to the same genus; they differ as species',[67] then what Nagao has sketched out in his reading of the mahavakya is the dynamics of self-transformation of the genus itself: nothing about Indian philosophy remains the same after the rise of the Absolutisms. In Murti's reconstruction of this transfigured genus, Madhyamika eventually comes to be domesticated as a subspecies of the anatman species, and the collective memory that this subspecies was once the universal negation that reconfigured the entire genus gradually sinks into oblivion.

Universal History Redux

What if we were to now return to Nancy's intercommunal configuration as a being-with, and once again pose the question of the emergence of an immanent dynamic, this time not through a dialectic of sublation but through a constitutive act of self-relating? But how—if the 'immanentism' of communal substantiality is purely illusory, and its truth that of a mutual exposure? Here, a small retreat from Nancy's own over-ontologization of community might be of some help. It is true that the communal substance possesses none of the density of the Hegelian *Sittlichkeit*, but to dismiss this substance as a 'reified' outcome of the individuals' own activity fails to account for why it is nonetheless experienced by them as a minimally transcendent substance irreducible to their interaction. Although the communal substance is kept alive entirely by the activity of individuals comprising the community, why is this substance minimally 'objectivized' and cannot therefore be rid of in the classical Marxist style of individuals recognizing behind it the product of their own activity?

The only answer to this puzzle is that the communal substance must be both virtual and real: virtual, because it has no independent existence of its own, it exists only insofar as individuals relate to it as their substance; real, because it makes its presence felt in regulating actual social processes and their outcomes. This duality of the real and the virtual is inscribed into the communal substance, and it is their mutual tension that explodes in the course of communal self-contraction. Through a reflexive relating to its self-difference, the community enacts its autonomy from external determination.[68] Precisely because it is neither a purely ontic entity nor an entirely illusory virtuality, the communal substance is susceptible of self-contraction, making possible an immanent dialectic capable of transforming an inert multiplicity of communities into a dynamic intercommunal web of self-aware relations, and redrawing the very contours of these communities. Only in this way can communities transacting across boundaries as ontic entities transcend their entityness and awaken to the Truth of their relationality.

But it is only thanks to its dependence on all the other substantive communities—which by default lend to it its outline form—that
a community can undertake self-voiding without disintegrating
altogether. What remains of the community, once it divests itself of
substance, is the pure form of community sustained by all other 'still
substantive' communities. By the time the community undergoes a
negation of this negation and returns to communal substantiality,
the very 'context' of intercommunal relations that had previously
determined it is subordinated to the dynamic of its self-contraction/
expansion, inducing convulsions in all the other communities and
recontextualizing the entirety of the socio-symbolic space.

'Representation' here dissipates in a blur because there is no longer any community with a set of positive attributes which abstraction
can adequate itself to because it is the 'concrete entity' of the community that itself turns abstract. This predicament of representation
is correlative to the extreme reflexivity of a community sundered
from its *differentia specifica*, and its mutation into the pure *form* of
community *qua* community. What is left as a remainder in 'reality'
is this pure communal form lacking any substantive content susceptible to representation. The emergence of this paradoxical 'concrete
abstraction' in reality also points to the limits of any attempt to hew
closely to the so-called 'real' persons, entities, and actions comprising such an event by directly soliciting categories from those
involved. Representation as such dissolves after the first negation,
and only re-emerges from its dissipation in concrete-abstraction
after the negation-of-negation and the community's subsequent
re-substantialization.

Not only is the community that undertakes the passage through
self-voiding therefore *not* the community that returns from it; the
communal self is constituted in the very movement of its 'return'.
The dynamic of return is what gives rise to the self to which the return
returns. The paradox proper to communality is that it is self-voiding
that reveals the self that undergoes the voiding: the communal self
only emerges as the retroactive effect of the process through which
the conditions that had previously determined communality are in
turn subordinated as a subsidiary moment of the dynamic process.
The entire prior world of intercommunal relations as a meaningful hermeneutic totality with a given disposition of affinities and

aversions, obligations and proscriptions, undergoes a dissolution to make way for a re-inscription of communities within a transformed horizon of relationality. This does not mean that every trace of the earlier substance is eradicated; many of the earlier practices may well persist into the new world—but these now present themselves as wholly mediated by the preceding Truth-Event.

The precipitating 'contradiction' in such a dialectic is not between infinite subjectivity and closed community, but between communal substance and *its own* non-coincidence. Thanks to the self-thwarting duality of real and virtual operative in the heart of community, every community is primordially enabled to relate not only to other communities but also to itself. Unlike the Hegelian dialectic of progressive history with the modern state as apotheosis, the state in this dialectic of backwater-ecstasis[69] is subsumed as a moment in the negation and negation-of-negation that runs transversal to universal history's sublatory logic and its subordination of communities under the aegis of the nation-state as meta-community.

This Madhyamika dialectic undercuts both universal history and communitarianism. Unlike universal history, the state is thoroughly decentered within a larger dynamic of intercommunality that is not beholden to any notion of 'progress'. And unlike a complacent communitarianism that seeks to freeze extant communities in their hypostatized forms, and freight them for eternity with their historically inherited substance of collective narratives, memories, and prejudices,[70] it founds itself on a confrontation with the non-identity of the communal substance, seeking to transform the inertia of this entrapped substance into a dynamic force of intercommunal regeneration. Indeed, from the Madhyamika perspective, the state's self-installation as the culminating accomplishment of community and the communitarian notion of a self-identical communal substance fully complement each other by turning communities into reified entities that may then be seamlessly integrated into the state's logic of power, recognition, and resource competition.

The modern state's subsumption of all other communities and its seeming current invulnerability in no way imply that it has tamed negativity once and for all and mediated the national collectivity into an eternally stable unity. Even if the state's coercive apparatus does manage to provisionally subdue other moments, the insistent negativity of the intercommunal dialectic will ever dog it, no matter how 'stable' the social constellation appears. In the Hegelian schema, negativity resurfaces periodically in the form of inter-state wars to undermine even the most well-ordered rational state. But since Madhyamika's next dialectical step—from external wars *between* states to its doubling back as the upsurge of internal negativity *within* each state— is not taken, Hegel leaves us with the state-form as the crowning sublation of community.

The Co-Destinal Analytic

And so finally back to the much maligned idea of communal 'destiny'. Without some concept akin to it, would the community not be left entirely at the mercy of an unrelenting contingency emanating from the state? To characterize the very notion of 'destiny' as 'crypto-fascist' the way many of Heidegger's liberal critics have done—is that also not to rob communities of their autonomous capacity for self-relating, leaving them only with the residual tasks of adjusting and accommodating to progressive universal history? These critics are certainly correct to identify the notion of *Volksgemeinschaft*[71]— the ethno-national community that would realize itself through the medium of the state—as the source of Heidegger's Nazi temptation. What they are loath to acknowledge, however, is that liberalism itself is wedded to an idea not far removed from Volksgemeinschaft: the state as 'national community' to whose imperatives every other community must bend.

The problem with Heidegger's notion of 'communal destiny' is therefore not any 'proto-fascism' intrinsic to it, but in its failure to conceptualize destining as a *co-destining with* other communities. Just as 'Dasein comes to realize that beyond Dasein-with and Dasein-in ... it must become Dasein-for'[72] (its own-most possibilities) by 'running ahead of itself', Mitsein too must become Mitsein-for by a 'running ahead of itself' that is disclosive of its destiny. 'Tradition' for Heidegger is never simply delivered over to Mitsein for the taking but must be reclaimed in its destining. What is missing, however, is any recognition that Mitsein can only become Mitsein-for as Mitsein-with (other communities).[73]

This matter of destiny may also be put in Madhyamika terms: any comprehensive account of the mutual exposure and dependence of communities would necessarily have to think relationality *and* emergence together. If we were to stop with the mere assertion of the anteriority of relationality to entitiness, we would not be properly seized of the doctrine of *pratitya-samputpada* (dependent co-arising). From the Madhyamika standpoint, relationality itself must come to self-awareness in the course of its passage from other-dependence (*paratantra*) of entities to dependent co-arising (pratitya-samutpada). This autonomous reconfiguring of the web of communal mutuality is precisely its *co-destining*.

Notes and References

1. Michael Ignatieff, 'Bosnia and Syria: Intervention Then and Now', 15 August 2013, available at https://bostonreview.net/world/bosnia-and-syria-intervention-then-and-now (accessed on 24 October 2016). Subsequent quotations are all drawn from this piece.

2. After this dispassionate account of the logic of 'humanitarian intervention', Ignatieff makes his own preferences known in the case of Syria in a subsequent article in the 15 February 2016 issue of *Financial Times*: 'establishing an aerial protection zone from the from the outskirts of Aleppo to the Turkish border, ensuring that the city is not cut off from its supply lines and protecting civilians seeking to flee the violence', 'further economic sanctions on Moscow', and 'rapid supply of anti-aircraft and anti-missile equipment to trusted rebel forces'.

3. In a confessional moment, Ignatieff writes, 'I let emotion carry me past the hard questions, like: Can Kurds, Sunnis, and Shiites hold together in peace what Saddam Hussein held together by terror?'

4. Martin Heidegger, *Being and Time* (New York: Harper Perennial, 2008). Derrida has characterized this analytic as 'uncircumventable' (Jacques Derrida, *Margins of Philosophy*, translated by Alan Bass [Chicago: University of Chicago Press, 1982], 22).

5. Being, for the later Heidegger, becomes a matter of 'epochal disclosure' rather than a phenomenology underlying the metaphysically structured experience of the everyday.

6. George Steiner, *Martin Heidegger* (Chicago: University of Chicago Press, 1987), p. 91.

7. Jean-Luc Nancy, *The Inoperative Community*, (Minneapolis & London: University of Minnesota Press, 1991), 3.

8. Nancy, *The Inoperative Community*, 3.
9. In Section 26 of *Being and Time*, Heidegger explicitly states that Dasein is co-original with Mitsein: that Dasein's there-being is always already a being-with.
10. This is laid out in the following passage:

> But if fateful Dasein, as Being-in-the-world, exists essentially in Being-with-Others, its historicizing is a co-historicizing and is determinative for it as destiny. This is how we designate the historicizing of the community, of a people. Destiny is not something that puts itself together out of individual fates, any more than Being-with-one-another can be conceived as the occurring together of several Subjects. Our fates have already been guided in advance, in our Being with one another in the same world and in our resoluteness for definite possibilities.
> (Heidegger, *Being and Time*, 436)

Theorists such as Hubert Dreyfus and John Caputo have asserted that it was Heidegger's conferring of a collective 'destinal' significance on politics that led Heidegger down the blind alley of his Nazi engagement. de Beistegui for instance, asks how being-toward-death as the resolute assumption of one's innermost possibility could possibly be transposed to the level of the collective without invoking some form of sacrificial death—since authentic death is uniquely one's own, not sharable with anyone else. 'How is a community to collectively take up an "authentic" stance toward its "death"? What could terms such as "death" and "resoluteness" possibly mean in the context of an entire community?' (Miguel de Beistegui, *Heidegger and the Political* [London: Routledge, 1998], 17–19).
11. Jean-Luc Nancy, *Being Singular Plural*, translated by Robert D. Richardson and Anne E. O'Byrne (Stanford, California: Stanford University Press, 2000), 204n81 (emphasis in original).
12. Nancy, *Inoperative Community*, 14.
13. Nancy, *Inoperative Community*, 29.
14. Jean-Luc Nancy, *The Sense of the World* (Minneapolis & London: University of Minnesota Press, 1998), p. 106.
15. Nancy, *Inoperative Community*, 7 (emphasis in original).
16. Nancy, *Inoperative Community*, 28.
17. Nancy, *Inoperative Community*, 26 (emphasis in original).
18. Nancy, *Inoperative Community*, 29.
19. Nancy, *Inoperative Community*, 29.
20. Nancy, *Being Singular Plural*, 1–99.

21. Nancy, *Inoperative Community*, 29.
22. Nancy, *Inoperative Community*, 35.
23. Nancy, *Inoperative Community*, x–xi.
24. Nancy, *Inoperative Community*, 35.
25. http://www.unhcr.org/576408cd7 (accessed on 17 September 2017).
26. http://www.unhcr.org/en-us/news/latest/2016/6/5763b65a4/global-forced-displacement-hits-record-high.html (accessed on 17 September 2017).
27. Echoing Hannah Arendt's famous remark that there are no dangerous thoughts, thinking itself is dangerous.
28. In India, one possible reason for this could be the long shadow cast by Gandhi's use of the word 'Truth' and the experimental-ascetic connotations evoked by it. Whatever else he or she may or may not know about Gandhi or about Truth, every schoolchild in India is aware that Gandhi conducted some experiments with Truth. (In a similar vein, every Indian knows that at the stroke of the midnight hour, India had a tryst with destiny even if no one has a clue what this destiny was.) Truth, in Gandhi's conception, is God—and self-purification through fasting and prayer is required to reach this Truth because such a God cannot, in Gandhi's words, be approached 'in the arrogance of strength, but (only) in the meekness of the weak and the helpless' (quoted in D.R. Nagaraj, *The Flaming Feet and Other Essays* [Ranikhet: Permanent Black, 2010], 49). Where do the dominant schools of Indian metaphysics stand with respect to such an ethico-religious conception of Truth? For an answer, we could turn to the last great (and unjustly neglected) dialectician of India, T.R.V. Murti: 'Even the spiritual discipline (marga) undertaken for attaining Nirvana, exalted and purifying as it is, is within *samvrti*. ... Those texts which speak of the means, of the path, of the reality of this and that (*atman, skandhas*, and so on) are *neyartha*; they are not to be taken as literally true; they are of secondary import only (*abhiprayaka*) and must be subordinated to the texts which speak of the Absolute' (T.R.V. Murti, *The Central Philosophy of Buddhism* [New Delhi: Munshiram Manoharlal Publishers, 2010], 252–4). Murti can hardly be more unequivocal here: as excruciating and self-mortifying as the path of purification may be, it cannot qualify as Truth. Parallel to the Madhyamika distinction between into *nitartha* and *neyartha*—depending on whether they deal with *paramartha-satya* or *vyavaharika-satya*—Advaita also makes a distinction of the *sruti* texts into *para* and *apara*.
29. Quoted in Peter Hallward, *Badiou: A Subject to Truth* (Minneapolis & London: University of Minneapolis Press, 2003), 26, 109.

30. 'What is thus found only comes to be through being left behind', as Hegel puts it (Hegel's Science of Logic [Atlantic Highlands: Humanities Press, 1969], 402).
31. Dieter Heinrich, Between Kant and Hegel: Lectures on German Idealism, edited by David S. Pacini (Cambridge, MA and London, England: Harvard University Press, 2003), 326 (emphasis in original).
32. Heinrich, Between Kant and Hegel, 327 (emphasis in original).
33. Hegel's Philosophy of Right (Oxford: Clarendon Press, 1965), 155.
34. Hegel's Philosophy of Right, 156.
35. Heinrich, Between Kant and Hegel, 32 (emphasis in original).
36. Self-interest, the hallmark of civil society, is mediated through the intermediate institution of 'estates' even before we reach the stage of the state.
37. Hegel's Philosophy of Right, 161.
38. The Volk is given a central place in his lectures on the philosophy of history.
39. Hegel's Philosophy of Right, 212.
40. Hegel's Philosophy of Right, 218–19.
41. Hegel's Philosophy of Right, 161.
42. G.W.F. Hegel, Philosophy of Mind (Oxford: Clarendon Press, 1971), 263.
43. This, in essence, is Hegel's critique of Kant.
44. T.R.V. Murti, The Central Philosophy of Buddhism (New Delhi: Munshiram Manoharlal Publishers Pvt. Ltd, 2006).
45. A brief aside on Murti: In what must undoubtedly be one of the most remarkable guru–shishya (teacher–student) bonds witnessed in modern India, T.R.V. Murti and Sarvepalli Radhakrishnan were locked in a relationship of 'incessant intellectual combat and instantaneous embrace' (to paraphrase Octavio Paz in a different context). Murti dedicates his book to Radhakrishnan, declaring in his preface:

> My deepest and most sustained obligations are to my revered teacher, Professor S. Radhakrishnan. He has very kindly revised the manuscript and sent me full and helpful suggestions from Oxford. He has also taken a keen interest in the publication of the book, encouraging me to hope that it may prove a useful work on the subject. I am very deeply indebted to him for all his kindness to me. The Central Philosophy of Buddhism is respectfully dedicated to him as a token of my gratitude and admiration.

What makes this dedication especially remarkable is that Murti was advancing nothing less than a wholesale debunking of the entirety of Radhakrishnan's narrative about Indian philosophy.

46. Murti, *Central Philosophy*, 20.
47. Murti, *Central Philosophy*, 20 (emphasis in original).
48. The ultimate proof of fidelity to a guru, Murti seems to be telling us through his book, is the shishya's willingness to commit 'gurucide'.
49. Murti, *Central Philosophy*, 13.
50. As Murti puts it, 'The Madhyamika dialectic, being a criticism of philosophical standpoints, can get under way only when the different systems have already been formulated. It cannot be an original system' (Murti, *Central Philosophy*, 217). Explicitly drawing a comparison with Kant's relation to rationalism and empiricism, Murti asserts that Madhyamika too could only have followed upon the metaphysical claims of earlier systems; in order to denounce the earlier systems as errors, these systems have to first have existed. It is, therefore, intrinsic to Madhyamika's Truth that it could not have been accessed from the get-go: the beginning is necessarily in error, and Madhyamika's role consists in tracing a path from the errors of preceding systems to their critical denunciation.

     Murti buttresses this claim with a number of assertions, which, from the standpoint of academic pedantry, cannot but give rise to a host of critical questions: How could Murti possibly be certain that Madhyamika is a response to the inner deadlocks of the ekatvavada of the Upanisadic tradition and the Abhidharma of the Buddhist tradition? Where is the evidence that Samkhya had any influence on Madhyamika or that Nagarjuna was even familiar with Samkhya? How can Murti be certain that Abhidharma grew out of a rejection of Upanisadic substantialism? How could Murti possibly extend the 'conflict in Reason' all the way back to the Buddha with his outrageous claim that 'to Buddha belongs the honor of having suggested the dialectic first, much before Zeno in the west?' Where is the evidence that the Buddha's refusal to answer certain kinds of questions (*avyakrta*) has anything to do with his awareness of the antinomical character of Reason? Is Murti not illegitimately importing ideas and frameworks from Western philosophers such as Kant and Hegel and distorting the history of Indian philosophy rather than studying it on its own terms? The first rejoinder Murti might make to the cultural purists and academic pedants would be that there are always two alternative modalities for reconstructing any process: from the standpoint of its 'becoming' (which is what Murti is doing) and from the standpoint of its completed 'being' (which is what the pedants are accustomed to).
51. Murti, *Central Philosophy*, 162n1.
52. According to Kierkegaard, there are always two different standpoints from which to observe a process: the standpoint of its 'being', that is, the

self-identical consistency of the result, or the standpoint of the dynamic of its generative process, that is, its 'becoming'.

53. Walter Benjamin also considers historical reality as being composed of traces which point toward the future; however, these traces become readable only after a future emancipatory event ('divine violence') has redeemed the hopes and dreams that were encoded in these traces, but which were crushed in the course of history's forward march (Walter Benjamin, 'Critique of Violence', in *Reflections*, edited by Peter Demetz [New York: Schocken Books, 1986], 294).

54. One could also risk putting the matter in quasi-psychoanalytic terms: Murti's procedure is to first locate the repressed trauma in Radhakrishnan's account of Indian philosophy, and to then reconstruct it on this basis by placing the trauma at its dead-centre.

55. T.R.V. Murti, *Studies in Indian Thought: Collected Papers of T.R.V. Murti*, edited by Harold G. Coward (New Delhi: Motilal Banarsidass Publisher, 1983), 5.

56. 'They are not merely different, but are opposed to each other as contraries; they explain all things from mutually conflicting points of view. And this conflict is not empirical in origin and scope' (Murti, *Central Philosophy*, 140).

57. Murti, *Central Philosophy*, 164–5.

58. 'What is thus found only comes to be through being left behind' as Hegel puts it (*Hegel's Science of Logic*, 402).

59. Murti, *Central Philosophy*, 230.

60. Murti, *Central Philosophy*, 230.

61. Murti, *Central Philosophy*, 155

62. Murti, *Central Philosophy*, 213.

63. Murti, *Central Philosophy*, 210.

64. Murti, *Central Philosophy*, 209.

65. Gadjin Nagao, *Madhyamika and Yogacara: A Study of Mahayana Philosophies*, translated by Leslie S. Kawamura (Albany: State University of New York Press, 1991), 194.

66. Nagao, *Madhyamika and Yogacara*, 194.

67. Murti, *Studies in Indian Thought*, 163–4. On p. 219, we read: 'Although their generic identity is undeniable, the specific differences are equally undeniable.'

68. As Hegel puts it: 'For it is only because the concrete does divide itself, and make itself into something non-actual, that it is self-moving' (G.W.F. Hegel, *Phenomenology of Spirit*, translated by A.V. Miller [Oxford: Oxford University Press, 1977], 13–14).

69. For an account of how this dialectic unfolded in the southern Indian 'backwater' state of Kerala, see Roby Rajan, 'Backwater Disclosure: Ontological Politics and the Dialectics of Intercommunality', in *India and the Unthinkable*, edited by Vinay Lal and Roby Rajan (New Delhi: Oxford University Press, 2016), 56–91.

70. In his highly regarded essay *Flaming Feet* (D.R. Nagaraj, *The Flaming Feet and Other Essays*, edited by Prithvi Datta Chandra Shobhi [Permanent Black, 2010]), Nagaraj is very critical of the wilful disowning of collective memory, which he sees being justified in some communities on account of the interwovenness of such memories with extreme collective humiliation. He believes that this is bound to prove self-destructive for such communities by robbing them of the gods, goddesses, spirits, and myths that have sustained them through millennia. At one point Nagaraj even adverts to Heidegger's notion of ontological difference, declaring that 'the theoretical project of this entire book draws its sustenance from the notion of ontological difference' (60). The word 'truth' also makes its appearance a number of times here because Nagaraj takes ontological difference to be the difference 'between contingent details of historical fact and the truth of a deeper historical concern' (59) Despite its brevity, there is indeed something of Heidegger in this assertion, but then in the line immediately following, Nagaraj asserts, 'At the level of deeper historical truth the conflicting fact disappears to reveal the underlying unity ... accepting and examining difference leads to the truth of dynamic unity' (60), turning Heidegger's thought into a version of Advaita in which conflicts at the level of phenomenal reality are revealed to be illusory because they spring from the same underlying unity. This Advaitic Heidegger—the first and last we hear of Heidegger in Nagaraj's book—is not a description in which the German philosopher is likely to recognize himself. The ontological difference between beings and being is indeed central to Heidegger but 'being', for him, is in no sense a unitive substratum that underlies phenomenal beings. For Heidegger, 'unity', if any, is that of a historical horizon of meaning within which entities disclose themselves. Nagaraj, however, wants to draw on two different sources that cannot possibly belong in the same universe: an ahistorical substratum in which illusory differences melt away in an overarching unity, and Heidegger's thoroughly historicized conception of being in which meaning is disclosed differentially in the different epochs of being. On the one hand, we have a proto-Advaitic conception of unitiveness for which the very idea of history is thoroughly alien; on the other hand, we have Heidegger's conception of being which has no

place for any cross-historical substratum of the kind Nagaraj appears to be referring to. In no sense can these two worlds belong together. What *is* lasting in Heidegger is his fundamental distinction between changes that occur *within* a given meaning horizon (say, in specific arts, crafts, and sciences) and the far more radical transformation *of* this meaning horizon itself.

71. 'Volksgemeinschaft' was the term used by the Nazis to designate the 'German national community' and which Heidegger also uses on occasion. See Martin Heidegger, 'Political Texts: 1933–1934', *New German Critique* 45 (1988): 98.

72. Steiner, *Martin Heidegger*, 100.

73. Therein also lies the source of Heidegger's *political* blindness: not in the idea of 'destining' as such, but in the inability to think a co-destining *with* European Jewry.

5

DARSANA AS THEORIA
Locations and Ends of Mnemopraxial Learning

D. VENKAT RAO

Thinking Pagan

Cultures are said to differ in different ways. So should, it is logical to assume, cultural thinking. This throws up the inevitable question: how, then, should one think of cultural difference today? If our task is to explore what difference India can make today, one kind of inquiry that can, perhaps, configure such cultural/civilizational difference is precisely an exploration into forms of reflection and being that cultures nurture and privilege. The so-called centres of higher learning—the universities—are barely in a position to grapple with the question of differential cultures of thinking today.

In order to pursue the risky question of cultural difference, the primary task perhaps is to examine how Europe thinks about itself and others. As is well known, Europe's distinction from other cultures is often traced back to the Greek 'event'—the event when thinking could think *about* itself: the emergence of thinking about thinking is seen as a singular event that is said to have happened only in European antiquity. This mode of thinking can be set apart from a thinking that does not probe into the phenomenon of thinking and objectively formulate what thinking is: a form that embodies and enacts thinking in its very modes of being or emergence. If the former posits objects of thinking for/by a subject, the latter displaces categorical thinking (thinking that divides itself into categories). If the former erects a hierarchy of forms of thinking (science, mathematics, philosophy/ myth, poem, performance-theatre, art), the latter undermines hierarchies and confounds them. If the former ascends through institutionalization and professionalization, the latter disperses a-centrically (without a centralized commanding altar) and heterogeneously. If the former enframes and regiments the latter, the latter lives on indifferently; that is, the former invests in thinking the latter whereas the latter moves on a-theoretically, a-conceptually (where terms are not abstracted from figurative uses, where metaphors are not turned into concepts).

Such differences among forms of thinking can be further multiplied. But the question that needs to be faced is: how should reflective modes of being respond to the all-pervasive specialized institutionalized forms of thinking *about* thinking? Every single concept that one is compelled to work with—concepts such as politics, religion, history, aesthetics, philosophy, law, science, literature, art, the university, and the state—is the product of the privileged pattern of thinking *about* thinking. At the very core of the object-oriented method of thinking seems to lurk the desire to determine the object of thought by means of some justifiable ground. But the institutions and the concepts they shelter and perpetuate hardly prepare one to receive and respond to the other reflective modes of being in the world—except as objects of a patterned representation. Such thinking can appropriate any other mode of thinking into its object-making apparatus. Pagan Greek thinking appears only in such European enframing today.

Thinking about thinking is a categorial thinking. Science and philosophy are said to exemplify this method of thinking about thinking and they are projected as the unparalleled signifiers of the 'event'— the Greek miracle. Plato is designated as the pioneering exemplifier of this discursive knowledge.[1]

Can European enframings exhaust Pagan thinking? Can we categorize Pagan thinking of antiquity to the binary muthos versus logos or the body and the soul? What is the epistemic place of *reason* in Pagan thinking? Can their inquiries be reduced to a foundationalist probing? What are the ends of Pagan modes of learning and how does this learning grapple with the question of being and going about in existence? Can one think of distinct Pagan trajectories for disseminating such learning? This chapter is an initial and risky attempt to address some of these questions from the very location of higher education—the university—which is a part of the problem. Moving with the heuristic of cultural difference (between Pagan and European) this chapter focuses on 'ends and locations of learning'. It is not, however, claimed here that it escapes the irony involved in the mode of presentation it is constrained to use.

Primal Rational

The foundation of the institution of higher learning in Europe (medi-eval or modern)—the university—is said to be the 'principle of rea-son'. The principle of reason requires exploration of effects through recourse to their grounding, root causes. The principle seems to underwrite continuity between the first principle of reason, cause, and the subsequent action or effect. The emergence of science and philosophy in antiquity and the coming forth of technosciences and the institution of rational discourses (the university) in the modern period are traced back to this 'first' principle. This 'absolute predomi-nance of the final cause'[2]—the domination of the principle of reason postulates the essence of beings as objects before a subject (ego), which represents the objects for itself and for others.[3] The modern university—the cherished abode of such postulates—is built on the principle of reason. Such a grounding of the essence of being as the representable object 'installs its empire', and covers up the question of being. Therefore, the question of the ground and being forever remain hidden in the empire of objectificatory discourse of knowl-edge, points out Derrida.

We no longer inquire into the grounding principle in the house that it erects: the university. Generalizing the impulse to search for the foundations, Heidegger avers that the quest for origins and ends is a universal human cognitive search and it is the principle of reason that motivates such cognitive inquiries. But is such a postulation necessar-ily universal? Do all cultures originate and terminate their inquiry in finding/founding such a 'principle'? Doesn't such a postulate ascribe to reason the status of sovereignty? Did Pagan Greeks accord such sovereign position to reason? Irrespective of the epistemic status of the principle of reason in Greek thought, the concept of sovereignty as the omnipotent entity appears more as a theological certitude. The cognitive inquiry of the Greeks does not appear to culminate in the search for and sublimation of the *archè* into a doctrinal principle. The search—theoria—seems to get reiterated more in *praxial* ethos than in an endeavour to normativize the relation between the principle of reason and beings and their actions: that the action ought to conform to and abide by the principle seems alien among Pagans.

The search for archè or determining causes appears to be a peculiarity of theological heritage. For it seeks to provide the foundational basis on reason—whether divine or human. Theology (*doctrina sacra*) alone appears to provide unity to inquiries into nature and into human society; it provides the foundation for the order of things. Theology draws on the scripture to establish and justify the foundation of human reasoning and human relationship to the world on divine reason and plan. It is precisely such a heritage that appropriates the Pagan *philosophia* as contemplative/observational reflective practice into propounding systematic accounts of divine reason. Philosophy was made to serve theology.[4] The Pagan theoria was converted into Christian theory.

The centrality of theology (its accounts of divine reason) was displaced by human reason in modern society and the university represented this new avatar of reason. Needless to say that the displacement of the divine (the 'death of god') did not entail the displacement of reason. Faith in reason reinforced the explanatory accounts on the basis of presumed principles. Consequently, the theological institution drawing on reason now spawned multiple sovereign inquiries and thus postulated principles for each regional inquiry. The fundamental modern concepts of state, ethics, society, legal code, and so on derive from the theo-epistemic model.[5]

At the foundation of such ('barely') secularized categories is the concept of god as the foundation or principle of reason. The medieval theological concept of the 'double truth' paves the way for the linear filial bonding between the divine and human. The concept implies that the same phenomenon can fall into earthly and human domain or truth and at the same time that of the divine domain or truth.[6] Thus, the relationship between the state and individual is modelled on the relationship between god and man. The proclamation of the death of god in this context is the declaration of man's usurpation of the position of god. Thus man's explanatory systems—man's inquiry/research—are modelled on the theological accounts about god's achievements. Man can manipulate or redesign nature now. Humanism is fundamentally a theological concept—man's murderous emulation of god. The university became a 'multiversity' of specializations: 'And yet without the all-pervasive principle [of reason] there would be no modern science and without such a science there would be no university', proclaimed Heidegger.[7] Given that the principle of reason is a universal cognitive necessity, Heidegger goes on to say: 'Only founded statements are intelligible and intelligent ... human cognition seeks ... the first and last reasons.'[8]

Heidegger, however, sees the recognition of the principle in Greek antiquity. But it took 2,300 years of gestation period for the principle to be so explicitly formulated, observes Heidegger. As can be seen here the Pagan and theological traditions are seen as continuous and the vantage for such a reading is provided by theological basis. Heidegger sees an explicit formulation of the 'fundamental principle of all fundamental principles' in Leibnitz's axiom: nothing is without reason: *nihil est sine ratione*.[9] One wonders whether the latter isn't just a dissimulated version of theological account of divine reason.

Heidegger, however, goes on to launch a concerted critique of the principle of reason as it manifests today in the manipulative scientific-technological reason and its concomitant social order. In other words, the critique targets the fragmentation and regional calculative manifestations of the principle of reason. Derrida too moves in Heidegger's path and designates it as the 'first principle, the principle of principles'.[10] He sees the principle as a 'requirement present since the dawn of Western science and philosophy', providing the impetus 'for a new era of purportedly "modern" reason, metaphysics, and technoscience'.[11] Derrida's reading, not unlike Heidegger's, too provides a continuist account from the Pagan antiquity to Protestant modernity. The triumphalism of the principle covers up in its progress the 'abyssal question of being' and 'the very question of the ground, of grounding' from its calculated inquiries, contends Derrida. The query 'can the ("forgotten") "question of being" escape the theological determinations of European heritage' remains equivocally answered in the works of Heidegger and Derrida.

Reason is, Derrida notes, after all, 'only one species of thinking'. Derrida underwrites the need for a new articulation of responsibility in the very abode of the university—responsibility which would reach out to 'what is beyond the principle of reason'—even while working with the principle. Despite the risks involved (nihilism of reason and obscurantism of the beyond), thinking requires both the archè of the foundation and the 'anarchy "of the unfounded"', he affirms. Curiously, one may note in passing that a thinking that does not emerge from archeo-theological foundation should be termed anarchic by Derrida. Only the 'enactment of this thinking can decide', points out Derrida, the difference between thinking that privileges the calculative principle of reason and the one that works in the double bind of archè and anarchy.

It is interesting to point out that the new responsibility of questioning the ground and the foundation, in Derrida's account, comes out as a practitional one. It must be practised by a 'community of thinking', which while questioning the ground of reason is open to the beyond of reason; and it would not provide 'discourses of knowledge' as such but enact 'performative discourses that produce the events of which they speak'.[12] Such events overturn and displace the hierarchy of the conscious and the unconscious, constative and performative, theoretical and practical, philosophical and the literary, and subject and object. In order to show the limits of the principle of reason which (onto)theology privileged in the production of discourses of knowledge, Derrida suggests that the praxial thinking-community must engage with literary fiction and poetry rather than informational value of language.[13]

Once again we are turned toward the 'event' and the antagonistic hierarchy between muthos and logs.[14] While working from within the theological heritage Derrida's work here, however, appears to aim not at a simple inversion of the hierarchy and privilege the literary but bring forth (what can be called) a performative episteme that suspends the archeo-theological foundation that supervened all the explanatory account/systems until now. It is in this context that, for Derrida, literature, fiction, and poetry appear to either suspend or function without the foundation of the absolute ground of their emergence. Literary work can perhaps be atheological. Therefore, from within the interstices of theological and theoretical (that which by aligning causes and effects builds systematic explanatory accounts of foundational thinking), Derrida affirms, the possibility of articulating new responsibility in the formation of praxial reflective collectivities. In this regard one can sense a gesture toward the Pagan traditions of performative reflection in Derrida's work on the university. In contrast to theory, Derrida points out, for the Greeks '*theoria* was the only highest form of praxis, and the mode, par excellence, of *energaia*' (work).[15]

Configurations of Learning

Theoria for the Greeks is more seeing or contemplative observation rather than foundational thinking. How one can reconcile the appropriation of Greek thought into Christian theological frame with Derrida's insight into the praxial reflection of Greek thinking is barely explored in the context of his work. The possibility of such an exploration into European thought in general is opened up by the work of S.N. Balagangadhara in today's context.

While grappling with the theological basis of Western culture and thought, Balagangadhara is precisely unravelling the aetiology of rendering account or rendering reason. In other words, he probes persistently into the 'reason' for the principle of reason— though he does not foreground the particular formulation of the principle the way Heidegger and Derrida do. Balagangadhara's characterization of religion—as rendering 'explanatorily intelligible account'—captures the urge to render an account or render reason. The difference between him and Derrida appears to be that the latter is involved in salvaging the concepts of the theological heritage (sovereignty, principle, and so on), whereas Balagangadhara works on this heritage—precisely with these very concepts to unravel their theological ground. For him there appears to be an outside to the theological enframing and that comes from his insight into (and theorization of) ritual.

In contrast to the dominant European configuration of learning stands another cultural configuration where knowledge emerges from observations of human practices, argues Balagangadhara. Such knowledge seeks coherence and compatibility of practices and alters or transforms practices on the run for the purpose of attaining such

coherence. Here practices are not sought to be explained or legiti-
mized on the basis of any presupposed rational foundation—divine or
human. Pagan cultures move with such practitional topoi, contends
Balagangadhara.

Pagan topoi form Pagan experience. Such praxial topoi,
Balagangadhara argues, have brought forth sciences in ancient
Greece (hydrostatics, geometry, and medicine) and in India (the
sciences of language, ritual, mathematics, medicine).[16] When such
topoi of commonsense, shared ideas and practices crystallize, they
evolve into theories. But before such consolidation of topoi could be
achieved, the Greek culture disintegrated and its praxial reflections
got appropriated into European theology as instruments of reasoning. The encounter between the Greeks, Roman Pagans and the early
church figures (Clement, Origen, and Lactantius up to Augustine
and from another tradition Philo), shows the incorporation of Pagan
philosophic topoi into European theo-logos. The rational and historical religion that Christianity claims itself to be conveniently owns up
the Pagan insights (about god, the prime mover, forms, and logos) as
already anticipated pre-figurations of the *arrivant* (Derrida's pregnant
word from theological sources) religion proper. Christian theology
crystallizes Greek/Roman topoi.[17]

In such a theo-logic, religion becomes a cultural universal: every
culture has a religion but Christianity is the only proper religion.
Christianity's proper model can incorporate and explain all other
pre-existing religions as fore-runners predicted already in the Bible.
While unravelling this theo-genea-logic, Balagangadhara contends
that it was necessary for Christianity to assimilate the pre-Christian
past. The assimilationist (or continuist) account was a calculated
Christian response to the fundamental Pagan questions that antiquity posed to Christians: *What are your traditions?* For, Pagans traditions are ancestrally imparted practices and they must be rendered
in practice and not in legitimizing discourses with pre-established
foundations. In response to this question, Christianity dexterously
incorporates Pagan traditions as a part of its own ancestry: to serve
the theo-logic.[18] As can be seen, Balagangadhara breaches a major
opening for unravelling the continuist accounts (between the Pagan
and Judeo-Christian cultures) of major thinkers such as Heidegger,
Derrida, Foucault, and Agamben.

If the Pagan Greco-Roman thought disintegrated at the beginning of the common era, the (other Pagan) Indian topoi dissipated with the Islamic invasions in the second millennium, speculates Balagangadhara. It is possible to find the Indian topoi beginning to get crystallized in the works of Sankara, Ramanuja, and Madhva—but the process got disrupted, he contends. Balagangadhara advances here a provocative hypothesis (only) and this cannot be refuted by means of adhoc superficial historical accounts concerning Akbar and Dara Shikoh's 'contribution' or 'cosmopolitanism'. We are yet to initiate inquiries that meet the rigour and depth that Balagangadhara's work demands.

Here, without rashly contradicting Balagangadhara's hypothesis, one may observe that unlike in the case of Greek–Roman Pagan topoi, the clusters of shared human practices of Indian topoi have not completely disintegrated or been erased during either the Islamic or later European invasions. Even if the Indian topoi were threatened and continued to be vulnerable they can be said to be at work in actions and responses: the topoi continue to be filiated to what can be called Indian experience. Such experiential topoi continue to be transmitted generationally in modes of being. How did such topoi receive the Semitic theologic and respond to it in the Indian context remains a major task for inquiries today. Another task that awaits engagement is more challenging: is it possible now to elicit heuristic potential from these surviving topoi and experience and formulate a theoretical alternative to the dominant theo-logos of European culture? How does one meet this challenge? Balagangadhara (like Derrida, though differently) affirms such a possibility.

Cultivable Locations

Now, in order to engage with these challenging tasks even minimally, it may first be necessary to inquire into the modes in which the experiential topoi were transmitted across generations. As is well known the foundational narrative of the principle of reason in Europe was institutionalized very early (in the Common Era) and the explanatory accounts were transmitted systematically through the institutional structures of the church, monastery, monastic, cathedral schools, and universities. The Bible, the church, and its expanded institutions themselves required accounts and the principle of reason multiplied such accounts in terms of histories, doctrines, personages, and discourses. Despite internal variations—say between the medieval universities and their modern counterparts—there is continuity of rendering accounts of reason across all these institutions. MacIntyre's work on the universities and the Catholic philosophic tradition provides one such extended narrative.

In contrast to the European narratives, the Pagan antiquity of Greeks on the one hand and the millennially extended Indian cultural heritage on the other do not have any such centralized institutions (let alone religions, if the word makes sense at all in the Pagan context) that imparted learning and contributed to the formation of cultural topoi of experience. None of the four types of schools of Greek antiquity (Plato's Academy, Aristotle's Lyceum, Zeno's school of Stoa, and Epicurus's Garden) was attached to any institution, either political or religious. Nor did the schools of the Hellenistic period associated with Pyrrho or Diogenes have any dogmatic credo. What appear to be common to all these Pagan schools, whatever their differences, are their praxial modes of being.

These schools privileged neither texts nor exegesis of doctrines. All these schools were nurtured in a praxial topos. However, it is possible to indicate a modification within the praxial topoi between the sixth and fourth centuries. Alteration in topoi can take two (non-exclusive) forms, suggests Balagangadhara. It can alter the prevailing set of human practices: some of the inherited practices may be dropped and newer ones may be incorporated. Thus, modes and forms of going about may change and these changes are not subjected to the requirements of a legitimizing narrative. Or, alteration in topoi can take the form of configuring heuristics for theoretical inquiries.

Perhaps, it is possible to show that between the sixth and fourth centuries the Greek topoi were modified in respect of practices and heuristics. The first sign of such modification is the institution of the 'first' school—Plato's Academy—for imparting ('new') learning. As the topi were undergoing changes during this period (one significant factor contributing to this is the emergence of inscriptional technics), the prevailing modes of cultural training were also exposed to questioning. The only source of cultural training until even the fifth century was the bardic compositions of Homer and Hesiod—and their modes were performative. The Muses bestowed sophia on these bardic visionaries. Along with the king of justice and the oracular sage the bards were regarded as 'the masters of truth in archaic Greece'.[19] Their modes of being and their forms of rendering truth quintessentially remained performative—embodied and enacted articulation of intimations. They were the guardians of mnemopraxial ethos.

Praxial Turns

As a lover one relentlessly pursues wisdom. The ways of this lover are different from the mnemopraxial ethos enlivened by the earlier masters of truth. One can notice a double move in Socrates/Plato in this regard: (*a*) if wisdom is in the cultivation of the ability to live a virtuous life, then the task is to figure out what virtue is and find ways to teach or impart it. The inquiry into the ontological question ('what is virtue?') may appear to be a significant modification in the mnemopraxial topoi of the Greeks. (*b*) Now the modification in the inquiry seems to initiate a different form of transmission of learning (pertaining to virtue). Here too Plato/Socrates forges an alternative to the performative-immersive modes of the bardic composers. A dialogue-argumentative form of inquiry into the question of 'what' and 'how' (of virtue) is put in practice. The bardic mnemocultures are more attuned to embodied and enacted modes of being and imparting these modes across generations; they do not evince any categorizing impulse. The principle of reason is not the regulative mechanism of modes of being in the world. Modes of being do not require such a determinate regulative relationship, as Plato's account of the Myth of Er at the end of the purportedly political treatise the *Republic* implies.

Pagan cultures of memory live in/on the body and no surrogate can sever virtuous life from embodied existence. Therefore, neither Socrates' 'theses' (raising questions—such as 'Is virtue teachable?' 'Is happiness the supreme good?' or 'How should one live?') nor his 'pedagogy' can be said to mark any break in the cultural topos of the Greeks. There certainly appears to be a modification, alteration, in the practices of reflection and the modification seems to circumscribe the praxial reflection among members of the school. Theoria is the philosopher's vocation in search of happiness. The philologos takes over the task of imparting/teaching—*paideia*—of virtue from the bard.

Perhaps it is possible to show that the thinking at work in the
Republic is not so much preoccupied with the politics of the state as
it is with the search for happiness. Throughout the treatise it pursues the questions: what gives happiness in the finite life and beyond
that? Can there be a lasting, eternal happiness that is not occluded
by wealth, fame and passions? The *Republic* seems to be more concerned with the states of beings than with the fates of political states.
Moreover, Plato's heuristic cannot be reduced to the specific political-
cultural movement of the fourth century.

It is with such heuristic about the state of being that Plato con-
ceives of a pedagogical model for cultural training of the guardians
proper. Such well-trained guardians as philosopher-rulers can attain
happiness and strive to make it possible for all, Plato surmises. The
fundamental aim of such training is to cultivate theoria—to lead a
contemplative praxial life. The end of this Pagan paideia is not the
erection of a sovereign state as such but to impart a *liveable learning*
that practises virtual modes of being.

Doubts about the reality or plausibility of such a pedagogical
model do not matter to Plato; it matters little even if such a model
is possible only in heaven, says Socrates.[20] What is significant is
that it is fundamentally a heuristic model deeply rooted in reflexive
praxis. Plato has no anxiety about its universal validity and therefore
does not endeavour to offer a legitimizing narrative about it. Such
a heuristic is extendable as a model for a cluster of finite beings:
only of such a 'community' of contemplative thinkers can he be a
part, says Socrates. In the absence of such a community it can be
practised as a mode of being by singular contemplative beings. Such
reflexive praxis is not contingent upon the prior establishment of
institutions.

Plato's heuristic is a turn within the (mnemo)praxial topoi. Such
heuristic suggests the possibility, without abandoning the praxial
matrix, of configuring what can be called a performative episteme—a
sharable knowledge whose efficacy is in embodied modes of being. It
may be noted that in moving towards such an episteme, Plato does
not turn to the cherished inheritance of bardic traditions.

As the bardic-poetic compositions can only flourish on the passional
upheavals, the poets and tragedians do not find the culturally trained
'good men'—who can bear devastation of existence with serenity and

equanimity—as worthy material for imitation. Even when such men are represented, 'particularly when the audience is the kind of motley crowd you find crammed into a theatre', such representations remain unappreciated, observes Plato. Virtuous existence is foreign to such crowds.[21] Therefore, such passion-provoking poetic-performative spectacles must be either exiled or regulated in the first phase of the cultural training of the guardians, Plato contends.[22]

Yet, Plato's composition embodies the mnemocultural ethos and modes which are accessible to everyone (even if in different ways). The *Republic* ends the composition with a seductive (if, for some, alarming) account of a wonderful myth. At the end of the work, the *philosophos* gives place to *mythologos*. Whether deliberated or not this mode of ending the *Republic* can be accessed by the entirety of genos who are nurtured in the mnemopraxial topoi. Socrates concludes the composition with the Myth of Er. This can be said to recount a non-theological culture's experience of the formations, disappearances, *and* returns of human existence.

European intellectual history shows an extended and concerted effort to demarcate the Greek antiquity from the Orient (Asia) and filiate the former to its own genealogy. The grand continuist narratives woven from the early Judaic and Christian thinkers Philo and Clement to their repetition in the German intellectual histories of the nineteenth and twentieth centuries (culminating in Nietzsche, Jaeger, and Heidegger) consolidate inexhaustible testimony to the distortions of the Pagan. No wonder at the end of his mangnum opus, *Philosophy as a Way of Life*, Hadot can only grudgingly concede that 'there really are troubling analogies between the philosophical attitudes of [Greek] antiquity and those of the Orient'.[23] Why are these analogies 'troubling'? Agamben too fervently engages (of course in a continuist narrative) with such praxial attitudes of antiquity, but he has nothing to say about the possible 'analogies'. Asia does not exist in Agamben's work.[24]

Can Pagans learn to receive and respond to Pagans?

Liveable Learning

Indian traditions over millennia brought forth an education that can only be called liveable learning. Liveable learning is in the service of life in existence; and existence itself, in this context, is without a primal cause or a final end; it is recursive in its formations and dissolutions, in its alternations and variations. Embodied existence is perpetually exposed to strife and grief, death and deprivation, pleasure and pain. Desire is the dynamic of actional movement of life in existence.

Desire prevents one from discerning the difference between object- or relation-oriented pleasure and object-less or relation-free happiness. On the contrary, it deludes and fixates one to the former as the only source of real pleasure. Now in the former case when the desired object or relation becomes inaccessible or one is deprived of it, desire binds one to the animal actional existence. It is in such a context that learning (*vidya*) can help the releasement of the embodied being in existence:

Karmanaa badhyate jantuh
vidyayaa cha vimuchyate[25]

(Actions bind animals and learning releases)

The cognitive significance of such learning is that it can transform modes of being in existence; the test of this learning is in living it in the existence of life.

Existence unfolds in terms of phenomenal entities, objectal beings, and relationships among them; and this relationship manifests in the way an objectal being relates internally to itself and externally to other phenomenal entities; and it is driven by the essential but subtle (and non-objectal) force of the impulsive desire; this force binds, unbinds the objectal beings with themselves and with others and repulses them.

Learning must take into cognizance the perceptual gravity of the objectal circuit, and at the same time it must attend to the dynamic of volatile desire that binds one to this shifting and ephemeral ensemble of the machinic circuitry. The illusory gratification of 'new' objects and relations keeps the circuitry intact and reinforces the binding relationships. Therefore, the task of the liveable learning is to enable one to sense the double bind: the entanglement of the desire-driven objectal circuitry and the need to cultivate an object-free relation or non-relational partaking of the circuit one finds oneself in.

Here the most irreducible medium of learning is the perceptual-phenomenal body complex itself: the body complex is the effect of actional learning—resulting from mutually constituted action and learning. Thus, the body complex is the medium and also the end of liveable learning.

The body is put to work to mediate its transformations. As medium and effect of desire, the body is simultaneously a part of the problem and a way out of the problem: as an objectal being it occludes a non-objectal, non-relational intimacy in the ensemble of beings in existence. But as a heterogeneous complex it also contains yet another force that is irreducible to the force of desire, which thickens the webs of binds and bonds as the only ends of existence. This other force at once inheres in the thickets of the binds but remains untouchable to them; it is at once proximate and remote from the complex. Although these heterogeneous elements can be designated as forces there is an irreducible and abyssal distance and difference between them. The desiring force forever attempts to homogenize the complex by projecting (*adhyasa*) itself as the only driving dynamic and disavows the inhering other. Whereas the latter inheres in and witnesses indifferently the goings on of the embodied entities.

The body complex has the propensity to assume all learning to be perceptual-apprehensive knowledge. In cultures where the body is seen as the means *and* the objectal entity that requires to be transformed, the preferred modes of generating and transmitting such learning are verbal-acoustic and gestural-performative ones. These modes fundamentally require the body to be put to work. Such mnemocultural formations articulate memory through embodied and enacted modes. But when the ends of learning are reduced to mastering these technics, despite their significance, the body complex may remain ignorant or even disavow the other force inhering in the body. The Upanisads which intensively and extensively annotate the ends and sketch scenes and locations of learning impel attention toward such ignorance-inducing and pain-enhancing acquisition of learning, however revered it might be.

Scenes of Learning

Sanskrit traditions had no use for concepts that can be set apart from reflective practices. They worked with praxial epistemic learnables (as the essential actional means) whose singularity is not contingent upon their definitional rigour but their interminable *usability* in life. Thus, none of the learnables such as *aatma, dharma, manas, ahankaara, buddhi, shareera, loka, karma,* and the modes of their symbolization has any doctrinal (crystallized concepts/ideas that are contingent upon a determinate order or plan based on apriori foundations) status.[26] That is why no justifying accounts are advanced in the tradition.

The poetic-narrative-performative compositions that are released by the reflective-imaginative trio Suta-Bharata-Seer persistently foreground how these learnables are put to work and the consequences of their abuse in existence. They unfold instantiations of differentiated ways of being. It is a misreading of these compositions to treat them as illustrations of doctrines or dogmas. With their essential concern for how one moves about in the loka, the cultural forms of *itihaasa, puraana, kaavya,* and *naataka* are fundamentally oriented toward addressing the *saadhaka,* the seeker-practitioner, and not a theologue.[27] Now, subjecting these compositions to the original foundational-doctrinal and derivative-illustrational (narrative) schema is to impose a theological frame on them. Whether they take the narrative-performative form or non-narrative or dialogical form, these compositions come forth as practitioners' modes of preparing practitioners. The question of what should be imparted does not get prioritized and segregated over how it should be taught. More significantly even this 'how' does not get wrapped up in any explanatory or justificatory account. The Upanishads embody and impart such learnable technics (knowhow and knowledge—what is learnt and the way it is learnt).

Scenes of Paideia–I

The learned Narada once approaches the sage Sanathkumara in a forest setting and bemoans that what all he learnt has not freed him from sorrow and he now seeks knowledge which gives him happiness. Sanathkumara asks him about what all he learnt until then. Narada recounts twenty-two subjects ranging from the Vedas, Puranas, the fifth Veda (the Mahabharata), the sciences of ritual, language, time, astronomy–astrology, argumentation, archery, and the performative forms (dance and music) and others. Narada's subjects move beyond the ancient and medieval European disciplines of Trivium and Quadrivium put together.

It may be noticed that all these domains of learning come forth in the form of enactable embodied knowledge. Yet, Narada complains: they have not freed him from pain; they have merely turned him into a reciter of efficacious utterances: *mantra videvaasmi*.[28] All that learning has not made him into a 'seer' of the mantras (*mantra drasta*). Now he seeks knowledge that goes beyond the apprehensive objectal learning of perceptual-apparatus. He seeks to learn of the other inhering force that is heterogeneous to the calculative mastery of technics. Narada refers to this other force as aatma. Now the exegetical gloss on aatma alludes to its perennial (non-relational) circulation within the extended circuitry of emergences and dissolutions of existence of beings in the loka:

Atati samsarateetyaatmaa
Ata saatatyagamane.

(The one that circulates in *samsaara* always)[29]

Atati shareereshu samvasateeti[30]

(the one that inheres in the bodies)

That is aatma, says Amara. This incalculable and irreducible other can also be called *para*: para inheres and circulates in samsaara and shareera. Narada seeks to learn *para-vidya* (knowledge of the other).

Now Sanathkumara does not discard the technics of Narada's learning. The other of the perceptual/apprehensive is not posited as transcendental here. The teacher turns him around in what appears to be a graded circle. He calls all the learning Narada acquired so far as the technics of naming and asks him to meditate upon para as the name. Here Narada's competence as reciter of utterances is reoriented to focusing upon the inhering other that cannot be reduced to actional-objectal knowledge (whether verbal or visual).

But Narada seems to operate with a hierarchy of technics; he asks Sanathkumara whether there is anything superior to the naming mode. The teacher points to the acoustic utterance (*vaak*); vaak alone, says the teacher, provides differential knowledge about the variegated objectal beings of the loka/existence, and he asks Narada to concentrate and meditate upon vaak as para. Narada seems to miss the point of the learning: any technics—any and every *means*—can open up the passageway to 'sense' para if only one pursues that means with ardour and attention. He asks for superior means to learn further.

In a series Sanathkumara mentions manas, resolve (*samkalpa*), strength, knowledge, food, water, memory, sky, aspiration, breath, and so on, and 'finally' comes to a state of perpetual cognitive-awareness free from objectal fixation (*Chandogya Upanishad* 7.24-25). *That* state alone can bequeath happiness, says Sanathkumara. Then he recalls, as if to dispel Narada's deluded investment in the differential hierarchy, all the differently 'graded' technics and tells the latter that para permeates and inheres in every apperceptual technics and can be accessed through differential means. Narada's mis-cognition was based on his fixation with the objectal which occludes the sense of the non-object, the non-relational, that which inheres in the objectal. A sort of screen of indolence comes in the way of sensing that difference within. Narada is said to have been freed from the distorting screen (adhyasa) by Sanathkumara (*Chandogya Upanishad*, 7.27.2.)

Test Drive

Indian traditions open up a complex scenario. Here existence appears to be a 'test drive'[31]—one which is flagged off by a re-originating/iterative force that neither determines nor regulates the drive. If existence is an ensemble of heterogeneous entities (animal, plant, stone, and human)—every single entity must expose itself to the drive—without terminus. On such drive without determination and teleological or terminal signposts, virtue lies in how best one navigates (in) existence. Here the trope 'drive' should not be confined only to mobile entities—objects that can move. Every non-moving entity (plant and mountain) is also exposed to the test: their endurance and faring in existence matter during the drive.

There is also a drive or impulse for auto-mobility with regard to their movement or endurance among all the entities of existence. Here one can lay stress on the Pagan prefix *auto*. Does faring well in the test depend on one's own self (*auto*) or some other all-powerful determining agency? Cultures with theological heritage by default in the final analysis conform to the omnipotent sovereign (divine or human) force and its grace at work in their *archè*/teleological test drive.

The Indian case provides an alternative to such determination of the test drive. Given that existence and the entities that compose it are always already re-originary or reiterative in their movement (*jagat* is that which moves or is on the move)—the players (*sthavara*, rooted, and *jangama*, the drifting) persistently get reloaded into the circuit. Every iterated entity is composed (endowed/accursed) of the residues or effects of the modes and moves that that entity had made in its earlier manifest play-drive. These residues are neither continuous nor determinable by any external agency—including the player himself/herself/itself. The player, neither determined nor controlled by any other, has no total sovereignty either. What seems to require attention in this relentless test drive of existence is the metonymic chain of modes and moves of the drive: and the chain is intractably transgenerational. No sovereign being can command and control such reiterated strings of existence.

If the metonymic modes and moves alone drive the test in existence, how one plays them in the instance of one's test-existence alone matters predominantly. In this entire theatre of testing, the re-originary force is very much a part of the theatre and remains untouched by it. The force has only a status of witness or spectator to the drama of testing. The force can even be said to divide itself into the theatre of testing and manifests in terms of heterogeneous entities on the one hand and at the same time remains immune to the effects of the theatre on the other.

This witnessing but invisible, this proximate but remote (without control), this innate but pervasive force is what we pointed out as para.[32] But para may be omni but non-potential (non-virile); para may be un-generated but imposes or bestows no sovereign power on any; para is non-agentive with regard to the repetitive emergences and dissolutions of entities in existence. A crucial aspect of the test is to drive without forgetting, without erasing and denying the fundamental difference between para and existence in the course of the drive.

When the drive indulges in itself, overtakes with impunity, ignores and disregards the non-assertive para recklessly, the narcissism of the drive compels one to repeat the test. In all this it is not the principles of driving as norms that matter but the performative learning of driving itself becomes crucial—where blinding narcissism does not delude one's chance into proclamations of one's abrasive autonomy (one's *ipseity*). Here para has no theo-conceptual status of an omnipotent prime-mover, but that of an uninvolved ('apathetic') unseen seer without power, lurking in a praxial matrix of existence. Para emerges from a tradition in which the grounding principle of reason is completely absent. The much coveted para-vidya is therefore not accumulation of explanatorily intelligible accounts based on foundational reason; it is a liveable learning that unlearns explanatory justifications, if any. Indian traditions transmitted such praxial learning over millennia.

Scenes of Paideia-II

As every scene of learning is also a test arena, the learner is exposed to a series of ordeals (rather than discursive conceptual accounts). Another scene shows the learning process in which the father Aruni tests his presumptuous son on his learning. In his learning from other teachers, asks Aruni, has Svethaketu (the son) learnt to differentiate between the ephemeral, unreal, phenomenal entities from the eternal, imperceptible real that nestles in the multitude of beings? Svethaketu is puzzled and humbled by the question. As his teachers did not impart such learning, he begs Aruni to teach him that.

Aruni later tells him that all the differentiated life forms born of egg, womb, and seed could not have come into existence without the non-existent *real* permeating and inhering in them and counsels Svethaketu to know the real nestling in the ephemeral. In a way existence is a transformative effect of the real, says Aruni (*Chandogya Upanishad*, 6.2.3). Svethaketu fails to grasp the import of the lesson. Aruni puts him through an ordeal to make him learn indirectly (and by way of negation) that the real cannot be confused with the existent perceptual apparatus.

He asks Svethaketu to live without food but only on water for fifteen days and asks him to recite the Vedas on his famished stomach. Svethaketu complains of the loss of memory—he cannot recall the Vedas. As the subtle part of food nurtures memory, the deprivation of food ends the life of memory; similarly the subtle part of water sustains life (breath) and the loss of which ends life. In contrast, the real is untouched by any of these nurturing or nurtured entities and conditions, says Aruni. The latter tries to make Svethaketu learn that the real inheres in his own body complex and make him learn this experientially—by putting his own body to work. But the latter fails to grasp once again.

Aruni continues with several analogies: how the divergence of flowers disappears in the honey that the bees gather; how the hydraulic cycle effaces the variety of waters in the sea (which turns into rivers through the rains induced by the heat and evaporation). Through such analogies Aruni tries to turn Svethaketu's attention towards the common among the heterogeneous. Even after nine such attempts of ordeals and analogies, Svethaketu fails to learn the lesson and gain knowledge.

The perceptual-phenomenal apparatus—the very means of knowing and being in existence along with others—comes in the way of grasping the real which is the alien guest in body. Then, suddenly, for some inexplicable reason the narrateme of the ordeal of a thief who is asked to hold a heated rod to prove his innocence enlightens Svethaketu. He realizes that the myriad afflictions that the body is exposed to cannot touch the embodied being (as was the case of the thief in the ordeal) when one senses the common real inhering in the differential entities. That mode of being can neither be reduced to nor exhausted by the embodied existence. Ignorance and disavowal occlude the experience of the real (para). But existence 'flourishes' precisely through such reigning occlusions. Liveable learning exposes one to ordeals and turns the double bind of life into a testing ground—an experimental-experiential chance for transformation of modes of being. Svethaketu learns this through multiple and repeated instances, which are analogous to the re-emergence of being in existence.

Scenes of Paideia–III

As we have seen, there is no guarantee that the exposure and the teaching achieve their goal(less goal) at once. The seductive power of ignorance is fed by the force of desire and at every turn the latter releases distortional screens. This is precisely what the 'first' teacher Prajapati-Hiranyagarbha makes his 'first' students Indra and Virochana learn. They both fail in the very first instance to sense the seduction of the occluding screen.

Inseparable cousins making each other envious with rage, Indra and Virochana approach Prajapati to learn of para (aatma, the real) in the singularity of its manifestations (*vishesha rupam*). After thirty-two years of studentship, Prajapati tells them that the figure in the eye is para. Is the reflection that we see in water para, they ask. The figure in the eye sees in all directions and manifests in all, says Prajapati: Para is all-seeing. But the mighty students mis-cognize this. They decide that the seen object of reflection is para. They reduce the invisible and imperceptible to the object grasped by the sight.

However, as in the other scenes of learning, Prajapati does not discard the sight. Here the seeing, perception, is a detour through which para's difference can be learnt. This is Prajapati's test and both the students fail the test. Virochana goes back celebrating the perceptual body as aatma and serves it. Whereas Indra wonders: if the perceptual body is prone to decay, if it is only a reflection of the perceptual, does aatma too suffer from it? Then he turns towards the dream state and surmises that one who circulates in the dream state is aatma. But, on reckoning again, he realizes that the being in dream state is also prone to afflictions of the world and doubts its status as aatma and returns to Prajapati.

Every visit retains him for thirty-two years. The first mis-cognition pertains to confusing the perceptual being in wakeful state with para; the second one results from confusing the perceptual being of dream state with para. The third one is where the being is in a dreamless sleep, freed from any apprehensions, and that must be aatma, presumes Indra. But he doubts that too. In such a state the being cannot identify and differentiate himself from others; therefore, this cannot have been the singular form of aatma, he thinks, and goes back to Prajapati, who in turn retains him for another five years.

Then Prajapati tells him, solving the riddle of his enigmatic teaching:

Syaashareera syaatmanodhishtana maatto

(That mortal body is the sheltering abode of aatma). (*Chandogya Upanishad*, 8.12.1)

The unreal, ephemeral, and afflictional circuitry cannot be discarded but must be attuned. The entire inquiry into the difference between real (*sat*) and unreal non-being (*asat*, finite) is initiated and is carried on in the pervasive context of the cognitive/perceptual complex (asat) in all the pedagogical scenes that we have seen so far.

Asat perhaps is sat's detour or test drive for everyone constituted by the cohabiting contraries: sat and asat (real and existence, para and shareera). The entirety of the heterogeneous formation (srshti) is brought forth through such related (without relation) contraries composing the topo-temporal formations. But the 'success' of the test cannot be measured by cognitive perceptual means. When there is a difference between the means and ends—the instrument and the goal—such means cannot teach of para. All verbal means of the Vedas have such an instrumental status (*apara*).[33] The verbal means can only impart through negation of the instrumental by contrasting para with all the perceptual means and instruments. Cognitive perceptual means are ineffective in rendering the knowledge of para. But can para be posited as an object knowledge at all? It can only be 'sensed' in the very heterogeneous modes of being—the very formations of asat.

The arena of test is life itself; and the differentiation of sat/asat can only be sensed experientially. Such experience cannot be made present—discursivized—by perceptual-cognitive means. This root model of sat–asat inquiry has no use for the hierarchic dualities of the body and soul/mind, intelligent/sensible, theoretical/practical, nature/culture, reason/emotion, empirical/transcendental, physical/ metaphysical, phenomenal/noumenal, and so on. The inquiry into the real-existence (*sadasad vivechana*) is not a pathos-determined inquiry. One is not in competition with any other in this inquiry. One's life is one's testing ground where there is no normative authority adjudicating the measure of one's success. The liveable learning one receives must be received in the embodied existence. But the body can also be mis-cognized as the end in itself. Such a mis-conception indulges it in the pleasures of existence gratificatory to the body itself. The apparatus is confused to be real. Another scene of learning focuses precisely on such a miscognition.

Scenes of Paideia-IV

Para permeates the entire phenomenal existence, says the learned Varuna to his son Bhrugu. Food, life (breath), seeing eyes, hearing ears, manas, and utterance are all *means* of accessing *para*, adds Varuna.[34] The son misses the point and focuses only on the phenomenal entities. He thinks since food is essential for the existence of every being para must be food. But soon Bhrugu realizes that this was inadequate for knowing para. Then Bhrugu focuses on life-breath (*prana*) as essential for existence and assumes that to be para, but soon finds it to be incomplete. Like Narada earlier, he goes through these various testing turns and misses the import of Varuna's counsel. Then the latter tells him to continue contemplative reflection (*tapas*) and after a few more turns Bhrugu contemplates on happiness (*aananda*) as para and learns that that is the source of all generativity—but at the same time senses that para cannot be reduced to what is generated.

Liveable learning affirms the possibility of happiness in existence. When the desire-driven, strife-ridden body complex learns the possibility of being in existence, unperturbed by the raging upheavals of the passional existence that the real (being) in existence is indeed the undemanding and non-relational para, then happiness may ensue. But what comes in the way of sensing this being in-difference is the seductive force of desire binding the being to objectal entities and relations. In such a framework the desire-driven being feels threat from other beings of the multitude and consequently indulges the path of domination as the only source of pleasure. Every other is seen as a subjugable object. Virochana's termination of learning after the first counsel can turn him towards such indulgence in projecting himself as para. Such an impulse has the potential to homogenize the divergent and unify them for subjugation. But crystallization of such an impulse into an absolute model with continuities is difficult to nurture from the liveable learning of Indian traditions.

Ends of Learning

The ultimate end of learning (if it can be called that) in these traditions is 'knowing' that that differential other is (in) you. But here one must be cautious with regard to this pronoun 'you': it cannot be designated as an object of perception; for the same pronoun can indicate a referent—an embodied entity. The difference between them is subtle and this must be discerned in the singular but deeply resonant (with the ends of learning) term *tat-tvam*: that you[(r)self]. This search for the ultimate learning (of the subtle but infinite difference between the 'same' as heterogeneous) is not a peculiarity of the humans.

Even gods too are in pursuit of it, says Yama to Nachiketa, when the latter asks him of the para-vidya and tries to dissuade the young learner from pursuing that path.[35]

Knowledge of tatvam is eminently teachable—but it will be effective only when taught by a practitioner—the one who has put to work his learning. The paradox, in the case of the scene of learning in the *Kathopanisad* is that if the teacher must be such an enlightened person, why is Yama still at the position which is a part of extended samsaara/existence? (After all, both *svarga* ['heaven'] and *naraka* ['hell'] are part of the recursive circuitry). One can suggest two answers: (*a*) Yama is only instantiating his actional effects, the results of his deeds, and he is aware that he will be deprived of that position (which is akin to the function of the goddesses in the Myth of Er (processing the journey of the souls on the basis of the consequences of their actional life) once he exhausts his endowments; (*b*) Yama is in the same position as any practitioner-teacher and they all reinforce the singular crucial point: the test of the learning is in its praxial rendering in existence without pathos.

In an existence deeply drenched in pathos (the afflictions of life: *avidya* [ignorance], *asmita* [egoism], *raga* [passion], *dvesha* [hatred], *abhinivesha* [will to live])[36] one cannot but put to work one's endowments. Any of the actional modes—recitation of the Vedas, rendering of rituals, examining multiple works other than the Veda, even listening to Upanishadic teachings several times[37]—have little power to impart the ultimate learning. The sole context of such praxial learning is loka—the alluring-afflicting colossus of existence itself. The fact that there are learned teachers (Yama, Varuna, Sanathkumara, and such others) still located in existence to impart such a learning indicates that their actional modes may have, perhaps, transgenerationally indulged in pathos of existence. But the delight or happiness that the learning entails cannot be confused with pathos of life: it is an apathetic delight or affirmative indifference which can regulate actional life without remainders.

The teacher–student figures in these scenes of learning have little psycho-biographical significance. They are eminently substitutable figures: Bhrugu can be Nachiketa or Narada or Svethaketu. They are all in search of the ultimate learning—para-vidya. They are all drawn first toward the pathos-ridden loka and as they persist in their inquiry they begin to differentiate the indulgent faculties of the body that come in the way of differentiating the other of the lively being. They are all taught to learn the need to temper the restive faculties (likened to horses in the *Kathopanisad*) and cultivate attentiveness of the vicissitudinal (formational and deformational) manas (akin to charioteer—the chariot being the body). That is, the entirety of the body's resources is to be cultivated in such a way that their effects and their reach can be discerned. Such discernment is crucial for distancing oneself from the pulls of pathos. Such a learning process—even when unfolded through singular (but repeatable) figures—cannot be drawn on to exemplify some identity narratives. These figures circulate as narratemes, but whose elaboration has no telos of unfolding the meaning of a singular individual's life story.

All the analogies drawn and ordeals specified in the scenes of learning reiterate the liveable learning concerning tat-tvam variedly. These analogies are pedagogical ways of reiterating the *upadesha* (praxial counsel). There is nothing in the context that distinguishes the particular instance (say the thief's ordeal) that enabled Svethaketu to understand the learning concerning the real (sat). In other words, analogies, narrative accounts, do not become privileged means of attaining the end and thus drawing attention to their meaning exclusively. For upadesha is not fundamentally contingent upon meaning, requiring understanding first for attaining a desired end as such.

The efficacy of liveable learning is not dependent upon its thematic/semantic interpretative content but on its persistent practice—its embodied rendering. No wonder why we do not get to hear how Svethaketu led his praxial existence after grasping it. For such existence has no use for narrative representations of it. What gets emphasized again and again is the necessity of attunement of embodied existence—persistent preparation of the faculties of the body for the embodied to sense or learn to differentiate the real from existence. In other words, the 'means'—the faculties *of* the body—themselves are the 'material'—the sources to be put to test first. What is the status of rhetoric here?

Rhetoric understood in the sense of metrical/acoustic figural composition, woven with anecdotal episodes and analogies can be said to have neither a persuasive nor epistemological status here. It cannot be said that one episodic analogy (the thief's ordeal compared to the sensing of the learned) was more appealing than the other one (the banyan kernel containing sat or the tree permeated by sat) in the case of Svethaketu. Conversely, even if the cognitive value of these elements of composition can be postulated in propositions, it remains ineffectual. For the ends of such compositions are to prepare pathos-free mode of being, a being which is cocooned in the cognitive perceptual modes of miscognition. That is, a liveable learning that attunes or prepares one for a praxial mode of being primarily and persistently tests the very means of learning—and delimits these (verbal/ visual means) as ineffective ways of learning. Rhetorical and cognitive schemas seem to remain in the shadow of pathos. This suspicion of cognitive-perceptual means may be one reason for the absence of the emergence of Platonic agonism (between poetry and philosophy) in Indian traditions. This could also be the reason why these traditions seem to have no use for literary interpretative or translational-comparatological schemas either.

Locations of Learning

Liveable learning as *tattva-jnaana* is open to all and it circulated for millennia in open, un-architectural locations. The practice of this learning can be undertaken in a forest, cave or on the sand-bank; such practice makes the learning habitual, says the *Nyaayasutra*.[38] Learning shines forth when the reflective-imaginative faculty (*chitta*) is refined and focused. Such refinement and focusing can be achieved through a series of bodily practices such as non-violent mode of living, celibacy, tempering of internal and external faculties, and cultivation of contemplative reflection. With such refinement of the means/ technics one may proceed to pursue the ends of learning.

Para-vidya is eminently teachable. Hence, the privileged place of the guru. But such teacher must not only be well-versed in actional knowledge but also its relationship (of non-relationship) with tattva-jnaana. The Upanishads proclaim praxial modes of being (not so much 'understanding' or 'interpretation') as the imperatives of learning:

Esha Aadeshah
Esha upadeshah

(This is the rule

This is the import). (*Taittiriya Upanishad*, 1.11, 29–34)

The first teacher of this mnemopraxial learning is Prajapati/
Brahma/Hiranyagarbha—the re-originating 'primal' phenomenal
being that can disperse itself into the multitude of objectal entities in/
as existence. He imparts it to Manu (a Prajapati) who in turn passes it
onto genos (*jana/praja*).[39] (This is a secret knowledge—but it is open
to everyone.) This is what the cultural forms of India have imparted
to the genos over millennia in immeasurably diverse ways. At three
different places, the *Brhadaaranyaka* provides lists of (about 192)
teachers who generationally imparted the liveable learning.[40]

Given that the material locations of learning were for millennia un-
architectural sites, no historical search has revealed the material forms
of the abodes of teachers (guru or *acharya kulas*). No ashrama sites
that the *Ramayana* and the *Mahabharata* describe can be unearthed
archaeologically. Such architectural absence does not negate the possibility that such teaching shelters associated with singular teachers
were spread across the forests, villages, towns and even the cities.
There was *never* a centralized institution that could bring all these
diversified clusters of mnemopraxial learners. Clusters of learning
proliferated for long without institutional structures.

As the Buddhists were the first ones to take lithic (inscriptional)
and iconic turn in Indian culture, they (along with Jains) also appear
to be the first ones to take to building educational institutions and
accumulating repositories of learning material. Asoka and the
Satavahana kings are credited with donating caves to Buddhists
(and Ajivakas).[41] By the time of the Common Era, Buddhism spread
across the Silk Route and Central Asia regions up to China. Large-
scale organization of education began with Buddhists and Jains.[42]
One of the earliest Buddhist educational centres identified is
Takshasila (now in Pakistan). But by Fa-Hsien's time (fifth century)
this institution was in decline. Yet, Buddhism continued to build
other such institutions in Bihar, Bengal, and Gujarat regions after
the fifth century. Even before Fa-Hsien's visit to India, twenty-five
Buddhist *bhikkus* (Buddhist practitioners living on offerings made
by people) were believed to have been in China translating Buddhist
works into Chinese.[43]

The Buddhist centres of learning were located in *viharas* and were
extensively spread across the country and beyond until about the
fifteenth century. Nalanda stands out as the model for all the major

centres of learning for over 1,000 years between the two millennia of the common era.

Heuristics of 'Seeing'

It is difficult to get insights into the nature and ends of learning practised at Nalanda from historical accounts. Huen-Tsang and I-tsing would not be of much help either, for they were only focused on Buddhism and would have no clue about the deeper extended traditions of learning within which Nalanda (and other such institutions) flourished. Scharfe's work is already shaped by the colonial stereotype about Buddhism as anti-Brahminical—where Buddhists appear as reformist Protestants: 'The Buddhists shared with Christian monks the desire to save the world (and out of *karuna* 'compassion') against the general Hindu concern with his own personal salvation. Hence Buddhists formed universities with universal appeal.'[44]

Buddhism and Nalanda received and responded to the traditions of liveable learning and they cannot be said to have radically departed from them. The ends of learning in these traditions were fundamentally to explore the ways of terminating sorrow in existence through embodied modes of being. The Buddha himself was essentially a mnemocultural being—putting his own body complex to test— dedicated to imparting mnemopraxial learning peripatetically without institutions.

As in the case of Socrates/Plato, who were nurtured in the Homeric mnemocultural milieu and turned toward *philosophia*, Buddhism (at least in the context of Nalanda) in its responsive reception to Vedic mnemocultures seems to have been involved in generating heuristics for systematic knowledge pertaining to the real (even when it is conceived as 'empty') and its (non)relationship to existence. This took the form of a rigorous inquiry into the means of knowing and ascertaining what is to be known. But Buddhism cannot be said to have begun such heuristic inquiry in a vacuum.

Ways of 'seeing' the real and configuring its inherence in, and its (non)proximity with, existence were the sole concern of a range of internally differentiated inquiries called Darsanas in Indian reflective traditions. Literally, darsana can mean meditative (non-perceptual)

seeing. The Darsanic compositions—themselves formed of in a chain
of responsive reception to Vedic inheritance (Vedas, Upanishads)—
do not, however, exhibit a demonstrative rationality to postulate their
seeing. They all share the common problem of inquiry: how to attain
happiness in existence and how to differentiate existence from real.
Their modes of inquiry remained unequivocally mnemopraxial: the
absolute effect and means of existence, the body complex, was the
site and target of their inquiry. The mnemopraxial darsanic inquiries
strikingly resonate with the other Pagan heuristic *theoria* of antiquity.
They both reinforce the necessity of transforming the modes of being
one finds oneself in.

Modern scholarship is yet to reorient our attention towards the
shared problematic of these mnemopraxdial traditions. On the contrary, ill-thought partisanism appears to have been reinforced (in a
completely different way from the earlier kinds of disputations) by the
alien tradition of the principle of reason. Colonial and postcolonial
inquiries sought to excavate a theory of rationality or cognition or
consciousness from the Darsanic traditions (especially from *Nyaaya/
Navyanyaaya*) in quest for some putative 'early modernity' that is
said to mark a 'break' with 'ancients'.[45] Such probes were alien to the
mnemopraxial traditions.[46]

If 'colonial consciousness' (to use Balagangadhara's phrase to refer
to internalized Europe-enframed understanding of India)[47] impelled
university teachers in India to force *Nyaaya* and *Navya-Nyaya* to speak
for a rational heritage of India, Buddhism was appropriated to bring
up an anti-Vedic, anti-Brahmincal (Lutheran) reformism in India. If
the former attempted at recovering an allegedly 'lost age of reason',[48]
the latter spawned victimhood narratives about oppression. Colonial
consciousness—an instantiation of what Europe or America says
about our traditions—continues to occlude us from reconnecting ourselves to the much-endured traditions of learning that circulated in
India over millennia. It would also foreclose the possibility of extending the heuristic inquiries into the question of existence and real that
were sustained with vigour and vitality through our own responsive
receptions to them. Our higher centres of learning—the centrally
organized universities—are nowhere near sensing the problem. They
carry the malaise from their inception—to stigmatize and disregard
the praxial learning of the Indian traditions.

Metonymic Dispersals

No other alien invasion in the Common Era has ruptured and dis-placed traditions of learning of India as decisively as the one initi-ated at the hands of Europeans. Even during the period of Islamic invasions centres of learning emerged and were sustained after their displacement. It would be important to inquire (beyond spurious victimhood syndrome) why Buddhist centres of learning did not re-emerge and sustain themselves in India after the fifteenth century.

Interestingly, without such large-scale institutionalization, the centres of Vaidika traditions spread across and sustained over long periods in this country. Located in forest settings, guru-kulas, *illams*, *ghatikas*, *mathas*, *salas*, and *tols* these totally decentralized but palpa-bly connected centres of learning invigorated (even if discontinuously) mnemopraxial learning for centuries. From Pallavas to Vijayanagara kings, from Zamorins to Sultanate kings, from Kakatiyas to Nayakas, a whole range of royal patronage contributed to the conditions of this learning to move on. Locations which look like dusty dots on the map today—Ennayiram, Thribhuanai, Kandalur, Kanchipuram, Gadag, Ballari, Shimoga, Haasan, Munganda, Gadvala, Kolachala, and count-less other such places—sheltered the energetic nodes of learning.

Ranging from different schools and branches of the Vedas, ritual sciences (*grhya*, *kalpa*), language sciences, Mimaamsa, Nyaaya, Vedangas, Vedanta and other Darsanas, *smritis*, kaavya composed the subjects of learning in these centres. But all these disciplines of thinking were rendered performatively. The sciences of utterance (*siksha*) was essentially for learning how to recite/perform the Vedas; *Vyakarana* was to comprehend the compositional and generative dynamic of Vedic utterances; kalpa was to impart the science of ritu-als to render them with precision contextually; and *aalamkara* was for learning the acoustic figural potential of received languages to gener-ate unprecedented poetic compositions and discern defective uses of language.

All such forms of learning are substantive and eminently impart-able, and they are ultimately oriented towards refining modes of being. Consequently, the epistemic is not sublimated in an exclu-sively theoretical—normative-universal vocation. The *Manusmriti*, for instance, which extensively annotates differentiated practices, does not culminate into a jurisprudential discourse. It has no place for any normative authority either in the form of a god or a law giver.

The Tamil Country, Karnataka, Kerala, and Telugu regions remained hospitable to such centres of learning—whether Buddhist, Jain, or Vaidika. Learning was not contingent upon textualization in such centres. On the contrary, putting the body complex to work was the imperative in this tradition of learning. Perhaps the most crucial factor that sustained their longevity and endurance even in adversity is their mnemoculturality. Mnemopraxial learning is not dependent upon surrogate bodies (scriptoria, library, museum, database, and so on); it circulates through the lively archives, 'archives' of learning embodied and enacted in contemplative and performative modes of being.

Such learning does not come to an end with the destruction of surrogate bodies. Thus, even though from the beginning of the second millennium centres of learning severely suffered, learning did not suffer annihilation. As the centres were invaded and devastated, the teaching families migrated to other places and ignited learning processes there. Thus, we see such migrations from the Punjab to Kashmir and Kashi in the eleventh century; from Nalanda and Vikramasila to Nepal and Tibet in the thirteenth century; from the Deccan to Kashi in the sixteenth century; and from Navadvipa to Puri in Odisha in the sixteenth century. Karnataka, Tamil Country, and Kerala did not record such devastations and migrations. What is remarkable—especially in the Vaidika learning tradition—is that these traditions of learning did not get obliterated.

One major factor for their survival and resurgence was that these centres were neither centralized with accumulations of institutional structures and indispensable repositories of externalized-recorded tomes of knowledge. They were largely un-archival. As embodiments of lively archives the displaced teachers and students carried their millennially nurtured learning in the fibres and molecules of their body and disseminated it. Literacy, as Plato feared,[49] had not succeeded in erasing these mnemocultural learning processes in India. As discussed earlier, despite the lithic turn Buddhism had taken, Nalanda was not devoid of lively archives alongside manuscript repositories. Text-less teaching sessions imparted learning to students.

Without centralized instructional command-control systems mnemocultural learning was disseminated in these traditions. It spread
across diversified but interconnected networks of nodes in proliferated clusters. Thus, even as their famed Buddhist centres were devastated, Mithila and later Navadvipa on the one side and Varanasi on the
other were vibrant with vigorous response to what they received from
the Darsanic tradition and Buddhist receptions of it. Precisely such
networked clusters disseminated this learning in Sanskrit across and
beyond the Kham cultural constellation into China, Myanmar, Laos,
Thailand, Vietnam, Indonesia, and Malaysian cultural formations in
earlier centuries.

Mnemocultures of Theoria

Although they both pursue praxial paths of inquiry, what differen-
tiates the Indian mnemopraxial learning from Plato's or Aristotle's
theoria is the persistence of mnemocultural modes of recitation, song,
and performance in inquiring into the ends of learning in the Indian
context. Plato treated the Homeric modes as impediments to gaining happiness by means of theoria, or contemplative reflection. Even
when they turned to heuristic inquiries, the Indian traditions have
not shown any kind of antagonism toward the performative modes of
puraana, naataka, and kaavya.

Liveable learning can be generated, practised, and transmitted
through immersive performative modes. In fact, one of the strongest
and most vibrant surviving manifestations of liveable learning can be
seen in the song-performative traditions. Performative song genres
such as the *saman, stotra, stuti, prashasti, vakh, geet, bol, bar-geet, kirtan,
bhajan, vacana, tevaram, padam, paddana, padatattva, pata, abhang,*
and countless others permeate lively currents across the entire Indian
mnemoscape.

As discussed earlier, the ultimate learning is the learning of para-
vidya. But this learning can be achieved only when one discerns
what occludes such learning. The primacy or the only condition of
this learning is that it has to be acquired solely in the context of bio-
cultural existence. Although this learning is open to everyone, it must
be pointed out that forms of learning are differentiated in accordance
with the formations of being. In the Indian context the formations of

being are none other than internally differentiated clusters of bio-
cultural entities called *jatis*. Thus, even when overcoming of
ignorance is a common task of all beings, forms of liveable learning
that impart the common task operate as divergently as the bio-cultural
formations. Indeed, the bio-cultural formations and the cultural forms
of liveable learning are mutually co-constitutive modes of beings in
the loka. One receives the learning as a member of a distinct cultural
formation (clan, jati, *varna*, and *jan-jati*.)

Consequently, the modes of receiving inescapably remain bio-
cultural. The bio-cultural formations, which are dynamic clusters
without necessarily forming into consolidated unities, have enriched
and disseminated the liveable learning across millennia. The sonic
compositions of Tirumaymoli and Tevaram continue to reverberate
in the temples of Tamil Country over a millennium (performed by
specific bio-cultural formations). It is important to note that these
mnemocultural currents moved along with (and without filiation
to) the other mnemocultural heuristics emerging from the Darsanic
traditions.

The Tamil Country song-cultural forms like the Marathi Warkari
creations and the Vachanakaras of Karnataka resoundingly affirmed
the possibility of grappling with the central question of the relation between existence and the real and accented sonic-perfomative
modes for articulating ends of learning in existence. As is well
known, the great *acharya*s (Sankara, Ramanuja, and Madhva) braided
the currents of heuristic inquiry with lasting acoustic measures. They
reinvigorated the *puraanic-itihaasic* heritage and wove extended per-
formative-recitational genres (let us recall Sankara's *Nirvaanashatka*
or *Dakshinamurthystotra*). Jnaneswar forged new idioms and tunes
and released haunting *abhanga* compositions.[50]

Only a few (academics these days) know the fame and glory of
Gangesha (Mithila) or Raghunatha Siromani (Navadvipa)—but
it is difficult to erase the memory of Vidyapati, who emerged in
Mithila between the times of the above-mentioned *Nyaaya-Navya-
Nyaayaikas*. The magnetic pull of his performative compositions
attracted Sankaradev from Assam (Kamrup), Chaitanya from Bengal,
and Ramanatha from Odisha over centuries. His idiom, evolved
into Braj, unleashed a whole literary movement. Similarly it was
not so much the Buddhist Valabhi that earned a cherished niche in

Gandhi's mnemopraxial existence but the glorious compositions of Narsimehta.[51]

Annamaya to Tyagaraja, Lal Deg to Akka Mahadevi, Allama to Nayanmars and Abhinavagupta, Nanak to Narsimehta, Kanakadasa to Kabir, Purandara Dasa to Ramadasa, Meera to Lallan, Chokha to Tuka—the mnemocultural learning dispersed and communicated across clusters of networks. They had no use for literacy and its surrogate bodies. They carved their bodies into immersive acoustic media and groomed their tongue and throat to release haunting melodies. They live on by means of the strings and fibres of our embodied existence and they have nurtured and enriched the enduring alithic musical traditions of India immensely. In contrast to these melopoeiac traditions, the fate of Homeric mnemocultures was sealed by the Platonic heuristics on the one hand and more decisively by inscriptional theological cultures of Europe on the other. As we know, Homer survives today (if he does) embalmed in the inscriptional enterprises of philologists (let us point to the famed work of Milman Parry and Albert Lord).[52]

If the Darsanic mnemopraxis turned towards (without, however, discarding or denying the other current) heuristic inquiries into the ends of learning and modes of being, how do the melopoeiac mnemocultures articulate these ends? Here taking chances and the concomitant risk it is possible to suggest that their performative episteme relentlessly grappled with certain thematics. Deferring further elaboration what can be specified here are mere pointers as follows for further inquiry: (*a*) filiation between bio-culturality (jati) and cultural forms in the recursive circuitry of existence; (*b*) formations of ephemeral (with remainders) or finite embodied existence in the loka; (*c*) heterogeneity of the body complex, the non-relational intimacy of shareera and para; and (*d*) epistemic status of the visual/verbal signifier (*nama/rupa*). The entire literary-reflective-performative heritage of India can be said to be a persistent engagement with these thematics. This engagement brought forth an immeasurable range of mnemocultural forms of the hetero-genos. Without these thematics one may not be able to configure the singularity of Indian experience. If such praxial ethos forms the genus of Indian cultural experience, European cultural invasion precisely targeted them and disrupted their lively currents.

Occluding Present

If culture is what we do and what we or others say about what we do, in the last 200 years what Europeans have said about the mnemopraxial modes of being and forms of articulation have become dominant in colonial discourses and institutions: discursive thinking has displaced embodied reflection. These discourses have stigmatized the bio-culturality of our modes of being and whipped up unexamined guilt among the educated. No writer or thinker in the Indian context today has been able to engage with these thematics of Indian experience beyond the symptomatics of colonial discourses. Irony, sarcasm, political correctness, and rage have taken the place of patient engagement with the lively mnemocultural formations of millennial inheritances. They harbour genus-erasing or genocidal impulses.

The Indian academy today is nowhere near to taking up the challenge or reconnecting to the clusters of cultural formations and their enduring cultural forms. Neither the discourse of philosophy nor that of literary studies has taken the risk to explore the ways of reconnecting to the most fundamental mnemopraxial inquiry brought forth by the Indian cultural formations: how to live the non-relational relationship between existence and real, shareera and para, in loka?

The crisis in higher education (in India) is due to neither economic or political factors but mainly the result of a crisis in thinking. If education is reception and response to generationally imparted learning, crisis sets in when there is a rupture in such generationally evolved responsive receptions. The rupture manifests in the form of radically altering conceptions of knowledge and learning and the modes of their articulation. In a word, this is an epistemic performative rupture. The rupture wrenches apart the epistemic from the performative and privileges the epistemic. Thinking *about* takes over and displaces thinking *as* formations in modes of being. Such a hierarchic division has a long history in European culture and it is derivative of a theological heritage. Although Plato and Socrates are seen as the classical philosophical models, one can see Plato/Socrates' difficulty/reluctance in configuring virtue as knowledge dissociated from a mode of being.[53] As shown in this chapter, the Pagan heritage gets appropriated into the Christian past. Rupture erupts when such a theo-epistemic heritage is imposed on cultural traditions that do

not share such a background. The deeper consequences of the rupture have barely received any attention in discussions about higher
education.

Now, it is certainly possible to discourse upon the modes of being
on the one hand and thematize the context of their learning on the
other; one can turn them into objects of discourse and talk *about* them.
This is precisely what the institutions of higher education impel the
heirs of ruptured inheritances to do. Our researches about liveable
learning and their performative modes of rendering take the forms of
information-retrieval, historical-philological, comparative-theoretical
accounts. The epistemic-performative forms and formations here
end up being objects of representation and they may barely touch the
investigator let alone transforming him/her; whereas the efficacy of
liveable learning is in transforming or changing the inquiring learner
from a sorrow-filled, pathos-ridden mode of being into a seeker of
happiness in existence.

If one is convinced of the prevalence of such an impulse of praxial
learning (for the purpose of further inquiries), and if one tolerates
the suggestion that such an impulse is a millennially nurtured live
current in Indian cultural formations, it has the possibility of opening up inquiries into different domains. Such inquiries (into the the-
matic specified earlier) drawing on the hypothesis of Indian cultural/
civilizational difference and Indian experience would go a long way
in reorienting sedimented institutions and their professionalized
modes of knowledge production. Such inquiries can be pursued
at individual, collaborative, and institutional levels in and *from* the
Indian contexts—and beyond that they may provide the possibility
of communicating with other displaced, subjugated, and discarded
Pagan mnemocultures of the planet.

Notes and References

1. Here among others, I am drawing on Alan Badiou's more recent retelling of this sedimented narrative about the 'event'. Badiou identifies the
   other mode of thinking with poetry and claims that Plato discarded
   the latter in advancing discursive thinking. For Plato, says Badiou, the
   poem 'ruins discursivity' (31). As is well known, this is a replay of the
   old agonism between muthos and logos. It must be pointed out here

that Badiou's effort is to make philosophy overcome the discord between the poetic and the mathematic (mythic and mathemic/dianoiac) thinking, after Heidegger. This can be achieved, he contends, by 'pairing' (what were claimed to be opposed and hierarchized) the sensible and the intelligible, muthos and logos, good and beauty (50–4). As I try to show in this chapter, without directly focusing on Badiou, this is a deeply entrenched plot that European intellectual history has institutionalized. Citations are from Alain Badiou, *The Age of the Poets: And Other Wrings on Twentieth-Century Poetry and Prose*, edited and translated by Bruno Bosteels (London: Verso, 2014).

2. Derrida, 'The Principle of Reason: The University in the Eyes of Its Pupils', in *Eyes of the University: Right to Philosophy vol. 2*, translated by Jan Plug and others (Stanford: Stanford University Press, 2004), 293 fn. 9.

3. Derrida, 'The Principle of Reason, 139.

4. Alasdair MacIntyre, *God, Philosophy, Universities: A Selective History of the Catholic Philosophical Tradition*, (Lanham: Rowman & Littlefield Publishers, 2011), 5–18. In the medieval universities, especially in Paris, E.R. Curtius points out, '*sacerdotium* had taken the possession of the *studium*'. See E.R. Curtius, *European Literature and the Latin Middle Ages*, translated by Willard R. Trask (London: Routledge & Kegan Paul), 55.

5. Derrida, 'Faith and Knowledge: The Two Sources of "Religion" at the Limits of Reason Alone', in *Acts of Religion*, translated by Samuel Weber, edited by Gil Anidjar (New York: Routledge, 2002), 63–4; S.N. Balagangadhara, *Pratyabhigyaana: The Indian Renaissance*, (Ghent: Ghent University, 2014). This document develops a series of projects inquiring into the theological basis of concepts of politics, ethics, history, law, human rights, and religion.

6. See Jacques Legoff and Jean-Maurice de Montremy, *My Quest for the Middle Ages* (Edinburgh: Edinburgh University Press, 2005), 53.

7. Heidegger quoted in Derrida, *Eyes of the University*, 293 fn. 11. The passage appears in Heidegger's book titled *The Principle of Reason*, translated by Reginald Lilly (Bloomington: Indian University Press, 1991), 24.

8. Heidegger, *The Principle of Reason*, 3.

9. Heidegger, *The Principle of Reason*, 3.

10. Derrida, *Eyes of the University*, 152.

11. Derrida, *Eyes of the University*, 137.

12. Derrida, 'The University without Condition', in *Without Alibi*, translated by Peggy Kamuf (Stanford: Stanford University Press, 2002), 209.

13. Derrida, *Eyes of the University*, 146–7.

14. It must be noted here that the overturning of muthos by logos in antiquity, in Heidegger's reckoning, was also at the same time the

displacement of Asia (associated with myth) by Europe (filiated to logos). See Heidegger cited in J.L. Mehta, 'Heidegger and Vedanta: Reflections on a Questionable Theme', in *India and the West: The Problem of Understanding: Selected Essays of J.L. Mehta* (Chico, California: Scholars Press), 245.

15. Derrida, *Eyes of the University*, 153.

16. Incidentally, Frits Staal contends that the original home of the humanities is India; for, Staal observes, it is in India that the first sciences of language (*vyakarana*) and ritual (*kalpa*)—which configure human activities—were developed. See Staal, *Rules without Meaning: Ritual, Mantras and the Human Sciences* (Delhi: Motilal Banarsidass, 1996), 350–71. Staal demolishes the ventures to impose the concept of religion on Indian traditions in a compelling chapter, 'Religions', 397–439. Balagangadhara builds his major work drawing on but going beyond Staal's contribution. Despite Staal's distinctive contribution it is difficult to accept that these sciences worked with any conception of the human. The *concept* of the human is deeply filiated to the concept of God and the Indian sciences have little to do with the concept of god.

17. In an unravelling of the theological heritage that resonates and differs from Balagangadhara's, Derrida too points out how Christian logic could apriori appropriate every other religion—Buddhism, Judaism, and so on. See Derrida, 'Interpretations at War', in *Acts of Religion*, 157.

18. For an illuminating critique of the deeply interested misreading of the Pagan (Cicero's) notion of *religio* as *traditio* by Lactantius, see Balagangadhara, '*The Heathen in His Blindness ...': Asia, The West and the Dynamic of Religion* (Leiden: E.J. Brill,1994), 240–7. Curiously, for a continued interested reading of the debate in recent times, see, Derrida, 'Faith and Knowledge', in *Acts of Religion*, 72–5.

19. Marcel Detienne, *The Masters of Truth in Archaic Greece*, translated by Janet Lloyd (New York: Zone Books, 2009).

20. Plato, *Republic*, translated by Robin Waterfield (Oxford: Oxford University Press, 1993), 343.

21. Plato, *Republic*, 358.

22. Plato, *Republic*, 70–102.

23. Pierre Hadot, *What Is Ancient Philosophy?* translated by Michael Chase (Cambridge, Mass.: The Belknap Harvard University Press, 2004), 278–9.

24. At the time of writing this chapter (in 2016) there were only stray parenthetical references to Asian (Indian) culture in Agamben's work. Only in 2018 does Agamben devote a whole treatise on the theme of Karma. See *Karman*, translated by Adam Kotsko (Stanford: Stanford University Press, 2018).

25. Citation attributed to Vyasa, quoted in the commentary on *Brhadaaranyaka Upanishad* (with Sankara's commentary), translated with commentary into Telugu by Suri Ramkakoti Sastry (Hyderabad, 1989), 2.4., 72. It must be noted that animals are not deprived of access to such learning and happiness in Indian traditions. See *Manusmriti*, translated with commentary into Telugu by Saraswati Venkata Subbarama Sastry (1928; Madras: Balasaraswati Book Depot, nd.), 11.240, 629–30.

26. Aatma: that which circulates within the body but not reducible to the body; dharma: cultivable endowments of an entity; manas: abode of desire and memory; ahamkaara: individuating faculty of an organism; buddhi: discernment; shareera: body complex (abode of [six] impulses); loka: location of beings.

27. Loka: location of beings; itihaasa: a compositional form configuring temporal happenings; puraana: A compositional form containing ancient accounts which are made novel in each rendering; kaavya: a poetic composition; naataka: A performative composition; saadhaka: seeker-practitioner.

28. *Chandogya Upanishad*, translated into Telugu with commentary by Rayasam Veerashwara Sarma (Hyderabad: Seetarama Adisankara Trust, 2002), ch. 7, 168. (The entire scene is sketched in 163–267).

29. *Amarakosa*, translated with commentary into Telugu by Saraswati Tiruvengadacharyulu (1859; Hyderabad: Jayalakshmi Publications, 2006), 1.4, 108.

30. *Amarakosham*, Part I, edited and compiled into Telugu by Chalamacharla Venkata Seshacharyulu, (Hyderabad: Jayalakshmi Publications, 1989), p. 201.

31. Avital Ronell's phrase. See her *Test Drive* (Urbana: University of Illinois Press, 2005). Although she passingly refers to Eastern traditions (especially yoga) as exemplifying the self-testing paradigm, her work is entirely focused on European–American literary-cultural life. Ronell, it may be noted, turned Derrida towards the end of his painful life to yogic meditation to seek relief from pain.

32. See *Ishaavaasya: tadejati tannaijati/taddure tadvantike/tadantarasya sarvasya/tadu sarvsyaasya baahyataha* ([Para] does not move but moves; it is remote and far away yet it is proximate; it inheres in every being and spreads across the entirety)(*Ishavaasyopanishattu*, translated with commentary into Telugu by Kompella Dakshinamurthy [Hyderabad: Seetarama Adhisankara Trust, 2003], 5.63–5).

33. *Mundakopanishad: Dve vidye vditavye ... paraa chaivaaparaa cha* (The learned say that there are two kinds of knowledge/learning: para and apara). See *Mundakopanishad*, translated with commentary into Telugu

by Pullela Sreeramachandrudu (Hyderabad: Surabharati Publications, 1984), 1.4, 137–8.

34. *Taittiriya Upanishad*, translated with a commentary into Telugu by Pullela Sreeramachandrudu (Hyderabad: Surabharati Publications, 1984), 3.1, 71–3 (the entire pedagogical scene is in 71–95).

35. *Kathopanishad*, translated with a commentary into Telugu by Kompella Dakshinamurthy (Hyderabad: Seetarama Adisankara Trust, 2001), 1.21–9, 91–113.

36. Patanjali, *Yogasutra*, in *Six Systems of Indian Philosophy*, translated by Madan Mohan Agrawal (Delhi: Chaukhamba Sanskriti Pratishthan, 2001), 2.3, 231.

37. *Kathopanishad*, 1.2.23, 178–81.

38. Gautama, *Nyaayasutra, Samadhi Visheshaabhyasaat*, in *Six Systems of Indian Philosophy*, 2.38, 69 (practice of meditation renders the knowledge of truth habitual).

39. *Chandogya Upanishad*, 8.15.1.

40. *Brahadaaranyaka Upanishad*, 2.6, where Hiranyagarbha is said to have learnt directly from para; 4.6; and 6.5.

41. Hartmut Scharfe, *Education in Ancient India* (Leiden: Brill, 2002), 163.

42. Scharfe, *Education in Ancient India*, 131.

43. B.N. Misra, *Nalanda: Sources and Backround* (Delhi: B.R. Publishing Corporation, 1998), 307.

44. Scharfe, *Education in Ancient India*, 132.

45. Ganeri, *The Lost Age of Reason: Philosophy in Early Modern India 1450–1700* (Oxford: Oxford University Press, 2014), 8–10.

46. Although traditional centres of learning continued to exist (in whatever form) until the first quarter of the twentieth century (at Mithila and Navadvipa), they were already displaced as sources of learning by the new institutions established by the British. At Calcutta, Benares, Lahore, and Maharashtra traditional learning was offered with 'a Western bent and with a large number of Western professors and principals'. See Scharfe, *Education in Ancient India*, 192. Also see Madhav Deshpande, 'Pandit and Professor: Transformations in the 19th Century', in *The Pandit: Traditional Scholarship in India*, edited by Axel Michaels (Delhi: Manohar, 2001), 119–53.

47. S.N. Balagangadhara and Marianne Keppens, 'Reconceptualizing Postcolonial Project: Beyond the Strictures and Structures of Orientalism', *Interventions* 11, no. 1 (2009): 50–68.

48. Ganeri, *The Lost Age of Reason*,10.

49. Plato, *Phaedrus*, translated by Benjamin Jowett (Chicago: Encyclopaedia Britannica, Inc. 1952), 138–9.

50. *Acharyas*: teacher-practitioners; *Nirvaanashatka*: a composition of six stanzas pertaining to releasement; *Dakshinamurthystotra*: invocatory composition about Shiva in the form of Dakshinamurthy; *Abhanga*: a Marathi compositional form celebrating the god Vithoba, in circulation from at least the thirteenth century. Literally, 'a-bhang' means that which is not interrupted or broken.

51. Gandhi's praxial insights are stunning. Commenting on the icon of the so-called Indian renaissance, Ram Mohun Roy, he says something penetrating: Roy, he said, sometimes appears as a giant; but sometimes he seems like a pigmy. For Gandhi, Roy becomes dwarfish compared to what Nanak and Kabir accomplished. (This comment is cited from memory and I cannot locate the reference. However Gandhi did refer to Roy as a pigmy, not in comparison with Kabir or Nanak [which I saw in an article in a newspaper] but with regard to something else: 'And when someone mentioned Ram Mohan Roy, I remember having said that he was a pigmy compared to the unknown authors, say, of the Upanishads.' See Gandhi, 'The Poet and the Charkha', *Young India*, 5 November 1925, available at http://www.gandhi-manibhavan.org/eduresources/article13.htm [accessed on 25 June 2016].)

52. Interestingly, it was precisely the Pagan mnemocultural Homeric impulse that the contemporary Albanian writer Ismail Kadare was trying to invoke at the time of the Kosovo massacres. He was appealing to a deeper European sense of genealogy (a retrospective continuist narrative now turning to the mnemocultural past that was never sustained). See Kadare, *Elegy for Kosovo*, translated from Albanian by Peter Constantine (New York: Arcade Publishers, 2012).

53. Plato, *Protagoras*, translated by W.K. Guthrie (London: Penguin, 1956), 99–100; Plato, *Republic*, 377–9.

6

HISTORY AND ALLEGORY
Affinities between the Puranas and Kabir

MILIND WAKANKAR

This essay is Gnostic in its impulse. I take as fundamentally opposed Indian nihilism and Indian secularism. My effort is to demonstrate the inability on the part of secularism to take into account the centrality of the mystic, apophantic current in our history, which is to say the tradition of *Nihil*, the act of uttering the No or the Not. Nihilism ceases to be objectionable to secularism once the former has been rid of its obscure and dark impulses, especially if those impulses have been turned toward social critique. Secularism does not and cannot understand any form of belief or faith that celebrates the event of the coming of God to man, especially if the event is addressed in the language of negative theology. Beyond this lies for secularism the *terra incognita* of orgiasm, mystery, and arcana. Nihilism is the other of secularism in that it dares to take seriously the historical emergence of reason from out of a dark impulse whose nature is obscure. The unquestioning affirmation of light, reason, and publicity blinds secularism to the integral relation between reason and unreason, being and non-being, God and death. What transpires in secular thinking is a disavowal of an account of freedom not linked to subjectivity; secularism is ignorant of the domain of the extra-subjective, of the radically other—it neglects to take into account the transcendental origins of generosity, which lie in a realm prior to freedom and entitlement. In what follows, I begin with an account of puranic obsession that yields for us an insight into a turning point in the late antique account of negativity. I see this is as a segue into the role that the negative will go on to play in Indo-Islamic allegory. With that transition signposted, the chapter will have recourse to the legacy of Kabir. My trajectory should, I hope, make plain my attempt to chart an alternative history of self-positing or subjectivity in India. Instead of projecting back into the past a secular viewpoint, and then retro-actively discovering in such moments the medieval devotionalism of Bhakti notions dear to secularism (such as the idea that religion can only every be self-surrender or protest, and the notion of 'tolerance') I try to go back to the origins of self-positing in something like the past of religion. Indian nihilism, I will try to show, is uniquely equipped with the ability to understand and excavate this 'past' before the past familiar to historiography.

* * *

I begin with the saintly life of the child-devotee Prahlada. Our excur-sus on the life of Prahlada will take us into the heart of a typically 'Puranic' text. The puranas, written in Sanskrit verse, were composed at various points in the first millennium of our common era. The timespan is enough to make us realize that what we have before us are not merely vast narrative sagas inflected here by doctrine and there by narrative. For there is nothing indifferent in the puranas: they attend at every step to the problem of the relation between the internal limit to human life which is the speculative spirit and the external limit which is the world of nature experienced in space and time. Coming as they do at the end of a long millennium of philosophical speculation on this question, they quite understandably devote themselves to a narrative resolution of this problem. But what does narrative imply in this context? We will have to understand nar-rative as more than doctrine but also more than myth. So that what is needed here is neither a mere listing of the philosophical schools the puranas make reference to; nor is this a matter of myth analysis. I will argue that the narratival project of the puranas is the work of *muthos* in the expansive sense of that Greek word: it is the recapitulation of a past prior to the past available to history. More to the point, it is the recovery of the 'fact' of that past. Not surprisingly, the miracle of such a past translates into what is in the puranas a remarkable set of theses on the problem of divinity. But as we know from the purana scholar whose book-length essay on Prahlada I will have occasional recourse to here—I am thinking of Paul Hacker, who wrote the essay in the late 1950s[1]—the puranas practice a peculiar form of ambivalence wherein, at every stage, one finds them unable to decide between the eternality of the inner world of the spirit and the transient but knowable outer world. The idea of divinity in the puranas is by this token couched in the narratival account of this ambivalence, often with deeply unsettling effects, as we will see in the case of Prahlada. I will go on to suggest that this ambivalence prepares the ground for Indo-Islamic allegory at the start of the second millennium of the common era. But by then the allegorical apparatus will have undergone a series of transformations whereby one can no longer speak of narrative without also referring to interiority. And, therefore, even more than the literature of the Indo-Persian *dastans* (narrative sagas) it is really Kabir in whom narrative and allegory coalesce under the force of the Nathpantha and under the imprint of Sufism.

Hacker's magisterial essay traces the Prahlada story in its many recensions from the Mahabharata down to the Bhagavata Purana, which is the *locus classicus* of what is known as Vaisnava or Bhagavata dharma, the tradition of Visnu worship. Let us stay with the story as it appears in its most developed form in Canto Seven of the Bhagavata Purana, which was composed in a deliberately archaic Sanskrit by Tamil Alwar (Vaisnava) poets at some point in the eighth century.[2] The myth itself is easily recounted. Enraged by Visnu's killing (in his boar avatar) of his brother Hiranyaksha, the demon-king Hiranyakashipu undertakes an unprecedented form of penance. Disconcerted by the sheer force of his ascetic passion, the gods appeal to Brahma to grant him a boon. Here is what the demon-king asks for:

Give me the power to be lord over all creatures. Grant that no created being, whether man or animal, organic or inorganic, god or demon can bring about my death. Grant that my death take place beyond the antinomies of outside and inside, day and night, caused by beings neither terrestrial nor otherwise, and neither on earth nor in heaven.

The boon is granted. Then begins a long period of tyranny characterized by Hiranyakashipu's persecution of brahmanical society, mostly
by the devastation of its ritual everyday. This is followed by the persecution of his own son Prahlada when, in catechism after catechism,
the latter betrays a profound knowledge and fealty to Visnu. He
cannot but deny the sovereignty of Hiranyakashipu, for he knows only
one lord, Visnu himself. His demon-father is enraged and subjects
Prahlada to a series of trials of a brutal variety, going so far as to throw
him into a pit of snakes. The child survives every test by dint of his
devotion to Visnu. As a final affirmation of his love for his devotee,
Visnu himself appears in an extraordinary deus ex machina. In this
well-known puranic scene, the god defies the limitations imposed by
Brahma's boon, but in a highly unusual way. He emerges from within
a pillar at twilight, though not as Visnu but as a creature half man and
half lion. In this anthropo-feline (Narsimha) avatar, having incised
the antinomic cordon around Hiranyakashipu, the god holds the
demon-king on his knee and proceeds to disembowel him. Prahlada
is anointed the new demon-king.

It should be clear from this sketch that the tale is steeped in a kind
of passionate intensity that can only produce an unprecedented dramatic conflict. There is the deep melancholy of Hiranyakashipu and
his family upon the death of his brother. This is followed by the ardour
of his penance, instituted to avenge himself on Visnu and to challenge
the latter's sovereign sway over the three worlds. Counterposed to this
range of passions is the fervour of Prahlada, whose sermons on the
nature and essence of Visnu as godhead acquire an almost apocalyptic
tenor under the force of his father's intransigence. All these signs
indicate that the text is not merely a Vaisnava hagiography. In point
of fact, it puts into play a central paradox that calls to be incised and
reconciled by the pacific figure of Prahlada.

The paradox is introduced by the text in the frame narrative that
has King Parikshit in conversation with Suka. This is how the issue is
broached at the very beginning of the Canto Seven (I present the two
verses in prose):

Parikshit: God (*bhagwan*) loves all beings (*priyaha ... bhutanam*), is in
empathy (*suhrida*) with them, wants to be non-indifferent (*sama*) with
them. Why then would he take sides, pitting himself against foes for

the sake of Indra, going so far as to enter into indifference (*visama*) with them? If God's essence is to be the unmediate salve (*saksan nihisreyasa*), he can have no sociality of interest (*hasyartha*) with gods. [Conversely,] as a being without qualities (*agunasya*) [which is to say, none derived from primordial matter], he cannot harbor any impetuosity (*udvega*) or enmity (*vidvesa*) toward demons. (BP 7:1:1–2)

For Parikshit as for Prahlada, Visnu is no doubt one with all beings, but this oneness is not indifferent in quality. He is not merely the common element in a manifold of beings. Visnu is qualitatively different, he is the highest of the high. For this reason, Visnu is nothing if not this movement between the one *in* the many and the one *as against* the many. Gods and demons inhabit the realm of the indifferent (visama)—gods as beings requiring other grounds for their authority, demons as the very instance of beings determined by different *gunas* (qualities, moods)—but Visnu's soteriology needs no mediation just as his being can have no connection with the sensible world of the three gunas (*sattva, rajas*, and *tamas*).

Now the question is: what explains God's need to descend into the polemical standoff between a friend and an enemy? By way of a response, Suka cites Narada, the messenger of the gods, who had replied to a similar query from King Yudhistir. (In the embedded narrative that follows from this point in Canto Seven, it is Narada who then proceeds to recite the saintly tale of Prahlada for Yudhistir's edification.)

> Narada: Yudhistir! It is my firm view that the extent to which man can unite (*tanmayata*) with God in a stance of enmity (*vairanubandhena*) is unmatched even by the yoking [with God] effected by [the participant devotion which is] Bhakti. A wasp having entrapped a worm on a wall, the worm in fevered anxiety contemplates (*tamanusmaran*) the wasp with fear—thus does the worm by turns acquire the same form (*tatsarupatama*) as the wasp. (BP 7: 1: 26–7)

By token of this contemplation (*smarana*, tanmayata), what is indifferent (visama) to God becomes non-indifferent (sama, tatsarupatama). Enemies of Visnu may well be reborn as his enemies in his successive avataras, but they will all by sheer force of this inimical obsession have finally merged with him (BP 7:1; 32–46). Following Schelling's use of the word in his *Ages of the World* drafts, we can think of this thinking-after as a kind of obsession, a *Sehnsucht*.[3] (I will explain shortly why the parallel with Schelling is both appropriate and useful.) It is almost as though the world of the enemies of Visnu, one that is at once inimical and polemical, asks at the very limit of its hateful passion to unite in infatuation with its object.

An obsessive hatefulness toward God is then not very different, is perhaps more effective, than an obsessively devotional comportment toward him. This is the gist of a framing device couching a tale that, at least on the face of it, is almost entirely about the obsessive devotion (smarana, tanmayata) of Prahlada! At this point it would be somewhat simplistic of us to imagine that the widening inclusiveness between frame and tale, enemy and friend, is merely an aspect of Vaisnava theology. What is more crucial here is what can be called the 'ontological' relation between men and gods. That relation is defined of course by the question of mortality. I mention 'gods' here; but the demonology of the text moves freely between gods and demons as two forms of being that surpass humanity and its limits. To be sure, the specific demonological stake here is to enter into the problem of the relation between the internal and external worlds. Unfortunately for us, the inculcation of Prahlada into the pantheon as a would-be martyr-devotee for Visnu has meant that the tradition tends to neglect the exact rationale for Hiranyakashipu's hubris. This may give one the mistaken impression that the latter's overleaping of demonic power by way of Brahma's boon finds its reversal, and therefore its neutral or resolved form, in Prahlad's interiorization of Visnu through his powers of reflective recall (smarana). It would seem as though the text is solely about the institution of God in Prahlada's inner world, a process that at its very limits draws an analogy between Brahman (the world as interiorized essence) and Visnu as sovereign deity over the external world. But if the setting up of this thesis as an axiom ('Visnu *is* Brahman') were the sole aim of Canto Seven we would lose sight of the philosophical *and* (I would argue) the historical problem the text sets into play.

That problem is best characterized as the obsessiveness of reason precisely in the way Schelling sought to explain it. It helps turns our sights away from Visnu as end to Visnu as the origin. Whether this origin is cosmological or cosmogonic in its implications is perhaps less important than the fact that the origin is that to which the whole trajectory of Vaisnava rationality returns. At the origin and at the end is Hiranyakashipu, not Prahlada. What is the significance of this circular return? It represents, to my mind, a specifically puranic response to questions the tradition as a whole had had to deal with in the momentous interface between early Upanisadic thinking and the first sermons of the Buddha in late antiquity. The results of that interface were twofold. (I rely here on the influential recent account of these issues by Toshifumi Goto.[4]) One, the *Brihadaranyaka Upanisad*, as the earliest of the Upanisads, established the problem of mortality as one that was first and foremost about the end of life, or the ends of human life in general. The notion of the afterlife (a temporary stay in heaven) for the *atman* became less crucial than the problem of the return to *samsara*. Here the atman becomes the internal limit of reflection on the problem of how to escape the cycle of rebirth; this atman is not the soul, nor is it the spirit; it is the point of reflexivity at which thought turns upon itself. And for this reason, samsara is not the world given historically (as a Christian scene of strife or redemption) but the world *as* the necessary and uncircumventible fall into rebirth. So the end of human life became co-terminus with the point of internal reflexivity (the point of institution of the atman). Another way of saying this is that the internal limit which was the atman was set in place at the point at which the external world was delimited, which is to say the natural or sensory world as the stage for the cycle of rebirth. This was the fertile ground for the theses on the atman put forth by the schools of Vedanta in the first millennium CE; they took as their point of departure some of the key theses (the *mahavakya*s) of the early Upanisads.

Second, if the emphasis in these early texts is on the reversal at the end (death as the 'end' that can also be a vestibule into a life free from death), the major shift that occurred with the Buddha was a renewed meditation not on the end that is death, but on the beginning that is birth. It was no longer the question of a life free from death (*amartya*) but of a life free from (re)birth (*jati*). If the atman marked the internal limit of bodily existence, a remnant of the eternal in the midst of all that is transient in the world, the notion of jati introduced a kind of fold in the internal limit. The atman as the negation of death had to give way to jati as the negation of birth. It was only a short but momentous step from this to the idea that all origin is derived from other origins, leading to the idea of the transience of origin itself.

This form of *pratityasamutpada* (dependent origination), which was the finding of the major Buddhist philosopher Nagarjuna, implied that all being passes over into nothing. Which is to say that we can free ourselves from the weight of all entanglements with the lived world if we train ourselves to focus on becoming itself. For what is retained in the eternal movement between being and nothing on the one hand, and nothing and being on the other, is minimally the transience of transience itself: this is the minimal element of life as it is lived in the awareness of perpetual movement, change, and becoming.

Despite their seeming heterogeneity of content, the puranas can be understood, as I have suggested above, to be a series of responses to these crucial ideas put in place and disseminated in late antiquity. What is the crisis that the puranas respond to? One might characterize this is as an emerging uncertainty with regard to the status of the lived world. Let us not understand this to be a 'traditional' response seeking to restore the certitudes of the Vedic period, such as were overturned by the Upanisads. The vast and complex machine of the puranas, with all its deliberate archaisms, its many digressions, its attention to doctrine and so on, seeks instead to return to the radical notion of worldly life that is at the heart of Vedic thinking, and of the Rg Veda in particular. What this notion specifies is not the necessary movement of life into death, being into nothing, and vice versa. It understands the negativity inherent in this transience, but it seeks to attend instead to the movement by which negativity itself is annulled, giving rise to some form of affirmation. We can see how there is an infinitesimal proximity here between the Puranas and the late Buddhist theses (as Hacker too has noticed). But if there is this family resemblance, there is also a crucial difference between the puranic and Buddhist accounts of negativity. If we think of the process by which being passes over into nothing as 'nihilation', we can define the movement between the two as abyssal or 'an-nihilative' of worldly life. This annihilative understanding of the world was the central contribution of Buddhist thinking since Nagarjuna, spawning a great number of variants in the Buddhist universe. But to highlight the minimal departure that the puranas seek to undertake, we will have to think of 'nihilation' somewhat differently.

At this point, we can return instructively to our own text. I remarked earlier that the trajectory of Vaisnava rationality in the text seeks to return not to the loving infatuation of Prahlada but to the obsessional animus of Hiranyakashipu. This is the upshot of the myth itself, especially in its final moment when Visnu as man-lion disembowels the prostrate Hiranyakshipu. Moving between friend and enemy, love and hate, Canto Seven of the Bhagavata Purana attempts to expand the idea of the non-indifference (sama) of Visnu outward to the lived world of the indifferent and transient beings that can only have a negative relation to each other (visama). But the question is: how does one explain the fact that Visnu as man-lion is in the text posited as a reality exactly halfway between Hiranyakashipu and Prahlada? Let us look at the man-lion's anomalous status as a creature that, although half-human, nonetheless bears a reference to animal life. This is to say that the man-lion is a figure for what we can call in line with recent debates, the problem of animality. Now, the status of the animal is paradoxical. We cannot say, as does Heidegger, that a stone entirely lacks the notion of 'being in the world' vouchsafed to human beings alone, but that the animal is 'poor in world'.[5] For to say that is at once to throw open animality to something worldly or human *and* to close that momentary aperture in the very same instance. In the same way, one could ask: why does Canto Seven present Visnu as a creature fundamentally non-indifferent (sama) but also and at the same time the very embodiment of the indifferent (visama)? It is not a matter of merely breaking through the antinomies soldered together by Brahma's boon. More is at stake, since Vaisnava thinking here wants to argue in the final instance for the non-indifference (sama) of friend and enemy here. Moreover, we are given to believe that at the moment when Visnu as man-lion drinks the blood of the demon-king, the latter *could not have been more proximal* than at any other time to Visnu himself. So whereas a cursory understanding of the myth would have us believe that it is Prahlada's ascendancy that is moot here, a closer look reminds us of the centrality of Hiranyakashipu to the philosophical (call it doctrinal) question at issue. The very passion of the monstrous man-lion is but a reflection of the monstrous antipathy of the demon-king. My point is that, rather than simply portray the effort of Visnu to rescue his child-devotee, Canto Seven takes pains to break through the representational possibilities made available by puranic myth. This is then a reflexive moment, one in which hate and love, friend and enemy are reflected in each other with their differences cancelled out by virtue of the unlikely union—or strictly speaking the being-with (*sayujya*)—of the demon-king with God. One could argue that a complete overthrow of representational constraints is necessary for this famous and much re-enacted scene to occur. Hiranyakashipu's hubris, which impels him to a lordship over the spatially available universe, finds its nemesis in a complete absorption in Visnu, an absorption that is at once anomalous and regulative within the Vaisnava frame. Regulative, because Visnu must break through all the constraints imposed by Brahma's boon, constraints that have to do with the world of space and time. And anomalous, because only through his own gory disembowelment can Hiranyakashipu find a place in that inner domain where, in this purana's Vedantic schema, Visnu and Brahman are one.

With this finding, it is time we returned to the question of nihilation. I have been arguing that the puranas are a response to the 'annihilative' dimension of Buddhist thought. I defined the latter in such terms as an insistence on the movement between being and nothing; annihilation involves an emphasis on the negativity inherent in this moment. From this perspective it is now possible for us to detect in the puranic text a minimally different emphasis. For in the trajectory of Canto Seven, as I have tried to show, there is a deeply disturbing embrace of animus. Note that this is an embrace: animus is retained in it, not effaced in favour of divine love. I believe the key to the puranic notion of the world lies in the fact of this retention. The implication is that the world that *is* Visnu emerges from out of the fundamental retention of the negative moment. Love and hate are not indifferently reconciled in him; we neglect the essence of divinity if we merely think of it as reconciliatory in its effects. This is in all probability an instance of our retroactive attempt to inject a humanized account of the world back into this text. For, the divine here oversees the emergence of worldliness from out of a prior negativity. Hence the central role accorded in this tale to the demonic. Its demonology, couched in the tale's dark core (which is the death of the demon-king), is the secret source of the luminous world that is finally affirmed at its culmination. Where the profound insight of Buddhist thought was to enter into the possibilities opened up by the question of annihilation, the puranic text seems to want to bring about a new relation to nihilation itself. The notion of the world that it unveils is assuredly 'inhuman', if one can use the word. The dark origin of this world is nihilation, which is to say (in the case of our myth) the unabsorbable negativity of Hiranyakashipu. The restoration of dharmic order that ensues cannot then but be a form of 'un-nihilation' (I borrow the phrase from Eugen Fink).[6]

We must remember, however, that this coming-from-out-of-the dark into the light is impelled by the obsessive force of Hiranyakashipu's demonic hatred of Visnu. This fatal obsession is counterpointed in the text by the enlightened ardour of Prahlada. The demon-king's is a passion from within the dark; it is the necessary condition for the tale of the child-devotee. It is almost as though a passion of the exterior world is made to serve as the very basis, the very ground for a passion of the interior world. In other words, a benighted passion from out of the puranic past serves as the threshold for the very instance of Vaisnava rationality that is Prahlada's brilliant series of sermons on the ontotheology of Visnu; this is the prelude to the puranic future. Schelling's notion of obsession as *Sehnsucht* is then an apt description of this emergence. Rather than assume that the earlier moment of darkness is eclipsed by the later moment of light, Schelling tells us the earlier moment seeks to be drawn into the later. But the force of this pull is unique to that earlier moment itself: it is by an act of 'love' (obsessive hate which is always already obsessive love) that it pushes itself into the open to embrace the light. More strictly, Schelling is speaking here of the relation between what he calls the prior 'potency' (*Potenz*) of the natural world and the ultimate potency of the world of the spirit. To put it differently, nature contains within itself both the ground for the mystery of its own sentience as well as the ground for the future emergence of the human mind or spirit; it is not supplanted by a (human) spirit gifted with the power to contemplate the assimilation of all things within the absolute. Instead, the natural world remains the necessary (and darkly obsessional) prelude to the historical advent of the spirit. (In this schema the virulence of the man-lion serves, one might argue, as an *interlude* between nature and spirit.) Obsession then is both intensely self-directed *and* passionately other-directed toward the object opposing it.

The fact is that Visnu as the seat of an interiorized reason is not averse to the inauguration of exteriority. One must understand the latter as first and foremost a question of limits. The qualitative infinite that is Prahlada's inner devotion finds its counterpoint in the quantitative infinite that is Hiranyakashipu's unbridled rage. Linking the two is of course Visnu himself, who is the paradigm for measure (*maryada*). The man-lion represents that which is immeasurable about measure, the point where measure is equal to the absolute. But what is measure itself (measure *as* Visnu) than the threshold for the emergence of the subject? This is because of the retentive nature of Vaisnava reason, itself the source of the movement from dark to light, and from hidden to open. And so the subject of the puranas appears as the 'I' that sought to keep to itself but was instead 'pulled' toward the world. The puranic text would seem to be a meditation on the nature of this compulsion. The compulsion has neither origin nor end but it nonetheless generates the world from out of the void of a self-related obsession. Is that process of generation tantamount to something affirmative? The puranas do not reply to this question: suffice to say that the entire elaborate machine of the puranas is an answer of sorts. What it offers is not a history of the world *per se* but a history of 'un-nihilation' as the scene for the emergence of the historical world.

* * *

A world can emerge *as* a world, that is to say it can inaugurate itself historically either in reference to the past or to the future. The great model for the work of the vernacular as the basis for a re-imagined 'future' for Europe after the Second World War was provided by Erich Auerbach, both in *Mimesis* as well as in his late work on *Latin and Its Public in Late Antiquity*, not forgetting the achievement of his essay on 'Figura' and his lifelong work on Dante.[7] It rested in literature's capacity to 'figure' the future in its 'fullness'. Figure in Auerbach is language in its ability to bring out the silhouette of a worldly life that is also the boundary to an uncharted future. The vernacular bears this figurality within itself, both the density of the present and the promise of the future. The difference between the scene of the European vernacular in Auerbach's great works and that of the

Indo-Islamic millennium is telling: here it is not a worldliness that is always already freighted with the eschatological—worldly life in Hindustan bears instead the imprint of a past before the past (which is the advent of the divine). In God's 'always having already arrived' the saint-poet experienced, more traumatically, an absence—God's having just been here (very much the way one travels to meet someone and, having arrived, learns that that person has 'just left'). The 'I' of the saint-poet is a response to precisely this event, as I will suggest below.

We have seen how the Bhagavata Purana points in the direction of the 'past' as a prelude to history. Which is to say, the past as an un-nihilative 'beginning' rather than an origin. Now, Hacker was drawn to the Bhagavata Purana because it represented what for him was the central ambivalence in the Vedantic tradition (Hacker, we should remember, was primarily a scholar of the long tradition of the Advaita Vedanta school),[8] which is to say its inability to reconcile the twin poles of abstraction and representation. For him the tension in the text between its purely conceptual moments (exemplified in the outstanding discourses of Prahlada) and its narratological-representational moments (as they come to fore especially in the final disembowelment of Prahlada's father by Visnu-Narsimh) is characteristic not just of this particular Puranic text but of Vedantic thought in general. Whatever the merits of Hacker's position, and disregarding his criticism that Indian 'monism' lacks an ethical standpoint (an outcome of Hacker's predilections as a Catholic theologian), we can take his work on Prahlada and on the Vedantic tradition as an important point of entry into the nature of allegory.

Two things are clear: first, his ambivalence between concept and metaphor is the very instance of the typically allegorical movement between the abstract and the concrete, the ideal and the material, and the inner and the outer. Second, the ambivalence itself is a salient aspect of Indo-Islamic allegory as it came to be elaborated from the fourteenth century CE onward in the work of Kabir pre-eminently, but also in Jayasi, Tulsidas, Manjhan, and other poets in the period 1300–1700 CE. My interfusion of Bhakti and Sufi poets is deliberate, since my point is to draw attention to their shared allegorical idiom. Under the millennial influence of Vedanta on the one hand and tantra and nathyoga on the other, this idiom implied

the possibility of an internal elaboration of the soul. The elaboration was at once interminable and narratival. Which is to say that
both Bhakti and the Indo-Persian love-sagas or *premakhyans* such
as Jayasi's implied an internal physiognomy of the soul that was
productive of narrative elaboration. Kabir's reliance on this internal
sign-system of *ida-pingla* and *sushumna* borrowed from nathyoga
is fairly well documented, as is his use of a kind of loose Advaite
Vedanta; the achemical logic underlying nathyoga transformation
has been described in ethnographic detail by David Gordon White.[9]
This persistent cross-hatching of idioms is precisely what makes
Bhakti and Sufi *fluent*—indeed the Indo-Islamic millennium is this
vast reservoir of traits made fluent, workable, current, set into play.
The name we have of late given to this inexhaustible fund of linguistic innovation, cutting across Avadhi, Bhojpuri, Braj, Persian,
Arabic, Old Marathi, Dakkani, and so on—the name we give to the
great worldliness of this idiom in its unsurpassable secularity—is
'Hindavi'.[10] Against this backdrop where fluency is both linguistic
and conceptual itinerancy, we can no longer think of allegory as a
form of reference that falls short of the symbol because it assumes a
mechanical relation between figure and meaning.[11] Allegory's inner
generativeness allows us to extrapolate from the nathyogic elements
in Kabir to Bhakti to the Indo-Persian premakhyans; indeed the
latter too are profuse within tantra and nathyoga. The work of the
late Aditya Behl and others such as Ramya Sreenivasan and Thomas
de Bruijn has helped us understand how Indo-Persian dastans
worked between a spiritual frame of reference and a set of narrative
turns that adhere to that basic frame.[12]

De Bruijn's characterization of the underlying structure of Jayasi's
Avadhi epic, *Padmavat*, usefully lays out the 'allegorical' frame of
the text (understanding allegory as always more than a mere correspondence of hidden and apparent). This is how the story looks from
the point of view of the protagonist, King Ratansen, who pines after
Padmavati, his beloved, who dwells in the southern fortress of the
mythical Simhal.

> The fortress of Simhal [is] the body that has to be conquered by yoga
> ... Ratansen's yoga of love is the force that subdues the passions
> that govern his body and stand as watchmen at the gates of Simhal.

Inside the fortress of the body are the secret channels through which one can reach the tenth door. By climbing the floors of the fortress, the yogi of love pierces the *cakras* [wheels, ascending nodes in the upward process of yogic self-transformation] and reaches the *brahmarandhra* [cleft of Brahman; fontanelle in the alchemical physiognomy of the soul], the point where the meeting with the beloved takes place. *The fortress is crooked, like your body; examine it and see that you are its mirror image. It will not be conquered by a determined fight; he who knows himself will get it.* ... The body is the base metal from which gold can be made through the process of [the] yoga of love.[13] [de Bruijn, 116–17]

That such an allegorical or interiorized elaboration of the soul is not uncommon in Bhakti can be gleaned from similar passages in the *Dnyaneswari*, as I have shown elsewhere. What de Bruijn goes on to describe as the final aim of the process is again shared across Bhakti and Sufi contexts: 'The penance and control leads to the effacement of the self, which opens up the "channel" for realising God in the world in its universal and pervasive aspect'.[14]

Given this interiorizing premise, it follows that we must ask after the link between the historical—or which is the same thing in this context, narratival—elaboration of the soul and the notion of 'un-nihiliation' which we detected in the Bhagavata. My point is not of course to tendentiously insist that Indo-Islamic allegory is by this token 'Hindu' in origin. I am trying to emphasize here the extent to which the basic impulse of this allegorical apparatus stems from a relation to negativity that is nothing if not puranic in its tendency. Puranic, not Vaisnava, although like all else in the Indo-Islamic millennium the drive toward Vaisnavization is ineluctable: it will come, it is the future. My point is: what we see as a pervasive Vaisnavization in the Indo-Islamic millennium is guaranteed by the puranic; it is not the puranic that is guaranteed by Vaisnavism. This lack of fit, or asymptote between puranic and Vaisnava begins at some point in antiquity (we could speculate after Jan Gonda that its precise origin as a non-relation may lie in early Krishna-worship in late antiquity).[15] But for our purposes we should note that the asymptote produces two possibilities that, as Jack Hawley[16] and others have noted, run continuously into each other, which is to say the anthropomorphic impulse that produces the *sagun* (replete with phenomenal

attributes) Ram and Krishna as an outcome of Vaisnavism, and the
aniconic (even iconoclastic) impulse that has as its outcome the idea
of the *nirgun* (devoid of phenomenal attributes)—which we should
now see as an outcome of the puranic. Sagun and nirgun, puranic
and Vaisnava, the relation between these terms is fourfold, crossing
over chiasmically. And so the stakes are much greater. The Bhagavata
does not just give us a clue to the historical impulse of Indo-Islamic
allegory. It takes us back to the anthropomorphization of deities in
late antiquity. Indeed, not only does the puranic make possible the
curious temporality of the 'having already arrived' nature of God; it
also reminds us of how *proximal* antiquity was to the poets of Bhakti.
Between the proximity (His having just left) of God and a past always
ready at hand we can see the work both of time as history and of time
as eternity. This juxtaposition is startling but essential: the religiosity
of Bhakti would otherwise seem anomalous (notably in the work of
literary historians such as Sheldon Pollock),[17] given that the saint-
poets of Bhakti were uniquely engaged in social critique; all their
God-talk could easily be seen as superfluous. What appears to be the
curious God-addiction of the Bhakti can instead be seen more specifically as the ability to negotiate the divide between time and eternity—
Bhakti is prayer because, first, it evokes antiquity synoptically (time
as history); second, because it invokes God in the transience of the
past (time as eternity).

We need look no further for an instance than Kabir, whose fluent
idiom travelled far over centuries (Kabir poems continue to be written) and embraced all manner of idiom from Hindavi to Hindustani;
Kabir, weaver of the fifteenth century from the Julaha community
steeped in nathyoga, convert to Islam and an untouchable. To use
a latter-day distinction, he epitomises Bhakti directed at a god without attributes (nirgun) which is to say his abstract inner 'Ram'. (In
twentieth-century discussions, the sagun Bhakti of Ram and Krishna,
a Bhakti with traits as in Tulsidas or Surdas, is often opposed to Kabir's
nirgun.)[18] But more crucially Kabir alone embodies this allegorical
tendency in its purest form, though this does not make it any easier
for us to adumbrate the tendency itself. The word of Kabir is like an
open secret, there for everyone to see but unavailable to all except
those who care to detect in it the archeological trace of the puranic.
This is the Word, the *shabad* of Kabir: *Mine is the One unblemished*

Allah(-Ram); Not for me Hindu–Turk as two.[19] Now, here is something we seldom attend to, except to note Kabir's unoriginal or shall we say weak Vedanticism of the 'One'. I refer instead to the bringing together in one utterance of Kabir's Allah-Ram, his God without traits (nirgun), *and* Hindu–Turk. We tend to interpret this all too quickly as Kabir's call for us to rise above religious difference and embrace his transcendent Ram. (How quickly do we project our modern sensibilities on to the materials of the premodern!) But does not this juxtaposition point elsewhere? For Kabir himself it would seem to be a question of how to think the nirgun and the overcoming of the Hindu–Turk distinction *at one and same time.* In other words, what are we to make of the shared time (co-temporality) of the negative as such which is the nirgun *and* the negative mutual determination or difference between Hindu and Turk? This refers us to the unprecedented juxtaposition of being-negative (the nirgun) and becoming-negative (*Hindu–Turk*). On the one hand, it is something like a Not that recedes into its own origin and makes possible Kabir's joyous experience of 'having-found (God)'. On the other hand there is the movement of negation that is 'not-Hindu, not-Turk'. The former is an 'un-nihilative' movement that opens out on to the event of finding the abstract Ram; the latter is annihilative in that it moves ceaselessly between the two poles of 'not-Hindu' and 'not-Turk'. In the latter, God is so to speak, 'dead', not in the sense that there is no longer piety or belief; God is dead because the valuation of all values (to paraphrase Nietzsche) is up for grabs. The former is Indian nihilism; the latter prefigures Indian secularism. Which is to say that nihilism is prior to secularism: Kabir points us to the undoing of nihilism in a joyous discovery of the inner Ram, who is not the Ram of the Ramayana. Kabir is a master of this nihilism, but how can one also say that he is a master of Indo-Islamic allegory?

The clue to this bond between allegory and individuation comes to us from an unlikely source: Ramchandra Shukla, the seminal Hindi-language philosopher who is notorious for his antipathy to Kabir. Writing in the 1930s in the heyday of anti-colonial nationalism, Shukla was committed to a generalizable form of social address in poetry and, therefore, favoured the more accessible tableaus of heroic action in the Ram-Bhakti of Tulsidas and the Krishna-Bhakti of Surdas to the inward and involuted mindset of Kabir. Now, when Shukla indicted

Kabir for his 'individualism,' he used the term *vyakti-vaicitrya-vad*, a
word that has rich implications for allegory as individuation.[20]

Vyakti implies an individual whose qualities have been universal-
ized. What Shukla faults in Kabir is the latter's proclivity for the
unexpressed, *avyakt*. The two words are related etymologically so
that one can say: Shukla weighs on the side of the universalizable
individual, bringing together humanity in cult and nation, whereas
Kabir stood for that which resists universalization, that is to say the
singular. Shukla's major criticism of Kabir and the Sufi tradition is
that they uphold the idea of a hidden, exoteric, secretive, mystical
access to God, drawing religion and aesthesis (which is for Shukla
the work of *bhava* or affect) away from its open, democratic, self-
evident social function. Adding the word *vaichitrya* to vyakti further specifies the individual, with a strong slant in favour of the
singular. This is now the unique individual, the singular person for
whom God is near. But this is also the frail, flesh-and-blood devotee
marked with the stigma of being a low-caste. The history of Bhakti
can be understood as this double movement. In one move, there is
world re-presented by the devotee who wills the deity into being.
This is the world of mainstream Bhakti, where the vyakti accedes
to nation and cult. In the second move, there is the event of God
(always having already arrived) that momentarily moves the devotee
out of the mainstream. This shuttle between the mainstream and
the marginal is typical of subaltern religious movements in the
Indo-Islamic millennium.

In the move away from the mainstream religion of deification
(Ram, Krishna) we can detect the momentary undoing of the entire
movement of representation, that movement where the individual
is set up as an individual and answers only to the needs of other
individuals like himself, all substitutable with each other in cult,
nation, and state. Not only did Shukla discern in Kabir an idea of the
'unsubstitutability', so to speak of character, he was entirely correct
to associate such a turn away from representation as a turn toward
the secretive. For here he was able, despite himself, to detect in Kabir
the catastrophic loneliness, the insupportable homelessness of the
singular being at a great remove from social, communal, or cultic
being-together, from every available possibility for the representation
of oneself as an individualized, empowered subject. In allegory, in the

secret secreted within, Shukla perhaps saw (and then turned away from) the nexus between character and violence in the Indo-Islamic millennium. Kabir experienced this as an outcaste, just as today we would think of this as the root of caste violence. Even more fundamental than what the state now calls an 'atrocity' is the reference to the margins. Herein would lie the point of departure for an Indian history of madness, or a psychoanalytically informed account of the subject of interiority in the Indo-Islamic world.[21] For Kabir's quest ends at the point where Majnun, beside himself with love and having lost his wits, walks into the wild.[22]

* * *

Note that the intense worldliness of medieval Indian life is not undercut (it is, if anything, enhanced) by the *other* worldliness that is ubiquitous in this the heyday of Bhakti and Sufi proselytization, a scene of competing faiths and creeds.[23] Something of Kabir's modernity for us resides in his immersion in the prosaic scene where religion works in secular ways, only occasionally withdrawing into itself to affirm an original experience of the arrival of God. *If Allah's in a mosque, whose is the rest? Hindus claim His Name's in an idol; God can't be found in either place. The south is Hari's home, the west Allah's hearth. Search your heart, your heart of hearts: that's His abode, His hangout. The brahmin fasts fortnightly, the qazi all Ramadan. Eleven months all to oneself, a mere month's fasting to accrue all merit. Wherefore Orissa for your holy dip? Why bowed head in mosque? You're a scamster to the core, your prayer a sham, you Haji to the Ka'aba!*[24] What we tend to overlook is that the limitations of the outer world are nothing like the limit of the inner world. The inner limit is the *eskhaton*, the internal border within which something like the 'I' persists. We saw how in the instance of the puranic the 'I' emerged—even as a primal obsession receded into the dark past. The emergence itself came with legible signposts all the way from Prahlada to Visnu, the demonological giving way to the shared lingo of Vaisnavism and Advaita Vedanta. There is in Kabir too this primal emergence and elusion, so to speak. We saw how there is at every point in Kabir an insistence on the *simultaneity* of two events, the insight into worldliness as a range of negative determinations and the event of having found the nirgun. The nirgun's Word is denial. It is apophatic. 'Ram' is the word for negativity itself. But to persist in this negativity is not possible, for this negativity is itself to be determined negatively; the abyss must be crossed for the 'I' to emerge, this time 'at the core' (heart of hearts, *dile dili*).

The nirgun stands at the internal limit—but this is not the threshold for interiority, reflexiveness, subjectivity, or individuality as it is made out to be, lamentably, in almost all modern scholarship on Kabir. The fact is, the psychological and cognitive tendencies in this tradition of criticism have distracted us from coming to terms with apophatic utterance in Kabir. The nirgun is a point of individuation, yes, but this is not yet the 'I'. Most crucially, the nirgun stands guard over the *transition* to the 'I', ineluctable as the latter is. This ought to explain my use of the word 'vestibule' earlier in the chapter. The puranic made possible a transition to the Vaisnava, in much the same way that Kabir's nirgun instituted a movement toward the 'I'. Again, the nirgun is *not yet* the 'I'. For this reason, the following traditional reading of Kabir is to my mind untenable: in such a reading Kabir would be asking us to look deep in our hearts to find that all is indifferently the same. No, Kabir is asking us to rethink the very idea of indifference; we are being asked to think the *non*-indifferent itself. Let us describe the non-indifference of the nirgun as the work of the 'Same', which is to say the work of identity as the incorporation of all otherness.

Admittedly, Kabir's nirgun is invested in the Same; but the point of the Same is not (as would be the case in a Vedanta-informed reading) to neutralize the negative in the interests of the eternality of the abstract Ram. It is analogous with the non-indifference of the sama, whose features we detected above in the puranic. Under the aegis of the Same what came together was first, the emergence from the dark core of the Not and second, the movement into the elusiveness of everyday determinations of the negative (Hindu–Turk, *shudra*–brahmin). We are asked to comport ourselves toward the Same understood in this sense, the bringing together of negativity as such (the dark core of the eternal Not, so to speak) and the movement of the negative which is also the inauguration of history and event, miracle and violence, memory and mourning. How to hold these together? The torsion of Kabir's One (*Ek*) should bring home to us the difficulty of this comportment, one that is strangely so 'easy' (*sahaj*) for dalits. The insight into negativity in Kabir was markedly unaffiliated to a transcendent or eternal idea of the truth. Like the puranic, Kabir's nirgun stood guard over the transition to interiority; it was, one should emphasise, *not* an instance of interiority itself.

* * *

The point of this excursus in the history of Indian nihilism has been to illumine a trait that runs from late antiquity into the heart of the medieval. It surfaces in the Puranic, has affinities with the Nathpanth, runs alongside *tantra*, and fuses easily with the most radical aspects of Sufism. Put differently, we might say the other-directed speech (the heterology) of the Not is interwoven with the perpetual heterogeneity of these tendencies in themselves; for, one could argue that tantra and the Sufi way themselves float over and mostly exceed the distinction between Hinduism and Buddhism, Shi' and Sunni, and perhaps between Shaiva and Vaishnava (the latter is certainly the case in the Varkari tradition of western India). Contrary to the modern Indian fascination with the eternality of the One, of which our latter-day exorbitation of Advaita Vedanta is a case in point, the tradition of the Not that we have traced in this essay is about the dark origin of the 'I' on the road to eternality. This primordial origin implies a form of non-freedom that is prior to the freedom to which the 'I' lays claim in modernity (in the modernity of electoral contests, identity, and political society). Now, if this is the case it is time we revisited a point made by David Lorenzen in a number of his influential essays.[25] Lorenzen has drawn attention to the social–historical importance of nirgun in that this variety of Bhakti has been espoused in almost all instances by low-caste communities that are most often also converts to Islam (again, Kabir is a prime instance): broadly speaking, we might characterize this as a dalit eschatology, with some allowance for my anachronistic use of the word 'dalit' for the original nexus of character and violence in the Indo-Islamic millennium. With the hindsight gained from our account of the Not, we may reformulate Lorenzen's notion, this time from the point of view not of social history but from the eschatological–historical (we might even say Gnostic) underpinnings of popular religiosity. For, eschatology requires an embrace of the uniquely individuated 'I' but from out of non-freedom, not freedom. This prior insight into the primordially dark origins of individuality ensures as though in advance the millennial reach of this nihilism. Here there is no epical Ram who stands behind the dalit in his time of need. His is not a religion of faith and succour.

What we have instead is a pre-cognitive, pre-psychological 'insight' into the origins of freedom from out of non-freedom, an insight vouchsafed to subaltern communities. I have described this elsewhere as the very 'incipience' of a (dalit) conceptuality that is yet to come.[26]

It refers to a form of soul-work that is prior to the arena of freedom, right, and duty. The anteriority of nihilism to history has been a closely guarded secret in the tracings of the Not across time, as we saw. It is in religious or literary history that these nuances are quickly dissipated with such distinctions as sagun–nirgun and puranic–Vedantic. The history of Indian nihilism is the perpetual prologue to the history of justice in the subcontinent; its secret past has been held in reserve productively by traditions of low-caste thought. But this esotericism finds its exact counterpart in the eschatological transformations whose history is older (it restores our antiquity to us) and whose traces lie deeper (they repose in the earth) than secularism would care to admit.

Notes and References

1. Paul Hacker, *Prahlada—Werden und Wandlungen einer Idealgestalt* (Wiesbaden: Franz Steiner, 1959).
2. *Atha Srimadbhagavatam* (Varanasi: Chaukhamba Vidyabhavan, 1993).
3. F.W.J. Schelling, *The Ages of the World (1815)*, translated by Jason M. Wirth (Albany: State University of New York Press, 2000).
4. Toshifumi Goto, 'Yajnavalkya's Characterization of the Atman and the Four Kinds of Suffering in Early Buddhism', *Electronic Journal of Vedic Studies (EJVS)* 12, no. 2 (2005): 71–85.
5. I am summarizing here Derrida's intricate reading of a passage in Heidegger's *Fundamental Concepts of Metaphysics* (a key lecture course from the period soon after *Being and Time* [1927]); see Jacques

Derrida, *Of Spirit: Heidegger and the Question*, translated by Geoffrey Bennington and Rachel Bowlby (Chicago: University of Chicago Press, 1989), 47–51.

6. See Ronald Bruzina, *Edmund Husserl and Eugen Fink: Beginnings and Ends in Phenomenology, 1928–1938* (New Haven: Yale University Press, 2004), 129.

7. See Auerbach's posthumously published book, *Literary Language and Its Public in Late Antiquity and in the Middle Ages* (Princeton: Princeton University Press, 1965); *Mimesis: The Representation of Reality in Western Literature*, translated by Willard Trask (Princeton: Princeton University Press, 2003 [1946]); 'Figura' (1938), in *Scenes from the Drama of European Literature* (Minneapolis: Minnesota University Press, 1984).

8. See Hacker's essays in *Philology and Confrontation: Paul Hacker on Traditional and Modern Vedanta*, edited and translated by Wilhelm Halbfass (New York: State University of New York Press, 1995).

9. David Gordon White, *The Alchemical Body* (Chicago: Chicago University Press, 1996).

10. For a provocative recent account of Hindavi, see Francesca Orsini, 'How to Do Multilingual Literary History? Lessons from Fifteenth and Sixteenth Century North India', *Indian Economic and Social History Review* 48, no. 2 (2012): 225–46.

11. In his final lectures at Cornell, Paul de Man hinted at this potential for the internal elaboration of narrative elements in allegory. See de Man's last lectures, written between 1977 and 1983 and collected in *Aesthetic Ideology* (Minneapolis: Minnesota University Press, 1996); see especially 'Pascal's Allegory of Persuasion' (51–69).

12. Thomas de Bruijn, *Ruby in the Dust: Poetry and History in the* Padmavat *by the South Asian Sufi Poet Muhammad Jayasi* (Leiden: Leiden University Press, 2012); Ramya Sreenivasan, *The Many Lives of a Rajput Queen: Heroic Pasts in India, c. 1500–1900* (Delhi: Permanent Black, 2007); Aditya Behl, *Love's Subtle Magic: An Indian Islamic Literary Tradition, 1379–1545* (Delhi: Oxford University Press, 2012).

13. de Bruijn, *Ruby in the Dust*, 116–17.

14. de Bruijn, *Ruby in the Dust*, 117.

15. See Jan Gonda, *Visnuism and Saivism: A Comparison* (London: Athlone, 1970); and compare the timeless class by Ramkrishna Gopal Bhandarkar, *Vaisnavism, Saivism and Minor Religious Systems* (Pune: Bhandarkar Oriental Research Institute, 1982 [1913]).

16. See John Stratton Hawley, *Three Bhakti Voices* (Delhi: Oxford University Press, 2005).

17. Sheldon Pollock, *The Language of the Gods in the World of Men* (Berkeley: University of California Press, 2009). The problem of the religiosity of the saint-poets recurs in this book and considerably undercuts its account of the vernacular millennium in India that began with Bhakti. At every point Pollock marvels at the linguistic virtuosity of the saint-poets; but he is unable to speak to or account for their relation with divinity. As I try to argue in the following pages, the gift of language and the advent of the divine are one and the same event in Bhakti.

18. For a discussion of these issues, see my book on Kabir, *Subalternity and Religion* (London: Routledge, 2010).

19. *Aik niranjan alah mera/Hindu turak dahun nain nera.* See *Pada* 423, Refrain, in *The Millennium Kabir Vani*, edited by Winand Callewaert, with Swapna Sharma and Dieter Taillieu (Delhi: Manohar, 2000), 532–3. I have interpolated '(-Ram)' in consonance with the poem I discuss in note 24.

20. See his 1933 essay, 'Sadharnikaran aur Vyakti-Vaicitryavad', in the first of the epoch-making two volume set of essays *Cintamani-1* (Agra: Hindi Sahitya Sarovar, 1992 [1939]), 151–60.

21. See especially Simon Digby's extraordinary discovery of the dream-visions of an Indo-Afghan soldier on the eve of the Mughal conquest, 'Dreams and Reminiscences of Dattu Sarvani, a Sixteenth Century Indo-Afghan Soldier', *Indian Economic and Social Economic and Social History Review* 2, no. 1 (1965): 52–80; and *Indian Economic and Social Economic and Social History Review* 2, no. 2 (1965): 178–94.

22. See the posthumously published Foucault-inspired history of madness in the Islamic world by Michael W. Dols, *Majnun: The Madman in Medieval Islamic Society* (Oxford: Clarendon Press, 1992).

23. The works of Simon Digby and Dirk A.H. Kolff are essential reading if we are to recreate this scene.

24. This is Vinay Dharwadkar's recent rendition, which I have considerably altered; see Dharwadkar, *Kabir: The Weaver's Songs* (New Delhi: Penguin, 2003), 129–30. Here is the complete poem (*Millennium Kabir Vani, Pada* 280, 386–9):

> *Aalha ram jivan teri nai/Tu kari miharmati sai* [Refrain]
> *Alahu eku masiti vastu hai avaru mulukhu kisu kera*
> *Hindu murati nami nivasi duhu mahi tatu nah era* [1]
> *Dakhan desi hari ka vasa pachhami alahu mukama*
> *Dil mahi khoji dile dili khojahu ehi thavari mukama* [2]
> *Birahman giyas karahi chauvisa kaji maha ramadana*
> *Yarah mah pasi kari rakhe eki mahi nidhana* [3]

Kiya udisai manjanu kiya masiti siru nivai
Dil mahi kapatu nivaj gujarai kia haj kabai jai [4]
Aite avarat marada saje ai sabhi rup tumhare
Kabira pugra ram alah ka sabhi gur pir hamare [5]
Kahu kamir sunahu nar naravai padahu ek ki saran
Eko namu japahu re purani ta nihachau hosi tarana [6]

25. See, among other places, David Lorenzen, 'The Historical Vicissitudes of Bhakti Religion', in *Bhakti Religion in North India*, edited by David Lorenzen (Albany: State University of New York Press, 1995), 1–32.

26. See my essay, 'Topics of the New Dalit Critique', *Comparative Studies of South Asia, Africa and the Middle East* 33, no. 3 (2013): 403–8.

7

RAHUL SANKRITYAYAN AND AMBEDKAR AS CONTRAPUNTAL CONTEMPORARIES
Unpacking Their 'Metaphysics and Politics'

MAYA JOSHI

Rahul Sankrityayan (1893–1963) was an Indian polymath who lived an extraordinarily rich life as scholar, traveler, translator, historian, political activist, and prolific writer across languages and genres. His life-journey was at one level singular; yet, it connected in vital ways with the dominant issues of his age. His writings reveal a dynamic approach to the self, which he fashioned in ways consistent with a changing world view that engaged intensively with two of the most powerful discourses on 'Liberation' that the world has produced: Buddhism and Marxism. His illustrious contemporary, Dr. B.R. Ambedkar, offers uncanny parallels and contrasts, though very little direct contact between the two men is recorded. The two lives seem parallel, though the ideological paths cross, while running in opposite directions. This story folds into itself other historical narratives, some as yet unfolding and thus not fully cognized, especially the complex story of the reception of Marxism/socialism and the revival of Buddhism in India and South Asia. Tensions and overlaps between the perceived binaries of textual and 'lived' traditions, religion and culture, spirituality and politics, faith and reason, tradition and modernity, 'east' and 'west', appear as recurrent themes and constitute the subtext of the narrative. Needless to say, this chapter cannot offer an exhaustive engagement with this richly suggestive field of enquiry; it does hope to posit the two lives as compellingly contemporary interlocutors.

* * *

Scholars treat Gautama Buddha as a saint and a religious thinker and not as a revolutionary or a political theorist. The responsibility of this cooptation and distortion lies with colonial as well as nationalist scholars. During the nationalist period except Mahatma Jotirao Phule and Dr. B.R. Ambedkar, all scholars of philosophy treated Buddhism as part of Hinduism.[1]

A comparison between Karl Marx and Buddha may be regarded as a joke. None-the-less a comparison between ... them just forces itself on me.[2]

Kancha Ilaiah's provocatively titled book, *God as Political Philosopher*, seems an apt place to begin a discussion on the Buddha's political import as imagined in the Indian context. The above cited statement invokes a binary between saint/revolutionary and religious thinker/political theorist that the example of the Buddha arguably demolishes. Ambedkar's statement points to the tension between an apparent disjuncture and a deeper conjuncture between the ancient 'spiritual' master and the nineteenth century political philosopher. As a polemically driven yet scholarly and nuanced reading of the Buddha's message as a systematic political challenge to contemporary orthodoxy, the second part of Kancha Ilaiah's statement is surprising since the lone indexed reference to Rahul Sankrityayan indicates at least an awareness of his work, though he is quoted in passing as a provider of a contextual detail. On the other hand, the review comment by Uma Chakravarti on the back cover lists Sankrityayan as part of a tradition—with Iyothee Tass and Ambedkar, and now Ilaiah—of 'interpreting Buddha for our times'. Neither Ilaiah's marginalization of Sankrityayan nor Chakaravarti's blending him into the tradition of Ambedkar quite does justice to Sankrityayan's engagement with Buddhism; he was, despite Ilaiah's claim, a powerful writer on

Buddhism as a heterodox school of thought that challenged, philosophically and even in empirically verifiable practice, most of the
central tenets of Brahminical orthodoxy. He also, however, diverges
from Ambedkar who reads the Buddha—however creatively—as
the complete answer to the world's social and political ills. In this
nuanced and evolving engagement with Buddhism, Sankrityayan is at
best an interlocutor in the debate on Buddhism socialism. He shows
us the challenges and possibilities of reading Buddha as a socialist.

Another one of Sankrityayan's illustrious (but poorly read) predecessors whom it is pertinent to recall here is the Goa-born scholar
Dharmanand Kosambi, who had become a practising and devout
Buddhist by 1899 and whose inspiring life as an itinerant autodidact
questing for Buddhist knowledge Rahul had read in Gujarati, and
whom he describes finally meeting in Karachi in 1931.[3] Kosambi had
translated and edited the *Vissuddhimagga* and wrote twenty-two books
on Buddhism. The attempt to read Buddhism as a politically emancipatory project, a feature of Ilaiah's own work and one that Ambedkar so
powerfully argued for, is something that one may also find in Kosambi,
who had encountered socialism as early as 1910 en route to Harvard
to teach Pali. More significantly, it was Kosambi's thesis—elaborated
in *Hindi Sanskriti ani Ahimsa* and in his play *Bodhisattva*—that the
Buddha's renunciation of his inherited legacy was prompted not by
the shock of witnessing sickness, old age, and death, as has been the
traditional narrative, but rather an act of compassion driven by the
need to avert the imminent clash between the Shakiya and Koliya,
the two prominent kshatriya clans of Gautama's time. Ambedkar,
who would go on to radically reinterpret many aspects of the received
traditions of Buddha Dhamma, echoes this interpretation.[4] For the
man responsible for the introduction of Buddhist Studies as an academic discipline in India, at the universities of Gujarat, Bombay, and
Calcutta, in the early decades of the twentieth century, and one who
wrote in Marathi, his apparent absence from the Ambedkar narrative
(at least in English) deserves some looking into.[5]

Continuing with Ilaiah's statement, Sankrityayan's life trajectory
bears testimony to a lifelong attempt to read Buddhism in ways
that made sense to his increasingly Marxist sensibilities, especially
after 1938. Unlike Kosambi, who encountered socialism *before* the
revolution of 1917, Sankrityayan had been deeply impressed by the

Bolshevik Revolution of 1917 and had initially sought a confluence of Marxism with his other great lifelong passion for Buddhist philosophy. This finds scholarly, and polemical, expression in his essay 'Buddhist Dialectics', which traces socio-economic views as well as Buddhist investigations into epistemology and ontology.[6] Indeed, attempts by the likes of Dr S. Radhakrishnan to deny Buddhism's radical 'difference' (what Ilaiah asserts in the above-mentioned) and to absorb it back into the Brahminical/*aastik-atmadvadi* fold are the object of Sankrityayan's sharp and stinging rebuke.[7] Thus, Ilaiah's contention that in *pre-Independence* India, there was an absence of scholars, barring Phule and Ambedkar, who would refrain from collapsing the difference between Buddhism and 'Hinduism', needs to be amended. What seems equally clear is that the characterization of scholarship in this area by Ilaiah and most academics as nationalist, colonial, or Marxist does not do full justice to the complexity and uniqueness of a Kosambi or a Sankrityayan.

I cite these few illustrative instances at the outset to indicate the gaps that exist in our understanding of this moment of India's intellectual and political history. Dharmananda Kosambi[8] and Rahul Sankrityayan, in particular, remain glaring absences in our collective scholarly and intellectual imaginary. The reasons for these are manifold, and here too Kosambi and Sankrityayan share much: their extraordinarily unconventional lives, resistance to facile classification, failure to fully conform to *any* orthodoxy, and last but not least, the choice of a 'vernacular' (Marathi for Kosambi, Hindi and occasionally Bhojpuri and Sanskrit for Sankrityayan) as a medium of expression, coupled with the fact that most of their voluminous oeuvre is unavailable in English.[9] Inserting them into this intellectual history helps set the historical record straight; it also invites further studies in the particular ways they received, revived, and responded to Buddhism in a period when a nation was being born and complex negotiations between modernity and tradition were underway.

There is also a larger theoretical issue—the issue raised by Ilaiah, and by the examples of Ambedkar and Sankrityayan, which is a hermeneutical one. Their respective interpretations of Buddhist ontology and epistemology also turn these issues back on themselves: their own ontological and epistemological presuppositions, their intellectual and cultural lines of descent and transmission, their relation to

existing disciplines and dogmas. Who speaks for Buddhism? How do
we establish the veracity of *Buddha vacana*? Is there an 'essence' to this
(non-essentialist) tradition? What is the status of varied textual traditions, and which ones do we privilege? Is it correct to read Buddhism
as a community-oriented political philosophy commensurate with
Enlightenment ideas of universal social justice and rationalism or are
we to see it primarily as a tradition of spiritual training that seeks
to lead *individuals* to *nirvana*? Are the two necessarily divorced from
each other? What, finally, is the nature of 'Liberation' (nirvana) in
Buddhism? Is it even a topic open to discursive elaboration, considering the famous silences with which the Buddha received 'metaphysical' questions? What kind of hermeneutical licence does this silence
give to those who follow him and those who do not?[10]

Encountering Ambedkar, who created 'Navayana', and Sankrityayan,
who gave his own interpretive edge to a long tradition of exegesis that
marks Buddhist scholarship in which one could include Ilaiah's book,
and indeed encountering Buddhism's long and complex transmission
through various lands, its division into many *yanas* or vehicles, one
encounters the troubled terrain of interpretation in which reading
and reception, memory and amnesia, discourse and dissemination,
appropriation and proprietorship, faith and reason play their part. It
is fitting that these questions should rise in all their complexity with
reference to Buddhism, arguably one of the most open of all existing
religio-spiritual traditions to the exercise of hermeneutical judgement. For, had not the Buddha enjoined upon his disciples to accept
nothing at face value, to subject all he had said and all they had heard
to the critical scrutiny of their own judgement? Were they not asked
to test all as a goldsmith tests the purity of gold, by cutting it, burning
it, and rubbing it against a touchstone?

Some sort of hermeneutical hard work, it would seem, is a condition of being a Buddhist, and all yanas endorse this to a greater or
lesser degree. In fact, Ambedkar and Sankrtiyayan found that to be
the most attractive aspect of this tradition, one that had continued to
attract 'modern' progressive and 'scientific-minded' individuals over
millennia, most recently supported in his public talks and writings
by the fourteenth Dalai Lama, who has been actively encouraging the
study of convergences between Buddhist doctrine and practice and
modern science, whether it be quantum physics, or neuroscience and

psychology. In order to do this, a 'secularized' version of Buddhist meditation practices, verifiable by the scientific method of brain-wave mapping or lab tests, has been evolved as a practical solution to contemporary problems of mental and psychological suffering in a language that the modern world wedded to 'the scientific method' can recognize.[11] But then, there are also 'esoteric' elements in Buddhism (their authenticity largely recognized by traditional practitioners of the faith) emphasizing direct perception, mystic intuition, personal deities, karma, even the paraphernalia of theistic traditions, of meta-physics, of magical feats, miracles, charms, and spirits.

And this latter aspect of Buddhism elicits divergent responses from these two men devoted equally to rationalism and logic: while one decides to leave Buddha Dhamma to embrace Marxism, the other sheds these elements as inessential excrescences to the true Dhamma.

* * *

I took ideas/knowledge as a raft to ferry me across, not as a load to be carried on the head.[12]

I start with Sankrityayan, arguably the lesser-known figure, at least outside the Hindi speaking world.[13] In conjunction with sundry essays and biographical writings to trace the curious dialectics of a deep engagement with the past and an equal commitment to the future, I use the following works by Sankrityayan: his multi-volume autobiography, *Meri Jeevan Yatra*; his monumental survey of philoso-phy across the world, *Darshan Digdarshan*; his fictionalized account of human history from 6000 BC to India in 1943, *Volga se Ganga*; and his remarkable treatise in praise of travel, *Ghumakkar Shastra*. In this journey, 'home' and the 'world', religion and politics, the personal and the public, Buddha and Marx form the chief matrices.

A brief sketch of the major events of his life shows the broad pat-terns of his philosophical growth. Born into an orthodox Brahmin peasant family in Azamgarh village in the current state of Uttar Pradesh, he goes from being a Hindu sadhu in diverse theistic tra-ditions to shedding ritual to embrace the Arya Samaj. His Buddhist phase began with his growing distance from the Arya Samaj, of which he had been a zealot between 1914 and 1915. In the 1920s, he systematically studied Buddhism, earning a degree as Tripitakacharya at Vidyalankara Perivena, a traditional monastic college in Sri Lanka. He moved on seeking a wider understanding of Buddhist traditions, and desiring to retrieve its lost treasures, particularly those later Buddhist epistemological texts mentioned by refutation in the Advaita Vedanta—works he had previously studied, which were lost to India but available in their Chinese or Tibetan translation. Buddhist scholarship recognizes him for his four travels in disguise to Tibet for this purpose, between 1929 and 1938, affecting madness and mendicancy as protective guises against the double hazard of ruthless local bandits and the British police. He retrieved over 1,600 Buddhist manuscripts and texts transporting them on mule, translating some of them along the way.

While his titles—Mahapandit and Tripitakacharya—indicate his mastery of Sanskrit and Pali texts, the changes to his name from Kedarnath Pandey to Baba Ramodar Das to Rahul Sankrityayan indicate a pull towards *ghumakkari*, a relentless journeying towards intellectual and spiritual clarity. His later Socialist phase, which started in the late 1930s, coincided with his visit to the USSR, where he learnt Mongolian and Russian, and taught Buddhist Logic at Leningrad University at the invitation of Tscherbatsky, the noted Russian scholar of Buddhist logic, who had heard of Rahul's dramatic discovery in Tibet of Dharmakirti's *Pramanavartika*, a classic of Buddhist logic. In 1937, 1944, and 1962, he revisited the USSR. In between, he returned to and travelled extensively in India, participating actively in the nationalist movement, which earned him several jail terms, which he effectively utilized to further his education and produce much of his voluminous oeuvre. In 1939, he had become a member of the Communist Party of India; he stayed within its fold for nine years, then opted out, before being re-inducted into the party in 1958. He spent the last phase of his life in Darjeeling, where he passed away in 1963.

The variety and volume of the written and translated work he left behind in Hindi, Bhojpuri, Pali, and Tibetan include nine novels, short stories, an autobiography published originally in five volumes, fifteen biographies of religious and political leaders—ranging from 'Vir Chandrasingh Garhwali' to 'Mao-Tse-Tung', 'Stalin' to 'Mahamanav Buddha'—travelogues documenting Asian and European journeys, essays, translated books, and several booklets on science, sociology, politics, philosophy, religion, and folklore in Hindi alone. His monumental *Madhya Asia ka Itihas*, three primers on the Tibetan language, two Bhojpuri plays, and last, but certainly not the least, fifteen volumes of classical Buddhist texts that he researched, edited, and translated make for a formidable oeuvre.

As told in *Meri Jeevan Yatra*, a multi-volume account of his various travels, literal and metaphorical, an important point in this narrative of growth is the encounter with, conversion to, and movement away from Buddhism. Here, the scholar and the believer have to be disentangled. It is also important to remember that his engagement with philosophy is increasingly coloured by an involvement with the anti-colonial nationalist struggle, and later, with the peasant struggle in Bihar. The addition to this, the class-angle to his analysis of the ills of Indian society has a dual effect: it both draws him towards the Buddha and distances him from Buddhism.

This scholar-traveller found it necessary to travel 'beyond' Buddhism to arrive at Marxism—a philosophy and a practice quite at variance at first glance. His continued scholarly interest in Buddhist Studies till the very end of his life, a vocation often involving considerable personal risk, both physical and financial, seems to refute this argument. He thus emerges as an apparently paradoxical figure—ideologically a Marxist, but also committed scholastically, academically, and even emotionally to Buddha and his legacy.

However, beyond these apparent binaries lies a position, a Middle Way, one that requires that we turn our attention to the philosophical *links* between Buddhism and Marxism. Indeed, it is precisely in the closeness of Buddhism to Marxism that Sankrityayan finds meaning in it. This involves an understanding of Buddhism that underplays the 'religion' in favour of the 'philosophy' and highlights the collective over the individual—a conception of Buddhism that is outward-looking and socially-engaged rather than focused on the inward-looking, meditative, or mystical aspects of some of its traditions. Insofar as Buddhism has deviated historically from these 'preferred' modes of being, he feels free to criticize it as inadequate as an answer to contemporary problems. In 'Buddha or Karl Marx', Ambedkar echoes much of this, though there are significant differences in their *investment* in Buddhism as (*a*) an article of faith and (*b*) a name/identity they wish to adhere to. While each highlighted the similarities and considered the differences between Buddha and Marx, Rahul *moved away* from Buddhism to embrace Marxism, while Ambedkar's trajectory *towards* Buddhism was the last statement he would make.

* * *

Rahul's first encounter with Buddhism was quite unconscious and steeped in ignorance wrought of generations of collective historical amnesia: the Buddha statue worshipped as 'Deehbaba' in his native village, its Buddhist genealogy lost in centuries of neglect. The educated Indian class's new-found appreciation of Buddhism, visible since the early twentieth century, he points out somewhat sardonically, is actually a reunion with its lost soul owing much to the academic interest of Western scholars, especially the Russians, followed by the French and the Germans.[14]

Beyond the 'few lines' taught at school, there was little awareness of Buddhism in his milieu. He recounts a tumbling journey into the heart of the tradition—living and dead—beginning with a pamphlet on Buddhism written in Sanskrit by a Sadhu Khunnilal Shastri that he encountered at age seventeen. Later, travelling via Sarnath, he met some Burmese monks at prayer, hindsight enlightening him to his ignorant failure to connect the root of the Pali word they used (*chakkhu*) with the Sanskrit for 'eye' (*chakshu*) to refer to the Buddha who is also known as *lok chakshu*. Later, in his Arya Samaji phase, he heard more about the views of the Buddhists, which an Arya Samaji proselytizer was obliged to study in order to refute them. Ironically, this had the opposite effect. Meeting the Buddhist monk Bodhananda Mahasthavir, he started an intellectual engagement with Buddhism which took him first to Sri Lanka, and then to Tibet, bringing him in close contact with the *bhikshus* (alm-seekers) Jagdish Kashyap and Ananda Kausalyayana, and of course Anagarika Dharmapala, with whom he made common cause for the restoration of Buddhism's lost glory in the land of its birth.

Buddhism, encountered on his inveterate travel-quest, reinforced Sankrityayan's favoured philosophy of *ghumakkari* or wandering, which he recommends to the nation's youth, encouraging them to revolt against all restrictive structures and orthodoxies, if needed.

This is not a self-justificatory appropriation of a tradition; it is testified to by Buddhist scholars who remind us that the Buddha 'commanded' in Buddhist scripture, the *Mahavagga*, 'Walk, monks, on your tour for the blessing of the many, for the happiness of the many, out of compassion for the world, for the welfare, the blessing and the happiness of *devas* and men. Monks, teach Dhamma.'[15]

As elaborated in *Ghumakkar Shastra*, his delightfully tongue-in-cheek 'treatise for roamers/travellers' that parodies the great shastric tradition to extol the virtues of a secularized variant on the Buddha's injunction, he first considers the various religious traditions that have fostered this 'supreme path': Christianity, Brahmanism, and Islam. Sankaracharya owed his greatness to *ghumakari dharm*, and his followers left their mark as far as Baku in Russia and by the banks of the Volga managed to convert many Christians.[16] But Buddhism is the gem amongst them all due to its radical freedom from the caste-ridden purity/pollution taboos that prevent a free mixing of human beings thus rendering the traveller's enterprise difficult and sometimes impossible. It is only in the Buddhist tradition that a Mongol and an Indian face, or an Asian or a European complexion, create no possibilities of discrimination, he asserts. *Samdarshita* (seeing all equally) and *atmiyata* (geniality/intimacy) are the fundamentals of this creed, as is *swawalamban* (self-reliance). For those who are bhikshus, *bhikshacharya* (alms-seeking), and *atmasamman* (self-respect) have to be balanced like the *mahaan ghumakkar* Buddha did.[17] He recommends everyone learn a handy trade—men can become barbers and women beauticians, for example—which will help earn a living and make for an icebreaker in strange lands. Incidentally, the trades chosen are all 'lower caste' by ascription and the model of travel prescribed is far removed from touristy consumption.

Quite contrary to the insulating effect of the Brahaminical taboos on travel across the oceans, Buddhism encouraged the spread of its rational and universal message via travel through the most difficult terrains, its missionaries heroically transcending all obstacles, be they the mighty Himalayas or the Gobi desert.[18] Likening Bauddha Dharma's universality to the merging of many rivers into one ocean, Sankrityayan celebrates its profoundly humanistic creed.[19] The disappearance of Buddhism from India meant the onset of a dark age of *koop mandukta* (frog-in-the-well mentality).[20]

Rahul's travels can be seen in term of his passionate quest for
knowledge about the origins of ideas and peoples, of which Buddhism
comprised a core element. In his encounter with the Buddha, there
is a shift in his attitude, from that of a devotee to that of a sceptic,
though each category is somewhat permeable. While there is an element of spontaneous *shraddha* (faith/veneration),[21] this is grounded
largely in a philosophical/intellectual regard for the Buddha and
appreciation of the sophistication of Buddhist philosophy, in concepts
such as *pratitya samutpada* (co-dependent origination), *kshanikavada*
(momentariness), and *anatmavada* (theory of no-self).[22]

In his essay called 'Buddhist Dialectics' (referred to earlier),
Sankrityayan explains the continuities between Buddhism and
Marxism. It is easier for someone with a Buddhist background to
understand Marxist philosophy, he says, and links the dialectical
method in Buddhism, its rejection of an eternal soul or a creator god,
and its human-centred approach with some Marxist ideas, though
Buddhism remains for him, in the final analysis, a kind of Hegelian
idealism. He also enumerates many 'irrationalities' that mark
Buddhism and separate the two traditions.

In his massive survey of philosophy from the East and West,
Darshan Digdarshan, he uses Marxist terminology to critique
Buddhism's historically status-quoist character, whereby societal
hierarchy is not actually challenged since debtors, soldiers, and slaves
were not allowed to join the *sangha* (the community of monks), thus
preserving the interests of the royalty and the ruling classes. However,
like fellow Marxists D.P. Chattopadhyay and D.D. Kosambi, and more
recently Uma Chakravarti and Kancha Ilaiah, he accepts, with qualification, Buddhism's socially transformative character. In an argument
one hears in Ambedkar as well, he stresses that the Buddha, born into
the republic of the Sakyas, valued the idea of *ganatantra-prajatantra*
(republicanism-democracy) as opposed to *rajtantra* (monarchy) and
was indeed dreaming of a socialistic world order, which he managed
to establish only in the monastic sangha,[23] though on the previous
page he asserts: 'Ordinary Buddha dharma too, *as religion*, is against
progress.'[24] Thus, while its *philosophical* foundations were radical,
Buddhism's subsequent *institutionalized, historical reality* suggests its
inefficacy to a revolutionary Rahul. The Buddha was a subject of, and
subject to, History.

The historical/materialist perspective with which he viewed Buddhism and its relevance was not merely a matter of an intellectual shift. It is also significant to note his disinterest in the individual *practitioner's* Buddhism, from the very beginning, *insofar as* practice is seen to imply psychological inner work through meditative practice. It is interesting to contrast here Ambedkar's emphasis on *individual* development (discussed later) as a focus, along with the social dimensions, of his choice of Buddhism. Bhikkhu Jagadish Kashyap's reminiscences confirm this. It underscores the nature of (the then bhikkhu) Rahul's interest in Buddhism, or rather his preferred way of serving its cause. In China, while studying Buddhism and translating texts, Bhikkhu Jagadish Kashyap, developing an interest in practising meditation, went to Sri Lanka to commence this project. Instead of supporting him, Rahul took him to task for taking to this 'sedentary' mode of practice. Urging instead that Kashyap engage himself in propagating Buddhism in Europe, he asked him to drop *vriddhyochit yogabhyas* as a practice appropriate for the old and infirm.[25]

Sankrtiyayan focuses on the public implications of Buddhist ideas, as the following excerpt from his essay 'Buddha Aur Gandhi' illustrates:

> Here we are not especially concerned with the issue of which philosophical concepts the Buddha contributed to the stream of human thought. Come, let us focus on his [views on] humanism, love, universal brotherhood, and generosity. Some people hold the wrong view that Mahatma Buddha was an individualist concerned with individual liberation alone. However, this view is deluded. He was not an individualist. One incident from his life proves this point. Once his foster-mother Prajapati Gautami presented him with a piece of cloth woven by herself. He responded by saying that it would be more fitting for her to give that cloth to the sangha (the community of monks) instead, as the sangha is greater than any individual. ... His bodhisattva ideal, according to which one sacrifices oneself over infinite births for the benefit of others, is not an individualistic ideal.[26]

Rahul Sankrityayan's mode of address here is public and focuses on the most universally and easily understood of the Buddha's teachings. The Buddha is for him a 'realist':

> He wants the good of all beings. But he was not a passive dreamer. He was a realist. Thus when he instructed his disciples to set out to work,

inspiring them to propagate the *dharma*, he did not say to them they should direct their efforts to the good of all beings; rather he said that they should travel far and wide for the good of the many. *He knew that the good of the many is sometimes contrary to the interests of some.* Society is divided along opposing interests. In his view, the way primitive man consumed worldly goods was the ideal mode of consumption.[27]

For Sankrityayan, Buddhism's significance lies in its proximity to ideals of an egalitarian social order and the practical problems of making such an order a concrete reality, combining as it did the possibility of social and political work with no reference to a Creator or a permanent Soul. In 1932, he records his nuanced position vis-à-vis Buddhism and the Buddha wherein he distinguishes between the two, marking his distance from the former while testifying to his eternal admiration and respect (shraddha) for the Buddha as the biggest thinker (*vichaarak*) of India.[28] It was a trajectory which gets summed up by one of his closest associates, Bhadant Anand Kausalyayan, as having been marked by three major stages, from soul-affirming theism to soul-denying atheistic idealism to the final one of soul-denying atheistic materialism:

Prayag ki Triveni ki tereh se Rahula ji ki mukhya vichar-sarniyan teen hi rahi hain:
1. *atmavadi, ishwarvadi, adhyatmavadi*
2. *anatmavadi, anishvarvadi, adhyatmavadi*
3. *anatmavadi, anishvarvadi, bhautikavadi.*[29]

The seeds of this philosophical shift can be found in the earlier quote from Rahul. His distinction between 'the good of all' and 'the good of the many' serves to highlight the centrality of class conflict. This growing conviction was fed by his involvement in the peasant's struggle in feudal Bihar, a move that had turned him away from Gandhiji's mainstream Congress movement, which he found riddled with elitism, especially in Bihar, where one of the worst oppressors of poor peasants was a feudal landlord who doubled as an elected Congress candidate. The 1917 revolution in Russia had had a profound impact on him; he had travelled in the Soviet Union, was impressed by what he saw, and his becoming a card-carrying communist underscored his belief in organized struggle as the only means of achieving a just social order.[30] Interestingly, Ambedkar would travel with him until stage three, except that he would reserve his judgement on the *bhautikavadi* part, insisting that 'religion' had an indispensible role in creating the ideal society. It is true that contours of his religion were shaped by the claim of an ethic that responded to a deep sense of historical, material wrong. But he would not give up on the conceptual and even emotive pull of religion, spiritedly taking on the communist charge that religion was an opiate of the masses.

* * *

Ambedkar is thus particularly evocative in the context of Sankrityayan, precisely because both brought to their engagement with Buddhism comparable considerations. At one level, Rahul Sankrityayan could not be further removed from Ambedkar's personal circumstances. Sankrityayan's education was also largely outside the fold of formal structures, especially Western ones, while Ambedkar was trained extensively at some of the premier universities in the West. However, each rejected in important ways the limiting circumstances of their birth and spoke for a kind of modernity that valued a non-theistic, non-ritualistic, egalitarian, and rationally satisfactory philosophical system that could offer social, economic, and political liberation for the downtrodden. While Sankrityayan literally ran away from his caste identity and spent considerable energy throughout his life ridiculing Brahminical taboos (vegetarianism being a particular favourite, but also extending to matrimonial choices), Ambedkar's was a more piquant and urgently felt need to annihilate caste, which he, like Sankrityayan, saw as endemic to Hinduism. Both focused largely on the social, the democratic, and collectivist aspects of Buddhism, to the detriment of the more inward-looking aspects of Buddhist practice. However, while Sankrityayan takes cognizance of Buddhism's multiplicity, warts and all, Ambedkar simply rejects as invalid those traditions and beliefs that do not conform to his notions of a fundamentally 'rational' Buddha.

It is axiomatic to say that Buddhism offers a highly developed psychology and philosophy for individual spiritual growth, while the ideals of *karuna* (compassion), *upaya* (skillful means), and *prajna* (wisdom), the core of Buddhist practice, have obvious social implications. Unlike Sankrityayan, who was content to analyse Buddhism

and, finding it wanting, moved on to Marxism, Ambedkar's harness-
ing of Buddhism to fight the curse of caste resulted in the creation
of Navayana, a fourth yana distinct from Hinayana,[31] Mahayana, and
Vajrayana, and an insistence that he interpreted the Buddha's true
intention therein. His investment in 'Buddhism' was thus of a different order. While he rejected quite categorically some key tenets
of existing traditions of the Dharma as it had been practiced (and
Sankrityayan's approach is living proof of that, else he would not
have felt the need to move away), I also hope to show that there is in
Ambedkar a deeper if muted appreciation of the 'spiritual' aspects of
the tradition, something that is also in keeping with some of the key
tropes in the revival of Buddhism in modern times and contemporary
developments such as 'Engaged Buddhism'.

Historically, Buddhism has combined a culture of inner reflection,
analytic acuity, and collective effort in its creation of a sangha, an envi-
ronment conducive to spiritual development of the hitherto marginalized and deprived. Despite some initial reluctance to the inclusion of
women, the sangha offered women the possibility of spiritual growth
free from the often oppressive institutional pressures of the family,
as the *Therigathas* written by these early converts so joyously indicate.
The *Dhammapada* also redefines the word 'Brahmin' to delink the
category from the idea of birth (inherence) to that of deed (understood
as being of the mind and body). By refuting the authority of the Vedas
and by disregarding caste as a criterion for entry, by the democratic
mode of its functioning (though nuns got short shrift here as well)
and its eschewal, at least at its inception, of private property, the
sangha was acting as a radical social institution.

Buddhist philosophy was innately dynamic and conducive to
change, especially change in rigid social denominations. As the
close textual analysis of Vincent Eltschinger has shown, only recently
made available in English translation, Buddhist philosophers such as
Dharmakirti, Aryadeva, Vasubandhu, Dharamapala, and Chandrakirti
were producing, as late as the sixth to the eighth century AD, long
after the Buddha was gone, sophisticated arguments against the realist interpretation of social denominations, which naturalized caste,
among other categories. As a result, Buddhist polemics against the
innateness of caste were provided with a more rigorous philosophical
foundation. This epistemological and ontological assault on the

notion of caste as 'innate' had limited efficacy, however. As Eltschinger puts it: 'Buddhism has not created a social reform in India, despite various elements in its literature that could have served such purpose. Nonetheless ... Buddhism has developed an original *explanation* of caste, several *arguments* against its naturalization, as well as an unfailing soteriological *abolitionism.*'[32]

Eltschinger's reading does account for the *ambivalence* produced by the theory of karmic retribution, which though never linked to *jati* (sub-caste) or *varna* (caste, but literally 'colour') does invoke the category of *kula* (clan), whereby, depending on one's karma, one may be reborn into a *nich* or *uccakula* (low or high-ranked clan). This would lead to a kind of social determinism, since in practice each family would have belonged to a caste and thus fallen under a statutory denomination, which however 'conventional' (as opposed to 'ultimate' or 'innate'), however defined by professional activity (as the Buddhists understood caste), would yet cause that statutory denomination to be linked to birth, and not just to one's deeds in one's own life. He also warns in conclusion that the polemical texts must be read in the light of historical and epigraphical facts, which lead us to ask questions of the kind that Sankrityayan asks: 'Would a real abolitionist engagement have presented the risk of alienating the monastic order from princely liberalities?'[33]

Sankrityayan, who was an expert on Buddhist logic and had read his Dharmakirti carefully, having recovered and restored the original version of his monumental treatise on logic, *Pramavartika*, would have concurred that there was much philosophical power in the Buddha's challenge to contemporary orthodoxies, caste-as-nature being just one of them. In fact, he deploys Dharmakirti time and again to challenge contemporaries such as a certain 'Karpatri-ji', whose defense of *ramrajya* and attack on communists in *Marxvad aur Ramrajya* he tore into mercilessly in his own *Ramrajya aur Marxvad.*[34] When 'Karpatri-ji' attacks Marx on the ground that he accepts only that as true knowledge which is arrived at with *prayog* (experimentation) and *anubhav* (experience), Sankrityayan reminds him that not only Marx but Dharmakirti too follows this principle for establishing true knowledge, and frontally attacks Karpatri for presenting his ignorance or cunning in the garb of innocence.[35] Contrary to the perception one gets in some writings, such as *Volga se Ganga*'s last chapter, where, in keeping with the dominant contemporary Marxist trends, considerations of class seem to override those of caste, here he takes Karpatri's regressive caste consciousness head on, though again, the category of shudras accompanies other groups such as slaves and women, all equally oppressed under '*ramrajya*'.[36] In his reckoning, Karpatri is a rusty relic, hopelessly behind the times, in an age when caste distinctions are melting away: '*aaj "shudron" ke saath brahmanon ki daal-roti ek ho gayi hai*',[37] he says, with characteristic optimism about progress, noting however that the next state of intermarriage amongst the castes had yet to be achieved.

Having said that, it cannot be denied that caste did not carry the primacy or singularity in Sankrityayan's deliberations as it did for Ambedkar; it was one amongst the many forms of backwardness that a progressive society must discard. The latter's focus on Buddhism was strongly driven by the need to find an indigenous spiritual tradition that offered a critique of caste hierarchy and offered subjective and collective emancipatory possibilities. The historical failures of Buddhism to meet the ideals he found in its *ur* form, he ascribed to later Brahmanical or monkish interventions. For Sankrityayan, Buddhism in its 'ur' form already contained (philosophically) idealist limits. He would have repeated with Marx that philosophers have long interpreted the world; the point is to change it, conceding that perhaps the 'Age' the Buddha lived in was not ready for these ideas to come to fruition. The present age had produced a philosophy suited for the times, namely *dvandvatmak bhautikvad* (dialectical materialism), and it was thus that, in his reckoning, the demands of History won.[38]

Ambedkar came from a location from where not only the ideological questioning of social inequality's *caste* variant but also the urgency to effect social change was a personally felt compulsion, a vocational calling, and a historical possibility. Having explored, employed, and put aside the discourses of law and politics for their inadequacy to effect the *social revolution* that he felt must precede a political and legally secured emancipation of the Untouchables, and convinced that the caste system was not a mere excrescence but a defining feature of the Hindu faith and practice, Ambedkar busied himself in building an argument for *leaving* the Hindu fold as the only way to ensure this social, and psychological, breakthrough.[39] But a 'secular' religion-less identity would not suffice. He agreed with Burke that 'true religion is the foundation of society, the basis on which all Civil Government rests, and both their sanction'.[40] As he put it in *The Annihilation of*

Caste, he thus chose a 'Religion of Principles' to replace 'the ancient rules of life'. Conversion was the Untouchables' *Swaraj*;[41] conversion was the way of breaking 'the chains of *Maharki*',[42] the identity into which his community was eternally fixed at birth; conversion was liberation from both material want and the way to spiritual rebirth. Conversion alone would give access to 'Sympathy, Equality and Liberty, the three essentials for the uplift of the individual'.[43] Ambedkar does not enter into the exact philosophical debates mentioned above, drawing instead extensively on his reading of Western liberal thought,[44] but it is in the Pali scripture that he reads an enabling radical social and political vision of democracy combined with communistic principles (more rigorously implemented in the Buddhist sangha than in the Soviet Union, he asserts), which would also be the 'safest and soundest alternative' to Marx.[45]

This required a considerable editing out of aspects of the received textual tradition, as we find in his treatise, *The Buddha and His Dhamma*, aspects he felt were neither practical nor logical, both criteria constituting for him the core of the Buddha's Way. But that pragmatism and that logic, his understanding of *prajna* (wisdom, knowledge, understanding), was of a mixed pedigree and, as Meera Nanda has argued, perhaps a little too forcefully, had a distinctly Deweyan character.[46] There is a Buddhistic echo—of the theory of momentariness, on being in the present—in Dewey that Ambedkar quotes in *The Annihilation of Caste*: 'An individual can only live in the present. ... The principle which makes little of the present act of living and growing, naturally looks upon the present as empty and upon the future as remote. Such a principle is inimical to progress, and is a hindrance to a strong and steady current of life.' However, one could argue that the robust American utilitarianism of the quote does not sit well with some of the currents of Buddhist meditation on the meaning of 'being present'. And the word 'progress' in the mid-twentieth century had acquired connotations that the Buddha had not dreamt of.

* * *

I regard the Buddha's Dhamma to be the best. ... If a modern man who knows science must have a religion, the only religion he can have is the religion of the Buddha.[47]

It is appropriate that Ambedkar's first memory of the Buddha be connected to 'progress', a moment of success in formal education, and an event that marked a personal achievement which was necessarily also a social and collective one. A Mahar had, for the first time, passed the Fourth Level English Examination, and to mark the event, a small ceremony took place at which the Marathi social reformer Dada Keluskar presented him with a book he had written on the Buddha. In his own narrative, this book moved Ambedkar deeply and impressed him enough to question the predilection of his father, who was a *kabirpanthi*, for telling his children stories from the *Ramayana* and the *Mahabharata*, books which irked him for their negative depiction of Untouchables and glorification of less than ethical conduct.[48]

One could say that a Western liberal notion of the individual segues into the Buddha's exhortation to test even his words against (even the follower's) experience and judgement. As we will see later, this has to be balanced with the idea of taking refuge (*sharana*) in the Triple Gem as a preliminary step to the practice of the doctrine of *anatta* (no self), as well as the parallel stress in the same tradition on community, on the sangha (one of the *Triratnas*).[49] Ambedkar goes on to adopt, adapt, and often downright reject many key tenets of the received Buddhist tradition in his posthumously published treatise *The Buddha and His Dhamma*, a move that earned him considerable criticism from various quarters. The *Maha Bodhi* journal called it a dangerous book that gave a 'new orientation' to Buddhism by seeing it only as a social system, and one which was 'based on hatred' rather than compassion. Dhananjay Keer suggests that it be called 'Ambedkarayan or Buddhist New Testament',[50] referring no doubt to Ambedkar's assertion of 'the need for the production of a Buddhist Bible'[51] since 'we must now copy some of the ways of the Christians in order to propagate our religion among the Buddhist people'.[52]

As is now well known, the revival of Buddhism in South Asia, and specially Sri Lanka, had a marked Christian connection. The *Light of Asia*, a poem in Victorian verse by Edwin Arnold published in 1879, became immensely popular and had inspired even Dharmanand Kosambi. The Theosophist Colonel Henry Olcott had published in 1881 the enormously popular and influential *The Buddhist Catechism* and a good deal of what followed in the name of Buddhist revival in Sri Lanka had clear Protestant Christian, as well as racist, elements. Most critical was the part played by Anagarika Dharmapala, a protégé of Olcott, who came to India on a mission to restore the control of Maha Bodhi Temple back to the Buddhists and to revive Buddhism. His understanding of Buddhism was already coloured by a reaction to Christian missionary activity and a resurgent Sinhala Nationalism, the full force of which has been visible in Sri Lanka lately. If Olcott, the white man, shouldered his burden by giving the Orientals back *The Buddhist Catechism*, Ambedkar, the empowered Untouchable, reclaimed that ancient legacy—with a rationalism that went quite counter to the 'healer–miracle worker' Theosophist—for his community and beyond with a 'Buddhist Bible' in the form of the *Buddha and His Dhamma*. In Ambedkar's stance, the implicit response to the power and threat of Christianity resulting paradoxically in a kind of mimicry of that which is repudiated, instead of being seen as an isolated and eccentric feature, should be understood within the frame of the larger history of Buddhist revival on the subcontinent.

Birth as motif and metaphor pervades the language of religious traditions. The caste system sees the upper caste as *dwija*, the twice born, consecrated via the sacred thread ceremony that performs the going forth of the young caste-Hindu male as *brahmachari* (a celibate student-seeker, entering the first *ashrama* [stage] of the traditional caste-Hindu male's life). Ambedkar's battle against caste exclusion interestingly enough reworked this motif in its own way. We know from *The Buddha and His Dhamma* that Ambedkar denied the Four Noble Truths their primacy in the received Buddhist tradition on the grounds that it made the faith 'pessimistic' and was a later accretion. He argued, in keeping with his world-affirming focus, that rather than seeing birth or existence itself as suffering, suffering was better seen as a social and material phenomenon that the Buddha wanted to end (and that nirvana was nothing but a just social order). Here, Ambedkar seems to be taking a rather literal view of the First Noble Truth.

It is important here to examine an interesting variation on the polyvalence of 'birth', found in the modern teacher Buddhadasa Bhikkhu's 1969 lecture delivered in Thailand, aptly titled 'Another Kind of Birth'. This can be seen as part of a larger trend towards readings of the

Buddhist scripture to meet pragmatic contemporary needs. His gloss goes as follows:

In *everyday language* the term birth refers simply to physical birth from a mother's body; in *Dhamma language* birth refers to a mental event arising out of ignorance, craving, and clinging. Whenever there arises the mistaken 'I', the 'I' had been born; its parents are ignorance and craving. The kind of birth that constitutes a problem for us is mental birth. Anyone who fails to grasp this point will never succeed in understanding anything of the Buddha's teaching.[53]

Identifying clinging to a delusory 'I' as the source of suffering, Buddhadasa Bhikkhu stays close to the Buddha's *ontological* statement on anatta as also the related *ethical* fallout of this principle in the sense of abandoning a false, clinging ego consciousness that leads to deluded, selfish behaviour. However, traditional exegeses have also seen this existential pronouncement on *dukkha* (the First Noble Truth, namely that existence is suffering) in a more literal sense, as a fundamental disillusionment with *samsara* (the world, with all its entanglements), which then supports the logic of *sanyas* or renunciation. Buddhadasa Bhikkhu performs a creative interpretive feat in rendering this teaching acceptably 'world-affirming' and 'non-metaphysical' insofar as birth becomes a metaphor and freedom from this birth-as-suffering requires a recognition of the false clinging ego as the root of suffering. The solution then is to cultivate 'clear awareness', by 'keeping close watch on the mind', not letting samsara be born, while continuing to inhabit the physical samsara.[54] 'If a person experiences dozens of births a day he has to suffer dozens of times a day; if he does not experience birth at all, he has no suffering at all.'[55] Now, this is a reading of the Buddha's (possible) metaphysics as metaphor, a reading which is also non-materialist. In this psychologized/internalized understanding of dukkha, suffering is understood as a subjective *mental* event, and not through the objective conventional interpretation of suffering as physical pain, loss, or deprivation. (The Tibetan tradition glosses suffering at multiple levels, where even conventional happiness is a form of disguised suffering.) Ambedkar, who was leaning towards reading dukkha as 'exploitation' or 'poverty' and celebrating the fact that the 'foundation' on which Marx rested was 'already laid' in Buddhism, would have, one guesses, little sympathy for such a view.[56]

For, in the rebirth that he fashioned for himself and which he so passionately and forcefully advocated for his community, is the willed annihilation of one socio-religious identity, the Hindu one, and a willed birth into a new social identity, as a Buddhist. It is public; it is, one could argue, egoic. Ambedkar does not denigrate the world; he just wants a world built on the slogans of Liberty, Equality, and Fraternity. This, he asserted, was derived not from the French Revolution but from Buddhist sources. Achieving this social nirvana is best done via the ancient (and significantly, indigenous) philosophy of the Buddha, after resurrecting the Buddha's *intended* meaning from under all the accretions of the ages, which he interprets through the filters of logic, reason, and efficaciousness.

He upholds the value of wealth, defending Buddhism against the communist charge that religion, specifically Christianity, 'sublimates poverty and weakness', since 'to acquire wealth legitimately and justly, earned by great industry, amassed by strength of the arm and gained by the sweat of the brow is a great blessing'.[57] He further asserts that 'a religion which does not recognize the individual is not acceptable to me ... individual welfare and progress (individual development) should be the real aim of religion'.[58] The question that might arise is: is the Buddha's teaching on anatta, so central to Sankrityayan's understanding of Buddhism, compromised by this focus on an assertive 'self'-consciousness that Ambedkar powerfully harnesses for his cause? Is there a chance of reification of the 'self', which the Buddha identifies as the root cause of ignorance and suffering? In his pressing need to focus on the decidedly worldly nature of the Untouchables' suffering (since *shastra*-recommended metaphysical 'other'-worldliness could and was used to defend the oppressive status quo), does Ambedkar forget something essential in the message of the Buddha, his *margadata* (the path-giver)?[59]

We saw that Sankritayayan's 'shraddha' has a rational component. How might one read Ambedkar's use of the word 'spiritual', oft-repeated in his speeches on conversion, especially in his denial of communism as the emancipatory path? Is his 'spiritual' a mental or rational faculty against which he often tests received Buddhist scriptural traditions? For he does seem to make a somewhat dualist

hierarchical distinction between spirit and matter in his 1936 speech
to the Mahars regarding conversion:

> For myself I have taken my decision. My conversion is sure. *My conversion is not for any material gain*. There is nothing I cannot achieve
> by remaining as an Untouchable. *Nothing but spirituality* is at the base
> of my conversion. The Hindu religion does not appeal to my reason.
> The Hindu religion does not appeal to my self-respect. However, *for
> you*, for spiritual as well as for material gains conversion is must.
> Some persons mock at the idea of conversion for material gain.
> I do not feel hesitant in calling such person as fools. A religion which
> preaches what will or will not happen to the soul after death, may be
> useful for the rich. They may entertain themselves by thinking over
> such religion at their own leisure ... *what is the use of this rich and idle
> people's Vedanta to the poor?*[60]

Much is worth noting here, strikingly, the fundamental distinction of social class, thus marking his conversion as affording the
'luxury' of a 'spiritual' raison d'etre. Notably, though, the 'spiritual'
here is construed in terms of the demands of 'reason' and of 'self-respect', *not* the transcendence of the rational or of the concept of
the self. Much spiritualism—Buddhist or otherwise—stresses surrender and the annihilation of the 'self' as the key to the spiritual
path. Not so for Ambedkar, though Dhananjay Keer stresses that
Ambedkar was deeply religious, that he thanked unseen powers in
times of difficulty, and that he bowed daily in front of the Buddha
image—all this suggesting spiritual surrender. Further, even
when differentiating between his spiritual and the poor Mahars'
economic reasons for conversion, though without denigrating the
latter, he underscores the primacy of the lived existential reality as
seen in material terms. He is careful to pragmatically balance the
spiritual and the material: 'Carlyle called Political Economy a Pig
Philosophy. Carlyle was of course wrong. For man needs material
comforts.'[61]

However, in developing his critique of Marxism and communism,
it is precisely the *surplus* need for the 'spiritual' that he emphasizes,
and again a 'progressive', hierarchical model of society is suggested
that curiously distinguishes between 'the backward countries' and
others. Further, a deeper sense of the Buddhist teaching on 'self'
emerges: after having proven that Buddhism contains the best and

most valid insights of Marxism *without* the violence endemic to
Marxism, he concludes:

> The Buddha's way is not to force people to do what they did not like to
> do although it was good for them. His way was to *alter the disposition* of
> men so that they would do voluntarily what they would not otherwise
> do. It has been claimed that the Communist Dictatorship in Russia has
> wonderful achievements to its credit. There can be no denial of it. That
> is why I say that a Russian Dictatorship would be good for all *back-*
> *ward* countries. But this is no argument for Permanent Dictatorship.
> *Humanity does not want only economic values, it also wants spiritual*
> *values to be retained.* Permanent Dictatorship has paid no attention to
> spiritual values.[62]

Earlier, Ambedkar explicates the nature of Buddha's teaching on
nibbana (Skt. nirvana), especially on the hindrances to Liberation:

> The Buddha called them the ten *Asavas*, fetters or hindrances. The
> first ... is the Delusion of Self. So long as man is wholly occupied
> with himself, chasing after every bauble that he vainly thinks will
> satisfy the cravings of the heart, there is no noble path for him. Only
> when his eyes are opened to the fact that he is but *a tiny part of a*
> *measureless whole*, only when he begins to realize how impermanent
> a thing is his *temporary individuality*, can he ever enter upon this
> narrow path.[63]

I quote this to point to the dialectical balance between the individu-
alist self-assertion that Ambedkar elsewhere upholds as essential
to his choice of a religion and a more profound Buddhist philosophical
understanding of the tenuousness of the self as a co-dependently
arisen non/entity. (And just as he celebrates the just accumulation
of wealth, and does not glorify poverty, he also points out that since
everything is impermanent, there ought to be no struggle for property.) *Both* assertions find support in Buddhist scripture. There are
two moves that Ambedkar is engaging in simultaneously: one is
aimed at raising dalit awareness which needs to stress the individual
self's capacities, its ability to be 'a sun unto itself', since a centuries-
deep denial of a 'self'-hood needs to be undone, and a (collective and
individual) self re-cognized and re-created. It is a move made earlier,
though under slightly different conditions and with somewhat different focus, by Iyothee Thass.[64]

However, the Ambedkar who sees the ethical and philosophical *limitations* of this individualism cites scriptural authority to uphold a profounder philosophic principle of anatta, one which is central to Buddha Dhamma, which posits the illusion of a separate, egoic self as a form of ignorance regarding the true nature of reality, *avidya*, which is ultimately the root cause of suffering, in Buddhist terms, in all traditions. One also has to understand the context in which these ideas are explicated. Ambedkar was speaking to ordinary men and women who had suffered much and whose primary needs he wished to address in simple terms. So the difficult task of bridging the two levels of 'self'—the conventional one with which we live and act, politically or otherwise, and the deeper truth of it being merely an aggregate of the *panchskandhas*—is his, and he manages it well here.[65] The dangers of the *reification* of that self in the form of an *identity* is a familiar paradox, and one that Buddhism, historically, has not been immune to.

Ambedkar's conversion was not without its ironies. The British Buddhist Sangharakshita, who knew Ambedkar personally, argued that 'his real significance consists in the fact that it was he who established a revived Indian Buddhism on a firm foundation', and suggested that 'the statue standing outside the parliament building in Delhi should really depict him holding *The Buddha and His Dhamma* underneath his arm and pointing—not for the benefit of the Untouchables only, but for the benefit of all mankind—in the direction of the Three Jewels'.[66] Bhikhhus like Mahasthavir Chandramani, however, issued a leaflet stating that Buddhism and Hinduism were branches of the same tree,[67] while the *Indian Express* (Bombay) congratulated Dr Ambedkar on becoming a good dwija via this religious rebirth and said: 'One is glad, however, that even while recoiling from the traditional Hindu social order, he chose another essentially Indian way which, like Sikhism, Brahmoism and the Arya Samaj, is only a variant of Hinduism.' Savarkar baldly declared that the Buddhist Ambedkar was a Hindu Ambedkar.[68] The *Hitwad* (Nagpur) hailed it as the most significant development of the century, noting that 'paradoxically enough, Dr. Ambedkar, a highly rationalistic and scientific thinker stands in line with Emperor Ashok and others of historic memory, as the *High Prophet* of Buddhist faith'.[69] The final irony, perhaps, was that Ambedkar, who lauded the Buddha for not claiming to be a prophet, should have been read in terms of this semitic category, and that for all the rationalism he wished to inculcate, to the extent of removing from his version of Buddhism all that offended 'reason', including the basic tenets of the Four *Arya Satya* (the Noble Truths), the theory of karma and rebirth, the traditional story of the Buddha's *parivraja* (renunciation of home to become a wandering mendicant), and the refuge in the Triple Gem,[70] he himself came to be deified.

But then, perhaps this reassertion of the category of 'faith' has a lesson vis-à-vis the limits of 'reason'. And to come back to the beginning, how does one determine the 'truth' of a particular reading of a religion? Who speaks for the 'authentic' Buddhism? Suffice it to say with Wilfred Cantwell Smith, and keeping in mind Ambedkar's argument against Gandhi's defence of Hinduism, and the subsequent exchange between them, that the beliefs and practices of the adherents of a faith rather than scholarly exegeses of textual traditions alone must determine what the faith 'means'. Buddhism's long history across a wide geographical spread, with concomitantly different modes of monastic and lay organization, make it difficult to talk about it in the singular, specially with reference to forms of social organization and the balance of 'rationality' and 'faith'. The debate on whether it is a religion or a philosophy rages on.[71]

It is precisely this rich and long tradition of hermeneutical diversity and instability, Christopher Queen argues, that allows us to read Ambedkar's version not as a deviation but as the latest in a long history of Buddhist exegeses.[72] The notion of the ur-tradition thus gets rendered irrelevant. Between and beyond Queen's invocation of postmodernism to understand Ambedkar (who rejects all available master narratives to forge his own amalgam), and Meera Nanda's reading of him creating an Enlightenment Deweyan Buddha (she following a decidedly anti-postmodern line of argument), lies the meaning of Ambedkar's multiple negotiations with religion and politics. Even as this is being written, the process of re-reading Ambedkar continues apace, in politically contentious and urgent ways, with red, blue, and saffron being deployed in multiple permutations and combinations on our university campuses, streets, and, not least, in the highest political office.[73] In the midst of much rhetoric and political posturing, historically situated and textually sound attempts, such as Anand

Teltumbde's most recent reclamation of an Ambedkar who can be in conversation with Marxism, make for compelling and thought-provoking reading, even if they go against the grain of certain dominant strains within dalit discourse.[74]

The ultimate significance of Ambedkar lies, perhaps, in what he means to the people he dedicated his efforts to, a community he helped forge and for whom he works both in the domain of spiritual affect and political effect. However, it is significant to consider that the 'community' he spoke for is not an unproblematic singular but contains several claimants, and those who look to him to light their path might well exceed those marked by caste-as-birth and take into its sweep a wider human one. He was of his time, and of 'his' people, but his relevance for our times and 'other' people might require dynamic acts of reading and re-reading that pay tribute to his own original, evolving, engaged, and defiant self-fashioning.

In this, like Sankrityayan, Ambedkar is true to the Buddha's message urging each of his disciples to be a lamp unto oneself and to travel, seek, test, and examine. Each is a significant actor in the story of Buddhist 'revival' in India. Each sought liberation here and now, in history, as a materially palpable goal, making light of much that was 'transcendental' in the received tradition. The urgency of this acutely felt and lived sense of injustices unites them, their divergent paths bridging Buddha and Marx, compelling a closer look at the continued relevance of the two seekers of liberation, individual and collective.

Notes and References

1. Kancha Ilaiah, *God as Political Philosopher*, 3rd ed. (Kolkata: Samya, 2010), 2.

2. B.R. Ambedkar, *Buddha or Karl Marx* (Delhi: Siddharth Books, 2009 [1945]), 5.

3. Rahul Sankrityayan, *Meri Jeevan Yatra II* (Delhi: Radhakrishna Prakashan, 2002 [1950]), 82.

4. Eleanor Zelliot (*Ambedkar's Conversion* [New Delhi: Critical Quest, 2005], 20) imputes from this that Ambedkar was familiar with the elder Kosambi's work, but there is a curious silence regarding him and his possible influence in discussions by or of Ambedkar.

5. One is led to believe that their varying attitudes to Gandhi might have something to do with this. Towards the end of his life, failing health led

Kosambi, who was deeply impressed with the confluence of Buddhist ideas of ahimsa and Gandhian thought, to choose the Jaina practice of *sallekhana* to gradually give up his life. He chose Sevagram Ashram where Gandhi, who demurred initially, agreed to accept him as an inmate. Also known as *santhara*, Sallekhana is a Jain practice of voluntarily fasting to death by gradually reducing the intake of food, especially when death is found to be approaching. The Jains see the practice as non-violent and do not consider it to be suicide.

6. Rahul Sankrityayan, *Buddhism: The Marxist Approach* (Delhi: People's Publishing House, 1970), 1–28.

7. Rahul Sankrityayan, *Darshan Digdarshan* (Allahabad: Kitab Mahal, 2007 [1944]), 408–10.

8. His avowedly Marxist son, D.D. Kosambi, has had much better luck with scholarly attention, though even there his unorthodox Marxism and polymathic persona make him a difficult case for orthodox Marxists.

9. Some of Kosambi's works have recently been translated into English by his granddaughter, Meera Kosambi. *Nivedan,* an autobiographical account of his travels, was published in 2012, while *Dharmanand Kosambi: The Essential Writings* came out in 2010.

10. Of the ten questions on which the Buddha is silent (*akathaniya*), four relate to whether the universe (*lok*) is eternal or not; two relate to whether *jeev* (soul substance) and *sharir* (body) are one or not; and four to what happens to the Tathagatas (lit. the 'Thus Gone Ones', the Liberated) after Nirvana. Sankrityayan vehemently critiques Radhakrishnan's attempt to read into these silences an implicit validation of the Upanishads (*Darshan Digdarshan,* 407–10).

11. Though the fourteenth Dalai Lama has had a personal fascination with science and endorses research projects worldwide such as the Mind-Life Project, he makes it clear that for *Buddhists,* the *pramana* need not be scientific empiricism, that *they* do not need scientists to validate their understanding. He also maintains that there are some spiritual experiences that escape scientific reason and machines. However, he has been willing to discard publicly certain textual Buddhist cosmological claims that modern astronomy has disproved.

12. Epigraph to Sankrityayan's autobiography, *Meri Jeevan Yatra,* paraphrasing the Buddha's advice in the *Majjhima Nikaya.*

13. Readers in Bengal, Kerala, and Maharashtra, especially of an older generation, are aware of some of his writings, primarily *Volga se Ganga,* especially as translated into these respective languages. Very recently, a biography in English has been published, the terms of its framing requiring considerable qualification.

14. Rahul Sankrityayan, 'Bhadant Bodhananda Mahastavir', in *Rahul Vangmaya—2.2: Jeevani aur Sansmaran* (New Delhi: Radhakrishna, 2008 [1994]), 402–3.

15. Lal Mani Joshi, *Studies in the Buddhistic Culture of India* (Delhi: Motilal Banarsidass, 1967), 350.

16. Rahul Sankrityayan, *Ghumakkar Shastra* (Allahabad: Kitab Mahal, 1992), 10.

17. Sankrityayan, *Ghumakkar Shastra*, 27.

18. Sankrityayan, 'Bhadant Bodhananada Mahastavir', 403.

19. Sankrityayan, *Ghumakkar Shastra*, 59.

20. Sankrityayan, *Ghumakkar Shastra*, 10.

21. His recollection of his first Buddhist pilgrimage when still a young man inspired by Fa-Hien's travels is deeply moving; but he recollects seeing the relics of Sariputra and Maudgalyayan at the Kensigton Museum in London in 1932, as a bhikku, with great 'shraddha' though in the same breath mentions not being able to take up Anagarika Dharmapala's desire to have him as a successor since he did not see such 'shraddha' in himself towards 'dharma' (*Meri Jeevan Yatra II*, 105).

22. Bhikku Jagdish Kashyap, who credits Sankrityayan with igniting his interest and faith in the Buddha, has an interesting episode to relate which points to what Sankrityayan considered significant in Buddhism. He recalls their first meeting, when Rahul Sankrityayan, a Bhikshu then, handed the younger man a text where the speaker urges his disciples to accept only that which has been proved by individual exercise of reason, rejecting the testimony of all texts, received opinion and teachers, even his own. This was, of course, as Jagdish Kashyap realized to his surprise, an episode from the life of the Buddha, an episode whose choice indicates how Sankrityayan would value this very spirit of enquiry in Buddhism ('*Rahulaji: Mere Gurubhai*', in *Rahula Smriti*, edited by Ramsharan Sharma 'Munshi' and Pushpamala Jain [New Delhi: People's Publishing House, 1988], 206).

23. '*Ve bhi duniya ke samyavaadi banane ka sapna dekhte the*' (*Meri Jeevan Yatra II*, 105).

24. *Meri Jeevan Yatra II*, 104 (emphasis added).

25. '*Rahulji: Mere Guru Bhai*', 208.

26. Sankrityayan, *Rahula Vangmaya*, 426. Ambedkar curiously quotes the same incident from Pali scripture, though he also takes greater pains to establish the value of 'the individual' in Buddhism.

27. Sankrityayan, *Rahula Vangmaya*, 426 (emphasis added).

28. Sankrityayan, *Rahula Vangmaya*, 105. The belief in rebirth held him for a while; at least till 1935 he records being unable to discard this view outright (*Meri Jeevan Yatra II*, 191).

29. 'Rahulji ka Bauddha Sahitya aur Daarshanik Chintan', in *Rahula Smriti*, 299.
30. Sankrityayan does not fully spell out his position on the question of vio-
    lence. As a communist, he was not committed to non-violence, though
    having been a satyagrahi, the actual modes of protest he had most
    adopted were those institutionalized by Gandhi. He suffered a serious
    head injury as a result of a police lathi-charge during a protest march. In
    his very late essay 'Buddha and Gandhi', written probably after Gandhi's
    assassination, he expressly brings the past and the present together to
    suggest how the two great individuals represent related yet different
    modes of tackling social and political problems. In this engaging analysis,
    which is also a tribute to both sons of India, the Buddha, described as the
    'greatest of India's sons', is yet found wanting in his egalitarianism. In
    a surprising shift from his Marxist critique of him as a bourgeois agent,
    he grew to find Gandhi going even further than the Buddha in actively
    opposing human inequality, but concedes that perhaps the historical
    circumstances in which the two functioned were different, making it
    unnecessary for Buddha to do what Gandhi did.
31. It is customary amongst several Buddhists to prefer the term 'Theravada',
    to avoid the connotations of 'lesser' or 'lower' in '*hina*'.
32. Vincent Eltschinger, 'Foreword', in *Caste and Buddhist Philosophy:
    Continuity of Some Buddhist Arguments against the Realist Interpretation
    of Social Denominations*, translated by Raynald Prévèreau, Buddhist
    Tradition Series (Delhi: Motilal Banarsidass, 2012), xvii, emphasis mine.
33. Eltschinger, *Caste and Buddhist Philosophy*, 173–4.
34. *Ramrajya* is literally 'Rama's rule'. In Karpatri's formulation, it is an idea
    of India based on an idealized conception of Rama's rule, including,
    here, traditionally 'Hindu', shastra-ordained beliefs and practices. This
    can be contrasted to M.K. Gandhi's use of the same term, which tended
    towards a more generalized set of spiritual ideals as guiding forces.
35. Rahul Sankrityayan, *Ramrajya aur Marxvad* (New Delhi: Peoples'
    Publishing House, 1959), 94.
36. Sankrityayan, *Ramrajya aur Marxvad*, 51–9.
37. Sankrityayan, *Ramrajya aur Marxvad*, 56–7.
38. 'Buddhist *vigyanvad*, like Hegel's, had also been performing *seersasana*
    (headstand) with the head below and feet above. Marx rid Hegel of this,
    and it is he who would liberate Buddhist *vigyanvad* as well' (Sankrityayan,
    Ramrajya aur Marxvad, 97).
39. B.R. Ambedkar, 'What Way Emancipation?', speech on 31 May 1936, in
    Conversion as Emancipation (New Delhi: Critical Quest, 2004), 20–1.
40. Dr Babasaheb Ambedkar, *Writings and Speeches (BAWS)*, vol. 1–17 (Bombay:
    Government of Maharashtra, Department of Education, 1982), 76.

41. Ambedkar, *Conversion as Emancipation*, 33.
42. Ambedkar, *Conversion as Emancipation*, 35.
43. Ambedkar, *Conversion as Emancipation*, 16.
44. It is interesting to note the eclecticism of Ambedkar's intellectual borrowings. The conservative Burke, harshest critic of the Jacobins, is quoted alongside the tripartite slogan of the French Revolution, to argue for his embrace of Buddhism in *The Annihilation of Caste*.
45. B.R. Ambedkar, 'Buddhism and Communism', speech at The Fourth Conference of the World fellowship of Buddhists in Nepal, 20 November 1956, in *Buddha or Karl Marx* (New Delhi: Critical Quest, 1987), 29.
46. B.R. Ambedkar, 'A Broken People Defend Science', in *Breaking the Spell of Dharma and Other Essays* (Gurgaon: Three Essays Collective, 2007), 31–83.
47. B.R. Ambedkar, 'Preface', in *The Buddha and His Dhamma*, edited by Akash Singh Rathore and Ajay Verma (Delhi: Oxford University Press, 2011), xxvi.
48. This contradicts his biographer Dhananjay Keer's rendition of this phase: 'Three personalities [Buddha, Kabir and Phule] influenced the life and actions of this great man, besides the stories from the *Mahabharata* and *Ramayana* which he heard with rapt attention in his childhood' (472). One gets the sense repeatedly that Keer is keen to absorb Ambedkar into an 'acceptable' Hindu devotional fold.
49. At his conversion in October 1956, Ambedkar was reluctant until the very end to take refuge in the sangha, convinced it was a bunch of 'idlers'. He made no effort to start an order of bhikkus in Maharashtra.
50. Dhananjay Keer, *Dr. Ambedkar: Life and Mission* (Bombay: Popular Prakashan, 1962), 518.
51. Zelliot, *Ambedkar's Conversion*, 21.
52. Ambedkar, 'Buddhism and Communism', 30.
53. Buddhadasa Bhikku, 'Another Kind of Birth', translated by R.B. (lecture delivered at Phatthalung, Thailand, 16 July 1969) (undated pamphlet printed at Shivporn Limited Partnership, Bangkok, Thailand), 1 (emphasis added).
54. Here samsara refers to the network (and net) of entanglements, especially mental constructions, attachment to which is seen as the root cause of suffering.
55. Bhikku, 'Another Kind of Birth', 16.
56. Ambedkar, *Buddha or Karl Marx*, 26.
57. Ambedkar, *Buddha or Karl Marx*, 21–2. Indeed, this would be the point of the difference between him and the Marxist Sankrityayan, as evidenced in fictionalized form in *Volga se Ganga*.

58. B.R. Ambedkar, 'What Way Emancipation?', speech delivered at Dadar, 31 May 1936, in *Conversion as Emancipation* (New Delhi: Critical Quest, 2004), 8. Interestingly, the fact that both Hinduism and Marxism (unlikely bedfellows!) do not recognize individuals but are 'based on a class concept' is given as a reason, separately, for rejecting both.

59. Ambedkar uses the term 'margadata' for his understanding of the Buddha, as contrasted to an understanding of him as *mokshadata* (the giver of salvation).

60. Ambedkar, 'What Way Emancipation?', 37–8 (emphasis added).

61. Ambedkar, *Buddha or Karl Marx*, 23.

62. Ambedkar, *Buddha or Karl Marx*, 22 (emphasis added).

63. Ambedkar, *Buddha or Karl Marx*, 10 (emphasis added).

64. See G. Aloysius' sociologically inflected exposition of anti-caste mobilization under Iyothee Thassar. In a monograph tellingly titled *Dalit-Subaltern Emergence in Religio-Cultural Subjectivity: Iyothee Thassar and Emanicipatory Buddhism* (New Delhi: Critical Quest, 2007), Aloysius makes a case for the dual process—confrontational as well as creative—involved in Iyothee Thassar's project of deploying a re-reading of history—the Untouchables were originally Buddhists, in his reading—and mass conversion as a return and recovery of a subjectivity-affirming Buddhism, a strategy for dalit emancipation in the Madras Presidency. Seeing the 'struggle for modern *subjectivity*' as also 'a quest for a *collective* identity', (27, emphases added), reminds us that this 'recovery of self' necessarily combines the 'individual' and the 'corporate' (29).

65. In Buddhist teachings, the *panchskandha*s are the Five Aggregates that come together to constitute the person: while different schools of Buddhism gloss them differently, simply put, they are: *rupa* (form), *vedana* (sensation), *samjna* (perception), *sanskara* (mental formation), and *vijnana* (consciousness). There is no concept of an eternal, essential *atman* (self) in the teachings of the Buddha.

66. Sangharakshita, *Ambedkar and Buddhism* (Glasgow: Windhorse Publication, 1986), 13.

67. Keer, *Dr. Ambedkar*, 500.

68. Keer, *Dr. Ambedkar*, 500.

69. Keer, *Dr. Ambedkar*, 500 (italics added).

70. Queen points out that 'Max Weber depicted ancient Buddhism as an anti-political status religion, more precisely a religious "technology" of wandering and of intellectually schooled mendicant monks'. He shows that most recent scholarship has upheld this view ('Introduction: The Shapes and Structures of Engaged Buddhism', in *Engaged Buddhism: Buddhist Liberation Movements in Asia*, edited by Christopher Queen and

Sally King [Albany: SUNY Press, 1996], 17). This is more in keeping with Sankrityayan's final understanding; Ambedkar turns this on its head, especially in his upholding of the householder's role. He is, however, not singular, as Queen's book shows, but part of the movement of modern Engaged Buddhists across Asia, who turn their attention from the 'supramundane to the mundane', and mould the tradition to socially and politically transformative ends.

71. Though the fourteenth Dalai Lama has resolutely and consistently emphasized the essential doctrinal similarities between Theravada and Mahayana, underscoring the fact that the essential truth of the Four Noble Truths and the doctrine of Dependent Origination and *Sunyata* are the core of Buddhist philosophy, just as compassion is the core of Buddhist practice, and that the *Vinaya* is as important for a *bhikshu* in the lamaistic tradition as it is for a Theravada one, and that we need to revive the 'Nalanda Tradition', the very fact that the point needs to be made reminds us of the historical fact that these streams have developed differently and often have made rival claims to authenticity in the past. Conversations between followers of Ambedkar and other schools are still rare due to the perceived difference of Navayana from existing Buddhist traditions. Significantly, groups such as the Triratna Bauddha Sangha (originally founded by Englishman Sangharakshita, close to Ambedkar) that work with neo-Buddhists have sought to bridge this gap somewhat and teach Buddhism with equal emphasis on *sila* (code of ethics), *Samadhi* (meditative awareness), and *prajna* (wisdom, knowing the true nature of reality) and to this end conduct meditation retreats as an essential part of their activities (interview with Dh. Subhuti).

72. Christopher Queen, 'Dr. Ambedkar and the Hermeneutics of Buddhist Liberation', in *Engaged Buddhism*.

73. The colours representing Marxism, Ambedkarite Buddhism, and a form of Hindutva, respectively. Interestingly, the international Buddhist flag that dalit organizations such as the Bhim Army also deploy quite visibly during their political rallies such as the large ones in Delhi held in May and June 2017 is a multi-coloured rainbow medley first designed in nineteenth-century Sri Lanka.

74. Speaking of 'Ambedkar against Marxism' as 'an axiom', he writes: 'It has become such a fixed idea that even if Ambedkar arrived today and took up cudgels for the Dalit masses, he would be condemned as anti-Ambedkar' ('Introduction', in *B.R. Ambedkar: India and Communism* [New Delhi: Leftword, 2017], 13).

8

M.G. RANADE AND BHAKTI AS A NEW GRAMMAR FOR INDIAN POLITICAL LIFE

APARNA DEVARE

In this chapter, I want to explore one instance of how ideas and practices of bhakti[1] were reinterpreted to influence new forms of political life in India during the colonial period. I look at the religious writings of M.G. Ranade, a prominent social reformer in nineteenth-century colonial India and one of the founding leaders of the Indian National Congress.[2] He was associated with what in Indian historiography are known as the 'moderates' in the nationalist movement in contrast to the 'extremists', such as Bal Gangadhar Tilak, who were more militant in their demands and methods against the British. Ranade, a high court judge (more popularly known as 'Justice' Ranade) in the colonial administration in the Bombay Presidency, focused primarily on social reforms dealing with matters of Hindu religious custom and practices.

The second half of the eighteenth century saw sustained efforts by upper-caste male 'reformers', especially in Bombay Presidency and Bengal—the epicentres of British rule—to bring about change in traditional Hindu practices drawing from colonial ideas with respect to upper-caste women in particular, though such reformers also questioned caste hierarchies more generally. What makes Ranade quite distinctive is that while he drew heavily from modern liberal ideas of egalitarianism, he was equally drawn to the life-world of bhakti as the basis on which might be fashioned what I refer to as a new grammar for political life in India in the backdrop of a modern colonial public sphere. This 'new' grammar relied heavily on bhakti to talk about caste equality, compassion, justice, morality, and fraternity with fellow beings.[3] In many ways he laid the ground for Gandhi, who extended some of these ideas such as selflessness, compassion, and love into the realm of mass politics, practising what Stuart Gray and Thomas Hughes call 'bhakti political philosophy'.[4]

There are several arguments or themes I wish to touch upon in this chapter with respect to Ranade's use of bhakti. First, his turning to bhakti, in contrast to the hyper-masculinist response that characterized the conduct of many of his fellow male upper-caste public figures, points to a different kind of masculinity privileging values of compassion and justice in the public sphere. Second, while Ranade was intervening in long-standing debates on social reform within Hinduism which were not entirely dependent on colonialism, he was also simultaneously responding to the colonial encounter which had brought forth many changes. Living in Bombay Presidency (present-day Maharashtra) as an upper-caste Brahmin employed by the British, the colonial impact was obviously a significant one on him. Third, I also wish to briefly explore the link between Ranade and Gandhi's use of bhakti and its engagement with modern politics. While Gandhi does not talk much about Ranade in his writings, he respected him particularly because his own 'political guru', Gopal Krishna Gokhale, was Ranade's protégé.[5] But I do believe that some of Ranade's ideas on bhakti 'travelled' (in part due to Gokhale's influence) to Gandhi, as I attempt to demonstrate in the chapter.

Ranade's Turn to Bhakti in Contrast to a Hyper-Masculine Reading of Hinduism

I argue in this chapter that Ranade's religious interventions can be seen as asserting an alternative masculinity or a 'softer' version of Hinduism in contrast to the hyper-masculine readings of his contemporaries such as Tilak. Ranade is drawing on a movement that sometimes questioned the mainstream Hindu canon by asserting values such as love, devotion, compassion, piety, and so on. His push to reform Hinduism by making it more egalitarian came via an interpretation of bhakti teachings by arguing that these values formed the core of Hinduism. In doing so, he was attempting to bring popular elements of Hinduism to its centre while pushing back the mainstream; and yet, he always used the language of continuity even as he tried to effect change.

Gender historians of nineteenth-century India have been quite critical of Ranade primarily for two reasons. First, despite his being at the forefront of the widow-remarriage movement and speaking strongly against child marriage, Ranade succumbed to family pressure and married an eleven-year-old girl shortly after his first wife died. His inability to marry a widow greatly undermined efforts of social reformers in that period who were facing considerable social ostracism for questioning age-old social practices. It forever tainted his reputation as an unflinching stalwart of social reform. Most critical of Ranade's decision to marry eleven-year-old Ramabai was Tilak, who ridiculed Ranade's inability to match his actions with his words. Second, some gender scholars have argued that social reformers such as Ranade and others were part of a patriarchal Brahminical structure that ensured Brahminic norms remained in place. They see little difference between the reformers (*sudharaks*) and the traditionalists (such as Tilak) as well as orthodox Brahmins.

Uma Chakravarti, who in her work on Pandita Ramabai has discussed Ranade quite extensively, points out that part of the reason he used the language of gradual change and talked of restoring a more glorious past history was because he and the reformers were unable to bring about any significant change and did not question Brahminical patriarchy. They were ineffective in bringing about transformations in their personal lives due to social pressures from within their families and they were often mute participants in the very oppression that they derided. She refers to the example of Ranade's own sister who was widowed early and had to live a life of 'restraint' and social exclusion while Ranade himself was socially pressured to marry a young girl within a month of his first wife's death. Ranade's only option then was to 'educate' his young bride, making her into what Chakravarti calls a model Hindu wife, educated and yet obedient and reverential towards her husband, thereby further upholding what she argues are new forms of patriarchal values.[6]

According to Chakravarti, the limitations of reformers such as Ranade were that in 'no way did they critique the entire structure of Brahminical patriarchy, the caste practices or the property structures in which they were embedded'[7] and that the 'shared assumptions were an outcome of a common upper-caste legacy, a largely Brahmanic Hindu world view where the differences lay in the emphasis on particular aspects of the legacy rather than in the structure as a whole'.[8] The larger differences, she argues, were with the non-Brahmanic castes, and she suggests that increasingly the reformers took more moderate positions on questions of caste, religion, and gender. This, she argues, can be seen in the manner in which upper-caste men dealt with Pandita Ramabai[9] and her conversion to Christianity. While traditionalists such as Tilak and orthodox Brahmins denounced Ramabai in harshest terms, the reformers also gradually distanced themselves from her.

Chakravarti concedes that one of the differences in emphasis between the orthodox/traditionalists and the reformers was on the writing of history where Ranade highlighted the place of bhakti in the Indian past whereas the traditionalists emphasized a more martial history rooted in saints such as Ramdas, a history that could uphold a combination of Chitpavan Brahminic and Kshatriya values.[10] While I do not dispute Chakravarti's point about Brahminical patriarchy being a common thread between various upper-caste groups, I think the similarities are overstated. The virulent manner in which Tilak attacked reformers such as Ranade, R.G. Bhandarkar, G.G. Agarkar, and later Gokhale attests to this because they were questioning many practices at the heart of Brahminical control and power. Their push to start schools for girls and make education compulsory for both boys and girls is an example of this, and was surprisingly not vehemently opposed by Tilak. Keeping an eye on ground realities, the reformers hoped for gradual change while eschewing abstract political ideals.[11]

While I am not trying to 'defend' Ranade for some of his actions, I believe some significant differences between Ranade and Tilak get flattened out when solely viewed through the prism of Brahminical patriarchy. Moreover, a gendered reading of Ranade will focus on the patriarchal nature of his relationship with his wife and the overall male upper-caste mindset towards women that placed certain limits on them (which is in itself useful and necessary). But how does one account for the *variation* in responses such as Tilak's hyper-masculinity versus Ranade's more sensitive one that stressed on bhakti via the Marathi bhakti traditions? Ranade's stress on compassion, self-abnegation and fellow feeling for others, which he recovers through the language of bhakti, does point to an alternative masculinity that is more inclusive, open, and just in contrast to the strands of hyper-masculinity emerging in the nationalist movement. A reading sensitive to gender should also take this into account. Tilak, for instance, saw an emphasis on bhakti as a passive, weak, and 'effeminate' response towards colonial power. He once called the reformers, including Ranade, 'eunuchs' like Shikhandi.[12] Anticipating Gandhian 'softer' values of non-violence, compassion, and love, Ranade talked about some of these principles in public life through his discussions on bhakti and its relevance for nineteenth-century India. However, unlike Gandhi, he did maintain a Brahminical distance from the 'masses' and mass politics, which he viewed with some scepticism.

Ranade's Use of Bhakti as the Basis of an 'Internal' and 'External' Critique of Hindu Society

Ranade's interventions were *both* 'internal' and 'external'; he was intervening in long-standing Hindu metaphysical debates that focused on the individual's relationship with God. Ranade was working within a long pre-modern tradition of discussing the merits and demerits of various paths such as *karmamarg* (path of action), *gyanmarg* (path of knowledge), *bhaktimarg* (path of devotion), or *yogamarg* (path of renunciation). In other words, *which amongst these should be the right or ideal path for the individual to come closer to God? And the path to liberation?* Traditional ideas of liberation (*moksha*) entailed freedom from the cycle of life and death and suffering. Bhakti saints such as Tukaram in turn were very critical of the link between moksha and karma (especially related to acts of previous births). Some of the saints rejected the idea of rebirth and talked about being devoted to God in the present life. But even for them the idea of liberation meant immersing oneself fully or becoming one with God or the divine and not the modern secular understanding of the term. And change happened at the personal level by the individual becoming a bhakta. One's immersion in God had to be purely an individual quest. There was no collective notion built into these metaphysical conceptions of liberation. But these views reflected long-standing debates between various schools of thought within Hinduism, broadly speaking.[13] Similarly, Ranade also took a position through his stress on bhakti on the centuries-old debate between non-dualism (Advaita) and dualism (Dvaita), arguing in favour of the latter. The bhakti saints rejected Advaita as laid out by Shankaracharya, who argued that the individual self (Atman) was only part of the Supreme Being (*Paramatman*) and that the world was *maya* or an illusion. They argued that man and God were separate entities so that man can worship God as a devotee and that the world is not illusory. They were critiquing what they saw as Brahminical metaphysical arguments that were far removed from their lives.

However, it is clear from Ranade's writings that he was not interested in bhakti purely for the sake of engaging in age-old metaphysical debates. He was especially interested in its *social* dimension, as one that questioned caste hierarchies and called for a more egalitarian and just order. And here the 'external' impulse of colonialism plays an important role. Ranade was profoundly concerned with what he unquestionably took to be the deeply inegalitarian nature of Hindu society. Colonial liberal rationalist ideas—articulated by colonial officials, intellectuals, and missionaries—that critiqued these hierarchies did have a profound impact on him and they did play a major role in the way in which he approached the problems of Hindu society. It is not surprising then that he is often called a 'liberal' in Indian historiography. For instance, he talks of Britain 'as the most gifted and free nation in the world, whose rule guarantees to us a long continuance of these favourable conditions. The reign of law is supreme'.[14] It was the British, he believed, who were uplifting Indians; he writes:

> Neither the old Hindu nor the old Mahomedan civilization was in a condition to train these virtues in a way to bring up the race of India on a level with those of Western Europe, and so the work of education had to be renewed, and it has been now going on for the past century and more under the *pax brittanica* with results ...[15]

For Ranade, these new ideas were allowing self-interrogation and self-critique, thereby opening up new ways of thinking which he saw as necessary. India, he argued, was in a state of decline because of the

> perception of fictitious differences between men and men due to heredity and birth, passive acquiescence in evil or wrong-doing. ... These have been the root ideas of our ancient social system. They have as their natural result led to the existing family arrangements where the woman is entirely subordinated to the man and the lower castes to the higher castes, to the length of depriving men of their natural respect for humanity.[16]

He writes: 'At present it is everybody's ambition to pride himself upon being a member of the smallest community that can be conceived, and the smaller the number of those with whom you can dine or marry, or associate, the higher is your perfection and purity.'[17] What is needed, he goes on, is to 'cast on the lines of fraternity, a capacity to expand outwards, and to make more cohesive inwards the bonds of fellowship ... tendency must be towards a general recognition of the essentially equality between man and man'.[18] However, while highlighting the positive impact of these ideas he could not embrace them fully as alternatives. While they made it possible to engage in necessary self-critique they lacked a religious and moral framework. Ranade was very critical of atheism or a rationalism that rejected spirituality. For him, it was important to talk about morality in public life through a religious or spiritual world view, and more specifically about piety linked to values such as compassion and self-abnegation. It was not surprising that he found these in the writings of the Marathi bhakti poets which were part of a strong living tradition in the region and one that he had also grown up with. He believed they were fundamentally egalitarian in their writings *and* sought a higher union with God. Ranade was interested in linking bhakti to the colonial 'public sphere' via his social reform agenda that included questioning certain oppressive religious practices such as widow remarriage and caste injustices. And in doing so he would also be providing an alternative ethico-spiritual basis to public life.

Of course, the lines between what is 'internal' and 'external' are often blurred and I have pointed to them more for analytical purposes to look at both continuity and change within Ranade. In the following

section, I examine Ranade's discussion of the significance of bhakti
for both the individual and society by drawing on some of his untrans-
lated Marathi religious essays titled 'Dharmapar Vyakhyaney'. Many
of these essays were delivered as speeches from the pulpit of the
Prarthana Samaj, a reformist organization he and other reformers
founded in 1867 in Bombay. He delivered a series of speeches there
in which he argued that the essence of Hinduism was 'bhaktimarg' or
the path of bhakti. He referred to the religion of the bhakti saints as
'bhagwat dharma'. This, he says, constituted *sanatan dharma* or eternal Hinduism. He was trying to reclaim bhakti as not a marginal set of
voices but as the core of Hinduism. Here he was trying to align bhaktis'
egalitarian impulses with modern ones but within the framework of
religion. Drawing on verses by Eknath and the *abhangas* (devotional
songs) of Tukaram, two very important Marathi bhakti saints, Ranade
argued that they strongly believed in the superiority of bhaktimarg
over all other paths or margs such as 'gyanamarg', 'karmamarg', or
'yogamarg'. The yogamarg was inappropriate for most people because
it called for severe austerities, control of emotions, and tremendous
physical hardships. Control of one's organs was not necessary to gain
union with God. He quotes Eknath who says: 'One should experience
and feel beauty and not try to deny oneself the sense of wonder and
awe. One should not renounce the world or shun it but feel it, live it
and absorb it.'[19] Even the Buddha, Ranade says, had to ultimately give
up this path because it ravaged his body and did little else. Moreover,
yogamarg only caused harshness in the person since it required
controlling all emotions including tenderness and softness. Yogis, he
writes, were often short-tempered and unemotional people. Ranade, in
deploying the insights of bhakti saints, was critiquing the over-emphasis
on renunciation in Hinduism.

Ranade talks about the limits of gyanamarg or the path of knowledge. According to him, the saints argued that this was not suitable
for common people. Under gyanamarg one had to know and recite
the Vedas, shastras, and all the commentaries. To begin with, this
knowledge was denied to lower castes or Shudras and women.[20] It
was assumed that Shudras and women, would, in the scathing words
of Eknath, 'keep drowning themselves and never attain moksha'.[21]
Second, there was no guarantee, according to Eknath, that even
if one mastered these texts it would bring a person closer to God.

Rather, reading these texts led to debates such as whether God was an illusion or form, and did not strengthen one's faith in God. Since this was a path open only to Brahmins, the saints rejected this path. Bhaktimarg, says Ranade, was superior 'because it is open and accessible to all whether it is a man or woman, a brahman or a shudra'.[22] It emphasized equality irrespective of caste and class differences. According to Ranade, Eknath said one does not need to be learned or know Sanskrit in order to be a bhakta. All that is required is devotion, which makes this the most accessible path for anyone. Here, Ranade was critiquing the privilege within Hinduism given to Brahmins via access to textual knowledge and the exalted status it enjoyed.

Similarly, with respect to karmamarg, Ranade argues that it is strongly criticized by bhakti saints. The focus on excessive rituals, offerings, and practices, bhaktas maintained, leads to rigidity, arrogance, and obscurantism.[23] For instance, according to Ranade, Eknath embraced the view that people who undertake rigid fasts and vows may believe this will bring them closer to God but they lose the devotional element in the process. They believe doing good deeds in this life will lead to a better next life and ultimately the chance of being born a Brahmin. This is the ultimate path to attain moksha, according to karmamargis. Ranade points out that the bhakti saints were very critical of this path. Common people, in Eknath's view, cannot be expected to wait endlessly for many rebirths to be born a Brahmin and then eventually attain moksha. He says, 'We do not believe we will get happiness in the next birth and must suffer in this one. With bhakti, anyone can achieve it in this life and not wait for the next. We want to attain God in this life but Brahmins say women and shudras cannot do so in one life time.[24] Moreover, he goes on, yogamargis and gyanamargis say do *punya* or good deeds in this life and it will help in your next life to come closer to god by becoming a Brahmin. But Eknath, Ranade submits, asks, 'How do you know you won't mess up in your next life? You make a mistake and you are back to square one and you will never be closer to god. We don't want to bother with all this.'[25]

After having argued against the other paths, Ranade discusses the strengths of bhaktimarg as laid out by the saints. It does not require mediators of any kind such as priests and caste or class is no barrier. God can be worshipped by anyone wholeheartedly with full faith. One does not have to physically torture oneself, restrain one's organs, or deny all worldly pleasures to come closer to God. Moreover, bhakti is also connected with ordinary people's daily lives. One can revel in God's glory in simple things such as seeing the ocean, mountains, and God's creations while worshipping the Creator. For Eknath, in Ranade's reading, God is all-pervasive and exists everywhere and in everything including in one's parents, in friendships, and in nature. The divine is present in all actions including walking, tasting, touching, and hearing. Even sounds reflect the presence of the divine.

Ranade asks, if God is all-pervasive, how does one worship Him? Rather, what is the bhakti mode of worship? In karmamarg, despite undertaking rigorous fasts, people are unable to control their lusts and desires. In bhaktimarg one can worship and sing praises of God through one's daily life and chores. What matters is pure devotion and nothing else. Most importantly, whatever one achieves should be offered to God without any expectations of returns. This, Ranade says, is the greatest dharma. Submerging oneself totally in the divine and becoming God's servant in a spirit of selflessness brings one closer to God. Such a person, he argues, achieves calmness, happiness, and enthusiasm about work. This also builds courage to face all obstacles including caste injustices. He quotes Eknath, who states that even in one's dreams one will not be shaken by criticisms including caste-related ones because of the inner confidence and courage that comes by adopting the path of bhakti. It allows an attitude of fearlessness. This path, Ranade argues, empowers ordinary people to gain tremendous inner confidence enabling them to live without fear or insecurities about not being knowledgeable enough or religious enough because they are not adhering to the rules laid down by gyanamarg and karmamarg.

Moreover, Ranade argues, it is only bhakti or devotion that satisfies the heart and evokes love, tenderness, and compassion unlike the other paths. For example, when one sees ascetics one does not see any love in them either for themselves or for others.[26] While bhakti is about asserting emotion, ascetics want to conquer their emotions including love. The search for God must come from within the heart and for this the conscience and instinct must be fully immersed in devotion. The main essence of bhakti, he argues, is love for God and for fellow humans. The other paths, he continues in a similar vein, has no place for fellow feeling.[27] Bhakti talks about sacrificing for others and to be giving. It has no gate-keepers unlike the other paths but has room for all. Its greatest strength, Ranade points out, is that there is no caste, no gender differences, no likes and dislikes.[28] Saints are drawn from all castes and central to bhakti is the assumption that love exists in everyone's heart including those who commit evil acts. Ranade does mention quite favourably that saints such as Eknath are not denouncing other paths altogether as being unworthy but saying that they are not suited for common people.[29] Here one can say his reading is more Brahminical than those who have read bhakti in more radical ways as decrying Brahmanism altogether.[30]

Ranade Laying the Ground for Gandhi's Use of Bhakti in Politics

In terms of Ranade introducing certain ideas that one also finds in Gandhi, the former took the first step by reinterpreting the message of the bhakti saints in order to create an ethical foundation for Indian public life by emphasizing piety, self-abnegation, love, compassion, and plurality. Ranade extended bhakti values into contemporary society by trying to reform Hinduism, particularly in its relation to caste and gender. He appropriated bhakti ideas into a social activist agenda even if not an explicitly political one. This is apparent in his interventions on the widow-remarriage movement, promotion of female education, stance against child marriage, and so on. His younger adversary Tilak recognized what Ranade was doing when he criticized the latter for using bhakti teachings as the basis of social transformation. As Tilak himself says:

> If the Samaj had been actually inspired by the *Bhakti* saints, it would not have kicked at the restriction that bound them. He (*a bhakta*) lived on too high a platform to think of either widow marriage or female education. ... A Bhakta works for his own salvation and not the salvation of the entire society ... I challenge Mr. Chandavarkar to name a single saint who has become such a utilitarian.[31]

Tilak recognized that bhakti interventions in the past may have been more individually oriented even if they had a social dimension of questioning caste injustices. Ranade's use of these ideas to shape a collective reformist agenda was perhaps something distinctive to suit the exigencies of an emerging modern colonial public sphere. But it took Gandhi to extend this to the next level of including these ethical values into the realm of politics through an active programme of non-violence that appealed for love. As Makarand Paranjape puts it, Ranade's 'model of saintly politics and spiritual activism'[32] did have an influence on Gandhi. Gandhi hardly had personal interactions with Ranade (who died early) but 'knew' him through Gokhale who often talked to Gandhi about his guru.[33] Gandhi mentions that Gokhale's 'reverence' for Ranade could be seen at every minute.[34] In a description of Gokhale's views that are strongly reminiscent of Ranade, Gandhi talks about how his guru believed religion did not reside in practising austerities but is a spiritualization of politics.

How does Gandhi go about the task of making bhakti values suitable for use in politics? Gandhi was drawn to the devotional element of the Bhagvad Gita, and from his childhood days was also drawn to Tulsidas's *Ramcharitmanas* which emphasized devotion to Ram.[35] Moreover, he was brought up in a Vaishnava household. In fact, as the Rudolphs, among many others, have argued, it was the bhakti element in the various competing strands of Gujarat's religious culture that had the greatest impact on Gandhi.[36] Gandhi talks about the example of Mirabai,[37] who lived a life of absolute love. Because of her unconditional and total devotion to Krishna, Gandhi writes, even her husband ultimately became her devotee. This, he says, is the ancient meaning of soul-force, an idea which became the bedrock of Gandhi's notion of satyagraha. He goes on to admit that it is he who has taken this idea of devotional love as exhibited by Mirabai into politically translatable terms. He writes about devotional love: 'But it may be stated that so far as its use on the political platform is concerned, the idea may have said to have originated with me. I knew nothing of it, but Tolstoy drew my attention to it.'[38] The search for truth, Gandhi avers, is the meaning of bhakti and it is the path that leads to God. This quest for truth involves the heart, self-suffering, and complete self-abnegation.

How bhakti's concept of 'love' is translated into political action is indeed Gandhi's innovation. And he does this, I argue—of course apart from the philosophy of ahimsa or non-violence—by introducing the Christian concept of service, which one does not find in traditional Hinduism. None of the various philosophical schools of thought

within the broad 'Hindu' umbrella outline an idea of service or welfare of others and here one could include the dissenting Sramanic traditions such as Buddhism as well.[39] In general, the preoccupation is
with the individual and his/her quest for liberation, union with God,
and so on, whether it is called moksha or nirvana, or something else.
Of course, that does not preclude change because here the individual
is seen as the primary agent of change, something that Gandhi did
not disagree with and in fact made central to his political philosophy
such as with his idea of the individual conscience.[40] But the idea that
service to others may be a way to serve God does not appear to have a
basis in Hindu texts including in bhakti writings. A concrete idea of
service was far more established in Christianity such as serving the
poor and downtrodden. Gandhi, as is well-known, engaged in extensive dialogues with Christian missionaries and admired their passion
for service, even if he was critical of their tendency to proselytize.

However, another less explored link between Ranade's ideas of
bhakti and Gandhi's use of the notion of service is Gokhale. Gandhi
talks admiringly about Gokhale's notion of service in public life
through his setting up the Servants of Indian Society. It was a small
group of dedicated 'selfless' workers who came together in 1905 in
Pune under the leadership of Gokhale who would engage in the
'national' cause through social work and public service. Gandhi took
the view, following the lead of Gokhale, that moksha could be realized
only when the spirit of ethics and ethical work infused politics. This
idea of moksha, Gandhi argues, was suited to the exigencies of the
times. He said Gokhale was such a person who although not religious
in any ritualistic sense of the term lived a life filled with the true spirit
of religion.

Thus, 'service' becomes the concept linking Ranade's ideas of bhakti
(via Gokhale) and Gandhi's active philosophy of non-violence because
it emphasizes not just the individual relationship with God (which
Gandhi retains) but also the importance of fellow feeling, working
for others and the larger community, as a way to realize God. So, for
Gandhi traditional ascetics could be of little worth. 'Political sanyasis'
or political ascetics were what was needed. He writes: 'In this age,
only political *sanyasis* can fulfil and adorn the ideal of *sanyasa*.'[41] He
goes on: 'No Indian who aspires to follow the way of true religion can
afford to remain aloof from politics. In other words, one who aspires

to a truly religious life cannot fail to undertake public service as his mission.'[42] He says this was possible in the olden days but not any longer even amongst masses and peasants. Gandhi's originality was to extend the idea of service not just to the social and religious realm like the missionaries but bring it into the realm of politics. Gandhi worked with a capacious conception of *seva*: it is not just about serving the poor but fighting injustice—not through violence or hate but through love and compassion, more so for one's enemy.

Gandhi's originality in extending these ideas of love and compassion into politics was recognized by Martin Luther King when he stated, 'Gandhi was probably the first person in history to lift the love ethic of Jesus above mere interaction between individuals to a powerful and effective social force on a large scale.'[43] Ideas such as self-abnegation or selflessness, devotional love, forgiveness, and compassion which can be found in bhakti but also in other religious traditions as well which Gandhi makes clear are joined by him with other non-bhakti ideas drawn from various civilizational sources such as self-suffering,[44] collective action, and service to other human beings as seeking God to yield the concept of non-violent satyagraha.

Gandhi extended Ranade's efforts to bring bhakti-infused values into the public sphere via social and religious reform into the realm of *mass* politics. Both Ranade and his protégé Gokhale remained 'constitutionalists' or favoured gradual incremental reform by pressurizing the colonial state through administrative and legislative changes and believing it would eventually respond to their demands. They were very cautious in their approach and sceptical of any kind of mass action. That may have contributed to the decline of the moderates in the nationalist movement in the first two decades of the nineteenth century. And it accounts for the appeal of someone like Tilak as a fiery mass leader who had no hesitation in drawing crowds with his call for 'swarajya'. Here, Tilak was tapping into a growing need for greater political intervention. People were getting impatient. But Tilak in his critique of colonialism wanted to keep the religious and social completely outside the political agenda, highlighting only one at the expense of the other. The religious and social were not left untouched by him. On the contrary, these were increasingly interpreted in defensive, socially obscurantist and masculinist terms. Tilak also strongly reinforced patriarchal Brahminical values.

His concern was primarily in legitimizing violence through a certain reading of religious texts, and in particular by a removal of customary constraints on the understanding of ritual and the sacral to effect a more secularized concept of action.[45] Tilak justified the need for action even if violent as part of karmayoga, which he said was the highest form of action as shown in the Gita. But he also argued that this was not violence for the sake of violence[46] but violence for a higher cause for which one should not expect any rewards or personal benefits.[47] Tilak was trying to find religious grounds to justify Indians organizing themselves through violent action against the colonial powers; Gandhi did just the opposite. But interestingly, what Gandhi does take from Tilak is the need for organized mass collective *action* while reversing the emphasis from violence to non-violence, which he borrows in part from bhakti advocates such as Ranade. In other words, Gandhi synthesizes aspects of Ranade and Tilak ('moderates' and 'extremists') by emphasizing values that draw partly from bhakti but transforms these into a collective action-oriented programme in politics that emphasizes both the social and religious dimensions of life.

After Ranade's death, the social reform agenda took a backseat in the Indian National Congress[48] with defensive nationalists such as Tilak at the helm who claimed internal reform could wait until after independence. When Gandhi came on the scene he demanded that both social reform issues and political independence be addressed on the same platform. He called for a full-scale rejection of untouchability without jettisoning caste, a position B.R. Ambedkar strongly opposed and criticized him for. On the caste question Ranade was unequivocal; he saw the treatment of lower castes as inhuman and degrading. He often denounced caste in many public speeches. He called for reforms to 'remove social deformities' and these reforms were to be 'in the matter of infant marriage and enforced widowhood ... inter-marriage between castes, the elevation of the low castes'.[49]

It is poignant that one of the early encounters Gandhi had with Ranade was at a public meeting held in the Framji Cowasji Institute in Bombay to discuss injustices being meted out to Indians in South Africa. Most of the Congress leaders were supportive of Gandhi raising this issue and wanted him to speak about it.[50] Ranade addressed the audience after Gandhi reminded them that before their hearts bled for Indians in South Africa they should turn inwards towards their own lower-caste fellow human beings. He asked, 'whether it was [becoming] for those who tolerated such disgraceful oppression and injustice in their own country to indulge in all that denunciation of the people of South Africa?'[51] The issue of caste inequality was always on Ranade's mind and, in many ways, he went further than Gandhi in repudiating caste hierarchies and calling for inter-caste dining and marriage. This may be one of the reasons why Ambedkar eulogized him in a speech commemorating Ranade's 101st birth anniversary in Pune by calling him a 'visionary' and 'prophet-like'. Amebdkar praised Ranade as someone who relentlessly campaigned for social reforms over everything else and attributed the coming of Western rule to the deficiencies within the Hindu social system. Ambedkar admired the personal courage of the social reformers including Ranade who had to face excommunication in their communities and ostracism from their own families to fight for their causes. This, he says, was more difficult than even political imprisonment because the entire society rejected them. They had to bear the brunt of the 'mad orthodoxy' and political religionists such as Tilak who hurled the vilest abuses at them.[52] Ranade, he says, wanted to 'vitalize the conscience of the Hindu society' and aimed to create a 'real social democracy'. Ambedkar's approbation for Ranade's contributions to social reform are apparent when he says in the same speech, 'It would be difficult to find in the history of India any man who could come up to Ranade in the width of his learning, the breadth of his wisdom and the length of his vision.'[53]

Bhakti and the Colonial Public Sphere

Nineteenth-century debates in the Bombay Presidency were defined either by scathing attacks on Hinduism and its backwardness or a growing defensive reaction that saw nothing wrong and vigorously defended 'tradition', which was later hitched to nationalism. Ranade negotiated between both these extremes: he was drawn to Western liberal ideas and was deeply aware of some of the deficiencies of existing religious practice but he framed some of these ideas through the language of bhakti. In Ranade's understanding of bhakti, it made available ideas and equally a sensibility which liberalism, for all its attractions, could not offer. Perhaps he was also being strategic since reformers were often accused of being Christians or Western imports. Bhakti was, after all, an indigenous discourse of dissent. But, Ranade wanted to maintain a religious world view which was beyond what liberalism could offer because he believed India was inherently a religious society where religion and morality could not be separated. Thus, he turned to bhakti to question hierarchy but also used it to assert plurality. Their message of inter-religious harmony, he wrote of the bhaktas, was needed for present-day co-existence between religions such as Islam and Hinduism. Bhakti, he argued, allowed different religions to come together because it advocated equality, friendship between communities, and belief in one God.[54] He also pointed out its convergences with Christianity such as 'a correct sense of the dignity of man and woman', an 'active philanthropy', and a 'feeling of fraternity'. Thus, 'the Bhagavata Dharma has many points of contact and kinship with the Christian system of faith'.[55]

In addition, by laying stress on bhakti, Ranade attempted to popularize religion and take it out of the hands of only the priestly classes. He could have stressed on Hinduism via Vedanta much as Vivekananda did but he appears to have thought that there was some-thing quite elitist about that claim because it was claiming superiority of that particular reading of Hinduism over all its other traditions including the 'little' ones. Even when Vivekananda talks about bhakti or bhakti-yoga, he emphasizes the individual immersion in the divine without highlighting its social dimension or talking about its various low-caste saints. He engages in a more Sanskritic textual reading of bhakti that also tends to be conservative because it attempts to recon-cile Advaita with bhakti arguing that 'the Personal God worshipped by the bhakta is not separate or different from the Brahman'. The reason people do not knowingly immerse themselves in Brahman, he says, is because it is too much of an abstraction to be loved.[56] Ironically, it was Vivekananda's spiritual guru Ramakrishna Paramhamsa who believed and fully practised the path of devotion.[57]

For Ranade, the social dimension cannot be divorced from the metaphysics of bhakti. Hence, his discussion of bhakti focuses pri-marily on the living traditions of bhakti centred around the low-caste

Marathi bhakti saints. He talks about the common individual and collective practices of bhakti worship such as singing and prayer while
rejecting rituals. Borrowing from Christianity, he introduced the
practice of collective prayer on every Sunday in the Prarthana Samaj.
The members would engage in collective prayer, singing of hymns,
and he would give sermons from a pulpit that drew on all the major
religious texts such as the Bible, Koran, Tukaram's *abhangas*, and so
on.[58] Achieving pure devotion and spiritual exaltation was not enough;
their discussions would focus on how to achieve social reform.

Ranade's critics accused him and other Samajists of promoting a
'soft', 'ineffective', and 'passive' Hinduism by emphasizing bhakti.
Tilak was the most well-known of these critics. He made it very clear
that what was required was a martial response when he wrote:

> For in the first place the extreme humanization of the spirit and tol-
> eration which was exhibited by some of the saints and the prophets
> in their best moments cannot be said to be virtues of the market
> place at any time in Mahratta history during the five centuries before
> Shivaji. Secondly, it is not these qualities but something perhaps
> nearly opposed to them that in our opinion stirred up the spirit of
> nationality in Maharashtra and it was supplied by saints like Ramdas
> and Brahmendra Swami. ... The regeneration was accompanied by the
> hands of their sword wielding disciples.[59]

It was the martial traditions, according to him, which had contributed
positively to society and not the 'humanizing' ones.

Tilak's disdain for Ranade's 'effeminate' promotion of bhakti ideals
as the basis of Indian public life in many ways mirrors the tensions
that were to come between Gandhi's talking about compassion, love,
and non-violence in politics and his Hindutva detractors.[60] His assas-
sin, a Hindu extremist, Nathuram Godse, made this point very clear
when saying at his own trial that Gandhian ahimsa was leading to
the emasculation of Hindus.[61] Godse held that a rigid adherence to
ahimsa had rendered Hindus unfit to resist Muslims and he saw it
as his duty to stop Gandhi from furthering the serious psychological
damage he was inflicting on Hindus.[62] The Hindutvadis or Hindu
extremists ought to privilege realpolitik and a violent response when
necessary. He writes: 'I could never conceive that an armed resistance
to the aggressor is unjust. I will consider it a religious and moral

duty to resist and if possible overpower such an enemy by the use of force.'[63] His mentor, V.D. Savarkar, also held a similar view. With reference to Gandhi's methods he would say: 'This doctrine of non-violence benumbed the revolutionary fervour, softened the limbs and hearts of the Hindus, and stiffened the bones of enemies. ... Revolt, bloodshed and revenge have often been instruments created by nature to root out injustice.'[64] What Hindus needed, he argued, was to gain greater masculine potency. This would prove their 'virility and fitness for survival in the universal struggle for existence'.[65] The gendered nature of his language is quite obvious here. Savarkar saw Hindus in general as hopelessly effeminate and wanted them to become masculine, much like their Western rulers who he saw as strong, powerful, tough, and successful.

* * *

Ranade's use of bhakti can thus be read as a counter to the hyper-masculinist reading of Tilak and his followers, who saw little room for these values in politics and stressed realpolitik instead. Moreover, by turning to bhakti he was intervening in long-standing debates questioning the textual, renunciatory, and ritualistic tendencies within Hinduism. This critique may or may not have been dependent on colonialism. However, he also used bhakti to respond to *external* critiques of Hinduism and Indian society, drawing out egalitarian currents. He turned to bhakti as a language of positive renewal of Indian public life in light of modern colonial criticisms. Here, he did not reassert the belief like many other Indian elites that Indians were a subject people because of their softness, tolerance, religiosity, passivity, and lack of martial vigour but rather turned these values around as a basis of dignity and self-assertion via the language of bhakti. He was injecting the egalitarian, humane, just, and inclusive language of bhakti into the modern colonial public sphere. By doing so he was trying to provide an alternative discourse that went beyond both the liberal secular–rationalist one and the extreme nationalist one that defended 'tradition' at all cost. He thus paved the way for Gandhi to transform bhakti values into an active political philosophy to fight colonial injustices.

Acknowledgements

I thank Ashis Nandy and Vinay Lal for inviting me to present this paper at the Backwaters Collective in Kochi, 2016. I really appreciate their support. It was a very enriching experience and I am thankful to all the participants who pushed me with their inputs and questions, especially Prithvi Datta Chandra Shobhi who was the discussant for the paper. I appreciate Vinay Lal's close reading of the paper both substantively and as an editor. A. Raghuramaraju and Sanjay Palshikar read early drafts. Jyotirmaya Sharma helped with materials on bhakti and Hema Devare with Marathi sources. My deep gratitude to all of them.

Notes and References

1. Bhakti refers to popular devotional movements that spanned across India from the seventh to the eighteenth century. Their supporters often cut across classes, castes, and gender although there was great variation in these movements in this regard. Some were more radical than others. For the distinction between a more conservative bhakti or *saguna* and a more radical reading or *nirguna*, see Krishna Sharma, *Bhakti and the Bhakti Movement: A New Perspective* (New Delhi: Munshiram Manoharlal Publishers, 1987).

2. For a good introduction to Ranade, see Richard Tucker, *Ranade and the Roots of Indian Nationalism* (Chicago: University of Chicago Press, 1972). For a very insightful overview of the Hindu social reformers in the nineteenth century, see Charles Heimsath, *Indian Nationalism and Hindu Social Reform* (Princeton: Princeton University Press, 1964).

3. Bhakti, as John Stratton Hawley argues, has not always been subversive in all places and contexts in its practices. Yet, he goes on to say, bhakti is democracy. He writes: 'It is a people's literature, a people's religion, and its expressions vary across the social spectrum, with new infusions all the time' (John Stratton Hawley, *Three Bhakti Voices: Mirabai, Surdas, and Kabir in Their Times and Ours* [New Delhi: Oxford University Press, 2005], 335).

4. Stuart Gray and Thomas Hughes, 'Gandhi's Devotional Political Thought', *Philosophy East and West: A Quarterly of Comparative Philosophy* 65, no. 2 (2015): 375–400.

5. Gandhi had very little interaction with Ranade as the latter died in 1901, much before Gandhi moved back to India from South Africa. Gandhi first met Ranade in 1896 when he visited Bombay to discuss the problems Indians faced in South Africa.

6. Uma Chakravarti, *Rewriting History: The Life and Times of Pandita Ramabai* (New Delhi: Kali for Women, 1998), 216–24.

7. Chakravarti, *Rewriting History*, 89.

8. Chakravarti, *Rewriting History*, 102.

9. Pandita Ramabai was a Brahmin Sanskrit scholar who married a lower-caste man. However, he died soon after their marriage and she had to raise a young daughter on her own. She defied many traditional customs that widows were supposed to follow and became a public intellectual in her own right in Pune denouncing harsh religious strictures on women. She was severely criticized by the orthodox and traditionalists for her views. She eventually converted to Christianity. Two scholars who have done good work on Ramabai are Uma Chakravarti in her *Rewriting History* and Meera Kosambi, who has translated many of Ramabai's writings into English. See Meera Kosambi, 'Women, Emancipation and Equality—Pandita Ramabai's Contribution to Women's Cause', *Economic and Political Weekly* 23, no. 44 (1988).

10. Chitpavans are a sub-sect of Brahmins originally from the Konkan Coast who were rulers in Maharashtra (known as the Peshwas) prior to the British. It was rare for Brahmins to be kings but in this case Brahmin and Kshatriya (martial and ruling castes) status was fused.

11. I owe this point to A. Raghuramaraju, personal communication, 28 June 2016.

12. Stanley Wolpert, quoted in Chakravarti, *Rewriting History*, 244.

13. This was not confined to Hindus alone as one could include the Sufis here too.

14. M.G. Ranade, *The Miscellaneous Writings of the Late Honourable Mr. Justice M.G. Ranade* (Bombay: The Manoranjan Press, 1915), 117. Ranade's strong liberal belief in the institution of the state and law to effect change is highlighted by Rinku Lamba, 'Political Institutions for Remedying Caste and Sex-Based Hierarchies', in *Accommodating Diversity: Ideas and Institutional Practices*, edited by Gurpreet Mahajan (New Delhi: Oxford University Press, 2012), 229–56. But while Ranade is attracted to liberalism, albeit perhaps an Indian variant as Lamba puts it, he also saw the limits of Western liberalism. Here Lamba herself says, 'he drew upon the conceptual resources of the Bhakti saints, particularly those belonging to the *Warkari sampradaya*', and 'his perspective represented a creative attempt to establish links between the conceptual resources of Western and Indian ideas, which *together* contributed to his rejection of caste and sex-based relations of subordination' (243; italics mine).

15. Ranade, *Miscellaneous Writings*, 226.

16. Ranade, *Miscellaneous Writings*, 192.

17. Ranade, *Miscellaneous Writings*, 193.
18. Ranade, *Miscellaneous Writings*, 193.
19. M.G. Ranade, *Nyayamurti M. Mahadev Govind Ranade Hyanci Dharmapara Vyakhyane* (Bombay: Dvarkanath Govind Vaidya, 1915), 7.
20. Ranade, *Nyayamurti M. Mahadev Govind Ranade Hyanci Dharmapara Vyakhyane*, 9.
21. Ranade, *Nyayamurti M. Mahadev Govind Ranade Hyanci Dharmapara Vyakhyane*, 9.
22. Ranade, *Nyayamurti M. Mahadev Govind Ranade Hyanci Dharmapara Vyakhyane*, 9.
23. Ranade, *Nyayamurti M. Mahadev Govind Ranade Hyanci Dharmapara Vyakhyane*, 28.
24. Ranade, *Nyayamurti M. Mahadev Govind Ranade Hyanci Dharmapara Vyakhyane*, 5.
25. Ranade, *Nyayamurti M. Mahadev Govind Ranade Hyanci Dharmapara Vyakhyane*, 13.
26. Ranade, *Nyayamurti M. Mahadev Govind Ranade Hyanci Dharmapara Vyakhyane*, 29.
27. Ranade, *Nyayamurti M. Mahadev Govind Ranade Hyanci Dharmapara Vyakhyane*, 29.
28. Ranade, *Nyayamurti M. Mahadev Govind Ranade Hyanci Dharmapara Vyakhyane*, 34.
29. This position is similar to what Lorenzen calls the 'doctrine of socially appropriate levels of worship' that suggests bhakti is appropriate for lower levels of society. While Ranade does paraphrase Eknath to make this point, his writings on bhakti go beyond this. He suggests bhakti for all and not just for the lower castes. He himself was a bhakta. See David Lorenzen, 'Introduction: The Historical Vicissitudes of Bhakti Religion', in *Bhakti Religion in North India: Community Identity and Political Action*, ed. David Lorenzen (New Delhi: Manohar, 1995), 1–32, 15. Ranade can be seen as fitting within the saguna tradition of bhakti (this reconciled with many mainstream Hindu practices) rather than the nirguna one, which Lorenzen argues was more subversive.
30. For a radical reading of bhakti, see Philip Constable, 'Early Dalit Literature and Culture in Late Nineteenth Century and Early Twentieth Century Western India', *Modern Asian Studies* 31, no. 2 (1997): 317–38.
31. Tilak quoted in Parimala Rao, *Foundations of Tilak's Nationalism: Discrimination, Education and Hindutva* (Hyderabad: Orient Blackswan, 2010), 285.
32. Makarand Paranjape, *Making India: Colonialism, National Culture and the Afterlife of Indian English Authority* (Dordrecht: Springer, 2013), 22.

33. See Parvate for the Ranade–Gokhale relationship. Parvate says Ranade treated Gokhale like his son. T.N. Parvate, *Mahadev Govind Ranade: A Biography* (New York: Asia Publishing House, 1963), 234.

34. See Aparna Devare, *History and the Making of a Modern Hindu Self* (New Delhi: Routledge, 2011), 104.

35. Gandhi called the Manas 'the greatest book of all devotional literature'. Quoted in Philip Lutgendorf, 'Interpreting Ramraj: Reflections on the "Ramayan," Bhakti, and Hindu Nationalism', in Lorenzen, *Bhakti Religion in North India*, 1995, 253.

36. Lloyd I. Rudolph and Susanna Hoeber Rudolph, *Gandhi: The Traditional Roots of Charisma* (Chicago: University of Chicago Press, 1983).

37. Mirabai was a well-known woman saint of north India who lived in the sixteenth century and was a devotee of Krishna.

38. Cited by Raghavan Iyer, *The Moral and Political Thought of Mahatma Gandhi* (New York: Oxford University Press, 2000), 25.

39. An exception is perhaps Sikhism which first emerged as a dissenting sect within Hinduism and carries some notion of seva or service. One such example in Sikhism is the *langar* where food is collectively cooked and served to all those who visit the gurudwara.

40. Ranade also highlighted the importance of the 'inner voice'. Ranade stressed the importance of listening to the voice of God 'within' even if it went against society. For a longer discussion about Ranade and Gandhi on the 'inner voice', see Devare, *History and the Making of a Modern Hindu Self*, 136.

41. *Collected Works of Mahatma Gandhi*, Gandhi Seva Gram Ashram, Volume 16 (1 September 1917–23 April 1918), available at https://www.gandhi-ashramsevagram.org/gandhi-literature/mahatma-gandhi-collected-works-volume-16.pdf (accessed on 16 April 2016), 269.

42. *Collected Works of Mahatma Gandhi*.

43. King, quoted in Vinay Lal, 'Gandhi's West, the West's Gandhi', *New Literary History* 40, no. 2, India and the West (Spring 2009): 281–313, 297.

44. This idea is not present in bhakti and is in fact rejected as part of the harsh yogic ascetic traditions.

45. Sanjay Palshikar, *Evil and the Philosophy of Retribution: Modern Commentaries on the Bhagvad Gita* (London, New York and Delhi: Routledge, 2014).

46. Tilak would not have supported this position even if his militant followers and successors did.

47. See Bal Gangadhar Tilak, *Sri Bhagavad Gita Rahasya*, English translation, vol. 1 (Poona City: R.B. Tilak, 1935).

48. Ranade led the social reform wing of the party.

49. Ranade, *Miscellaneous Writings*, 196.

50. Gandhi, it appears, was too shy to speak and had D.E. Wacha, a Congress leader read out his statement at the meeting.

51. Gandhi quoted in Ramachandra Guha, *Gandhi before India* (New Delhi: Penguin, 2013), 104.

52. 'Ranade, Gandhi, Jinnah', address delivered on the 101st birthday celebration of M.G. Ranade, held on 18 January 1943 in Gokhale Memorial Hall, Poona, by B.R. Ambedkar. Available at http://www.columbia.edu/itc/mealac/pritchett/00ambedkar/txt_ambedkar_ranade.html (accessed on 5 November 2016).

53. 'Ranade, Gandhi, Jinnah'.

54. This he believed was closer to Islam's monotheism without denying polytheism.

55. M.G. Ranade, 'Philosophy of Indian Theism', in *The Wisdom of a Modern Rishi: Writings and Speeches of Mahadev Govind Ranade*, edited by T.N. Jagadisan (Madras: Rochhouse and Sons Limited, 1900–88), 77.

56. Vivekananda, in *The Complete Works of Swami Vivekananda*, Vol. 3 (Kolkata: Advaita Ashrama, 2011), see chapter on Bhakti-Yoga, 31–100, 37.

57. Jyotirmaya Sharma argues that Ramakrishna's giving primacy to bhakti was brushed aside by his disciple. For the differences between the two, see his *Cosmic Love and Human Apathy: Swami Vivekananda's Restatement of Religion* (Delhi: Harper Collins, 2013), 14. Vivekananda says: 'Your bhakti is sentimental nonsense, which makes one impotent. ... Who cares for your Bhakti and Mukti? ... I will go into a thousand hells cheerfully, if I can rouse my countrymen immersed in Tamas, to stand on their own feet and be *men* inspired with the spirit of Karma-Yoga', quoted in Sharma, *Cosmic Love and Human Apathy*, 15.

58. The bhakti saints in Maharashtra in precolonial times belonged to a sect known as the Varkari sampradaya. They were Vaishnava saints who worshipped a deity known as Vithoba, whose shrine lies in the ancient town of Pandharpur. Collective singing was an important part of bhakti worship. They would sing devotional poetry known as abhangas. Going by foot, carrying the *palki*s or palanquins of the saints to Vithoba's shrine on a pilgrimage at least once a year, is an important part of Varkari belief. The saint Namdev would preach through songs known as *kirtan*s and would dance wildly while preaching his radical principles to the crowd. See Balchandra Nemade, 'The Revolt of the Underprivileged: Style in the Expression of the Warkari Movement in Maharashtra', in *Tradition and Modernity in Bhakti Movements*, edited by Jayant Lele (Leiden: E.J. Brill, 1981), 113–23, 117. *Kirtankar*s tell stories and often the audience is asked

to join in loud collective singing. Ranade was trying to introduce some of these elements in the Samaj along with some church practices.

59. Tilak quoted in Parimala Rao, *Foundations of Tilak's Nationalism: Discrimination, Education and Hindutva* (Hyderabad: Orient Blackswan, 2010), 286.

60. Nandy points out that it was Gandhi's 'effeminacy' that greatly irked Hindu nationalists. See Ashis Nandy, 'Final Encounter: The Politics of the Assassination of Gandhi', in Ashis Nandy, *At the Edge of Psychology: Essays in Politics and Culture* (Delhi: Oxford University Press, 1980). For a detailed discussion of the nature of Gandhi's 'effeminacy', see Vinay Lal, 'The Mother in the "Father of the Nation"', *Journal of Peace and Gandhian Studies* 1, no. 4 and 2, no. 1 (July–Dec 1996): 44–8.

61. Nathuram Godse, *May It Please Your Honour* (Delhi: Surya Prakashan, 1977), 42.

62. Godse, *May It Please Your Honour*, 42.

63. Godse, *May It Please Your Honour*, 67

64. 'Savarkar's Last Press Interview', in *Savarkar Commemoration Volume* (Bombay: Savarkar Darshan Pratishthan, 1989), 240.

65. 'Savarkar's Last Press Interview', 163.

9

THE TRANSFORMATIVE POWER
OF THE ONE WORLD VISION
OF SRI NARAYANA GURU

GEORGE THADATHIL

In this chapter I intend to present the 'one world vision' presented by the Sri Narayana Guru Movement (SNGM)[1] and trace its origin to the socio-philosophical tenets of Sri Narayana Guru. 'One in God, One in Religion, and One in Kind is the Human being' (*oru jati, oru matam oru daivam manushyanu*) was the rallying call around which a movement arose in the early twentieth century that transformed the social space of Kerala. The potential of this vision as elaborated in their cumulative literature by two generations of his key disciples— Nataraja Guru and Nitya Chaitanya Yati—spanning a century, comes under scrutiny in this chapter. The potential is assessed in terms of the power it has given to its subscribers to transform their lives, where 'transformation' may be viewed as akin to 'an increased ability to alter the course of one's life, (and) the nature of one's self', through the 'unfettered setting of priorities and goals'.[2] This study in four parts shall focus, first, on the person of Narayana Guru and his literary contributions; second, on his one world vision; third, on locating this vision within the philosophical trajectory in India; and, last, on its transformative power.

SNG: The Mystic Revolutionary

The uniqueness of the personality of Sri Narayana Guru and the leadership he provided consists of the ingenious combination of socially revolutionary action from within a mystically oriented philosophical perception. The society of Kerala in which Sri Narayana Guru made his appearance was one where 'neither social freedom nor equal opportunity or economic justice prevailed'.[3] It was a time of acute caste discriminations and practice of untouchability; a time when the separation between the high and low being extreme, the higher castes inflicted innumerable atrocities upon the Dalits.[4] He is remembered today as one who showed a non-violent approach to revolution even before Gandhi hit upon the idea and as one who challenged any spiritual vision as incomplete when faced with the sufferings of the masses.

Narayana Guru, locally known as Nanu, was born on 20 August 1854 at Vayalvaram house in Chempazhanthy, a village 10 miles north of Trivandrum, the capital city of the present-day Kerala state in India. Before Travancore came under the hegemony of the Maharaja Marthanda Varma there were eight feudal chiefs who were politically powerful and opposed to the ruling prince. Chempazhanthy was the seat of one such chief. Nanu's father, Madan Asan—the word *asan* being used for teacher in Malayalam—was a local teacher who doubled as an astrologer. His mother was Kutty Amma, but there were several other females in the household—his three sisters Kochu, Kochammu and Devi. He had his early education in Malayalam with from father, and in Sanskrit from his uncle, Krishnan Vaidyar (a word for a physician practicing Ayurveda). He had formal schooling at the school of Chempazhanthy Pillai. After his mother passed away in 1872, he continued his education from 1877 at Varanapally in central Travancore. Before his father died in 1884, he had been married although, as local tradition has maintained, the marriage was not consummated.

Narayana Guru spent his young adult years as a wandering yogi, and during this phase often associated with Chattambi Swamigal (1853–1924), a one-time classmate and associate. They trained in Yoga and asceticism under the guidance of Swamy Ayyavu of Thaikkat. Chattambi Swamigal, who was just a tad bit older than

Sri Narayana Guru, gave the impetus for the social revolution that the latter would eventually spearhead. Most of Narayana Guru's wanderings were either along the coastlines of Kerala or in the interior villages of the present-day Tamil Nadu and these gave him first-hand knowledge of the life and deprivations of the people of the area. While Chattambi Swamigal worked for bringing equality between Brahmins and Nairs, Narayana Guru worked for equality between Nairs and Ezhavas. Narayana Guru was urged by his followers, among them Dr Palpu[5] and Kumaran Asan,[6] to begin a protest movement for the social recognition of the Ezhavas. The social front of the activities of Narayana Guru originated from forthrightly pursuing his universalistic and mystical stand on fundamental issues. Besides, on realizing that the very organization initiated for overcoming caste barriers on humanistic lines was eventually turning out to be casteist, he disowned it and distanced himself from leading the same.[7] The philosophic-mystical appropriation of the advaitic insight through his meditations and the compassionate outreach to the poor and deprived in concrete measures of involvement in their lives characterized his unique personality. His travels through the length and breadth of the present Kerala and the adjacent districts of neighbouring Tamil Nadu was with the mission of spreading the good word of the possibility for people to stand up for their rights and recreate their life through creative health care measures, economic activities, and, above all, investment in education. In his days he stood out as a spiritual leader and social reformer with a wide following within the state and eventually even beyond. Sri Narayana Guru died in 1928.[8]

In focusing on the course to social reformation chosen by Narayana Guru, one finds a non-sectarian and non-anti-Brahmin stand. It is a measure of his achievement as 'one of the greatest reformers of the last hundred and fifty years' that he accomplished the task of uplifting the lives of millions without recourse to violence. Faced with the reality of unequal treatment by people who professedly proclaimed the equality of all beings, his strategy was to redefine the very core of the tradition that had degenerated, in order to reform society. According to one of his biographers, Moorkoth Kumaran,

> he attained the higher levels of spiritual awareness by immersing himself in the teachings of the Upanishads. ... As he attained these

levels, his entire life became a refutation of the claims of the orthodox as to their superiority; his beatific state became a refutation of the assertions of the orthodox that the esoteric lore was closed to the lower castes.[9]

He has thus made a contribution not only to the deprived in giving them a true sense of worth but also succeeded in rewriting the norms of holiness and non-duality by revaluing and re-normalizing the very tradition for contemporary times.

Narayana Guru wrote in Malayalam, Sanskrit, and Tamil with equal ease and proficiency. The extant works attributed to him are nearly sixty, of varying length. Some of them are triplets (*muktakam*) and others of five verses (*panchakam*), and yet others of eight verses (*ashtakam*) or of ten verses (*dasakam*), and still others of hundred verses (*satakam*). His works include poetry as well as prose. He also has some translations from Sanskrit and Tamil to Malayalam. Some works attributed to him are yet to be traced. His extant works can further be classified under five headings: hymns (*stotram*), exhortations (*anusasanam*), philosophies (*darsanam*), translations (*vivartanam*), and prose (*gadhyam*).[10] However, such a system of classification often obscures more than it reveals, presupposing as it does the idea that these are genres that can always be distinguished with ease from one another. Some of the hymns have a markedly philosophical component and similarly some philosophical works can also be considered as exhortations, as in the case of *Atmopadesa Satakam*. The hymns which are in praise of gods and goddesses are basically supplications. Within hymns, which constitute nearly half his works, one could further see subgroups such as those written for particular deities, those composed with no specific deity as the focus, those penned with the intention of helping the mind to concentrate, and those written to mark some special occasion.

Sri Narayana Guru's writings were mostly extempore. Often the more serious works were dictated by him and transcribed by his disciples. Besides the above classification, his works can also be regarded as containing mystical hymns of inspired exultation, simple teaching for the common folk, philosophical renditions for the elite, and translations. The philosophical works are *Atmopadesa Satakam* (One Hundred Verses of Self Instruction), *Advaita Dipika* (Lamp of Nondual

Wisdom), *Brahmavidya Pancakam* (Five Verses of the Knowledge of the Absolute), *Municarya Pancakam* (Five Verses on the Practices of the Sage), *Arivu* (Knowledge), and *Darsanamala* (Garland of Visions). Significant as these literary works are in understanding the vision of Narayana Guru, it is just as important to acknowledge the cultural impact his initiation and quiet leadership of a social movement has had on society.

The inheritors of the Narayana Guru Tradition are threefold: (*a*) the Sri Narayana Dharma Paripalana Yogam (SNDP), which could be considered as the continuators of the socio-political wing of the Narayana Guru tradition with a pan-Kerala and even India presence; (*b*) Sri Narayana Dharma Sangham (SNDS) Trust established at Sivagiri in the vicinity of Varkala, Kerala; and (*c*) the Narayana Gurukula Foundation, established by Nataraja Guru at Sivagiri, Sreenivasapuram, Varkala, with networked units in different parts of Kerala, India, and abroad. While the second group focused on the religio-cultural changes effected by Narayana Guru disciples, the third group concentrated on the philosophic-mystical intent contained in the teachings of the Guru. This latter lineage in its appropriation of the teaching and practice of Narayana Guru includes Nataraja Guru, Nitya Chaitanya Yati, and Muni Narayana Prasad, all exponents of the philosophy and vision of Narayana Guru in their writings.

The popularity of the movement initiated by Narayana Guru is visible in the innumerable associations and initiatives begun in his name across the state, the country, and in the world. It is interesting to note that the stature of Narayana Guru has been steadily growing in and outside Kerala. His personality, socio-religious activities, and literary accomplishments come together in placing him among the sages on the cultural scene of contemporary Kerala. The growth of a person's fame after his lifetime is greatly dependent on his followers and admirers. A growing network of institutions and projects associated with his name reveals his inspirational power and the manner in which the Guru lives on in the minds and hearts of his followers and admirers.

Coming from within a region of India that has had over a millennia of history of the confluence of more than one religious tradition, Narayana Guru's primary dictums, 'one Kind, one Faith, and one God for Man', and 'whatever the religion, it is good enough if it makes a person better', have a liberating tone. They liberate the essence and truth of religion from the sedimentation it inevitably gathers over a period of time. It is a radical critique not to negate but to redefine the core of religion from within and because of which alone individual religions as paths, *margas*, ways of salvation have a relevance and *raison d'être*. The goal of the human is to strive for liberation, this being nothing other than 'deliverance from every constraint, from all limitation, for any limit stands like a wall, blocking us, preventing our flowering'.[11] The act of critically exercising freedom is the religious act by which a person is saved or doomed. The religious act is the act of freedom. It is such freedom which makes the assertion that 'One of Kind, One of Faith, and One in God is Man'. A rereading of this dictum within the totality of the teaching of Narayana Guru contains great potential for resolving contemporary paradoxes within India as well as globally.

In his years as a wandering revolutionary, Narayana Guru established many temples and made them instruments of reform. Unusually for Hindu temples, they were shorn of deities: in some, he had the words *satyam* (truth), *daya* (kindness), and *dharmam* (righteousness) inscribed; in another, there was just a burning lamp at the altar; and in still another there were just the words *Aum Tat Sat* (Aum, That is the Existent). He had no rivalry with any religion. He taught that whatever may be a person's religion, one should be good. In the *Atmopadesa Satakam*, he stated that the many faiths have but one essence (verse 44) and revealed the common goal of all humanity: 'all beings are making effort in every way, all the time, for the happiness of the Self; in the world, this is the one faith' (verse 49).[12] The word he uses in Malayalam for 'happiness of the Self' is *atmas-ukham*. This common goal of humanity is that in which and through which all of Humankind realizes to be of 'One God, One Kind and One Religion'.

The One World Vision

This vision placed against the emerging global awareness provides insights into attitudinal and policy level changes called for in social living especially for the preservation and promotion of harmony in society. The divisions in society, old as well as contemporary, of peoples on the basis of race, sex, religion, region, and language are premised on assumptions of inequality. The traditional ancient wisdom,[13] in contrast, was that of equality and its recurrent resurgence is what one finds as the ingenuity of Indian civilization. This resurgence, it is argued, is premised on the social consciousness as well as global awareness combined in a creative way so as to resist any move to divide society, and, instead, in seeking harmony through dialogue.

The search for the foundations of social consciousness in contemporary society entails looking into the sources of violence that underlie all types of segregation, discrimination, and marginalization. This cannot but be identified as rooted within differences of religious identities construed, constructed, and preserved for the purposes of sectarianism and its advantages for vested groups. The pre-modern religious identities and their demarcations got a fresh lease of life in the order of creed, code, and cult which are inventions of modern Europe in the wake of its own theological battles between Catholicism and Protestantism. Demarcations along these lines have urged the people elsewhere too to define themselves as identifiable in terms of religious categorizations against others around them.[14] This has given rise to that part of modern India's problems which began with the bizarre logic that informed the Partition of the subcontinent along religious lines to establish Hindu–Muslim identities and has now reached the heights of identity politics and vote bank calculations. The forcible enforcement of the logic of Partition in the Punjab as opposed to its inability or non-enforceability in the east/Assam where the Muslim population is the highest in India and reminiscent of pre-Independence days points to the grossness of the problem.[15]

It is in the context of these socially definable complexities of the identities drawn around language, region, religion, and ethnicity that new modes of thinking are imperative. The Narayana Guru tradition offers a possible entry into such thinking beyond the confines of a given religion or even culture. The post-secular and post-religious nature of the religiosity proposed by Narayana Guru's vision or contained therein has been elaborated by me elsewhere.[16] Here I would like to focus on the transformation that the writings of Narayana Guru underwent in the hands of two generations of his disciples represented in the two successive heads of the Gurukula Foundation:

Nataraja Guru (1895–1973), the founder, and Nitya Chaitanya Yati (1924–1999), the second generation head of the organization.

It is noteworthy that Narayana Guru, who had a mystic religious experience in the hidden solitude of the mountains, came down to the plains in order to awaken an illiterate mass from its miseries, which were often self-imposed if not coercively perpetuated by agents who benefited from the system. This social tenor of his involvement in society and the religious fervour of his writings got transformed in nuanced ways in the hands of his successors.[17] In this transformative process a couple of features are prominent: first, there is the link between concrete programmatic action and the idealistic goal of eradicating inequality and its accompanying discriminations. Narayana Guru, with his philosophico-spiritual compositions as well as social reformation drive, Nataraja Guru with his commentaries on Narayana Guru's texts and his foundation of Gurukula work, Nitya with his missionary tours around the world preaching the word of the Guru and reinterpreting his writings[18] in Malayalam and English from Fernhill[19] and Varkala[20] reveal the adeptness with which opposites—the outward move for expansion and the inward move for in-depth analysis—were brought into unity.

Second, for a community deprived of the access to education, the role of written literature became highly significant in the generation and spread of social consciousness. The cumulative impact of the literature produced by the three generations of *guru–sishya parampara* over the minds of people across class, caste, sex, and the religion divide is phenomenal.[21] The studies that are on across the globe on the *guru parampara* are indicative of this fact. Internally, within Kerala, too, the impact of the gurus has been constantly substantiated by academics of diverse political and ideological persuasions. The hermeneutical attempt to discover and reinterpret the tradition for contemporary times is an ongoing process.

Third, in the case of Nataraja Guru, the distance he maintained from those followers of the guru who wanted to exclusively politicize his role in the transformation of Kerala society, and the effort in turn he made to highlight the Guru's vision as having a broader, deeper, and more lasting contribution deserves scrutiny. He highlighted the universality of his Guru's message for persons across the world and believing in its power laid the foundations of Gurukulam (a commune

of disciples around a Guru), bringing about a new appreciation for
the movement. This is evinced in the manner persons were drawn to
him from all over the world. He was instrumental in the beginning of
Values, a monthly initiated by John Spiers,[22] the very first disciple of
Nataraja Guru, which later became the inspiration for the *Gurukulam*
magazine, and the sprouting of Gurukulas with persons committed to the cause in Kerala, Tamil Nadu, and other parts of the world
such as Singapore, Sydney, Fiji, and New York. Eventually, owing to
the efforts of Nitya Chaitanya Yati, the Guru's disciples would make
their presence felt in the United States, particularly in San Francisco,
Portland, and Bainbridge Island, Washington State.

Fourth, his writings such as *One World Education Manifesto, One
World Economics, Unitive Philosophy*[23] and participation in the ideas
mooted for a World Parliament and World Citizenship along with
Gary Davis, and the attempt to organize a world congress of religions
are indicative of a thinking and philosophy that arose out of the seeds
sown by the vision of Narayana Guru, who envisaged 'oru jati, oru
matham, oru daivam manushyanu' (oneness of caste, religion, and
godliness for the humankind) and even further visualized a form of
communal/societal living wherein 'whatever be the religion', the goal
is 'to better the human person' (*matam etayalum manushyan nannayal
mati*). It could also be translated or paraphrased to mean 'regardless
of his/her religion man/woman has to uphold his/her worthiness'.
The purport of the Guru Vision has been to provide impetus for such
a perception gripping individuals strongly enough so as to create a
new wave in society.

The transition from the leadership that Nataraja Guru gave to the
Gurukula Foundation to that of Guru Nitya probably marked a shift
from the attempts to make the vision of Narayana Guru globally known
to that of reinventing his image within Kerala and then beyond. This
is evident in the corpus of writings that Guru Nitya generated in the
Malayalam language bringing the vision of the Guru to a contemporary audience in a linguistic style that appealed to and captured the
imagination of an upcoming generation, urging it to think beyond its
given borders of psychic as well as religious perceptions.

One of the chief characteristics of the guru parampara, after
Narayana Guru, has been its attempt to show the universality of the
vision of the guru with its applicability across cultures. This was the

goal with which Nataraja Guru and Nitya endeavoured to link the knowledge base of the contemporary world with guru vision in their respective masterpieces of *Integrated Science of the Absolute* presently being re-edited for a new reprint by Scott Teitsworth[24] of Portland Gurukula and *The Psychology of Darsanamala*.[25] The following both the gurus received from persons of diverse backgrounds from across the world indicates yet again Narayana Guru's receptivity beyond the shores of Kerala where it originated. The twofold trend of showing its connectedness with a past heritage as well as its receptivity in contemporary thought frames—be it of structuralism or poststructuralism, or in the application of the principles of feminism and psychoanalysis to reinterpret tradition—defined their efforts to make known the guru vision.[26]

Positioning the Vision of SNG

The third part of this chapter attempts to bring to focus the relevance of the guru parampara in terms of its contributions for revitalizing contemporary Indian society in more ways than one: the caste problem, the issue revolving around appreciations and resistances to colonial modernity, the emergence of indigenous rationality, the critique of tradition and its dominance in keeping peoples subjected, the emergence of vernacular as a medium, and discourses revolving around power are all areas that will stand to gain in engaging with the parampara. In all these, two gains can be identified: first, the recovery of the value of tradition for its inherently 'modern' components; and, second, in highlighting the uniqueness of the leadership that Narayana Guru offered in and through his apparently non-confrontationist attitude and yet challenging postures to the dominant.[27] These postures offer new scope for mitigating the continued conflict-ridden scenarios, whether in cultural, religious, economic, or political arena. As a result one outcome would be a renewed emphasis on his message of universal brotherhood and equality of humankind and compassion for all beings. It can be argued that his leadership also had a second unique feature: unlike other nationalist figures Narayana Guru stands out as a team collaborator and leader by consensus rather than being a trailblazing loner. This characteristic of his leadership, therefore, calls for positioning him along with his contemporaries who teamed up with him as well as his followers who championed his cause along with him and after him. Therefore, a scrutiny of his significance has to be based in the context of the movements he left behind or which were initiated with his concurrence.

The world of Indian philosophers of modern India can be grouped broadly under three categories: revivalists, reformers, and transformers. The first group may be described as being concerned with the preservation of tradition and that too in all its purity. They would prefer to remain within the sanskritic or vernacular traditions within which the schools emerged and have continued. For them, it is in preserving this tradition and its orthodoxy that the credit for being a truly Indian philosopher is premised.

The second group attempts to reform the conceptualizations of the traditional schools by trying to modernize and reform them by applying schemes of modern Western philosophy to the classical philosophical schemes and framework. This has brought about a freshness and new lease of life considering the overall goal any branch of philosophy has of winning over adherents from across the world. Reformists, however, move within the fixed grooves of one or the other traditional schools and one or the other modern Western philosophical trends. These mergers, comparisons, and contrasts do pave the way for attempting similar juxtapositions between other schools and traditions. Here the familiarity is assumed with the classical language of philosophy as well as with one or the other modern European languages with which the respective philosophers are engaging their reformist philosophical enterprise.

The third group of transformist philosophers consists of indigenous initiators of new paths that are an answer to the cultural socio-ethical dead ends that a society experiences in epochs of great transition. The arrival of colonial modernity and the varied responses to it across the country gave rise to many a transformist philosopher of repute. The manner in which each in their own times and circumstances challenged status quo and orthodox traditions in order to make way for the liberation of people in their respective times and contexts is yet to be recorded in all its details. The Narayana Guru vision under reference in this chapter is one such ingenious attempt to transform a people by applying indigenous wisdom to the requirements of modern age.

In order to position the significance of the guru vision, it needs to be placed along with other visionaries and their contributions. In terms of quantity, the writings of Narayana Guru do not remotely compare to what an Ambedkar or Gandhi has left behind. However, the impact he made in the transformation of a people, and the potential that inheres in his life for becoming a norm in transforming other similarly placed contexts, suggests that the comparison of the Guru with Gandhi and Ambedkar is not only reasonable but requisite. It is all the more significant in terms of strategic decisions and postures undertaken in the face of problems that challenged them and continues to challenge Indian leadership in the socio-political arena.

Among the many makers of modern India, Sri Narayana Guru, Gandhi, and Ambedkar represent three strands[28] of envisioning the future of the country. Gandhi, despite having had full exposure at a mature age to Western civilization, was not enchanted by it; rather, the exposure brought him back to ground himself in some of what he believed to be eternal values of the Indian civilization, which he found could offer a new model for a new world. Gandhi's strategies of non-violent resistance in South Africa and India having been emulated by political activists across the world with varying degrees of success, it may be said that he has found a prominent place among world leaders who have offered grand schemes with a view to transforming the world. The growing scholarship on Gandhi from across the world is indicative of his undisputed stature. One recognizes as well that, of late, there have also been highly critical reviews and biographies of him and a reassessment of his role in giving a direction to modern India, especially vis-à-vis his stand towards, and responses to, the Dalit cause espoused by Ambedkar.[29] As for India, Gandhi dreamt of a *ramrajya* of harmonious and participatory governance to be achieved based on the principles of *swaraj* applied at the grass-roots village level.

Ambedkar had an exposure to the Western world and took to being an ardent admirer of the same, coming as he did from a background of victimization resulting from segregation and exclusionary social practices prevalent in Indian society. The possibility of a brighter future for his countrymen (those excluded from the brahminic scheme as he had been) became the moving force behind his concerted action to transform Indian society by taking up the radical challenge, which he perceived as the inevitable option, to extricate himself and the Dalit communities from the weight of brahminic tradition. His deeply analytical assessment of India's past and the pragmatic and programmatic attempt to reverse the wrongs of the past met with stiff opposition from a Gandhi who was not able to see eye to eye with Ambedkar as regards the future he envisaged for India. On the other hand, the proposal for 'self-purification' of the tainted tradition that Gandhi attempted as a 'troubled insider' was not acceptable to Ambedkar, who wanted to spearhead a project of massive 'self-respect' among a people described as 'outcasts', himself having been a 'struggling victim' in a caste-ridden society that perpetuated the iniquities of caste. While Gandhi worked for a 'civilized society where people do not humiliate one another' by reforming the old, Ambedkar laboured for a 'decent society where institutions do not humiliate people' by dismantling the old.[30] Most likely, the destruction of social structures, however comprehensive, never succeeds to totally annihilate or wipe out the evils that surrounded them, as they resurface within the same society in and through the memories of the past, in new resuscitated forms. Ambedkar envisioned an egalitarian society where opportunities are denied to none as in the best of then existing welfare state models in the West, at least in their avowed efforts to create such a salubrious state of affairs.

Narayana Guru's exposure to the West came in the form of the colonial masters who were making their presence felt in the Hindu kingdom of Travancore and in and through the foreign disciples and visitors he had on and off. His equal appreciation for Sanskrit as well as English as fundamental to the training of the younger generation and his own initiative in encouraging Nataraja Guru to undertake a travel to Europe to complete his studies are indicative of the way he envisaged the arrival of modernity impacting the Kerala society in particular and the preparedness the Indian subcontinent needed to face the transition the entire culture was to undergo. As a transformist spiritual leader of the time his own inspirations are *desi* more than 'derivative' and his goals seem to challenge tradition with its own cards as it were from a 'beyond' standpoint.[31] He is not easily classifiable as a patriot nor as a nationalist in ordinary parlance. Yet, he was an ardent promoter of *atmasukham* (soul happiness), an interior self-defining characteristic as the point of reference for well-being both at the individual and collective level. This outlook is best displayed in his most seminal work, *Atmopadesa Satakam.*

In order to situate Narayana Guru among the transformist philosophers/leaders and to bring him to the front stage of prevailing discourse, the categorizations used by Gopal Guru come to aid. He gives five reasons for the distinctive character of the 'beyond' in contrast to the 'desi' and the 'derivative': first, it seeks 'to render visible the thinking that otherwise is pushed beneath and beyond the public imagination'; second, it is 'different both in terms of style and substance'; third, as a socio-political conceptualization it plays 'an important role of recasting the real (largely un-thought) into reflection'; fourth, its articulation 'adopts a vocabulary, which might appear to be negative or grotesque' to the 'desi' and 'derivative'; and finally, as most important for our present consideration, it goes 'beyond', 'particularly in terms of its search for an alternative normative ideal'.[32]

The encounter with colonial modernity gave rise to the hitherto well-documented twofold reactionary responses: one that of outrage due to other lands occupying the hallowed landscape of India without legitimacy as couched in the 'desi' stand, and, the other, in the claim held up for a nation becoming ready to take on the full responsibility of self-rule demanding swaraj in the 'derivative' discourse built around the aspirations of imitating the developments in Europe. Both these discourses felt uncomfortable with the truth of an excluded India of the 'untouchable', Dalit, *bahiskrut bharat*, and its own version of the articulations of what India ought to be is what the 'beyond' category intends to bring to focus. In articulating the 'alternative normative ideal' of what the nation, or the world itself ought to be, there are divergences between Phule, Periyar, Ambedkar, and Narayana Guru. This difference is one reason why probably even among the Dalit intellectuals there is a reservation in bringing to sharp focus the role played by Narayana Guru.

Narayana Guru outlines an alternative normative ideal without taking on the anti-stand that one finds ordinarily associated with most Dalit ideologues. Though the negative language of the Dalit can be a strategic stand and a propaedeutic one and therefore has to be acknowledged for its constructive potential, Narayana Guru's posture was different: first, in the fact that he admonishes the oppressor and the oppressed in the same breath; second, he thereby lifts the problematic to a level that touches the core of the issue—overcoming the stigma of caste in a person, as well as among a people: both by way of self-belief or acceptance and by way of attribution onto the other. We shall take a closer look into this transformative vision in the next section.

Transformative Power of SNGM Vision

The 200 odd pages of the original writings of Narayana Guru in Malayalam, Tamil, and Sanskrit have been elaborated upon in commentaries and interpretative renderings by Nataraja Guru, Nitya Chaitanya Yati, and Muni Narayana Prasad into a little more than 200 works. The spiritual vision as a philosophical enterprise gives rise to literature (prose and poetry, religious and secular) and the literature in turn evokes and mobilizes a people towards a new direction in life—individually and collectively—to achieve transformative goals. In order to measure the impact of this literature a study had been undertaken on the evolution of the movement with special reference to the Gurukula Foundation. One of the issues of discontent by a few who went through the research undertaken by the author into the SNGM and its vision has been built around the attempt to concretize the person and the message in a socio-historical context. This effort has been critiqued as 'narrowing the vision of the guru' contrary to his stated and avowed intention. It is true that the 'one world vision' of Narayana Guru is a universal message meant as an ideal and for the application across the globe. However, the perspective of the present study is aimed at showing how it originated in a particular time and space, just as the other universal messages associated with the Buddha, Zoroaster, Christ, Confucius, the Prophet Mohammed, or Guru Nanak also originated at particular moments of history and in specific geographical locations. Therefore, the socio-historical contextualizing is no disservice to the Guru or his vision, but rather an attempt to empirically ground the vision into the particular context from where its universal relevance originates.

The grounded thinking that Narayana Guru forthrightly expressed is evident in the question that he put forward to Gandhi: 'In the name of caste and superstition, money, force and denial of opportunity when the majority of the population called "low" were considered as slaves by the so-called Brahminic elite for centuries, what right does India have to ask freedom from the British?'[33] This happens in the context of Gandhi's prevarication on the issue of Vaikom Satyagraha about which Dr Palpu, Narayana Guru's voice and right hand, wrote to Gandhi in no uncertain terms that 'the right to walk through public roads is one that even dogs and pigs enjoy everywhere without having to resort to any *satyagraha* at all. Besides, the present *satyagraha* at Vaikom is only a year old, but our struggle here has been going on for some centuries now'.[34] Despite such strong language, the overall tenor of the writings of the Guru gives the impression of moving in a realm in which change can be effected irrespective of the happenings in the ordinary world. This combination of the representation of the emotional content of the struggle in an evocative language coupled with the philosophical insights into the spiritual dimension of the inner world is what gives shape to the unique vision of Sri Narayana Guru and its transformative power.

What Narayana Guru draws attention to in his 'one world vision' is the layered depth to the problematic—the age-old hegemonic ideo-logical impact on a people and their self-perceptions needing a cor-rective at the very root where the impact has been the most intense. He was drawing attention to the 'unending struggle at the core of consciousness', and at the 'contradictory consciousness' derived out of the double bind of 'acceptance and resistance to definitions of self' imposed by caste ideology. This struggle and search for the unen-cumbered self-definition though couched in a mystical–philosophic language of poetry[35] thereby exposes the political aspirations of a people desiring to move from being assigned to the periphery to the recognition that they are the centre.

The one world vision encapsulated in the dictum oru jati, oru matam, oru daivam manushyanu envisages a world where other con-siderations dwindle into nothingness. The promotion of harmonious living between men and women and between humankind and rest of creation endeavouring to find their place in the divine realm, all three as intertwined, is at the core of the vision. Of all the evils that hampered harmonious living in society he found the caste prejudices as playing the greatest havoc and found them to be unscientific and baseless. Nevertheless, the hold of caste over people's imagination needed a radical critique, which he provided through his reinterpretation of *advaita* (non-dualism).

The advaita that he mooted and that is at the core of his vision is 'an attitude and an approach'; an intuition into 'the way things are, reality is, and perception functions'. For him, it is not merely one of the systems of philosophies circulating in India, rather it is 'the yardstick of all systems, as the core of Indian religiosity-rationality: it is an intellective intuition into reality gaining ever new religious sanction and adherents'.[36] Confronting the problem of deeply embedded caste consciousness and seeking a solution to liberate the oppressed as well as the oppressor, he has recourse to 'advaita' as a key: to open up the possibilities of self-definition, escaping the burden of 'other-imposed' conceptualizations of who one is or who one can be. One may think of it as a key that enabled the victim of casteist society to move away from having to 'live in a shifting zone of interpretations between dominant conceptions and their own' towards fashioning 'one's own conception of the world'. Sukumar Azhikode refers to Narayana Guru 'on his journey carrying the cross of caste' coming to discover advaita as a tool. It acts as a key in as much as it enables one to contain differences and yet be 'oneself'—as self-possessed and determined as one can be.

The key to social transformation lies in the transformation of the self-understanding of people as neither inferior nor superior, neither as dominated nor as dominating any one. This self transformation has to be effected through a change in the prevailing self consciousness. The transformation of consciousness is the route to social transformation. How this can be achieved is what the vision of SNGM shows.

Notes and References

1. The movement under reference is the Narayana Gurukula Foundation begun by Nataraja Guru (1895–1973) in order to carry forward the spiritual and philosophical ideals espoused by Narayana Guru (1854–1928).

2. Mathew Adams, *Self and Social Change* (New Delhi: Sage Publications, 2007), 50.

3. Kilimanoor Visvambaran, *Kerala Samskara Darsanam* (Kilimanoor: Kanchanagiri Books, 1990).

4. Though atrocities against Dalits continue in different parts of the country, and their collective status is yet to attain the desired equality as enshrined

in the constitution, in the case of Kerala some significant gains have been achieved over the past century. It is in expanding this egalitarian outlook and inclusive social space that the Kerala Model of social change and its ideological undercurrents need wider discursive circulation.

5. Son of Taccukudy Palpu of Trivandrum, he was the first to procure the licence from Madras Medical College to be a medical practitioner from among the Izhava community. He was denied a job in the Cochin and Travancore States due to his caste identity, and this discrimination urged him to mobilize around Narayana Guru the demand for the legitimate rights of the community from the state through the signature campaign and memorandum submitted on 13 May 1895 to the Dewan of Travancore.

6. Kumaran Asan (1873–1924), the celebrated poet of Malayalam literature, was well versed in Malayalam and Sanskrit having studied in Bangalore and Kolkata. He was the secretary of Yogam, the association set up for the promotion of the Izhava community from its inception in 1903 until 1919. He was the editor of the journal *Vivekodayam*, the ideological mouthpiece of the community.

7. He made a declaration on 28 May 1916 from his Advaithashram in Alwaye, Kerala, that he had neither caste nor religion: 'Already some years have passed since I gave up caste, but I have come to know that still some particular groups consider me as belonging to their sect and behave accordingly. Because of that, an awareness is generated which is against truth. I don't belong to a particular caste or religion.' Compare SNGCC, *Oneness* (March–August 2017), 40, available at http://www. sreenarayanaguru.in/content/advaithashramam-chapter-%E2%80%93-9 (accessed on 9 April 2019).

8. Nitya Chaitanya Yati, *Narayana Guru* (Delhi: ICPR Studies on Classical and Contemporary Builders of Indian Philosophy Series, 2005).

9. Moorkoth Kumaran, *Biography of Narayana Guru* (Calicut: PK Brothers, 1971).

10. T. Bhaskaran, *Sreenarayana Guruvinte Kavyasarani* (Kottayam: DC Books, 1991), 10.

11. Kilimanoor Visvambaran, *Kerala Samskara Darsanam* (Kilimanoor: Kanchanagiri Books, 1990).

12. Muni Narayana Prasad, 'The Overall Structure of *Atmopadesasatakam*', in *Gurukulam* (September 2016), 5–11.

13. The two sources of ancient wisdom referred to here are, first, the sangam literature and the call for egalitarianism found therein, and second, the upanishadic insights of the mahavakyas that give rise to the Advaita Vedanta.

14. David Scott, 'Toleration and Historical Traditions of Difference', in *Subaltern Studies XI, Community, Gender and Violence*, ed. Partha Chatterjee and Pradeep Jeganathan (Delhi: Permanent Black, 2005), 290.

15. Sanjib Baruah, 'Assam: Confronting a Failed Partition', *Seminar 591*, November 2008.

16. George Thadathil, 'Sri Narayana Guru's Vision of Liberative Religiosity: A Post Secular Approach to Religion', *Divyadaan Journal of Philosophy and Education* 16, no. 2 (2005): 195–228.

17. Nitya Chaitanya Yati, *Narayana Guru* (New Delhi: Indian Council of Philosophical Research, 2005).

18. A detailed account of the works of all three gurus is found in my *Vision from the Margin* (Sonada and Bangalore: Salesian College & Asian Trading Corporation, 2007).

19. A hamlet in the outskirts of Ooty, a hill station in the state of Tamil Nadu, India, has easy access from Kerala and Karnataka, the two other neighbouring states, which makes it a popular tourist destination in south India. It was developed by the British due to its soothing climatic conditions and suitability for tea cultivation. Nataraja Guru had a 3 acre plot with a house gifted him at Fernhill and lived most of his years there, except when visiting other Gurukula centres or their headquarters at Varkala. Nitya Chaitanya Yati, too, in the latter part of his life settled in Fernhill and has his Samadhi there.

20. The Narayana Guru Movement though began with the installation of the idol at Aruvipuram in Trivandrum district of Kerala, the headquarters of the Sree Narayana Dharma Paripalana Yogam and eventually that of the Sree Narayana Dharma Sangham (the monastic order) and the Gurukula Foundation initiated by Nataraja Guru (with his Samadhi, the Brahmavidya mandiram) being there. Varkala, in the Quilon district of Kerala, has come to be the centre of Sri Narayana Guru Movement.

21. The word 'parampara' describes the intellectual lineage under which, over generations, knowledge is transmitted from a teacher (guru) to a disciple (shisya); in time, the latter takes over the mantle of the guru and in turn transmits knowledge to his students.

22. Compare P.R. Sreekumar, 'The Life and Values of John Spiers', *Gurukula* (May 2017), 39–45.

23. Nataraja Guru, *Unitive Philosophy* (New Delhi: DK Printworld, 2005). It is a combined volume of three earlier publications which were originally serialized articles of the magazine *Values*.

24. Scott Teitsworth is a lifelong student of Indian philosophy and modern science under the guidance of Nitya Chaitanya Yati, himself a disciple of Nataraja Guru. Teitsworth hosts the Portland branch of Narayana

Gurukula along with his wife, Deb Buchanan. He is the author of *Krishna in the Sky with Diamonds* and *The Path to the Guru: The Science of Self-Realization according to the Bhagavad Gita* (2014), besides having re-edited *Love and Blessings: Autobiography of Nitya Chaitanya Yati* (2003). *The Integrated Science of the Absolute* (3 vols) was originally published by Gurukula Publication, Varkala in 1977 with a reprint by DK Printworld, Delhi, in 1982.

25. Nitya Chaitanya Yati, *The Psychology of Darsanamala* (Varkala: Gurukula Publication, 1987).

26. For example, in commenting on verse 5 of *Advaita Dipika*, Nitya says, 'What is the world the Guru is speaking of? He is speaking of your world and my world—the world that is being structured in, around, and through every person' (Nitya, *Narayana Guru*, 127).

27. See, in this regard, the interpretation given by Satheese Chandra Bose, '(Re)construction of "the Social" for Making a Modern Kerala: Reflections on Naryana Guru's Social Philosophy', in *Kerala Modernity: Ideas, Spaces and Practices in Transition*, edited by Satheese Chandra Bose and Shiju Sam Varughese (Delhi: Orient Blackswan, 2015), 59–73.

28. See two other works of mine, one published in Johnson J. Puthenpurackal, ed., *Enhancing Our Home: Re-reading Gandhian Vision of Life* –Festschrift in honour of Dr A Pushparajan (Bangalore: ATC, 2016), entitled, 'Reading Gandhi in Ambedkar's Shoes: Reclaiming Democracy'; and the other a paper presented at the Cochin Conference of the Backwaters Collective held at Le Meridien, Cochin from 14–17 July 2016, entitled, 'A Conciliatory Gaze: Sri Narayana Guru on BR Ambedkar and MK Gandhi'.

29. Aishwary Kumar, 'The Ellipsis of Touch: Gandhi's Unequals', *Public Culture* (Spring 2011): 449–69. See also Aakash Singh, 'Gandhi and Ambedkar: Irreconcilable Differences?', *International Journal of Hindu Studies* 18, no. 3 (2014): 413–49.

30. Thadathil, *Vision from the Margin*, 199. See also George Thadathil, 'A Conciliatory Bridge: The Gaze of SNG at BR Ambedkar and MK Gandhi', presented at the Backwaters Collective's Cochin Conference, Le Meridien, 14–17 July 2016; Aishwary Kumar, 'Ambedkar's Inheritances', *Modern Intellectual History* (July 2010), available at https://www.cambridge.org/core/journals/modern-intellectual-history/article/ambedkars-inheritances/25536ABA831C58F679C3B7C4D9E4CF04 (accessed on 9 April 2019).

31. Gopal Guru makes the resourceful distinctions between the 'desi' and 'derivative' drawing upon Partha Chatterjee and adds a 'beyond' category to insert the Dalit interventions into the study of nationalist discourses.

32. Gopal Guru, 'The Idea of India: "Derivative, *Desi* and Beyond"', *Economic and Political Weekly* 46 (2011): 36–42, 37.

33. Nitya Chaitanya Yati, *Guruvinte Matruka* [The Example of the Guru] (Ooty, Tamil Nadu: Nitya Books), 18 (translation mine).

34. Private papers of Dr Palpu, file no. 7, quoted in T.K. Ravindran, *Vaikom Satyagraha and Gandhi* (Trichur: Sri Narayana Institute of Social and Cultural Development, 1975), 5. It is also to be noted that, commencing with the Vaikom incident, the temple entry issue became an all-India agenda of the Congress social reform project, especially with Gandhi at the helm.

35. Besides *Atmopadesasatakam* and *Darsanamala*, one can also get the pulse of his vision in *Arivu, Jatinirnayam, Daivadasakam, Kalinatakam*, and other poems.

36. Thadathil, *Vision from the Margin*, 210.

10

SREE NARAYANA ICONOGRAPHY
Its Transformation and Impact
on Society and Politics

SUJIT SIVANAND

Towards the end of the nineteenth century, as sage and philosopher Sree Narayana Guru (see Figure 10.1) gained acclaim for his spiritual and social reform initiatives, the publication of visual imagery and the iconographic characterization of Narayana Guru also gained momentum across south India and Ceylon (Sri Lanka). Moreover, the public use, display, and undertones of the Sree Narayana genre of imagery and characterization have gone through much transformation over the last century.

Although iconography refers more specifically to the pictorial material or physical imagery that represents a religious or legendary subject, this chapter attempts to extend the relevance of iconography to include the personal and social reverence implied in the iconic characterization of Narayana Guru. Whilst many surviving photographs evidence the persona, life, and times of the Guru, this study of visual imagery (including sketches, paintings, and sculpture) characterizing the Guru,

Figure 10.1 A popular portrait of Sree Narayana Guru (1855–1928)
Source: https://commons. wikimedia.org/wiki/.

since the turn of the twentieth century up to the present, also aims to trace the role of such imagery in driving the different storylines of this guru in the spiritual and political domains.

Since Narayana Guru is seen as one in the continuum in the lineage of poet-sages from ancient times, combined with his role as a social reformer in pre-independent India, he has a large following in the country across conservatively religious as well as rationally liberal segments of the population. A philosophical reasoning of Sree Narayana iconography could be applied to distinguish the *objective* reality of any man-made physical and visual imagery on the one hand and on the other the Guru as an iconic phenomenon in the *subjective* realm of a follower's mind. This physical and conceptual argument could further be applied to larger groups of people. From a politically conservative perspective, the objective and representative physical icon, when placed in an appropriately divine surrounding, such as a place of worship, creates an empowerment in the icon to take a certain control over those who hold faith in the icon. The icon in this situation becomes the object of a wishful and auspicious sight (*darsan*) for a group of steadfast believers. The icon further serves as the glue melding the group that shares a common faith and, nevertheless, also as dyke and fertile ground for furthering political objects of those in leadership and control. So, also from a liberal perspective, such an iconic phenomenon helps groups to take inspiration from the value-sets attributed to the icon. Though liberal groups may have a lesser commitment to leaders, the very spirit of freedom that the icon helps to instil in people's minds results in their collective empowerment by the icon, such as in the case of minorities and those who were historically socially underprivileged. Interestingly, Narayana Guru as an icon seems to hold appeal in all such political domains, particularly in Kerala, be it conservative, liberal, or people in between.

Besides visual imagery, of equal or greater interest to a serious researcher on Sree Narayana iconography is the evolution in the characterization and representation of the Guru through the use of Sree Narayana images by different social groups. Social organizations and even opposing political parties sometimes simultaneously use the Guru's image as an icon that bridges diversity and attracts and bonds their ranks, with individuals in most cadres identifying their values and ideology to one or more facets of the Guru's multifaceted personality and legacy. For instance, in the most recent state elections in Kerala in May 2016, all three prominent fronts, the United Democratic Front (UDF), Left Democratic Front (LDF), and Bharatiya Janata Party (BJP) alliances went to lengths linking and correlating their value sets to Narayana Guru and widely used imagery associated with the Guru in their election campaigns. It could be argued that the use of Narayana Guru as an icon by these ideologically opposed forces could have been with the intention to capture the votes of the state's single largest Ezhava community, which more closely lays direct claim to and motivational lineage from the Guru; but despite that obvious intent, somewhere underlying the ideological fences, Narayana Guru's value system stood as that firm common ground of political freedom and empowerment of the individual that all groups equally cherished.

Visual Iconography

Traditionally, realistic paintings, charcoal sketches, and sculpture were popular methods used to create iconography. Unlike the iconic images of Gautama Buddha or Jesus Christ that have originated from the imagination of artists and evolved into widely accepted forms of visual expression, the pictorial imagery of Narayana Guru has been largely guided by photorealism, a genre of art where realism is created to perfection based on photographs.

Narayana Guru's birth in the mid-nineteenth century coincided with inventions and development of black-and-white plate photography as a popular new medium of art. There are several real-life photographs of the Guru that have been in use in the public domain over the last century. Besides the works of photographers from the past, over the decades, numerous independently working artists, sculptors, filmmakers, graphic editors, and even government mints have created and replicated Narayana Guru imagery in diverse forms—such as portrait paintings, sketches, statues, relief works, character adaptations, digitally edited pictures, stamps and coins, and so on.

Reputed professional artists attempting to create portraits of Narayana Guru have had to ensure realism in the Guru's facial features, as any deviation from realism or 'likeness' would predictably result in rejection of the work by observers already familiar with the photographs of the Guru.

Figure 10.2 The earliest photograph of Nanu Asan in Anchuthengu
Source: Courtesy of the author.

The earliest surviving photograph of Narayana Guru dates back to 1880–5, presumably taken while the Guru was between the ages of 25 and 30 (Figure 10.2). This photograph entered the public domain at least a decade or more into the twentieth century. The photograph is said to have been taken during the days when young Nanu Asan, as he was known (Nanu is a diminutive for Narayana), worked as a teacher (*asan*) at a primary school in the coastal village of Anchuthengu, south of Thiruvananthapuram. Although what exists today is a heavily edited version of the photo, observably this frame captures the subject's attire comprising a simple white loincloth (*dhoti* or *mundu*), tied around the waist and extending to cover most of the legs, and a shawl (*thorthu*) loosely covering the upper body. Based on the social customs of those times, the addition of the shawl to the upper torso indicates the stature of the young man as a teacher or otherwise respectable person. The photo also draws attention in particular to his partly shaven head and hairdo knot (*kudumbi*), which no other photograph of his has captured. The subject at this point in time had a small build and an obviously demure appearance in the manner he sat for the photographer. A close observation of chronological photographs of Narayana Guru henceforward would unfold the dramatic transformation of the Guru's personage in the years to come.

Into his mid-40s, Narayana Guru had become recognized as a saintly person. Having initially attracted a following of local villagers seeking his skills in traditional Ayurvedic cures, he had by then set up the Aruvippuram *ashram* and the Siva temple by 1888, thence followed by the establishment of other temples in southern Travancore, wherever local underprivileged village folk needed a place of worship and sought his spiritual guidance. A noteworthy photograph from this period exists, in which Nanu Asan, as he was still known, has no tuft or kudumbi anymore but just the natural stubbly hair growth on

Figure 10.3 Photograph from the days when Nanu Asan had gained recognition as a saintly person
Source: Courtesy of the author.

an occasionally shaven head (Figure 10.3). Here he seems to sport an unshaven beard, slightly greying, along with his pectosternal pattern of chest hair. Besides the body and posture of the subject conforming to that of a yogi, what are noticeable from this photograph onward is his conscious effort to maintain an unemotional stare and alertness to slow-speed plate photography of the early days. Being seated on a deerskin could not have been for any reason other than it was befitting of the reputation as a *rishi* that he had gained by then.[1] There is yet another surviving photograph (Figure 10.4) from the same period, but apparently the subject is getting older (than in Figure 10.3) as seen from his receding hairline.

In a small chapel at the Sree Narayana Ashram in Pillayarpatti near Madurai there is a surviving print of a rare photograph of Nanu Asan assumed to be taken around the year 1895. The photograph shows Nanu Asan seated on a leopard skin with his head covered

Figure 10.4   Nanu Asan's photo showing a receding hairline
Source: Courtesy of the author.

(Figure 10.5). He looks tired and weathered from the effects of nature during meditative penance in the Aruvippuram area, which

was his base in those days. There exists yet another photograph in the public domain in which the subject appears to be in the same physical condition and bearing similar facial features (Figure 10.6), which point to these two pictures being from the same period. It is even possible that both photographs were captured in a studio setting on the same occasion.

On 25 January 1903, Narayana Guru, as he would have been already known by then, was the esteemed guest at the ancestral family home named Adipparambil in the coastal village of Valapad, in southern

Figure 10.5   Nanu Asan's photograph at Pillayarpatti, dated circa 1895
Source: Courtesy of the author.

Malabar. At a photo session arranged by the head of Adipparambil, a portrait of Narayana Guru was captured for the family. The only surviving print, still at Adipparambil, has a partly damaged emulsion layer.

Figure 10.7 shows a lightly restored version of the print. The Guru, 48 years old by then, poses for the picture in a casual manner, dispassionately seated on a chair decked with heavy drapery and with his hands coyly tucked between his knees.

Figure 10.6 Nanu Asan's photograph from circa 1895
Source: Courtesy of the author.

Figure 10.7 The only surviving copy of the Adipparambil portrait from 1903
Source: Courtesy of the author.

With the Guru's growing reputation as both an inspiring social change agent and a tolerant negotiator of pluralistic coexistence, he emerged as a newsmaker in community circles and political power centres. In 1904, the then Maharajah of Travancore exempted Narayana Guru from personal appearances in court, an honour recognizing the Guru as a distinguished living personality.[2] From this stage of his life onwards more portrait photographs appear to have been captured in studio settings. Each of these portraits, when closely reviewed, helps relate the progressing story of his remarkable life.

Figure 10.8 shot in a studio setting with an artwork background shows the subject consciously posing, standing erect, tall and confident of his stature as a recognized guru. He is clean-shaven and does not sport the beard from his days as a wandering ascetic. His attire has turned more formal, apparently in the manner in which his shawl flows from the shoulder and is partially wrapped around one the elbow.

Figure 10.8   Studio photo of Narayana Guru taken at the turn of the twentieth century
Source: Courtesy of the author.

In many respects the living Guru's esteem proliferated to such a high point that he was transformed as the subject of adoration at a personal level in the underprivileged commoners' spiritual realm—which until then was largely prostrated towards Brahminical dominance and restricted idolatry.

Photographs and art portraits of Narayana Guru have evidently played a role in raising the stature of the Guru in the minds of a growing population of followers, who were able to draw upon these objective portrait images of this living iconic personality as recorded in their minds, to be recalled from memory with reverence and as hope for resolving their social issues, and further as the image of strength behind their spiritual and other social reform initiatives. Narayana Guru himself has postulated that the *world* as *reality* is represented in the human mind by the bipolar relationship between *names* (subjective ideas, thoughts, and percepts) and *objects*. He penned this verse, setting out his line of reasoning as follows:

> *Names in their thousands*
> *Concepts in their thousands*
> *And the externally existing*
> *Objects in their thousands*
> *Corresponding to each of them –*
> *These together form the 'world'.*[3]

In other words, in the absence of such Guru imagery (the objective portraits) the Guru narrative at that point in history would not have been the same and as effective had it been fully left to peoples' subjective imagination or 'abstraction' of the person with the name Narayana Guru.

In the initial days of the Guru's popularity (1888–1905), the placement of a Narayana Guru image (painting, sketch, or photograph) in a follower's home was still a wishful thought for most, as there were no commercial channels that would make affordable prints available to the common man. It is assumed that in 1905 at the time of the industrial exhibition in Quilon (Kollam), commercially reproduced lithographic prints of the Guru's pictures became available, making them affordable. Then onward, lithographic reproductions of many photorealistic paintings, including one titled 'Sree Narayana Paramahamsan' (Figure 10.9), have been widely displayed across homes and establishments in (erstwhile) Travancore, Cochin, and Malabar states.

The Kolathukara temple is located in Kulathoor on the outskirts of Thiruvananthapuram city. It was originally a Bhagavaty temple often visited by Narayana Guru during his days as a wandering ascetic. In 1892 it was renovated and re-established as a Shiva temple under the Guru's guidance. In 1916, owing to the long association of Narayana Guru with the Kolathukara temple and as a mark of respect to the Guru on the occasion of his 60th birthday, the local townsfolk in charge of the temple commissioned an artist, Oruvathilkotta Kunjukrishna Kurup, to paint a portrait of the Guru. The oil painting portrays the Guru in a seated posture (Figure 10.10). The posture and even the folds of the subject's clothing closely resemble the

Figure 10.9   Fine art portrait titled 'Sree Narayana Paramahamsan'
Source: Courtesy of the author.

Sree Narayana Paramahamsan portrait. It is said that Narayana Guru
was present at the portrait's installation at Kolathukara temple, and
observing his followers rushing away from him to gather around the
portrait about to be installed at a chapel in the temple premises, the
Guru quipped, 'See, they are rushing away to see an image while the real
one stands here!'

Figure 10.10   The 1916 portrait painting at Kolathukara temple
Source: Courtesy of the author.

The present canvas at Kolathukara has undergone retouches and repair over the century as is visible from the contours of the subject's image and the background artwork.

Bodhananda Swamikal (1883–1928) was an ordained *sanyassi* (monk) from the order of the *Uttarāmnāya matha*, or the northern monastery at Joshimath, one of the four cardinal monasteries established by Adi Sankara. In 1908, Bodhananda Swamikal met

Figure 10.11   Surviving image of Bodhananda Swamikal's visit to Ceylon.
Copy of a portrait similar to the Kolathukara portrait is seen in the photo
Source: Courtesy of the author.

Narayana Guru and not much later he joined the path of Narayana
Guru, from then onwards becoming a trusted disciple and taking a
lead role in many of the Guru's spiritual and social reform initiatives.
Photographs of portraits similar to the Kolathukara portrait are visible in certain other photographs and publications that originated
in Ceylon during the life of the Guru and beyond (Figure 10.11).
A framed photograph of such a portrait can be seen in the group
photograph shot in Ceylon during the visit of Bodhananda Swamikal
in 1918. Another similar image was also used in 1947 as the cover picture of a publication by Sree Narayana Guru Celebration Committee
of Ceylon (Figure 10.12). All these
similar images discussed here
point to the possibility of there having existed an actual photograph
of Narayana Guru in this posture,
though no such photograph seems
extant in the public domain today.

1916 was a notable year as the
Sree Narayana Movement[4] celebrated
the Guru's 60th birthday as an auspicious event at that time. It was a
year filled with formal receptions

Figure 10.12   Cover of the 1947
publication in Colombo
Source: Courtesy of the author.

and celebrations across Travancore, Kochi, Malabar and in the larger cities of Madras, Calcutta, Bombay, Coimbatore, Bangalore, and Mangalapuram, and even beyond India in Ceylon, Singapore and Burma. In September, Narayana Guru and his entourage of monastic disciples had visited Madras, after which they were in the city of Kancheepuram in connection with establishing the Sree Narayana Sevashram. One of the most widely published photographs at that time was a seated portrait of the Guru, shot during this tour, captured and processed at the then renowned Klein & Peyrel studio in Madras (Figure 10.13). As Narayana Guru also visited a young Ramana Maharshi at Thiruvannamalai during this tour, this portrait most closely picturizes the Narayana Guru that Ramana sat face to face with. This is a powerful and striking portrait in which the Guru casts a piercing look at the camera. In most of the Guru's portrait photographs he has a characteristic unemotional stare for the camera, and this could have been the result of his deliberate concentration during the photoshoot, in an era of

Figure 10.13   Sree Narayana Guru at the age of 60 in 1916
Source: Courtesy of the author.

slow-speed plate photography, to avoid a subject-shake. A subject-shake in photography is the blurring caused by the subject moving during a shoot using slow-speed film/plate, even though the camera might be held steady or fixed to avoid any camera-shake.

Nataraja Guru, Narayana Guru's disciple, has recorded his vivid recollection of a photographing session he witnessed:

> *The cameraman had already arrived, but Narayana Guru raised his usual objections. On the insistence of all, he sat on a leopard-skin. Murmuring protests about something or other that was not right, he was at last prevailed upon to sit in the usual cross-legged posture of repose, confronting the camera. His casual countenance dropped its former mild indifference and became deep and clear. The eyes seemed to be looking into pure space. The corners of the lips curved downwards a little, in an expression which was neither a smile nor a serious frown, but connected, it seemed, with something unrelated to the events that went on around him, something which absorbed him to its very depths. Evidently, on merely being asked to assume the posture of the yogi, sensitive as he was to each little suggestion in the air, Narayana Guru had lapsed into the traditional yogi state.*[5]

In the Guru's portrait and group photographs the leopard skin is an often-used prop (see Figure 10.14). The leopard skin was placed as a mat for the cross-legged seated posture on the floor, or for resting the Guru's feet when he was seated on a chair. Artists too have used the leopard skin as an integral part of the imaginary space they have created in paintings of the Guru. Why would the Guru, a votary of ahimsa, have used or at least posed on animal skins is a likely modern-day question that would arise if one is not aware that the Guru's *ishta devata* (favourite deity) was none other than Pashupati, the lord of animals and beloved to all creatures—the reason Shiva wears and sits on a leopard skin or sometimes a tiger skin. In verse 5 of his poem 'Song of the Kundalini Snake' (*Kundalini Pattu*), Narayana Guru uses words to paint the space around Shiva as follows:

> *A spotted leopard skin surrounds*
> *His form of tender bloom.*
> *'Within the Self he dances' say, and*
> *(repeat refrain) Dance, cobra, dance!*

Figure 10.14 The Guru seated on leopard skin
Source: Courtesy of the author.

Nataraja Guru further narrates on the rationale of the leopard skin used at the aforesaid photoshoot:

Behaviour-teaching becomes as essential as the spoken instruction. To those who stood around him the actions of the Guru spoke the Word-language, while he himself remained neutrally withdrawn within his own sphere of inner meditation. He was the yogi and had no objection to the animal skin on which he sat because, for one reason, the leopard was no longer alive, and for another reason, it was part of the recognized paraphernalia or tradition-ally-fixed appointments of the yogi, adopted as essential and inherited from the days of the prehistoric Shiva—belonging to what had become, through ages of association and habit, part of the necessary being of people's lives. In this case the Guru's objections would have been unavailing. Helpless to abolish the past, he therefore accepted it with graceful resignation, while using it as a pedestal from which to declare his revalued Guru-Shiva message—one of the principles of which was a strong disapproval of killing. But to break totally with the past under these circumstances would have made him a destroyer who could not fulfil. The Guru-message has thus to use even dead letters to express its living truth.

During the life of Narayana Guru, paintings of his images and real-life photographs were already venerated in ashrams, shrines, households, and other establishments that honoured him. At a shrine in the Sivagiri Ashram, where a life-size image of his was installed, a young devotee, loudly chanting the traditional *Guru Stotram*,[6] made his offerings. Among the onlookers was Narayana Guru himself. In subtle humour, the Guru is said to have remarked, 'Look at that. Here I stand in reality without my breakfast and still waiting for it; but my picture gets all the elaborate ritualistic attention. That is due to faith!'[7]

In 2010, a portrait from the 1920s that went unnoticed for many decades was identified by this author as unique and not in the public domain. The deteriorating print at the Alummoottil Meda (manor) at Muttom, Mavelikara (Figure 10.15), was carefully restored, re-photographed, digitally reprocessed, and released by this author to the public with the permission of the Alummoottil family.

Further enquiries on the provenance of the photograph revealed that the original version is one that was shot outdoors, in the premises of the Jagganatha Temple in Thalassery. The Thalassery version is evidently shot with Narayana Guru seated on a chair in the temple premises, with parts of the temple's protruding basement visible in the background. As the photo shot at Thalassery has captured more areas of the Guru's attire in the frame, compared to the version at Alummoottil House, it can be safely assumed to be the source and original image. It would be reasonable therefore to conclude that the existing version of the picture at Alummoottil House is a 'superimposed' version created by Sree Krishna Photos, Kayankulam, using the original picture from Thalassery. The cluttered background of the original picture would have prompted the studio artist to 'cut-out' the subject, replace the background and 'touch-up' the contours to create the neater Alummoottil portrait.

It was rather common practice in the early days of black-and-white plate photography that photo studios employed artists to literally 'cut and paste' the subject on to new backgrounds and to give finishing touches to portraits, sometimes doing the 'touch-up' work directly on

Figure 10.15 The portrait at Alummoottil Meda in Mavelikara. It is originally from a photograph captured in Thalassery
Source: Courtesy of the author.

the large-format negative plates themselves. Where the original shot was not under ideal lighting conditions or pleasant background settings, these artists often replaced the background by overlaying. They would painstakingly blend the cut-out edges, by touch-up artwork, to a backing paper, and finally re-photograph the collage on a second negative plate. Thus were achieved the kind of results easily attainable today with a software application such as Photoshop. Many of the Guru's currently available photographs have been the subject of this type of editing (see Figure 10.16).

Many of Narayana Guru's social and spiritual reform initiatives were made possible with the patronage of wealthy families that subscribed to the Guru's philosophy of equality and spiritual freedom. The Guru was never reluctant to visit the homes of his followers and patrons. It was a privilege for many such families to arrange photo sessions. Some of the prominent portraits of Narayana Guru that exist today have originated from such sessions.

In 1928, a few months before the Guru's *mahasamadhi* (end of a grand mortal life and merger with the Absolute), he was in Madras to undergo treatment for his deteriorating medical condition. The Guru was the esteemed guest at Bhuvana, the bungalow on 1, Rosary

Figure 10.16 The last of the living Guru's photographs. Photo superimposed on artwork background
Source: Courtesy of the author.

Church Road, Mylapore, owned by prominent businessman T.A. Arumugha Mudaliar, a fervent Narayana Guru devotee. As arranged by Mudaliar, the Guru sat through photo sessions at Bhuvana and at Marina Beach.

Some commentators have observed that these could be the last of the photographs of the living Guru. One of the photographs captured in that instance portrays an emaciated Guru in an unusual posture, seated cross-legged on the ground, wearing a single loincloth wrapped around the body and one knotted behind his neck (Figure 10.16). The striking aspect here is the waning physical attributes of the Guru's body and face as compared to older photographs. With a completely clean-shaven face and head, the eyes more sunken and the ears sharply protruding upwards, the Guru maintained his classic stare at the camera, but also observable is the deterioration and drooping of his facial muscles and lips. This picture, superimposed on artwork of background scenery, is one that is apparently manually coloured. The photograph in its surviving form was placed in the prayer room at Bhuvana for decades after the Guru's passing away. It seems there was also a British-India one rupee coin preserved in that prayer room, as it was gifted by the Guru to Arumugha Mudaliar during the days of Mudaliar's humble beginnings as a railway employee. Mudaliar attributed the coin as the amulet of blessing that brought fortunes to his successful type-foundry manufacturing business, one that was initiated with the encouragement of the Guru.[8]

There is yet another photograph of the Guru that could have been part of the same photoshoot at Bhuvana, as inferable from the attire and weakened physical attributes that closely match the photograph referred to above. However, the second photograph (Figure 10.17) appears to have been taken either unawares, as the Guru is in a dismissive mode as it seems from the way he looks away from the camera while seated, or, it is possibly a reflection of his waning alertness and physique.

Figure 10.17 Possibly from the photoshoot at Bhuvana, the weakened guru poses in a dismissive mood
Source: Courtesy of the author.

Figure 10.18 On the occasion of the formation of Sree Narayana Dharma Sangham in January 1928
Source: Courtesy of the author.

Historical public events in the life of Narayana Guru have also been occasions for capturing his photographs. Group photographs are on record from events such as the All Religions Conference at Aluva in 1924, and the formation of the Sree Narayana Dharma Sangham at Thrissur in 1928. In the 1928 group photograph (Figure 10.18), the Guru is passing through a phase of severe illness but also sharing a moment of contentment together with his close disciples for whom it was the Guru's long-standing desire to establish a formal monastic order.

Established in 1906, Krishnan Nair Brothers, a Thrissur-based photo studio was often engaged in photographing the Guru during his life's events in the Thrissur area. Two of the negative plates from those days still exist as confirmed by Ajith Krishnan Nair—a current member of the Krishnan Nair family and proprietor of their studio in Kochi, which was recently closed down in the process of the partition of the family's business. In 2005, the studio in Kochi, where most of their old negative plates were stored, suffered almost a total loss of their stock of rare and valuable photographic prints and negatives on account of an accidental fire, but fortunately, a few months prior to that Ajith had moved these two negative plates to another location where he was operating a training centre. Ajith recollects that unplanned move as an act guided by providence. Ajith holds great respect for Narayana Guru and says that it has been the same with his predecessors in the Krishnan Nair family, who, like him, considered Narayana Guru as the pioneer of Kerala's social renaissance and the liberator of the underprivileged masses. Ajith takes pride in saying that as a mark of respect for the great yogi Narayana Guruswamy, he keeps the Guru's photograph in a prominent place in his home in Thrippunithura.

Bodhananda Swamikal was a creditable disciple and confidant of Narayana Guru. Although Bodhananda moved from Sivagiri ashram to live as a recluse in the Nilgiris near Ootacamund, he maintained his rapport with the Guru and thereby his position as the trusted

Figure 10.19 The Guru with a group of followers
Source: Courtesy of the author.

disciple to be chosen by the Guru as his spiritual successor. On occasions Narayana Guru visited Ootacamund to spend time with Bodhananda and other disciples and followers in the Nilgiris. A photograph survives from around 1926, when Narayana Guru visited Ootacamund (Figure 10.19). Hosted by a group of local businessmen and townsfolk, the Guru is seen clad in a dark-coloured woolen shawl, which is different from his usual attire.

Many other group photographs exist from other public occasions, particularly in the Kannur–Thalassery areas, taken during the Guru's visits to those places. Some of the Guru's portrait images in use today are artists' recreations and enhanced extracts from these group photographs (Figure 10.20). A careful review of the original photographs of Narayana Guru in chronological order will show that the pictures from Narayana Guru's youth, which perhaps later re-surfaced, are casual photographs without any idolizing touch-ups or excessive contrasting; whereas photographs from his later life show elements of preparation (by photographers) for idolization, such as the 'halo glow' light effect and other props added around the subject prior to the studio or outdoor photoshoot. However, this might not always be the case, as it is also understandable that the Guru lived for a long four decades as a most revered spiritual leader; so the organizers of auspicious events, or hosts who prepared a venue for the Guru would

Figure 10.20   Extract from an old group photograph, now reprocessed
Source: Courtesy of the author.

have, with the intention of honouring him, laid the leopard skins to
rest his holy feet.[9]

Another revelation in the chronological collection of the Guru's
portrait photographs is the waxing and waning of his physical health
and other features. The earliest of his photographs show a simple
village youngster with ordinary small-built physical attributes and a
rather shy demeanor. This is followed by images possibly from his
late-30s onwards with a beard and a lean body, from his days as a

meditative recluse and during his life of social interaction at Aruvippuram. Into his middle age, the Guru displays an erect posture and is observably a far more self-confident subject for the camera. His piercing yogic eyes from mid-life onwards is another notable change from the early days. Photographs from the last three years of his life show the gradual waning of his health, with visible changes like sinking eyes, protruding facial structures and the left arm visibly drifting downwards, indicating muscle weak-

Figure 10.21 Narayana Guru appearing retired and unwell in the twilight of his life
Source: Courtesy of the author.

ness (Figure 10.21). When closely observed, the photos relate untold parts of the Guru's life story, which contemporary writers chose to remain silent about, perhaps because of their disbelief in time's natural transformation affecting their most revered Guru's body, which then had to succumb to the ravages of age and illness.

Of particular interest to a student of these photographs from the Guru's twilight years are those taken during the Guru's stay at Bhuvana (Figures 10.16 and 10.17) and selected other photographs that display the waning health conditions of the Guru's mortal body (Figures 10.21 and 10.22). Figure 10.22 is presumed to be shot in a makeshift studio setting in the Guru's last months in 1928. What interests the reviewer of this picture is that the Guru, despite ill health, was willing and cooperative in allowing portrait photography to continue and thus satisfying the wishes of his followers and disciples. He makes his best attempt to sit still and maintain the stare, from his sunken eyes, to help create the best of photographs in that age of slow-speed plate photography. He is clad in more linen than usual, with his head covered by the shawl or mundu with the visibly broader border design (*kara*) which is different from his usual attire. A larger shawl than usual is used possibly due to his lowered resistance to cold weather. His best efforts are visible in the manner in which he clutches his fists, maybe to avoid a shivering or shake. With the usual leopard skin absent in the scene, he retains his footwear—the elevated wooden slipper (*methi-thadi*).

Figure 10.22   The Guru weakened by illness in 1928
Source: Courtesy of the author.

Commercial Art and Portrait Paintings

In the low-priced commercial art market,[10] there has never been
an end to the possibilities of adding to the idolizing attributes of
Narayana Guru—halo, glow, colour, and ornamentation. Some of
the excessively idolized artwork, such as those displayed in picture-
framing shops, are painted by commercial artists who also paint most
religious icons for lithographs in south India. Lithographs for framing and wall calendars to be used as promotional gifts were mostly
crafted and printed in Sivakasi in the days before large-format digital
print shops started operating in Kerala. Sivakasi, with its characteristic dry weather, was traditionally the location of choice for the printing
industry in south India. In this genre of art, there are accepted idolizing exaggerations—the 'windmill-like' rays of the sun as halo, or

slightly distorted facial features, unrealistic colours, and so on. For instance, Narayana Guru never wore yellow robes, but most sketches and digitally edited photographs wrongly portray the Guru in yellow attire. In recent years, digital editing ('photoshopping') opportunities are resulting in extensive make-overs to Narayana Guru's old photographs, which are transformed into many idolizing configurations and then appear on different websites.[11]

There is a large consumer base for framed pictures of Narayana Guru, especially in Kerala,[12] as he remains the most broadly acceptable icon of either spiritual or social renaissance, or both. As commonly seen in Catholic homes where the niche on the wall is the perceivable extension of the Church into the home, a picture of Narayana Guru plays the role of the 'guardian' in the home of the believer; while the very same picture in the home (usually entrance) of a non-believer or rationalist is often connotative of his rejection of all other Hindu deities and a statement of his unreligious but righteous outlook. Interestingly, some atheists seem to command social respect by placing the Guru's picture in their houses; and at the same time representing it as idolization of the one who dared to confront religion and neutralize its socio-political ferocity!

You might find only a few Hindu homes with crucifixes or images of Jesus, but in Kerala you will not find an icon commanding, among the general population, such a broad idolatry value as Narayana Guru does. There is indeed an expansive 'Sree Narayana effect' that creates demand for his images.

At the entrance to the home of Mohan Sankar in Kollam is prominently placed the charcoal sketched portrait of Narayana Guru (Figure 10.23). It was custom-made for his father, the late R. Sankar, who built the house during his illustrious career initially as a lawyer and later as General Secretary of the Sree Narayana Dharma Paripalana Yogam (SNDP Yogam) and as Chief Minister of Kerala.

Customer segmentation (by assumed income levels) indicates a shift over the last fifty years in the sales of Narayana Guru's images. Sales of commercial prints remain high, but the more affluent families which could easily commission an oil painting or drawing for their new home—a common practice in the past—are also preferring prints today despite the fact that even an original canvas is easily affordable to them. In this case, affordability may be understood as

Figure 10.23   Portrait at Mohan Sankar's house in Kollam
Source: Courtesy of the author.

a criterion based on the current price of a custom oil painting as a proportion of the estimated value of the new house. It was noted that affluent new homeowners have also 'moved' the Narayana Guru images (prints mostly) into their prayer rooms as compared to their parents who normally placed the Guru's picture at the entrance of their home or at another prominent place in the living area.[13] This change in the placement of the Guru image by affluent newer home-owners could also be on account of changing social attitudes. First, Narayana Guru images today tend to be directly associated with the Ezhava community, with fewer non-Ezhavas placing the Guru's image in prominent places of their homes. This tendency, however, does not necessarily imply any rejection of the Guru by non-Ezhavas, but could be prompted by the excessive possessiveness and unwrit-ten ownership claims over the Guru legacy and iconography that is displayed by the Ezhavas through their organizations, such as the SNDP Yogam, which today would hardly include non-Ezhavas in its activities with the exception of invited dignitaries at events. Second, to some extent, the current generations of Ezhavas who have gained upward social mobility try to avoid promoting their community tag, for whatever reasons—stigma or broadmindedness—and may consider the public display of a Guru image to be that Ezhava tag they might wish to avoid, though without implying any rejection of the Guru legacy. Lastly, the devotion towards the Guru and his elevation as another Hindu icon for adoration and daily darsan is apparent in the placement of the Guru image in their prayer rooms, as compared to placement of an image in a prominent public place in the home as an open expression of reverence—without any faith or caste inhibitions.

Displayed in the Thiruvananthapuram home of septuagenarian Usha Sahadevan is a portrait of Narayana Guru from the 1950s, by artist V.M. Balan of Cherai. The oil painting was a gift to Usha's late father, Kalavampara Ikkannan Gangadharan of Cherai, who was a close relative of the Guru's best-known rationalist disciple, the social reformer Sahodaran Ayyappan. When this author showed an interest in the history of the painting, the now ageing Usha was elated that someone in current times continues with the same interests in Narayana Guru and art that her late father cherished. Balan's 1950s painting shows the transformation in artists' imagination of the Guru's attire, as Balan has portrayed the Guru in a yellowish robe as compared to early twentieth-century paintings, such as the Kolathukara portrait, which shows the Guru in white robes. It is evidently the yellow robes used by pilgrims in the annual Sivagiri pilgrimage since 1933 that has caused mid-century artists to transform the Guru's attire to yellowish robes as well.

The fine art higher-quality portraits of Narayana Guru, such as sketches, pencil drawings, and oil paintings, have graced many older homes for over three quarters of a century. In many Kerala homes of affluent Narayana Guru devotees who are over fifty years in age, it is still evidently commonplace to have a unique (commissioned) painting or pencil portrait of Narayana Guru placed close to the entrance.

Artist Laji Nass spoke to this author about his work, a fine 1992 portrait of the Guru, displayed on his blog. Laji opined that the demand for original oil paintings has fallen drastically in recent years, mostly because of high-quality prints that can be made at a nominal price, with a choice of printing on paper or canvas. Home owners are generally concerned only about having a picture on the wall, more for decorative value and less moved by pride or considerations of aesthetics that come to the fore with an original painting—and that holds even if it is a good painting of Narayana Guru. Laji gave permission to use his image for this chapter as shown in Figure 10.24.

Figure 10.24   Artist Laji Nass's fine portrait of the Guru
Source: Courtesy of the author.

On his website Laji displays a watermarked image, as it can be easily downloaded and misused.

There are several professional artists such as Vakkom Sahadevan, who have made a mark mostly from Sree Narayana portraiture. The older homes in Cherthala town are notable for unique portraits of Narayana Guru that grace their entrances. Many of these date back to the 1930s and 1940s, and were done mostly by art teachers. Retired art teachers continue to paint or sketch as a hobby. Narayana Guru is often a favourite subject for their portraits, but many are unable to sell their works, or even get a fair reward for their efforts.

In the small town of Aranmula, a large framed portrait of Narayana Guru adorned a wall in the living room of the house of the late Bhaskaran Nair. In 2006, as a long-retired military man and senior member of a joint family, many members of which visited him regularly, Nair said he took great pride in Narayana Guru's philosophy. He had placed the picture in his house in the early 1950s, when he used to work closely with local SNDP Yogam leaders such as Edathara Kesavan Vaidyan on social issues. The picture of Narayana Guru was Nair's outward expression of solidarity with the socio-cultural renaissance that gripped a newly democratic and free Malayalee society at that time. Nair also knew by heart many verses of Narayana Guru's work *Atmopadesa Satakam*. His son Ajayan, who passed away in 2018, retained the picture in the house, although he did not know as much as his father did about Narayana Guru.

In 1931, an artist named Mary Longworth pencil-sketched a profile portrait of Narayana Guru. It was originally done in support of one of Nataraja Guru's articles in *The Sufi Quarterly*, published in Geneva. Not much could be traced about Mary Longworth, but her name was included in the credits to the article titled 'The Way of the Guru—Being Pen Pictures from the Life of the Sri Narayana Guru', published by Geneva Sufi Pub. Association, 1931. Kerala Kaumudi publications have over the years occasionally engaged the famed artist Namboodiri to sketch the Guru's outline images to illustrate features in their journals. Namboodiri often chose to depict the Guru in non-traditional styles, using his freedom of expression to sketch the Guru with minimal line structures and without much consideration for 'likeness' or realism that conforms to actual photographs of the Guru.

In 2007, art teacher-turned-filmmaker R. Sukumaran took this author through the rooms in his house, all stacked with his paintings in storage. The walls also displayed three of his paintings of Narayana Guru. One of them was based on the photograph of the Guru at Marina Beach, arranged by Arumugha Mudaliar of Mylapore. Starting from the discussion of those paintings, Sukumaran explained his then ten-year long ambition and groundwork for making a mega film on Narayana Guru. Sukumaran started with painting portraits of Narayana Guru and ended by 'painting' him on celluloid—scripting and directing the biographical feature film 'Yugapurushan'.

Statues

The earliest statue of Narayana Guru was created while the Guru lived. It is a bronze statue placed in an octagonal chapel in the premises of the Jagannatha Temple at Thalassery (Figure 10.25). In January 1926, the idea for the statue was conceived by Moorkkoth Kumaran, a prominent writer (later biographer) and contemporary disciple of Narayana Guru. Kumaran initiated a successful fundraising drive and commissioned the then famed Italian sculptor Professor C. Tavaroli to craft it. Tavaroli sculpted the statue using several photographs of the Guru that were shot specifically for this purpose by professional

photographer P. Shekharan of Thalassery. The photographs captured for this purpose are distinct in that the Guru had to pose from different angles, including frontals and profiles. The same attire, marked by the seam design on the possibly the woollen shawl donned by the Guru, is seen across these photographs, pointing to that collection being from the same photoshoot.

The completed statue was being shipped from a port in Ceylon in 1926, when Narayana

Figure 10.25 Earliest statue of Narayana Guru at Jagannatha Temple, Thalassery
Source: Courtesy of the author.

Guru was on his second visit to Colombo. On seeing the statue there, the Guru, it is said, quipped: 'Needless of food, it can live forever!'[14] On 12 March 1927, the statue was consecrated by Bodhananda Swamikal[15] and formally unveiled in a public function the next day.

Statues of Narayana Guru are most commonly venerated in hundreds of 'Guru-mandirams' (chapels dedicated to the Guru) across Kerala and other parts in India. Most of these statues, installed in Guru-mandirams, are moulded from mortar, with little care taken for realism, aesthetics, or decorative content. However, a few are exceptionally appealing, for instance, those that are crafted and overlaid with fine artwork to complete the facial features and other details.

The statue in the Guru-mandiram attached to the Ponekkara Subramanyaswamy Temple in Edappally is an example of a statue with fine artwork overlay that renders likeness and life to an otherwise moulded mortar statue (Figure 10.26).

Figure 10.26 Statue at the Guru-mandiram attached to the Ponekkara Subramanyswamy Temple, Edappally, Ernakulum
Source: Courtesy of the author.

Telefilm-maker Ramesh Swamy (V.K. Ramesh) has built his own Guru-mandiram in Chennai. Distinctive about its iconography is that the statue portrays the Guru as a continuum of past gurus. The statue incorporates imagery of Gautama Buddha and Jesus Christ as predecessors of Narayana Guru.

The 1953 *Souvenir*, published for SNDP Yogam's Golden Jubilee celebrations, had a cover illustration portraying Narayana Guru as the last in a lineage of gurus (Figure 10.27). That illustration inferably included the image representing Prophet Muhammad

Figure 10.27 Cover illustration of the 1953 *Souvenir* published for SNDP Yogam's Golden Jubilee celebrations
Source: Courtesy of the author.

Figure 10.28   Marble statue at the Mahasamadhi Mandapam at Sivagiri, Varkala
Source: Courtesy of the author.

as one of Narayana Guru's predecessors along with Ramakrishna Paramahamsa, Guru Nanak, Jesus Christ, and Gautama Buddha. Interestingly, six decades ago that illustration did not create any furore about the depiction of Prophet Muhammad in art, as it almost certainly would today in context of the present-day politics of religion.

Besides Guru-mandirams, there are several other prominent statues of the Guru placed in the premises of various institutions. A few noteworthy ones in the spiritual domain are as follows:

- The marble statue installed in the sanctum of the Mahasamadhi Mandapam (the eternal mausoleum) of Narayana Guru at Sivagiri, Varkala (Figure 10.28). Commissioned by M.P. Moothedath, the statue was crafted in white marble in Varanasi by the master sculptor Pasupathinath Mukherjee, as part of the construction of the mausoleum that was completed in 1968. Ironically, during the eight-month period that was planned for crafting the statue and soon after the most essential parts of the statue was chiselled, Mukherjee unexpectedly passed away, making the Guru's statue his last masterpiece. It was his wife who then arranged for its completion and delivery.

- The bronze-finished concrete statue installed at the Narayana Gurukula, in Varkala (Figure 10.29). This statue, portraying the emaciated Guru in the twilight of his life, is modestly placed on a high pedestal in the front yard as a mark of respect but not as a subject of adoration or ritualistic *pooja* (worship). The statue and its replica were crafted, circa 1995, by sculptor Hariharan Master of Aluva. The replica of this statue is installed at the Fernhill Gurukula.

- Another statue worth mentioning is the one originally placed in Narayana Gurukula, Varkala, from circa 1951 to 1995. This

Figure 10.29 The bronze-finished concrete statue installed at the Narayana Gurukula in Varkala
Source: Courtesy of the author.

seated statue of the Guru adorned the Gurukula locale for major ceremonial events, including the acceptance of sanyassa (monastic life) by Nataraja Guru, and the giving of *deeksha*[16] to John Spiers, Swami Mangalananda, and Nitya Chaitanya Yati. The statue, crafted in mortar by Messrs O.V. Arts of Trivandrum, was moved and installed at Vakayar, Konni, in 1995. It now faces the mausoleum of Vamakshy Amma, mother of Guru Nitya Chaitanya Yati. After the demise of Vamakshy Amma, she was interned at Vakayar, Konni. A Sharada Pratishta (Saraswathy statue) was erected over her resting place. As per Guru Nitya's wish, it was deemed appropriate to install the most beautiful statue of Narayana Guru available at that time to face the Sharada Pratishta.

Since the early 1950s, white porcelain statuettes of Narayana Guru were mass-produced by Messrs Kundara Ceramics and made very popular in southern Kerala. Although it is out of production now, the statuette is still seen in many homes of the Guru's devotees. The original cast of the statuette was crafted by artist and sculptor P. Hariharan Master of Bangalore.[17] There were both glazed and unglazed porcelain versions of the statuette available in the market. Though rarer, the unglazed ones were, aesthetically, the 'real masterpieces' in the opinion of those who recollect those statuettes. The glazing, as it appears, rounded-off the sharper features of the subject's face and other fine edges.

The Jñāna Vigraham, a distinctive statue of Narayana Guru crafted in Thiruvananthapuram in 2006, was intended to infuse possible aesthetic and storytelling elements around Sree Narayana iconography (Figure 10.30). The aesthetic elements of the design of the Jñāna Vigraham followed ancient Eastern philosophic and religious iconography and sculpturing styles. All relief artwork decorating the statue have specific legends connected with the Guru and his life and works. Conceived and initially sketched by this author, the statue was crafted in wood by the chosen sculptor Mani Mesthiri of Thiruvananthapuram. The work signified the period commemorating one-and-a-half centuries since Narayana Guru's birth, as well as the 75th anniversary of the annual pilgrimage to Sivagiri.[18] The statue's pedestal incorporates a verse, in Sanskrit, from the ancient

Figure 10.30 The Jñāna Vigraham
Source: Courtesy of the author.

Indian scripture *Bhagavata Purana* to venerate Narayana Guru. The verse translates as follows:

In pursuit of Spiritual Knowledge,
Some persons renounce all material activities and,
Having thus become peaceful, perform
The sacrifice of philosophic investigation to worship You,
The Embodiment of all Knowledge (i.e. Jñāna Vigraham).[19]

Following the Jñāna Vigraham, some craftsmen have moved to incorporate aesthetic elements into Sree Narayana iconography. Obvious recent trends include the addition of decorative and corniced pedestals, and the inclusion of the idolizing *Prabha*[20] to statues. The material used for new statues for Guru-mandirams have progressed from mortar to metal. The five-metal alloy (*panchaloha*), of which the principal metal is usually copper, is sometimes used to cast statues that have been installed at certain Guru-mandirams in Kerala. One panchaloha statue of the Guru has been subject to theft from a Guru-mandiram, most likely on account of its high-priced metal alloy content. It was recovered by the police and was intact.

Contemporary artist and curator Riyas Komu's sculpture titled 'The Cult of Dead and Memory Loss' (2006) is an installation based on Narayana Guru and contemporary Kerala. Incidentally, it held the record as Komu's highest-priced work in March 2015.[21]

Most recently, a bronze statue of Narayana Guru was installed at the Vayalvaram house replacing an old mortar statue placed in the room where the Guru was born. There is apparent variety in the types and purposes of Narayana Guru statues made today. They can be broadly classified as: first, purely idolizing statues commissioned and installed to facilitate the practice of religious rituals at places of worship; second, statues of reverence of the kind commissioned by Narayana Gurukula and other institutions and placed in outdoor surroundings; and, lastly, the expressions of abstract art with underlying messages as in the case of Riyas Komu's sculpture.

The Guru's Views on Idolatry

As part of this study, the comments by Narayana Guru and his disciples on idolatry were briefly reviewed. It is evident that these gurus were not against idolatry, provided there was conception of the Absolute in the idol. Prior to the consecration of the Sharada Prathista at Sivagiri Ashram, there was a symbolic golden spear (*vel*) placed as the object of worship. One of Narayana Guru's overly passionate devotees replaced the spear with a pair of the Guru's own wooden footwear and flung the spear into the bushes! When the Guru questioned his action, the devotee said: 'It is my penance that none other than thy divine footwear should be idolized.' The Guru's retort was a question: 'If I can be the footwear, then why can't I be the spear!?'[22]

Narayana Guru's intimate disciple and younger contemporary Swami Dharmatheerthar[23] (1891–1976), who has recorded the above incident further explains that essentially what matters is the necessity for a devotee to have a conceptualization of the power of the Absolute behind the idol, no matter what the object or the idol itself may be. Dharmatheerthar also records an anecdote about a Hindu preacher who put this question to Narayana Guru:

Preacher:	Other religions are rejecting idolatry. They are asking, what did your God, sitting in the idols, do when Muslims and others demolished your idols?
Narayana Guru:	That, God is omnipresent and exists in the hearts of human beings—do they agree?
Preacher:	Yes (they agree).
Narayana Guru:	When human beings are slaughtered, what is God's reaction, in their view?
Preacher:	That in the final judgment, they will be punished.
Narayana Guru:	Well, then why not say that the demolishers of idols, the same way, will be finally punished?

Nataraja Guru, in discussing traditions in Indian iconographic symbolism, says: 'Not even the simplest idolater in India takes the idol to be just matter. It says something to him, however crude or vague it may be.' He further cites that even in Islam, despite its hatred of idols and idolatry, sacred objects still persist within the body of such protestant religions, such as that Mecca has its Ka'aba, to take one example.

Sree Narayana Iconography and Politics

Statues for veneration in Guru-mandirams across Kerala appear in the news occasionally, when politically motivated mobs or covert operators engage in vandalizing these statues, mostly under cover of darkness. Such attacks on Guru-mandirams have occurred on various instances, including at least eleven alleged attacks in the year 2005 alone. Online news archives have records of several such acts of vandalism, such as at Kalluvathukkal in February 2000, at Cherai in July 2002, at Nedumangad in April 2006, at Karunagapalli in July 2006, at Kappil, Kayankulam, in February 2007, at Kodungaloor in July 2008, at Palluruthy in 2010, at Balaramapuram in May 2011, and most lately, Guru statues at different sites in Varkala were vandalized in February 2017.[24] In a 2015 incident reported by major news media houses such as Mathrubhumi and Madhyamam, three Rashtriya Swayamsevak Sangh (RSS) activists were arrested by the police in connection with the destruction of the statue of Narayana Guru at Nangarath Peedika in Thalassery.[25] Vandals caused damage to the statue and a hand of the statue was severed and thrown on the wayside.[26] This list, although incomplete, is broadly indicative of the misuse and politicization of Sree Narayana statues in recent times. Each incident would have had its then current political motive, but by and large these incidents are perpetrated as a trigger for flaming passion and rivalry within the loose fabric of Kerala's party politics—which is woven with a combination of party ideology, religion, and communal partisanships, often defeating true democratic morals.

Over the years, images of Narayana Guru and his quotes have been cleverly used by various political parties to enhance their image as champions of equality. So also in recent years with the advent of the Hindu political front the Guru is more often than before represented as a Hindu saint. This front also credits the Guru as the saviour of Hinduism in Kerala, at a time in history when a majority in the underprivileged strata of the population was on the verge of mass conversions to Christianity and Islam. It is a frequent sight in Kerala to see the picture of Sree Narayana Guru used, or lined up with other iconic characters such as Karl Marx, Lenin, and Bhagat Singh in Leftist political party hoardings and posters, and on occasions such as party conventions. As a widely acceptable icon across various social and political groups, the inclusion of Narayana Guru on an equal footing in the panel of other iconic characters apparently renders credibility and acceptability in the minds of the masses. Most socio-political groups in Kerala and outside the state nowadays also use Narayana Guru imagery to represent an iconic defender of the rights of the underprivileged. Beyond Kerala, this has happened more visibly in the state of Uttar Pradesh, after chief minister Mayawati came to power.[27] While in office, Mayawati installed at least four statues of Narayana Guru in public parks in Uttar Pradesh as follows:

- Statue of Narayana Guru installed at Ambedkar Park, Lucknow (2008);
- Statue at B.R. Ambedkar Samajik Parivartan Sthal, Lucknow (2009);
- Statue at Samta Mulak Chowk, Gomti Nagar, Lucknow (2010); and
- Statue at Rashtriya Dalit Prerna Sthal, in Noida (October 2011).

The Ambedkar Samajik Parivartan Sthal in Lucknow houses many statues and relief sculptures depicting prominent people from history. The statues are set out in two separate mausoleums. The first mausoleum houses, on an equal footing, the statues of modern-day reformers B.R. Ambedkar, Narayana Guru, Jyotiba Phule, Chhatrapati Shahuji Maharaj, and Shri Kanshiram. The second mausoleum houses statues of sages, mystics, poets, and reformers. They include Gautama Buddha, Sant Kabir Das, Sant Ravidas, Guru Ghasidas, and Shri Birsa Munda. From the grouping of these historical figures, it is apparent that Narayana Guru was bracketed in the category of social reformers, perhaps not recognizing the facets of his relevance in the second group, that is, of sages, mystics, poets, and reformers. By and large, those honoured at the Ambedkar Park are figures who upheld equality and came to prominence for attempting to debunk class distinctions between the privileged and the underprivileged.

In August 2015, a 24 foot high statue, supposedly the tallest one of Narayana Guru in Kerala, was unveiled by Kodiyeri Balakrishnan, Communist Party of India-Marxist (CPM) state secretary, at the SNDP Yogam conference, an event which was inaugurated by then chief minister, Oommen Chandy, a Congressman of the UDF alliance and a Christian. Approaching the state election year in 2016, the race for openly embracing Narayana Guru by two opposing political fronts was more than apparent at this event.

In 2015, the portrayal of Narayana Guru in a political tableau presented by the leftist CPM in Kerala aroused widespread anger and allegations of blasphemy from the right-wing BJP party and the leadership of SNDP Yogam, who joined in the protests against the portrayal of the Guru as being crucified by the right political front. The tableau was part of a procession in Thaliparambu, Kannur district, during the Onam festival. It was aimed at highlighting the growing religious radicalism in Kerala, but what made it controversial was that one of the men crucifying the Guru wore a saffron headscarf, while the other wore a yellow one. The saffron and yellow represent the Sangh/BJP and SNDP Yogam respectively.[28]

Mind, Space, and Iconography—an Epilogue

After a century of Sree Narayana iconography, I have attempted to argue, we now have something of a map of how this iconography has been conceived in subjective space, created and applied in the physical space, and its impact on individuals as much as collectives. As prospective leaders of religious groups and the state perpetually aim to gain control over the human mind, win their collective acceptance to gain power and then in turn to control both human bodies and minds, the power of iconography is alluringly brought to mind. Iconography could also be a cleverly conceived object to place in the physical space to win sympathizers to subscribe to underlying ideologies.

Much like photographs, paintings, statues, and other objets d'art that can represent Narayana Guru, there also are the physical spaces like the Guru's birthplace—the Vayalvāram house at Chempazhanthy, the Mahasamadhi Mandiram (mausoleum) at Sivagiri, and various other spiritual spaces adding to icons of the Guru's life and value system. When individuals with an affinity for Narayana Guru walk into that space, it empowers them by providing a privacy or protected space for freedom of religion, for being empowered even as minorities, and best of all for free thinking, temporarily liberated from the complexities of our current social order, at all times.

While a large part of the Guru's followers remain complacent with the use of physical imagery and physical space, the Guru also prevails as the *Word-wisdom*,[29] beginning from the very name or reference to

Narayana Guru that projects an array of concepts and percepts in a multitude of minds, to the messages and knowledge encapsulated in his literary works. Despite the subjectivity among followers and well-wishers, these minds in aggregate hold elevated niches for placing superlatives of the 'Guru image' ranging from Nanu the sensitive child to a simple village teacher, a wandering acsetic-sanyassi to the icon of righteousness, of social freedom, of spiritual freedom, and so on, progressing onward to the abstraction and non-image of that alone—the Absolute. It is this subjective realm of Guru iconism that is difficult to stratify, categorize, or catalogue due to its transcendent and transforming nature, often remaining as private impressions within individual seekers, changing along with the acquisition of an increasingly deeper knowledge of the Guru, his literary works, and his value system.

Notes and References

1. In 1901 the 'Census of India—Report on Travancore' recorded Nanu Asan as a good Sanskrit scholar and pious religious reformer.
2. C. R. Kesavan Vaidyar, *Gurucharanangalil* (Kerala: Vivekodayam Books, 1984), 118.
3. Sree Narayana Guru, *Advaita Dipika*, verse 1.
4. 'Sree Narayana Movement' is a generally accepted broad term used by various authors representing the spiritual and social reform movement (1888 to circa 1939) that took shape inspired by Narayana Guru. See T.M. Thomas Isaac and P.K. Michael Tharakan, *Sree Narayana Movement in Travancore, 1888–1939: A Study of Social Basis and Ideological Reproduction* (Trivandrum: Centre for Development studies [1986].)
5. Nataraja Guru, *Life and Teachings of Narayana Guru* (Kerala: Narayana Gurukula Foundation, 1990), 167–8.
6. Verses from 'Guru Gita' in Uttarakhand section of '*Skanda Purana*' in the form of a dialogue between Shiva and Uma (Shakti). The verses commence 'Guru Brahma, Guru Vishnu, Guru Devo Maheshwara'.
7. Nataraja Guru, *Life and Teachings of Narayana Guru*, 265.
8. Based on the 1936 observations, interviews and later recordings of K. Swaminathan, Retired Superintendent, Kerala Government Presses.
9. Worship at the feet of a guru is part of the age-old Gurubhakti tradition in India.
10. This author's survey of sales and use of Sree Narayana Guru's images are limited to the state of Kerala in India.

11. A Jabalpur-based Malayalee, Prasad Panicker, has a collection of over 1,000 pictures related to the Guru's life in his Facebook photo albums. Many of these are digitally edited versions of old photographs or paintings.

12. In 2006 and 2016 this author surveyed framing shops in three representative towns in Kerala enquiring about which customer segment most purchased these pictures. Around 39 per cent were said to be purchased by shopkeepers and stores/businesses. When it is a non-Ezhava owned store that displayed a Narayana Guru picture, it perhaps implies openness in their attitude towards all customers. Known households from the vicinity of a picture vendor purchased about 24 per cent, while the rest were sold to walk-in visitors or strangers to the town, including (multiple copies) for resale at temples and festivals—most of which can be assumed to end up in households. Despite the proliferation of the social media and digital printing capabilities within the reach of the end user by 2016, the sale of Narayana Guru images did not seem to have fallen (as compared to 2006).

13. Based on survey of a sample of new and old homes in six towns across Kerala.

14. Chambadan Vijayan, *Kerala Kaumudi: Sree Narayana Guru Souvenir edition for the Sivagiri Pilgrimage* (Thiruvananthapuram, Kerala: Kerala Kaumudi Press, 1993), 73.

15. Bodhananda Swamikal (1883–1928) was the creditable disciple and nominated spiritual successor to Narayana Guru. Bodhananda, ironically, lived only for three more days after Narayana Guru's passing.

16. Formal initiation into full-time spiritual life.

17. P. Hariharan Master was the son of Dr P. Palpu and the youngest brother of Nataraja Guru. Dr Palpu had taken interest in training Hariharan and his elder sister Anandalekshmy in handicrafts. Hariharan's wife was a Japanese lady known by the name 'Sethako' (from the recollections of J. Muraleemohan Lal, a long-time disciple of Nataraja Guru).

18. More information on the Jñāna Vigraham is available on Wikipedia.

19. Śrīla Vyāsadeva, *Śrīmad Bhāgavatam*, verse 10.40.6.

20. Prabha is the radiance board or decorative arch used as a backing for a religious figurine or statue, originally from Eastern spiritual schools of art like Gandhara.

21. See at http://indiatoday.intoday.in/story/riyas-komu-colour-of-politics-mahatma-gandhi-congress/1/440844.html (accessed on 12 April 2019).

22. Swami Dharmatheerthar, *Sree Narayana Gurudevante Thiruvachanangal* (Kerala: Sree Narayana Dharmashram Neeleeswaram), 20.

23. Swami Dharmatheerthar was also the first chosen General Secretary of Sree Narayana Dharma Sangham.

24. http://www.thehindu.com/todays-paper/tp-national/tp-kerala/gurus-statues-vandalised/article17338386.ece (accessed on 12 April 2019).

25. See http://www.mathrubhumi.com/tv/ReadMore/18789/vandalising-guru-statue-in-thalassery-3-rss-men-held/E (accessed on 12 April 2019). Also see http://www.madhyamam.com/en/kerala/2015/sep/8/three-rss-activists-arrested-vandalisingguru%E2%80%99s-statue-kannur (accessed on 12 April 2019).

26. List complied in October 2011 and updated in February 2017 from online news archives.

27. Mayawati Prabhu Das was chief minister of Uttar Pradesh from May 2007 to March 2012. She continues to head the Bahujan Samaj Party, which represents the Bahujans or Dalits, historically the weakest strata of Indian society.

28. See http://www.thenewsminute.com/article/cpims-tableau-sree-narayana-guru-being-crucified-angers-bjp-sndp34081 (accessed, 30 August 2017).

29. *Word-wisdom* is a phrase that originates from the writings of Nataraja Guru, the direct disciple of Narayana Guru. Like the usages in Greek philosophy and theology of the two terms *Logos—the word of God*, and *Nous—the faculty of the human mind as necessary for understanding what is true or real*, Nataraja Guru postulates that *Word-wisdom* represents the Indian (Eastern) counterparts of these terms, where wisdom that is perennial is arrived at and gained through the contemplative process, and re-evaluated and restated or explained through the *Words* of sages from time to time. For example, commenting on Narayana Guru's work 'A Critique of Caste', Nataraja Guru says: 'By his status in contemplative *Word-wisdom* the Guru Narayana had the right to revalue and restate the position. He fulfilled this role with that characteristically wistful touch of mysticism.'

EDITOR AND CONTRIBUTORS

Editor

Vinay Lal is a cultural critic, blogger, public commentator, and professor of history and Asian American studies at the University of California, Los Angeles. He writes widely on the politics of knowledge systems, Indian history, public culture, the Indian diaspora, cinema, colonialism, contemporary American politics, and Gandhi. His books include *Empire of Knowledge* (2002); *Of Cricket, Guinness, and Gandhi: Essays on Indian History and Culture* (2003); *The History of History: Politics and Scholarship in Modern India* (rev. ed., 2005); and, co-edited with Ashis Nandy, *The Future of Knowledge and Culture: A Dictionary for the 21st Century* (2005). More recent books include two co-edited volumes: one with Roby Rajan, *India and the Unthinkable: Backwaters Collective on Metaphysics and Politics I* (2016), the other with Ellen Carol DuBois, *A Passionate Life: Writings by and on Kamaladevi Chattopadhyay* (2017).

Contributors

Aparna Devare teaches courses in international relations theory, colonialism and international relations, Indian political thought and introductory international relations in the Department of Political Science, University of Hyderabad, India. She is the author of *History and the Making of a Modern Hindu Self* (2011), and has published articles in *Postcolonial Studies, Contexto, International Political Sociology,* and the *International Journal of Political Theory*. She also has several chapters in edited books, the most recent being 'Dialogical International Relations: Gandhi, Tagore and Self-Transformation' in the *Routledge Handbook of Postcolonial Politics* (2018).

Vivek Dhareshwar is scholar-in-residence at Srishti Institute of Art, Design & Technology, Bengaluru. He earned his PhD from the History of Consciousness program at the University of California, Santa Cruz, USA, in 1989. From 1993 to 1997, he was at the Centre for Studies in Social Sciences, Calcutta, where he was Fellow in the Social Basis of Culture and Sociology, and he then joined the Centre for the Study of Culture and Society, Bengaluru, as a senior fellow before serving as its director from 2001–4. His work for some time now has revolved around reconceptualizing the human sciences through the resources of Indian intellectual traditions.

Maya Joshi is associate professor of English at Lady Shri Ram College, University of Delhi, India. In part due to her family background, she carries on a parallel life as researcher in the field of Buddhist history and thought. During a stint in Tibet House, New Delhi, over several years, she co-edited a volume on Dharmakriti and Pramana. Her inter-disciplinary doctoral work includes a study of Rahul Sankrityayan— along with several notable contemporaries—as an autobiographer. She recently completed a stint as a Fulbright Post-Doctoral Research Fellow at the School of Arts and Sciences, University of Pennsylvania, working towards an intellectual biography of Rahul Sankrityayan.

Ashis Nandy has worked in the area of cultural psychology, the politics of culture, and the culture of politics for over four decades. He has had a lifelong association with the Centre for the Study of Developing Societies, Delhi, as fellow, senior fellow, director, and now distinguished fellow. He is the author of over twenty books, most of them published by Oxford University Press, Delhi. His works include *The Intimate Enemy: Loss and Recovery of Self under Colonialism* (1983), *Tyranny, Traditions and Utopias: Essays in the Politics of Awareness* (1987), *The Tao of Cricket: On Games of Destiny and the Destiny of Games* (1989), *The Savage Freud and Other Essays on Possible and Retrievable Selves* (1995), and *The Romance of the State and the Fate of Dissent in the Tropics* (2008). Oxford University Press (India) has honored him with a 3-volume Omnibus Edition which reproduces nine of his books, and among his many accolades are the Grand Prize of the Fukuoka Asian Culture Prize (2007).

Roby Rajan is professor of quantitative methods at the University of Wisconsin-Parkside, USA, but that does not mean he shies away from qualitative matters. Indeed, he holds the very division of the world into quantitative and qualitative to be suspect. To those habitually given to characterizing large parts of the Third World as 'failed states', his rejoinder is: *There are no failed states; state itself is failure.* Or rather, it is the entire vision with the state as the crowning accomplishment of community which has failed. In his search for a truer universalism, Rajan believes he has stumbled upon one in the south Indian backwater state he hails from, and has lately been preoccupied with trying to unravel its many discreet charms and mysteries.

D. Venkat Rao is professor at the English and Foreign Languages University, Hyderabad, India. He publishes widely in both Telugu and English. He has translated into Telugu Ashis Nandy's *The Intimate Enemy*, published as *Priya Shatruvu* (2009), and earlier translated into English the Telugu intellectual autobiography of Rani Siva Sankara Sarma under the title *The Last Brahmin: Life and Reflections of a Modern-Day Sanskrit Pandit* (2007). *Cultures of Memory in South Asia: Orality, Literacy and the Problem of Inheritance* (2014) reflects his interests in literary and cultural studies, image studies, comparative thought, and mnemocultures. He also edited the volume *Critical Humanities from India: Contexts, Issues, Futures* in 2018.

Sujit Sivanand, a management consultant by profession, was the Partner heading KPMG's consulting practice in Kuwait, offering advisory services in strategy and process improvement. An MBA from ENPC Paris, Sujit also holds a diploma in international business from the University of Bristol and a master's degree in financial management. He has, over the course of the last fifteen years, been reading, occasionally writing, editing, and speaking on philosophy as expounded by Narayana Guru. Sujit and some friends are organized under the Narayana Philosophy Society (NPHIL), a knowledge-based network engaged in researching, scoping, authoring, and creating imagery-applied lecture modules on Narayana Guru's life, works, and philosophy.

Father (Professor) George Thadathil is presently the principal of Salesian College at its Sonada, Darjeeling, and Siliguri campuses in West Bengal, India. Besides college administration, he is engaged in coordinating the research projects of the various departments of the college where he has been serving the cause of education for the past twenty-five years. He has authored *Vision from the Margin: Study of Sri Narayana Guru Movement* and edited seven books and published over thirty papers, both as articles in journals and as chapters in edited volumes. He is also the series editor of the *Salesian Journal of Humanities and Social Sciences*, now in its ninth year, and the founder director of Salesian Research and Translation Centre.

Milind Wakankar is associate professor in the Department of Humanities at Indian Institute of Technology Delhi, India. He earned his PhD in English, comparative literature, and postcolonial theory at Columbia University in 2002, and previously taught at the State University of New York, Stony Brook, USA; Centre for the Study of Culture and Society, Bangalore; and Ambedkar University, Delhi. His intellectual interests also include Bhakti literature, Indian philosophy, and German philosophy. He is presently working on a book on the highly influential Hindi critic Ramchandra Shukla, and a critical commentary on the *Dnyaneshvari*. He is the author of, among other works, *Subalternity and Religion: The Prehistory of Dalit Empowerment in South Asia* (2010).

INDEX